THE LOEB CLASSICAL LIBRARY

FOUNDED BY JAMES LOEB 1911

EDITED BY

JEFFREY HENDERSON

EDITOR EMERITUS

G. P. GOOLD

STRABO

VI

LCL 223

STRABO

GEOGRAPHY

BOOKS 13–14

WITH AN ENGLISH TRANSLATION BY

HORACE LEONARD JONES

HARVARD UNIVERSITY PRESS

CAMBRIDGE, MASSACHUSETTS
LONDON, ENGLAND

First published 1929
Reprinted 1954, 1960, 1970, 1989, 2000

LOEB CLASSICAL LIBRARY® is a registered trademark
of the President and Fellows of Harvard College

ISBN 0-674-99246-6

Printed in Great Britain by St Edmundsbury Press Ltd,
Bury St Edmunds, Suffolk, on acid-free paper.
Bound by Hunter & Foulis Ltd, Edinburgh, Scotland.

CONTENTS

LIST OF THE BOOKS OF
THE GEOGRAPHY OF STRABO

Showing their place in the volumes of this
edition and in the edition of Casaubon of 1620

LIST OF THE BOOKS

THE

GEOGRAPHY OF STRABO

BOOK XIII

ΣΤΡΑΒΩΝΟΣ ΓΕΩΓΡΑΦΙΚΩΝ

ΙΓ΄

I

C 581   1. Μέχρι μὲν δεῦρο ἀφωρίσθω τὰ περὶ τῆς
Φρυγίας· ἐπανιόντες δὲ πάλιν ἐπὶ τὴν Προποντίδα καὶ τὴν ἐφεξῆς τῷ Αἰσήπῳ παραλίαν τὴν
αὐτὴν τῆς περιοδείας τάξιν ἀποδώσομεν. ἔστι
δὲ Τρωὰς πρώτη τῆς παραλίας ταύτης, ἧς τὸ
πολυθρύλητον, καίπερ ἐν ἐρειπίοις καὶ ἐν ἐρημίᾳ
λειπομένης, ὅμως πολυλογίαν οὐ τὴν τυχοῦσαν
παρέχει τῇ γραφῇ. πρὸς τοῦτο δὲ συγγνώμης
δεῖ καὶ παρακλήσεως, ὅπως τὴν αἰτίαν τοῦ
μήκους μὴ ἡμῖν μᾶλλον ἀνάπτωσιν[1] οἱ ἐντυγχάνοντες ἢ τοῖς σφόδρα ποθοῦσι τὴν τῶν ἐνδόξων
καὶ παλαιῶν γνῶσιν· προσλαμβάνει δὲ τῷ
μήκει καὶ τὸ πλῆθος τῶν ἐποικησάντων τὴν
χώραν Ἑλλήνων τε καὶ βαρβάρων, καὶ οἱ
συγγραφεῖς, οὐχὶ τὰ αὐτὰ γράφοντες περὶ τῶν
αὐτῶν, οὐδὲ σαφῶς πάντα· ὧν ἐν τοῖς πρώτοις
ἐστὶν Ὅμηρος, εἰκάζειν περὶ τῶν πλείστων
παρέχων. δεῖ δὲ καὶ τὰ τούτου διαιτᾶν καὶ τὰ

---

[1] ἀνάπτωσιν, Kramer, for ἀναπτωεῖν F, ἀνάπτοιεν other
MSS. ; so the later editors.

---

[1] The translator must here record his obligations to Dr.
Walter Leaf on his monumental works on the Troad : his
Troy, Macmillan and Co., 1912, and his *Strabo on the Troad*,
Cambridge, 1923, and his numerous monographs in classical

2

THE GEOGRAPHY OF STRABO

BOOK XIII

I

1.[1] LET this, then, mark the boundary of Phrygia.[2]
I shall now return again to the Propontis and the
coast that comes next after the Aesepus River, and
follow the same order of description as before. The
first country on this seaboard is the Troad, the
fame of which, although it is left in ruins and in deso-
lation, nevertheless prompts in writers no ordinary
prolixity. With this fact in view, I should ask the
pardon of my readers and appeal to them not to
fasten the blame for the length of my discussion
upon me rather than upon those who strongly yearn
for knowledge of the things that are famous and
ancient. And my discussion is further prolonged
by the number of the peoples who have colonised
the country, both Greeks and barbarians, and by
the historians, who do not write the same things
on the same subjects, nor always clearly either;
among the first of these is Homer, who leaves us
to guess about most things. And it is necessary
for me to arbitrate between his statements and

periodicals. The results of his investigations in the Troad
prove the great importance of similar investigations, on the
spot, of various other portions of Strabo's "Inhabited
World."

[2] The reader will find a map of Asia Minor in Vol. V. (at
end).

3

τῶν ἄλλων, ὑπογράψαντας πρότερον ἐν κεφαλαίῳ τὴν τῶν τόπων φύσιν.

2. Ἀπὸ δὴ[1] τῆς Κυζικηνῆς καὶ τῶν περὶ Αἴσηπον τόπων καὶ Γράνικον μέχρι Ἀβύδου καὶ Σηστοῦ τὴν τῆς Προποντίδος παραλίαν εἶναι συμβαίνει, ἀπὸ δὲ Ἀβύδου μέχρι Λεκτοῦ τὰ περὶ Ἴλιον καὶ Τένεδον καὶ Ἀλεξάνδρειαν τὴν Τρωάδα· πάντων δὴ τούτων ὑπέρκειται ἡ Ἴδη τὸ ὄρος, μέχρι Λεκτοῦ καθήκουσα· ἀπὸ Λεκτοῦ δὲ μέχρι Καΐκου ποταμοῦ καὶ τῶν Κανῶν λεγομένων ἐστὶ τὰ περὶ Ἄσσον καὶ Ἀδραμύττιον καὶ Ἀταρνέα καὶ Πιτάνην καὶ τὸν Ἐλαϊτικὸν C 582 κόλπον· οἷς πᾶσιν ἀντιπαρήκει ἡ τῶν Λεσβίων νῆσος· εἶθ' ἑξῆς τὰ περὶ Κύμην μέχρι Ἕρμου καὶ Φωκαίας, ἥπερ ἀρχὴ μὲν τῆς Ἰωνίας ἐστί, πέρας δὲ τῆς Αἰολίδος. τοιούτων δὲ τῶν τόπων ὄντων, ὁ μὲν ποιητὴς ἀπὸ τῶν περὶ Αἴσηπον τόπων καὶ τῶν περὶ τὴν νῦν Κυζικηνὴν χώραν ὑπαγορεύει μάλιστα τοὺς Τρῶας ἄρξαι μέχρι τοῦ Καΐκου ποταμοῦ διῃρημένους κατὰ δυναστείας εἰς ὀκτὼ μερίδας ἢ καὶ ἐννέα· τὸ δὲ τῶν ἄλλων ἐπικούρων πλῆθος ἐν τοῖς συμμάχοις διαριθμεῖται.

3. Οἱ δ' ὕστερον τοὺς ὅρους οὐ τοὺς αὐτοὺς λέγουσι καὶ τοῖς ὀνόμασι χρῶνται διηλλαγμένως, αἱρέσεις[2] νέμοντες πλείους. μάλιστα δὲ αἱ τῶν Ἑλλήνων ἀποικίαι παρεσχήκασι λόγον· ἧττον μὲν ἡ Ἰωνική· πλείονι γὰρ διέστηκε τῆς Τρωάδος· ἡ

---

[1] δή, Corais, for δέ; so the later editors.
[2] Meineke, following conj. of Corais, emends αἱρέσεις to διαιρέσεις.

those of the others, after I shall first have described in a summary way the nature of the region in question.

2. The seaboard of the Propontis, then, extends from Cyzicenê and the region of the Aesepus and Granicus Rivers as far as Abydus and Sestus, whereas the parts round Ilium and Tenedos and the Trojan Alexandreia extend from Abydus to Lectum. Accordingly, Mt. Ida, which extends down to Lectum, lies above all these places. From Lectum to the Caïcus River, and to Canae,[1] as it is called, are the parts round Assus and Adramyttium and Atarneus and Pitanê and the Elaïtic Gulf; and the island of the Lesbians extends alongside, and opposite, all these places. Then come next the parts round Cymê, extending to the Hermus and Phocaea, which latter constitutes the beginning of Ionia and the end of Aeolis. Such being the position of the places, the poet indicates in a general way that the Trojans held sway from the region of the Aesepus River and that of the present Cyzicenê to the Caïcus River,[2] their country being divided by dynasties into eight, or nine, portions, whereas the mass of their auxiliary forces are enumerated among the allies.

3. But the later authors do not give the same boundaries, and they use their terms differently, thus allowing us several choices. The main cause of this difference has been the colonisations of the Greeks; less so, indeed, the Ionian colonisation, for it was farther distant from the Troad; but most of

---

[1] On the position of this promontory, see Leaf, *Ann. Brit. School at Athens*, XXII, p. 37, and *Strabo on the Troad*, p. xxxviii.

[2] See Leaf, *Strabo on the Troad*, p. xli.

δὲ τῶν Αἰολέων παντάπασι· καθ' ὅλην γὰρ
ἐσκεδάσθη ἀπὸ τῆς Κυζικηνῆς μέχρι τοῦ Καΐκου
καὶ ἐπέλαβεν ἔτι πλέον τὴν μεταξὺ τοῦ Καΐκου
καὶ τοῦ Ἕρμου ποταμοῦ. τέτρασι γὰρ δὴ
γενεαῖς πρεσβυτέραν φασὶ τὴν Αἰολικὴν ἀποικίαν τῆς Ἰωνικῆς, διατριβὰς δὲ λαβεῖν καὶ
χρόνους μακροτέρους. Ὀρέστην μὲν γὰρ ἄρξαι
τοῦ στόλου, τούτου δ' ἐν Ἀρκαδίᾳ τελευτήσαντος
τὸν βίον, διαδέξασθαι τὸν υἱὸν αὐτοῦ Πενθίλον
καὶ προελθεῖν μέχρι Θρᾴκης ἑξήκοντα ἔτεσι τῶν
Τρωικῶν ὕστερον, ὑπ' αὐτὴν τὴν τῶν Ἡρακλειδῶν εἰς Πελοπόννησον κάθοδον· εἶτ' Ἀρχέλαον,
υἱὸν ἐκείνου, περαιῶσαι τὸν Αἰολικὸν στόλον εἰς
τὴν νῦν Κυζικηνὴν τὴν περὶ τὸ Δασκύλιον· Γρᾶν
δέ, τὸν υἱὸν τούτου τὸν νεώτατον, προελθόντα
μέχρι τοῦ Γρανίκου ποταμοῦ καὶ παρεσκευασ-
μένον ἄμεινον περαιῶσαι τὸ πλέον τῆς στρατιᾶς
εἰς Λέσβον καὶ κατασχεῖν αὐτήν· Κλεύην δέ, τὸν
Δῶρον, καὶ Μαλαόν, καὶ αὐτοὺς ἀπογόνους
ὄντας Ἀγαμέμνονος, συναγαγεῖν μὲν τὴν στρα-
τιὰν κατὰ τὸν αὐτὸν χρόνον, καθ' ὃν καὶ Πενθί-
λος· ἀλλὰ τὸν μὲν τοῦ Πενθίλου στόλον φθῆναι
περαιωθέντα ἐκ τῆς Θρᾴκης εἰς τὴν Ἀσίαν, τούτους δὲ περὶ τὴν Λοκρίδα καὶ τὸ Φρίκιον ὄρος
διατρῖψαι πολὺν χρόνον, ὕστερον δὲ διαβάντας
κτίσαι τὴν Κύμην τὴν Φρικωνίδα κληθεῖσαν ἀπὸ
τοῦ Λοκρικοῦ ὄρους.

4. Τῶν Αἰολέων τοίνυν καθ' ὅλην σκεδασθέν-
των τὴν χώραν, ἣν ἔφαμεν ὑπὸ τοῦ ποιητοῦ
λέγεσθαι Τρωικήν, οἱ[1] ὕστερον οἱ μὲν πᾶσαν
Αἰολίδα προσαγορεύουσιν, οἱ δὲ μέρος, καὶ Τροίαν

---

[1] δ', after οἱ, Corais suggests ; so the later editors.

all that of the Aeolians, for their colonies were
scattered throughout the whole of the country from
Cyzicenê to the Caïcus River, and they went on
still farther to occupy the country between the
Caïcus and Hermus Rivers. In fact, the Aeolian
colonisation, they say, preceded the Ionian colonisation by four generations, but suffered delays and
took a longer time; for Orestes, they say, was the
first leader of the expedition, but he died in
Arcadia, and his son Penthilus succeeded him and
advanced as far as Thrace sixty years after the
Trojan War, about the time of the return of the
Heracleidae to the Peloponnesus; and then Archelaüs[1] the son of Penthilus led the Aeolian expedition
across to the present Cyzicenê near Dascylium; and
Gras, the youngest son of Archelaüs, advanced to
the Granicus River, and, being better equipped, led
the greater part of his army across to Lesbos and
occupied it. And they add that Cleues, son of
Dorus, and Malaüs, also descendants of Agamemnon,
had collected their army at about the same time
as Penthilus, but that, whereas the fleet of Penthilus
had already crossed over from Thrace to Asia, Cleues
and Malaüs tarried a long time round Locris and
Mt. Phricius, and only later crossed over and
founded the Phryconian Cymê, so named after the
Locrian mountain.

4. The Aeolians, then, were scattered throughout
the whole of that country which, as I have said,
the poet called Trojan. As for later authorities,
some apply the name to all Aeolis, but others to
only a part of it; and some to the whole of Troy,

---

[1] Pausanias (3. 2. 1) spells his name " Echelas."

7

STRABO

οἱ μὲν ὅλην, οἱ δὲ μέρος αὐτῆς, οὐδὲν ὅλως ἀλλήλοις ὁμολογοῦντες. εὐθὺς γὰρ ἐπὶ τῶν κατὰ τὴν
Προποντίδα τόπων ὁ μὲν Ὅμηρος ἀπὸ Αἰσήπου
τὴν ἀρχὴν ποιεῖται τῆς Τρωάδος· Εὔδοξος δὲ
ἀπὸ Πριάπου[1] καὶ Ἀρτάκης, τοῦ ἐν τῇ Κυζικηνῶν
C 583 νήσῳ χωρίου ἀνταίροντος τῷ Πριάπῳ, συστέλλων
ἐπ᾽ ἔλαττον τοὺς ὅρους· Δαμάστης δ᾽ ἔτι μᾶλλον
συστέλλει ἀπὸ Παρίου· καὶ γὰρ οὗτος μὲν ἕως
Λεκτοῦ προάγει, ἄλλοι δ᾽ ἄλλως· Χάρων δ᾽ ὁ
Λαμψακηνὸς τριακοσίους ἄλλους ἀφαιρεῖ σταδίους, ἀπὸ Πρακτίου ἀρχόμενος· τοσοῦτοι γάρ
εἰσιν ἀπὸ Παρίου εἰς Πράκτιον· ἕως μέντοι
Ἀδραμυττίου πρόεισι· Σκύλαξ δὲ ὁ Καρυανδεὺς
ἀπὸ Ἀβύδου ἄρχεται· ὁμοίως δὲ τὴν Αἰολίδα
Ἔφορος μὲν λέγει ἀπὸ Ἀβύδου μέχρι Κύμης,
ἄλλοι δ᾽ ἄλλως.

5. Τοπογραφεῖ δὲ κάλλιστα τὴν ὄντως λεγομένην Τροίαν ἡ τῆς Ἴδης θέσις, ὄρους ὑψηλοῦ
βλέποντος πρὸς δύσιν καὶ τὴν ταύτῃ θάλατταν,
μικρὰ δ᾽ ἐπιστρέφοντος[2] καὶ πρὸς ἄρκτον καὶ τὴν
ταύτῃ παραλίαν. ἔστι δὲ αὕτη μὲν τῆς Προποντίδος ἀπὸ τῶν περὶ Ἄβυδον στενῶν ἐπὶ τὸν
Αἴσηπον καὶ τὴν Κυζικηνήν, ἡ δ᾽ ἑσπερία θάλαττα ὅ τε Ἑλλήσποντός ἐστιν[3] ὁ ἔξω[4] καὶ τὸ
Αἰγαῖον πέλαγος. πολλοὺς δ᾽ ἔχουσα πρόποδας

---

[1] καὶ Ἀρτάκης . . . Ποιάπῳ, Leaf, in *Journal of Hellenic
Studies*, XXXVII., p. 22, would delete; so in his *Strabo on
the Troad*, p. 2 (see his note on p. 47).
[2] ἐπιστρέφοντος Ex, ἐπιστραφέντος other MSS.
[3] ὁ, before ἔξω. Kramer inserts: so the later editors.
[4] ἔξω EF, ἐν ᾧ other MSS.

---

[1] *Iliad* 2. 824. See § 9 following.

but others to only a part of it, not wholly agreeing with one another about anything. For instance, in reference to the places on the Propontis, Homer makes the Troad begin at the Aesepus River,[1] whereas Eudoxus makes it begin at Priapus and Artacê, the place on the island of the Cyziceni that lies opposite Priapus,[2] and thus contracts the limits; but Damastes contracts the country still more, making it begin at Parium ; and, in fact, Damastes prolongs the Troad to Lectum, whereas other writers prolong it differently. Charon of Lampsacus diminishes its extent by three hundred stadia more, making it begin at Practius,[3] for that is the distance from Parium to Practius ; however, he prolongs it to Adramyttium. Scylax of Caryanda makes it begin at Abydus ; and similarly Ephorus says that Aeolis extends from Abydus to Cymê, while others define its extent differently.[4]

5. But the topography of Troy, in the proper sense of the term, is best marked by the position of Mt. Ida, a lofty mountain which faces the west and the western sea but makes a slight bend also towards the north and the northern seaboard.[5] This latter is the seaboard of the Propontis, extending from the strait in the neighbourhood of Abydus to the Aesepus River and Cyzicenê, whereas the western sea consists of the outer Hellespont[6] and the Aegaean Sea. Mt. Ida has many foot-hills, is like

[2] See Leaf, *Strabo on the Troad*, p. 47.
[3] Whether city or river (see 13. 1. 21).
[4] See Leaf's definition of the Troad (*Troy*, p. 171).
[5] See Leaf, *Strabo on the Troad*, p. 48.
[6] On the meaning of the term Hellespont, see Book VII, Frag. 57 (58), and Leaf (*Strabo on the Troad*), p. 50.

ἡ Ἴδη καὶ σκολοπενδρώδης οὖσα τὸ σχῆμα
ἐσχάτοις ἀφορίζεται τούτοις, τῷ τε περὶ τὴν
Ζέλειαν ἀκρωτηρίῳ καὶ τῷ καλουμένῳ Λεκτῷ, τῷ
μὲν τελευτῶντι εἰς τὴν μεσόγαιαν μικρὸν ὑπὲρ
τῆς Κυζικηνῆς· καὶ δὴ καὶ ἔστι νῦν ἡ Ζέλεια
τῶν Κυζικηνῶν· τὸ δὲ Λεκτὸν εἰς τὸ πέλαγος
καθήκει τὸ Αἰγαῖον, ἐν παράπλῳ κείμενον τοῖς ἐκ
Τενέδου πλέουσιν εἰς Λέσβον.

Ἴδην δ᾿ ἵκανον πολυπίδακα μητέρα θηρῶν,
Λεκτόν, ὅθι[1] πρῶτον λιπέτην ἅλα

Ὕπνος καὶ ἡ Ἥρα, τοῖς οὖσιν οἰκείως τοῦ ποιητοῦ
φράζοντος τὸ Λεκτόν· καὶ γὰρ ὅτι τῆς Ἴδης ἐστὶ
τὸ Λεκτὸν καὶ διότι πρώτη ἀπόβασις ἐκ θαλάττης
αὕτη τοῖς ἐπὶ τὴν Ἴδην ἀνιοῦσιν, εἴρηκεν ὀρθῶς,[2]
καὶ τὸ πολυπίδακον· εὐυδρότατον γὰρ κατὰ ταῦτα
μάλιστα[3] τὸ ὄρος, δηλοῖ δὲ τὸ πλῆθος τῶν
ποταμῶν,

ὅσσοι ἀπ᾿ Ἰδαίων ὀρέων ἅλαδε προρέουσι,
Ῥῆσός θ᾿ Ἑπτάπορός τε

καὶ οἱ ἑξῆς, οὓς ἐκεῖνος εἴρηκε καὶ ἡμῖν νυνὶ
πάρεστιν ὁρᾶν. τοὺς δὴ πρόποδας τοὺς ἐσχά-
τους ἐφ᾿ ἑκάτερα φράζων[4] οὕτως τὸ Λεκτὸν καὶ
τὴν Ζέλειαν, οἰκείως τούτων καὶ ἀκρώρειαν
ἀφορίζει Γάργαρον, ἄκρον λέγων·[5] καὶ γὰρ νῦν

---

[1] ὅθι, Xylander, for ὅτι; so the later editors.
[2] καὶ τὸ . . . ὁρᾶν, ejected by Meineke.
[3] κατὰ ταῦτα μάλιστα, Leaf brackets (see his note, *op. cit.*,
p. 49).
[4] φράζων, Meineke, from conj. of Kramer, for ὁρᾶι.

the scolopendra[1] in shape, and is defined by its two extreme limits: by the promontory in the neighbourhood of Zeleia and by the promontory called Lectum, the former terminating in the interior slightly above Cyzicenê (in fact, Zeleia now belongs to the Cyziceni), whereas Lectum extends to the Aegaean Sea, being situated on the coasting-voyage between Tenedos and Lesbos. When the poet says that Hypnos and Hera "came to many-fountained Ida, mother of wild beasts, to Lectum, where first the two left the sea,"[2] he describes Lectum in accordance with the facts; for he rightly states that Lectum is a part of Mt. Ida, and that Lectum is the first place of disembarkation from the sea for those who would go up to Mt. Ida, and also that the mountain is "many-fountained," for there in particular the mountain is abundantly watered, as is shown by the large number of rivers there, "all the rivers that flow forth from the Idaean mountains to the sea, Rhesus and Heptaporus"[3] and the following,[4] all of which are named by the poet and are now to be seen by us. Now while Homer thus describes Lectum[5] and Zeleia[6] as the outermost foot-hills of Mt. Ida in either direction, he also appropriately distinguishes Gargarus from them as a summit, calling it "topmost."[7] And indeed at the present

---

[1] A genus of myriapods including some of the largest centipedes.
[2] *Iliad* 14. 283. [3] *Iliad* 12. 19.
[4] The Granicus, Aesepus, Scamander, and Simoeis.
[5] *Iliad* 14. 284. [6] *Iliad* 2. 824.
[7] *Iliad* 14. 292, 352; 15. 152.

---

[5] λέγων, Kramer, for τέρων CF*moz*, τερον D with ε above τ *man. sec.*, whence ἕτερον *hi* and Tzschucke.

Γάργαρον ἐν τοῖς ἄνω μέρεσι τῆς Ἴδης δείκνυται
τόπος, ἀφ' οὗ τὰ νῦν Γάργαρα πόλις Αἰολική.
ἐντὸς μὲν οὖν τῆς Ζελείας καὶ τοῦ Λεκτοῦ πρῶτά
ἐστιν ἀπὸ τῆς Προποντίδος ἀρξαμένοις τὰ[1] μέχρι
τῶν κατ' Ἄβυδον στενῶν· εἶτ' ἔξω τῆς Προποντίδος τὰ μέχρι Λεκτοῦ.

C 584   6. Κάμψαντι δὲ τὸ Λεκτὸν ἀναχεῖται κόλπος
μέγας, ὃν ἡ Ἴδη ποιεῖ πρὸς τὴν ἤπειρον ἀναχωροῦσα[2] ἀπὸ τοῦ Λεκτοῦ καὶ αἱ Κάναι, τὸ ἐκ
θατέρου μέρους ἀντικείμενον ἀκρωτήριον τῷ
Λεκτῷ· καλοῦσι δ' οἱ μὲν Ἰδαῖον κόλπον, οἱ δ'
Ἀδραμυττηνόν. ἐν τούτῳ δὲ αἱ τῶν Αἰολέων
πόλεις μέχρι τῶν ἐκβολῶν τοῦ Ἕρμου, καθάπερ
εἰρήκαμεν. εἴρηται δὲ ἐν τοῖς ἔμπροσθεν ὅτι τοῖς
ἐκ Βυζαντίου πλέουσι πρὸς νότον ἐπ' εὐθείας
ἐστὶν ὁ πλοῦς, πρῶτον ἐπὶ Σηστὸν καὶ Ἄβυδον
διὰ μέσης τῆς Προποντίδος, ἔπειτα τῆς παραλίας[3]
τῆς Ἀσίας μέχρι Καρίας. ταύτην δὴ φυλάττον-
τας χρὴ τὴν ὑπόθεσιν ἀκούειν τῶν ἑξῆς, κἂν
λέγωμεν κόλπους τινὰς ἐν τῇ παραλίᾳ, τάς τε
ἄκρας δεῖ νοεῖν τὰς ποιούσας αὐτοὺς ἐπὶ τῆς
αὐτῆς γραμμῆς κειμένας, ὥσπερ τινὸς μεσημ-
βρινῆς.

7. Ἐκ δὴ τῶν ὑπὸ τοῦ ποιητοῦ λεγομένων
εἰκάζουσιν οἱ φροντίσαντες περὶ τούτων πλέον τι,
πᾶσαν τὴν παραλίαν ταύτην ὑπὸ τοῖς Τρωσὶ
γεγονέναι, διῃρημένην μὲν εἰς δυναστείας ἐννέα,

[1] τά, before μέχρι, Groskurd inserts ; so the later editors.
[2] ἀναχωροῦσα E, ἀποχωροῦσα other MSS. ; so Leaf.
[3] τῆς παραλίας is indefensible ; perhaps παρὰ τὴν παραλίαν
(Kramer).

[1] See Leaf, Strabo on the Troad, p. xliv.

12

time people point out in the upper parts of Ida a place called Gargarum, after which the present Gargara, an Aeolian city, is named. Now between Zeleia and Lectum, beginning from the Propontis, are situated first the parts extending to the straits at Abydus, and then, outside the Propontis, the parts extending to Lectum.

6. On doubling Lectum one encounters a large wide-open gulf, which is formed by Mt. Ida as it recedes from Lectum to the mainland, and by Canae, the promontory opposite Lectum on the other side. Some call it the Idaean Gulf, others the Adramyttene. On this gulf[1] are the cities of the Aeolians, extending to the outlets of the Hermus River, as I have already said.[2] I have stated in the earlier parts of my work[3] that, as one sails from Byzantium towards the south, the route lies in a straight line, first to Sestus and Abydus through the middle of the Propontis, and then along the coast of Asia as far as Caria. It behooves one, then, to keep this supposition in mind as one listens to the following; and, if I speak of certain gulfs on the coast, one must think of the promontories which form them as lying in the same line, a meridian-line, as it were.

7. Now as for Homer's statements, those who have studied the subject more carefully[4] conjecture from them that the whole of this coast became subject to the Trojans, and, though divided into nine dynasties, was under the sway of Priam at the

---

[2] 13. 1. 2 (see Leaf's article cited in foot-note there).

[3] Strabo refers to his discussion of the meridian-line drawn by Eratosthenes through Byzantium, Rhodes, Alexandria, Syenê, and Meroê (see 2. 5. 7 and the *Frontispiece* in Vol. I).

[4] Strabo refers to Demetrius of Scepsis and his followers.

STRABO

ὑπὸ δὲ τῷ Πριάμῳ τεταγμένην κατὰ τὸν Ἰλιακὸν
πόλεμον καὶ λεγομένην Τροίαν· δῆλον δὲ ἐκ τῶν
κατὰ μέρος. οἱ γὰρ περὶ τὸν Ἀχιλλέα τειχήρεις
ὁρῶντες τοὺς Ἰλιέας κατ᾽ ἀρχάς, ἔξω ποιεῖσθαι
τὸν πόλεμον ἐπεχείρησαν καὶ περιιόντες ἀφαιρεῖσθαι τὰ κύκλῳ·

δώδεκα δὴ σὺν νηυσὶ πόλεις ἀλάπαξ᾽ ἀνθρώπων,

πεζὸς δ᾽ ἕνδεκά φημι κατὰ Τροίην ἐρίβωλον.

Τροίαν γὰρ λέγει τὴν πεπορθημένην ἤπειρον·
πεπόρθηται δὲ σὺν ἄλλοις τόποις καὶ τὰ ἀντικεί-
μενα τῇ Λέσβῳ τὰ περὶ Θήβην καὶ Λυρνησσὸν
καὶ Πήδασον τὴν τῶν Λελέγων καὶ ἔτι ἡ τοῦ
Εὐρυπύλου τοῦ Τηλέφου παιδός·

ἀλλ᾽ οἷον τὸν Τηλεφίδην κατενήρατο χαλκῷ,

ὁ Νεοπτόλεμος, ἥρω Εὐρύπυλον. ταῦτα δὴ πεπορ-
θῆσθαι λέγει καὶ αὐτὴν τὴν Λέσβον·

ὅτε Λέσβον ἐϋκτιμένην ἕλεν [1] αὐτός·

καὶ

πέρσε δὲ Λυρνησσὸν καὶ Πήδασον·

καὶ

Λυρνησσὸν διαπορθήσας καὶ τείχεα Θήβης.

ἐκ μὲν Λυρνησσοῦ ἡ Βρισηὶς ἑάλω

τὴν ἐκ Λυρνησσοῦ ἐξείλετο·

ἧς ἐν τῇ ἁλώσει τὸν Μύνητα [2] καὶ τὸν Ἐπίστροφον
πεσεῖν, φησίν, ὡς ἡ Βρισηὶς θρηνοῦσα τὸν Πάτρο-
κλον δηλοῖ·

14

time of the Trojan War and was called Troy. And
this is clear from his detailed statements. For
instance, Achilles and his army, seeing at the outset
that the inhabitants of Ilium were enclosed by walls,
tried to carry on the war outside and, by making
raids all round, to take away from them all the
surrounding places: " Twelve cities of men I have
laid waste with my ships, and eleven, I declare, by
land throughout the fertile land of Troy."[1] For by
" Troy " he means the part of the mainland that was
sacked by him ; and, along with other places, Achilles
also sacked the country opposite Lesbos in the neighbourhood of Thebê and Lyrnessus and Pedasus,[2] which
last belonged to the Leleges, and also the country of
Eurypylus the son of Telephus. " But what a man was
that son of Telephus who was slain by him with the
bronze,"[3] that is, the hero Eurypylus, slain by Neoptolemus. Now the poet says that these places were
sacked, including Lesbos itself: " when he himself
took well-built Lesbos " ; and " he sacked Lyrnessus[4]
and Pedasus " ;[5] and " when he laid waste Lyrnessus
and the walls of Thebê."[6] It was at Lyrnessus that
Briseïs was taken captive, " whom he carried away
from Lyrnessus " ;[7] and it was at her capture,
according to the poet, that Mynes and Epistrophus
fell, as is shown by the lament of Briseïs over

---

[1] *Iliad* 9. 328.　　　　[2] *Iliad* 20. 92.
[3] *Odyssey* 11. 518.　　 [4] *Iliad* 9. 129.
[5] *Iliad* 20. 92.　　　　 [6] *Iliad* 2. 691.
[7] *Iliad* 2. 690.

---

[1] ἔλεν, Xylander, for ἔλες ; so the later editors.
[2] καὶ τὸν Ἐπίστροφον, Meineke ejects.

οὐδὲ μὲν οὐδέ μ' ἔασκες, ὅτ' ἄνδρ' ἐμὸν ὠκὺς
Ἀχιλλεὺς
ἔκτεινεν, πέρσεν δὲ πόλιν θείοιο Μύνητος,
κλαίειν·

C 585 ἐμφαίνει γὰρ τὴν Λυρνησσὸν λέγων πόλιν θείοιο
Μύνητος, ὡς ἂν δυναστευομένην ὑπ' αὐτοῦ, καὶ
ἐνταῦθα πεσεῖν αὐτὸν μαχόμενον· ἐκ δὲ τῆς Θήβης
ἡ Χρυσηὶς ἐλήφθη·

ᾠχόμεθ' ἐς Θήβην ἱερὴν πόλιν Ἠετίωνος·

ἐκ δὲ τῶν ἀχθέντων ἐκεῖθέν φησιν εἶναι τὴν
Χρυσηίδα. ἐνθένδε δ' ἦν καὶ ἡ Ἀνδρομάχη[1]

Ἀνδρομάχη θυγάτηρ μεγαλήτορος Ἠετίωνος·
Ἠετίων, ὃς ἔναιεν ὑπὸ Πλάκῳ ὑληέσσῃ,
Θήβῃ Ὑποπλακίῃ, Κιλίκεσσ' ἄνδρεσσιν ἀνάσ-
σων.

δευτέρα οὖν αὕτη δυναστεία Τρωικὴ μετὰ τὴν
ὑπὸ Μύνητι. οἰκείως δὲ τούτοις καὶ τὸ ὑπὸ τῆς
Ἀνδρομάχης λεχθὲν οὕτως,

Ἕκτορ, ἐγὼ δύστηνος· ἰῇ ἄρα γεινόμεθ' αἴσῃ
ἀμφότεροι, σὺ μὲν ἐν Τροίῃ Πριάμου ἐνὶ οἴκῳ,
αὐτὰρ ἐγὼ Θήβῃσιν,

οὐκ οἴονται δεῖν ἐξ εὐθείας ἀκούειν, σὺ μὲν ἐν
Τροίῃ, αὐτὰρ ἐγὼ Θήβῃσιν ἢ Θήβηθεν,[2] ἀλλὰ καθ'
ὑπερβατόν· ἀμφότεροι ἐν Τροίῃ,[3] σὺ μὲν Πριάμου
ἐνὶ οἴκῳ, αὐτὰρ ἐγὼ Θήβῃσι. τρίτη δ' ἐστὶν
ἡ τῶν Λελέγων, καὶ αὕτη Τρωική,

Ἄλτεω, ὃς Λελέγεσσι φιλοπτολέμοισιν ἀνάσ-
σει·

οὗ τῇ θυγατρὶ συνελθὼν Πρίαμος γεννᾷ τὸν

16

Patroclus: "thou wouldst not even, not even, let
me weep when swift Achilles slew my husband and
sacked the city of divine Mynes";[1] for in calling
Lyrnessus "the city of divine Mynes" the poet
indicates that Mynes was dynast over it and that he
fell in battle there. But it was at Thebê that
Chryseïs was taken captive: "We went into Thebê,
the sacred city of Eëtion";[2] and the poet says that
Chryseïs was part of the spoil brought from that
place.[3] Thence, too, came Andromachê: "Andromachê, daughter of great-hearted Eëtion; Eëtion
who dwelt 'neath wooded Placus in Thebê Hypo-
placia,[4] and was lord over the men of Cilicia."[5]
This is the second Trojan dynasty after that of
Mynes. And consistently with these facts writers
think that the following statement of Andromachê,
"Hector, woe is me! surely to one doom we were
born, both of us—thou in Troy in the house of
Priam, but I at Thebae,"[6] should not be interpreted
strictly, I mean the words "thou in Troy, but I at
Thebae" (or Thebê), but as a case of hyperbaton,
meaning "both of us in Troy—thou in the house of
Priam, but I at Thebae." The third dynasty was
that of the Leleges, which was also Trojan: "Of
Altes, who is lord over the war-loving Leleges,"[7] by
whose daughter Priam begot Lycaon and Polydorus.

[1] Iliad 19. 295.   [2] Iliad 1. 366.
[3] Iliad 1 369.   [4] The epithet means "'neath Placus."
[5] Iliad 22 477.   [6] Iliad 22. 477.   [7] Iliad 21. 86.

[1] ἐνθένδε . . . Ἀνδρομάχη, found only in the Epitome.
[2] σὺ μὲν . . . Θήβηθεν, Meineke ejects.
[3] ἐν Τροίῃ Epitome, ἐκ Τροίης MSS.

Λυκάονα καὶ Πολύδωρον. καὶ μὴν οἵ γε ὑπὸ τῷ Ἕκτορι ἐν τῷ καταλόγῳ ταττόμενοι λέγονται Τρῶες·

Τρωσὶ μὲν ἡγεμόνευε μέγας κορυθαίολος Ἕκτωρ.

εἶθ' οἱ ὑπὸ τῷ Αἰνείᾳ·

Δαρδανίων αὖτ' ἦρχεν ἐῢς παῖς Ἀγχίσαο·

καὶ οὗτοι Τρῶες· φησὶ γοῦν·

Αἰνεία, Τρώων βουληφόρε.

εἶθ' οἱ ὑπὸ Πανδάρῳ Λύκιοι, οὓς καὶ αὐτοὺς καλεῖ Τρῶας·

οἳ δὲ Ζέλειαν ἔναιον ὑπαὶ πόδα νείατον Ἴδης,
Ἀφνειοί, πίνοντες ὕδωρ μέλαν Αἰσήποιο,
Τρῶες· τῶν αὖτ' ἦρχε Λυκάονος ἀγλαὸς υἱός,
Πάνδαρος.

ἕκτη δ' αὕτη δυναστεία. καὶ μὴν οἵ γε μεταξὺ τοῦ Αἰσήπου καὶ Ἀβύδου Τρῶες· ὑπὸ μὲν γὰρ τῷ Ἀσίῳ ἐστὶ τὰ περὶ Ἄβυδον·

οἳ δ' ἄρα Περκώτην καὶ Πράκτιον ἀμφενέμοντο,
καὶ Σηστὸν καὶ Ἄβυδον ἔχον καὶ δῖαν Ἀρίσβην,
τῶν αὖθ' Ὑρτακίδης ἦρχ' Ἄσιος·

ἀλλ' ἐν Ἀβύδῳ μὲν υἱὸς τοῦ Πριάμου διέτριβεν, ἵππους νέμων, πατρῴας δηλονότι·

ἀλλ' υἱὸν Πριάμοιο νόθον βάλε Δημοκόωντα,
ὅς οἱ Ἀβυδόθεν ἦλθε παρ' ἵππων ὠκειάων·

C 586 ἐν δὲ Περκώτῃ υἱὸς Ἱκετάονος ἐβουνόμει, οὐκ ἀλλοτρίας οὐδ' οὗτος βοῦς·

18

And indeed those who are placed under Hector in the *Catalogue* are called Trojans: "The Trojans were led by great Hector of the flashing helmet."[1] And then come those under Aeneias: "The Dardanians in turn were commanded by the valiant son of Anchises";[2] and these, too, were Trojans; at any rate, the poet says, "Aeneias, counsellor of the Trojans."[3] And then come the Lycians under Pandarus, and these also he calls Trojans: "And those who dwelt in Zeleia beneath the nethermost foot of Ida, Aphneïï,[4] who drink the dark water of the Aesepus, Trojans; these in turn were commanded by Pandarus, the glorious son of Lycaon."[5] And this was the sixth dynasty. And indeed those who lived between the Aesepus River and Abydus were Trojans; for not only were the parts round Abydus subject to Asius, "and they who dwelt about Percotê and Practius[6] and held Sestus and Abydus and goodly Arisbê[7]—these in turn were commanded by Asius the son of Hyrtacus,"[8] but a son of Priam lived at Abydus, pasturing mares, clearly his father's: "But he smote Democoön, the bastard son of Priam, for Priam had come from Abydus from his swift mares";[9] while in Percotê a son of Hicetaon was pasturing kine, he likewise pasturing kine that

---

[1] *Iliad* 2. 816. [2] *Iliad* 2. 819.

[3] *Iliad* 20. 83.

[4] Aphneïï is now taken merely as an adjective, meaning "wealthy" men, but Strabo seems to concur in the belief that the people in question were named "Aphneii" after Lake "Aphnitis" (see 13. 1. 9).

[5] *Iliad* 2. 824.

[6] Whether city or river (see 13. 1. 21).

[7] On Arisbê, see Leaf, *Troy*, 193 ff.

[8] *Iliad* 2. 835. [9] *Iliad* 4. 499.

πρῶτον δ' Ἱκεταονίδην ἐνένιπεν [1]
ἴφθιμον Μελάνιππον· ὁ δ' ὄφρα μὲν εἰλίποδας
βοῦς
βόσκ' ἐν Περκώτῃ·

ὥστε καὶ αὕτη ἂν εἴη Τρωὰς καὶ ἡ ἐφεξῆς ἕως
Ἀδραστείας· ἦρχον γὰρ αὐτῆς

υἷε δύω Μέροπος Περκωσίου.

πάντες μὲν δὴ Τρῶες οἱ ἀπὸ Ἀβύδου μέχρι Ἀδραστείας, δίχα μέντοι διῃρημένοι, οἱ μὲν ὑπὸ τῷ
Ἀσίῳ, οἱ δ' ὑπὸ τοῖς Μεροπίδαις· καθάπερ καὶ ἡ
τῶν Κιλίκων διττή, ἡ μὲν Θηβαϊκή, ἡ δὲ Λυρνησ-
σίς· ἐν αὐτῇ [2] δ' ἂν λεχθείη ἡ ὑπὸ Εὐρυπύλῳ
ἐφεξῆς οὖσα τῇ Λυρνησσίδι. ὅτι δὲ τούτων
ἁπάντων ἦρχεν ὁ Πρίαμος, οἱ τοῦ Ἀχιλλέως
λόγοι πρὸς τὸν Πρίαμον σαφῶς ἐμφανίζουσι·

καί σε, γέρον, τὸ πρὶν μὲν ἀκούομεν ὄλβιον
εἶναι,

ὅσσον Λέσβος ἄνω Μάκαρος πόλις ἐντὸς
ἔεργει,

καὶ Φρυγίη καθύπερθε, καὶ Ἑλλήσποντος
ἀπείρων. [3]

---

[1] ἐνένιπεν, Kramer, for ἔννεπεν x, ἐνέειπεν other MSS.
[2] For ἐν αὐτῇ, Madvig conj. ἐνάτῃ.
[3] After ἀπείρων Müller-Dübner add another line (546) from
Homer, τῶν σε, γέρον, πλούτῳ τε καὶ υἱάσι φασὶ κεκάσθαι, as
necessary to the sense; so Leaf (Strabo on the Troad, pp. 6
and 57).

---

[1] i.e. the kine belonged to Priam. This son of Hicetaon,
a kinsman of Hector (Iliad 15. 545), "dwelt in the house of
Priam, who honoured him equally with his own children"
(Iliad 15. 551).

belonged to no other:[1] "And first he rebuked
mighty Melanippus the son of Hicetaon, who until
this time had been wont to feed the kine of
shambling gait in Percotê";[2] so that this country
would be a part of the Troad, as also the next
country after it as far as Adrasteia, for the leaders of
the latter were "the two sons of Merops of Percotê."[3] Accordingly, the people from Abydus to
Adrasteia were all Trojans, although they were
divided into two groups, one under Asius and the
other under the sons of Merops, just as Cilicia[4] also
was divided into two parts, the Theban Cilicia and
the Lyrnessian;[5] but one might include in the Lyrnessian Cilicia the territory subject to Eurypylus,
which lay next to the Lyrnessian Cilicia.[6] But that
Priam was ruler of these countries, one and all, is
clearly indicated by Achilles' words to Priam : "And
of thee, old sire, we hear that formerly thou wast
blest; how all that is enclosed by Lesbos, out at
sea, city of Macar, and by Phrygia in the upland,
and by the boundless Hellespont."[7]

---

[2] *Iliad* 15. 546.   [3] *Iliad* 2. 831.

[4] The *Trojan* Cilicia (see 13. 1. 70).

[5] See 13. 1. 60–61.

[6] The eight dynasties were (1) that of Mynes, (2) that of
Eëtion, (3) that of Altes, (4) that of Hector, (5) that of Aeneias,
(6) that of Pandarus, (7) that of Asius, and (8) that of the two
sons of Merops. If, however, there were *nine* dynasties (see
13. 1. 2), we may assume that the ninth was that of Eurypylus (see 13. 1. 70), unless, as Choiseul–Gouffier (*Voyage
Pittoresque de la Grèce*, vol. ii, cited by Gossellin) think, it
was that of the island of Lesbos.

[7] *Iliad* 24. 543. The quotation is incomplete without
the following words of Homer: "o'er all these, old sire,
thou wast pre-eminent, they say, because of thy wealth and
thy sons."

8. Τότε μὲν οὖν τοιαῦτα ὑπῆρχεν, ὕστερον δὲ ἠκολούθησαν μεταβολαὶ παντοῖαι. τὰ μὲν γὰρ περὶ Κύζικον Φρύγες ἐπᾠκησαν ἕως Πρακτίου, τὰ δὲ περὶ Ἄβυδον Θρᾷκες· ἔτι δὲ πρότερον τούτων ἀμφοῖν Βέβρυκες καὶ Δρύοπες·[1] τὰ δ' ἐξῆς Τρῆρες, καὶ οὗτοι Θρᾷκες· τὸ δὲ Θήβης πεδίον Λυδοί, οἱ τότε Μήονες, καὶ Μυσῶν οἱ περιγενόμενοι τῶν ὑπὸ Τηλέφῳ πρότερον καὶ Τεύθραντι. οὕτω δὴ τοῦ ποιητοῦ τὴν Αἰολίδα καὶ τὴν Τροίαν εἰς ἓν συντιθέντος, καὶ τῶν Αἰολέων τὴν ἀπὸ τοῦ Ἕρμου πᾶσαν μέχρι τῆς κατὰ Κύζικον παραλίας κατασχόντων καὶ πόλεις κτισάντων, οὐδ' ἂν ἡμεῖς ἀτόπως περιοδεύσαιμεν, εἰς ταὐτὸ συντιθέντες[2] τήν τε Αἰολίδα νῦν ἰδίως λεγομένην τὴν ἀπὸ τοῦ Ἕρμου μέχρι Λεκτοῦ καὶ τὴν ἐφεξῆς μέχρι τοῦ Αἰσήπου· ἐν γὰρ τοῖς καθ' ἕκαστα διακρινοῦμεν πάλιν, παρατιθέντες ἅμα τοῖς νῦν οὖσι τὰ ὑπὸ τοῦ ποιητοῦ καὶ τῶν ἄλλων λεγόμενα.

9. Ἔστιν οὖν μετὰ τὴν τῶν Κυζικηνῶν πόλιν καὶ τὸν Αἴσηπον ἀρχὴ τῆς Τρωάδος καθ' Ὅμηρον. λέγει δ' ἐκεῖνος μὲν οὕτω περὶ αὐτῆς·

οἳ δὲ Ζέλειαν ἔναιον ὑπαὶ πόδα νείατον Ἴδης
Ἀφνειοί, πίνοντες ὕδωρ μέλαν Αἰσήποιο,
Τρῶες· τῶν αὖθ' ἦρχε Λυκάονος ἀγλαὸς υἱός,
Πάνδαρος.

C 587 τούτους δὲ ἐκάλει καὶ Λυκίους· Ἀφνειοὺς δὲ ἀπὸ

---

[1] For Δρύοπες Leaf conj. Δολίονες.
[2] EFmxz have συνθέντες.

---

[1] Leaf (*Strabo on the Troad*, p. 61) makes a strong case for emending "Dryopes" to "Doliones," but leaves the Greek text (p. 7) unchanged.

8. Now such were the conditions at the time of
the Trojan War, but all kinds of changes followed
later; for the parts round Cyzicus as far as the
Practius were colonised by Phrygians, and those
round Abydus by Thracians; and still before these
two by Bebryces and Dryopes.[1] And the country
that lies next was colonised by the Treres, themselves
also Thracians; and the Plain of Thebê by Lydians,
then called Maeonians, and by the survivors of the
Mysians who had formerly been subject to Telephus
and Teuthras. So then, since the poet combines
Aeolis and Troy, and since the Aeolians held
possession of all the country from the Hermus
River[2] to the seaboard at Cyzicus, and founded
their cities there, I too might not be guilty of de-
scribing them wrongly if I combined Aeolis, now
properly so called, extending from the Hermus
River to Lectum, and the country next after it,
extending to the Aesepus River; for in my detailed
treatment of the two, I shall distinguish them again,
setting forth, along with the facts as they now are,
the statements of Homer and others.

9. According to Homer, then, the Troad begins
after the city of the Cyziceni and the Aesepus River.
And he so speaks of it: "And those who dwelt in
Zeleia beneath the nethermost foot of Ida, Aphneii,[3]
who drink the dark water of the Aesepus, Trojans;
these in turn were commanded by Pandarus the
glorious son of Lycaon."[4] These he also calls
Lycians.[5] And they are thought to have been

---

[2] See 13. 1. 1, and p. 40 of Leaf's first article cited in foot-
note there.

[3] See foot-note on Aphneii in 13. 1. 7.

[4] *Iliad* 2. 824.　　　　　　　　[5] See 13. 1. 7.

τῆς Ἀφνίτιδος νομίζουσι λίμνης· καὶ γὰρ οὕτω
καλεῖται ἡ Δασκυλῖτις.

10. Ἡ μὲν δὴ Ζέλεια ἐν τῇ παρωρείᾳ τῇ
ὑστάτῃ τῆς Ἴδης ἐστίν, ἀπέχουσα Κυζίκου μὲν
σταδίους ἐνενήκοντα καὶ ἑκατόν, τῆς δ᾽ ἐγγυτάτω
θαλάττης, καθ᾽ ἣν ἐκδίδωσιν Αἴσηπος, ὅσον
ὀγδοήκοντα. ἐπιμερίζει δὲ συνεχῶς τὰ κατὰ τὴν
παραλίαν τὴν μετὰ τὸν Αἴσηπον·

οἳ δ᾽ Ἀδρήστειάν τ᾽ εἶχον καὶ δῆμον Ἀπαισοῦ,
καὶ Πιτύαν εἶχον[1] καὶ Τηρείης ὄρος αἰπύ,
τῶν ἦρχ᾽ Ἄδρηστός τε καὶ Ἄμφιος λινοθώρηξ,
υἷε δύω Μέροπος Περκωσίου.

ταῦτα δὲ τὰ χωρία τῇ Ζελείᾳ μὲν ὑποπέπτωκε,
ἔχουσι δὲ Κυζικηνοί τε καὶ Πριαπηνοὶ μέχρι καὶ
τῆς παραλίας. περὶ μὲν οὖν τὴν Ζέλειαν ὁ
Τάρσιός ἐστι ποταμός, εἴκοσιν ἔχων διαβάσεις
τῇ αὐτῇ ὁδῷ, καθάπερ ὁ Ἑπτάπορος, ὅν φησιν ὁ
ποιητής.[2] ὁ δ᾽ ἐκ Νικομηδείας εἰς Νίκαιαν τέτταρας καὶ εἴκοσι, πολλοὺς δὲ καὶ ὁ ἐκ Φολόης εἰς
τὴν Ἠλείαν . . . Σκάρθων πέντε καὶ εἴκοσι,

---

[1] Πιτύειαν ἔχον is the reading of the Homeric MSS., but see
Πίτνα in § 15 below.
[2] ὁ δ᾽ ἐκ . . . Ταύρου, Meineke ejects.

---

[1] On the site of Zeleia, see Leaf, *Strabo on the Troad*, p. 66.
[2] *Iliad* 2. 828.
[3] The places in question appear to have belonged to
Zeleia. Leaf (*op. cit.*, p. 65) translates: "are commanded by
Zeleia"; but the present translator is sure that, up to the
present passage, Strabo has always used ὑποπίπτω in a purely
geographical sense (*e.g.*, cf. 9. 1. 15, and especially 12. 4.
6, where Strabo makes substantially the same statement

called "Aphneii" after Lake "Aphnitis," for Lake
Dascylitis is also called by that name.

10. Now Zeleia[1] is situated on the farthermost
foot-hill of Mt. Ida, being one hundred and ninety
stadia distant from Cyzicus and about eighty stadia
from the nearest part of the sea, where the Aesepus
empties. And the poet mentions severally, in continuous order, the places that lie along the coast
after the Aesepus River: "And they who held
Adrasteia and the land of Apaesus, and held Pityeia
and the steep mountain of Tereia—these were led
by Adrastus and Amphius of the linen corslet, the
two sons of Merops of Percotê." [2] These places lie
below Zeleia,[3] but they are occupied by Cyziceni and
Priapeni even as far as the coast. Now near Zeleia
is the Tarsius River,[4] which is crossed twenty times
by the same road, like the Heptaporus River,[5] which
is mentioned by the poet.[6] And the river that flows
from Nicomedeia into Nicaea is crossed twenty-four
times, and the river that flows from Pholoê into the
Eleian country[7] is crossed many times . . . Scarthon
twenty-five times,[8] and the river that flows from the

concerning Zeleia as in the present passage). But see Leaf's
note (op. cit.), p. 67.

[4] On this river see Leaf, work last cited, p. 67.

[5] Strabo does not mean that the Heptaporus was crossed
twenty times. The name itself means the river of "seven
fords" (or ferries).

[6] *Iliad* 12. 20.

[7] *i.e.* Elis, in the Peloponnesus.

[8] The text is corrupt; and "Scarthon," whether it applies
to a river or a people, is otherwise unknown. However, this
whole passage, "And the river that flows from Nicomedeia
. . . crossed seventy-five times," appears to be a gloss, and
is ejected from the text by Kramer and Meineke (see Leaf's
Strabo and the Troad, p. 65, note 4).

πολλοὺς δὲ καὶ ὁ ἐκ Κοσκινίων εἰς Ἀλάβανδα,
πέντε δὲ καὶ ἑβδομήκοντα ὁ ἐκ Τυάνων εἰς Σόλους
διὰ τοῦ Ταύρου.

11. Ὑπὲρ δὲ τῆς ἐκβολῆς τοῦ Αἰσήπου σχεδόν
τι . . .[1] σταδίοις κολωνός ἐστιν, ἐφ' ᾧ τάφος
δείκνυται Μέμνονος τοῦ Τιθωνοῦ· πλησίον δ' ἐστὶ
καὶ ἡ Μέμνονος κώμη. τοῦ δὲ Αἰσήπου καὶ τοῦ
Πριάπου μεταξὺ ὁ Γράνικος ῥεῖ, τὰ πολλὰ δι'
Ἀδραστείας πεδίου, ἐφ' ᾧ Ἀλέξανδρος τοὺς
Δαρείου σατράπας ἀνὰ κράτος ἐνίκησε συμβαλών,
καὶ πᾶσαν τὴν ἐντὸς τοῦ Ταύρου καὶ τοῦ Εὐφράτου παρέλαβεν. ἐπὶ δὲ Γρανίκῳ πόλις ἦν Σιδηνή,
χώραν ἔχουσα πολλὴν ὁμώνυμον, κατέσπασται
δὲ νῦν. ἐν δὲ τῇ μεθορίᾳ τῆς Κυζικηνῆς καὶ τῆς
Πριαπηνῆς ἐστὶ τὰ Ἁρπάγια[2] τόπος, ἐξ οὗ τὸν
Γανυμήδην μυθεύουσιν ἡρπάχθαι· ἄλλοι δὲ περὶ
Δαρδάνιον ἄκραν, πλησίον Δαρδάνου.

12. Πρίαπος δ' ἐστὶ πόλις ἐπὶ θαλάττῃ καὶ
λιμήν· κτίσμα δ' οἱ μὲν Μιλησίων φασίν, οἵπερ
καὶ Ἄβυδον καὶ Προκόννησον συνῴκισαν κατὰ
τὸν αὐτὸν καιρόν, οἱ δὲ Κυζικηνῶν· ἐπώνυμος δ'
ἐστὶ τοῦ Πριάπου τιμωμένου παρ' αὐτοῖς, εἴτ' ἐξ
Ὀρνεῶν τῶν περὶ Κόρινθον μετενηνεγμένου τοῦ
ἱεροῦ, εἴτε τῷ λέγεσθαι Διονύσου καὶ νύμφης τὸν
θεὸν ὁρμησάντων ἐπὶ τὸ τιμᾶν αὐτὸν τῶν ἀνθρώπων, ἐπειδὴ σφόδρα εὐάμπελός ἐστιν ἡ χώρα καὶ

[1] After τι there is a lacuna in the MSS. except Fi, i reading ἐν εἴκοσι.
[2] Ἁρπάγια, the spelling in Stephanus; Ἁρπάγεια F, Ἁρπα-
χεια (unaccented) D, Ἁρπαχεῖα other MSS.

---

[1] The number of stadia has fallen out of the MSS.

country of the Coscinii into Alabanda is crossed many times, and the river that flows from Tyana into Soli through the Taurus is crossed seventy-five times.

11. About . . .[1] stadia above the outlet of the Aesepus River is a hill, where is shown the tomb of Memnon, son of Tithonus; and near by is the village of Memnon. The Granicus River flows between the Aesepus River and Priapus, mostly through the plain of Adrasteia,[2] where Alexander utterly defeated the satraps of Dareius in battle, and gained the whole of the country inside the Taurus and the Euphrates River. And on the Granicus was situated the city Sidenê, with a large territory of the same name; but it is now in ruins. On the boundary between the territory of Cyzicus and that of Priapus is a place called Harpagia,[3] from which, according to some writers of myths, Ganymede was snatched, though others say that he was snatched in the neighbourhood of the Dardanian Promontory, near Dardanus.

12. Priapus[4] is a city on the sea, and also a harbour. Some say that it was founded by Milesians, who at the same time also colonised Abydus and Proconnesus, whereas others say that it was founded by Cyziceni. It was named after Priapus, who was worshipped there; then his worship was transferred thither from Orneae near Corinth, or else the inhabitants felt an impulse to worship the god because he was called the son of Dionysus and a nymph; for their country is abundantly supplied with the vine, both theirs

[2] See Leaf, work last cited, p. 70.
[3] The root *harpag* means "snatch away."
[4] On the site of Priapus, see Leaf, p. 73.

αὕτη καὶ ἡ[1] ἐφεξῆς ὅμορος ἥ τε τῶν Παριανῶν
καὶ ἡ τῶν Λαμψακηνῶν· ὁ γοῦν Ξέρξης τῷ Θεμιστοκλεῖ εἰς οἶνον ἔδωκε τὴν Λάμψακον. ἀπεδείχθη
δὲ θεὸς οὗτος ὑπὸ τῶν νεωτέρων· οὐδὲ γὰρ
C 588 Ἡσίοδος οἶδε Πρίαπον, ἀλλ᾽ ἔοικε τοῖς Ἀττικοῖς
Ὀρθάνῃ καὶ Κονισάλῳ καὶ Τύχωνι καὶ τοῖς
τοιούτοις.

13. Ἐκαλεῖτο δ᾽ ἡ χώρα αὕτη Ἀδράστεια καὶ
Ἀδραστείας πεδίον, κατὰ ἔθος τι οὕτω λεγόντων
τὸ αὐτὸ χωρίον διττῶς, ὡς καὶ Θήβην καὶ Θήβης
πεδίον, καὶ Μυγδονίαν καὶ Μυγδονίας πεδίον.
φησὶ δὲ[2] Καλλισθένης ἀπὸ Ἀδράστου βασιλέως,
ὃς πρῶτος Νεμέσεως ἱερὸν ἱδρύσατο, καλεῖσθαι
Ἀδράστειαν. ἡ μὲν οὖν πόλις μεταξὺ Πριάπου
καὶ Παρίου, ἔχουσα ὑποκείμενον πεδίον ἐπώνυμον,
ἐν ᾧ καὶ μαντεῖον ἦν Ἀπόλλωνος Ἀκταίου καὶ
Ἀρτέμιδος κατὰ τὴν . . . .[3] εἰς δὲ Πάριον μετη-
νέχθη πᾶσα ἡ κατασκευὴ καὶ λιθία[4] κατα-
σπασθέντος τοῦ ἱεροῦ, καὶ ᾠκοδομήθη ἐν τῷ Παρίῳ
βωμός, Ἑρμοκρέοντος ἔργον, πολλῆς μνήμης
ἄξιον κατὰ τὸ[5] μέγεθος καὶ κάλλος· τὸ δὲ μαντεῖον
ἐξηλείφθη,[6] καθάπερ καὶ τὸ ἐν Ζελείᾳ. ἐνταῦθα
μὲν οὖν οὐδὲν ἱερὸν Ἀδραστείας δείκνυται, οὐδὲ δὴ

---

[1] ἡ, Meineke inserts.
[2] καί, before Καλλισθένης, Corais and Meineke omit.
[3] κατὰ τὴν Πυκάτην (omitted by Cx), after Ἀρτέμιδος, is
corrupt; κατὰ τὴν τύκατιν Dhi; κατὰ τὴν ἐπακτίαν, conj. Voss
on Scylax, p. 85; κατὰ τὴν ἀκτήν, conj. Berkel on Stephanus,
s.v. Ἀκτή (Kramer approving); κατὰ τὴν πυμάτην ἀκτήν,
Groskurd; κατὰ τὴν Πακτύην, conj. Meineke; κατὰ τὴν
Πιτυᾶτιν, conj. Corais.
[4] λιθία, Meineke emends to λιθεία.
[5] Instead of τό moxz read τε; so Corais and Meineke.

and the countries which border next upon it, I mean
those of the Pariani and the Lampsaceni. At any
rate, Xerxes gave Lampsacus to Themistocles to
supply him with wine. But it was by people of later
times that Priapus was declared a god, for even
Hesiod does not know of him; and he resembles
the Attic deities Orthanê, Conisalus, Tychon, and
others like them.

13. This country was called "Adrasteia"[1] and
"Plain of Adrasteia," in accordance with a custom
whereby people gave two names to the same place, as
"Thebê" and "Plain of Thebê," and "Mygdonia"
and "Plain of Mygdonia." According to Callisthenes,
among others, Adrasteia was named after King
Adrastus, who was the first to found a temple of
Nemesis. Now the city is situated between Priapus
and Parium; and it has below it a plain that is
named after it, in which there was an oracle of
Apollo Actaeus and Artemis. . . .[2] But when the
temple was torn down, the whole of its furnishings
and stone-work were transported to Parium, where
was built an altar,[3] the work of Hermocreon, very
remarkable for its size and beauty; but the oracle
was abolished like that at Zeleia. Here, however,
there is no temple of Adrasteia, nor yet of Nemesis,

---

[1] On the site of Adrasteia, see Leaf, p. 77.
[2] Three words in the Greek text here are corrupt. Strabo
may have said that this temple was "on the shore," or "in
the direction of Pityeia" (the same as Pitya; see § 15 following), or "in the direction of Pactyê" (see critical note).
[3] This altar was a stadium (about 600 feet) in length
(10. 5. 7).

---

[6] ἐξηλείφθη is emended by Müller-Dübner and Meineke to
ἐξελείφθη.

Νεμέσεως, περὶ δὲ Κύζικόν ἐστιν Ἀδραστείας ἱερόν.
Ἀντίμαχος δ᾽ οὕτω φησίν·

ἔστι δέ τις Νέμεσις μεγάλη θεός, ἣ τάδε πάντα
πρὸς μακάρων ἔλαχεν· βωμὸν δέ οἱ εἴσατο
πρῶτος
Ἄδρηστος ποταμοῖο παρὰ ῥόον Αἰσήποιο,
ἔνθα τετίμηταί τε καὶ Ἀδρήστεια καλεῖται.

14. Ἔστι δὲ καὶ τὸ Πάριον πόλις ἐπὶ θαλάττῃ,
λιμένα ἔχουσα μείζω τῆς Πριάπου, καὶ ηὐξημένη
γε ἐκ ταύτης· θεραπεύοντες γὰρ οἱ Παριανοὶ
τοὺς Ἀτταλικούς, ὑφ᾽ οἷς ἐτέτακτο ἡ Πρια-
πηνή, πολλὴν αὐτῆς ἀπετέμοντο, ἐπιτρεπόντων
ἐκείνων. ἐνταῦθα μυθεύουσι τοὺς Ὀφιογενεῖς
συγγένειάν τινα ἔχειν πρὸς τοὺς ὄφεις· φασὶ δ᾽
αὐτῶν τοὺς ἄρρενας τοῖς ἐχιοδήκτοις ἄκος εἶναι
συνεχῶς ἐφαπτομένους, ὥσπερ τοὺς ἐπῳδούς,
πρῶτον μὲν τὸ πελίωμα εἰς ἑαυτοὺς μεταφέροντας,
εἶτα καὶ τὴν φλεγμονὴν παύοντας καὶ τὸν πόνον.
μυθεύουσι δὲ τὸν ἀρχηγέτην τοῦ γένους ἥρωά τινα
ἐξ ὄφεως μεταβαλεῖν· τάχα δὲ τῶν Ψύλλων τις
ἦν τῶν Λιβυκῶν, εἰς δὲ τὸ γένος διέτεινεν ἡ
δύναμις μέχρι ποσοῦ. κτίσμα δ᾽ ἐστὶ τὸ Πάριον
Μιλησίων καὶ Ἐρυθραίων καὶ Παρίων.

15. Πίτυα¹ δ᾽ ἐστὶν ἐν Πιτυοῦντι τῆς Παριανῆς,

¹ Instead of Πίτυα, the Epitome, following the Homeric
MSS. (see § 10 above), reads Πιτύεια.

---

¹ A not uncommon appellation of the gods.
² Note the variant spelling of the name.
³ "Serpent-born."
⁴ See Leaf, work last cited, p. 85.   ⁵ See 17. 1. 44.
⁶ See Fraser, *Totemism and Exogamy*, 1. 20, 2. 54 and 4. 178.
⁷ According to the Scholiast on Apollonius Rhodius (1.

to be seen, although there is a temple of Adrasteia near Cyzicus. Antimachus says as follows: "There is a great goddess Nemesis, who has obtained as her portion all these things from the Blessed.[1] Adrestus[2] was the first to build an altar to her beside the stream of the Aesepus River, where she is worshipped under the name of Adresteia."

14. The city Parium is situated on the sea; it has a larger harbour than Priapus, and its territory has been increased at the expense of Priapus; for the Parians curried favour with the Attalic kings, to whom the territory of Priapus was subject, and by their permission cut off for themselves a large part of that territory. Here is told the mythical story that the Ophiogeneis[3] are akin to the serpent tribe;[4] and they say that the males of the Ophiogeneis cure snake-bitten people by continuous stroking, after the manner of enchanters, first transferring the livid colour to their own bodies and then stopping both the inflammation and the pain. According to the myth, the original founder of the tribe, a certain hero, changed from a serpent into a man. Perhaps he was one of the Libyan Psylli,[5] whose power persisted in his tribe for a certain time.[6] Parium was founded by Milesians and Erythraeans and Parians.

15. Pitya[7] is in Pityus in the territory of Parium,

933), cited by Leaf (*Troy*, p. 187), "Lampsacus was formerly called Pityeia, or, as others spell it, Pitya. Some say that Phrixus stored his treasure there and that the city was named after the treasure, for the Thracian word for treasure is 'pitye'" (but cf. the Greek word "pitys," "pine tree"). Strabo, however, places Pitya to the east of Parium, whereas Lampsacus lies to the west (see Leaf, *l.c.*, pp. 185 ff.; and his *Strabo on the Troad*, p. 87). In § 18 (following) Strabo says that "Lampsacus was formerly called Pityussa."

STRABO

ὑπερκείμενον ἔχουσα πιτυῶδες ὄρος· μεταξὺ δὲ
κεῖται Παρίου καὶ Πριάπου κατὰ Λῖνον, χωρίον
ἐπὶ θαλάττῃ, ὅπου οἱ Λινούσιοι κοχλίαι ἄριστοι
τῶν πάντων ἁλίσκονται.

16. Ἐν δὲ τῷ παράπλῳ τῷ ἀπὸ Παρίου εἰς
Πρίαπον ἥ τε παλαιὰ Προκόννησός ἐστι καὶ ἡ
νῦν Προκόννησος, πόλιν ἔχουσα καὶ μέταλλον
C 589 μέγα λευκοῦ λίθου σφόδρα ἐπαινούμενον· τὰ γοῦν
κάλλιστα τῶν ταύτῃ πόλεων ἔργα, ἐν δὲ τοῖς
πρῶτα[1] τὰ ἐν Κυζίκῳ, ταύτης ἐστὶ τῆς λίθου.
ἐντεῦθέν ἐστιν Ἀριστέας,[2] ὁ ποιητὴς τῶν Ἀρι-
μασπείων καλουμένων ἐπῶν, ἀνὴρ γόης, εἴ τις
ἄλλος.

17. Τὸ δὲ Τηρείης[3] ὄρος οἱ μὲν τὰ ἐν Πειρωσσῷ
ὄρη φασίν, ἃ ἔχουσιν οἱ Κυζικηνοὶ τῇ Ζελείᾳ
προσεχῆ, ἐν οἷς βασιλικὴ θήρα κατεσκεύαστο
τοῖς Λυδοῖς, καὶ Πέρσαις ὕστερον· οἱ δ' ἀπὸ
τετταράκοντα σταδίων Λαμψάκου δεικνύουσι
λόφον, ἐφ' ᾧ Μητρὸς θεῶν ἱερόν ἐστιν ἅγιον,
Τηρείης[4] ἐπικαλούμενον.

18. Καὶ ἡ Λάμψακος δ' ἐπὶ θαλάττῃ πόλις
ἐστὶν εὐλίμενος καὶ ἀξιόλογος, συμμένουσα καλῶς,
ὥσπερ καὶ ἡ Ἄβυδος· διέχει δ' αὐτῆς ὅσον

[1] πρῶτα, Corais, for πρῶτον; so the later editors.
[2] Ἀριστέας, Casaubon, for Ἀρισταῖος; so the later editors.
[3] Τηρείης, in margin of E, for ρείης C, τῆς ρείης other MSS.
[4] Τηρείης, the editors, for τῆς ρείης.

---

[1] Leaf (l.c.) translates, "hill shaped like a pine tree,"
adding (p. 187) that "the resemblance to a pine tree, so far
as my personal observation went, means no more than that
the hill slopes gently up to a rounded top." However, the
Greek adjective probably means in the present passage

32

lying below a pine-covered mountain;[1] and it lies between Parium and Priapus in the direction of Linum, a place on the seashore, where are caught the Linusian snails, the best in the world.

16. On the coasting-voyage from Parium to Priapus lie both the old Proconnesus and the present Proconnesus, the latter having a city and also a great quarry of white marble that is very highly commended; at any rate, the most beautiful works of art[2] in the cities of that part of the world, and especially those in Cyzicus, are made of this marble. Aristeas was a Proconnesian—the author of the Arimaspian Epic, as it is called—a charlatan if ever there was one.[3]

17. As for "the mountain of Tereia,"[4] some say that it is the range of mountains in Peirossus which are occupied by the Cyziceni and are adjacent to Zeleia, where a royal hunting-ground was arranged by the Lydians, and later by the Persians;[5] but others point out a hill forty stadia from Lampsacus, on which there is a temple sacred to the mother of the gods, entitled "Tereia's" temple.

18. Lampsacus,[6] also, is a city on the sea, a notable city with a good harbour, and still flourishing, like Abydus. It is about one hundred and seventy

---

"pine-covered" (cf. the use of the same adjective in 8. 6. 22, where it applies to a sacred precinct on the Isthmus of Corinth).

[2] *i.e.* buildings, statues, and other marble structures (see 5. 2. 5 and 5. 3. 8, and the foot-notes on "works of art").

[3] See 1. 2. 10, and Herodotus, 4. 13.

[4] The mountain mentioned in *Iliad* 2. 829.

[5] Xenophon (*Hellenica* 4. 1. 15) speaks of royal hunting-grounds, "some in enclosed parks, others in open regions."

[6] Now Lapsaki. On the site, see Leaf, p. 92.

ἑβδομήκοντα καὶ ἑκατὸν σταδίους· ἐκαλεῖτο δὲ
πρότερον Πιτυοῦσσα, καθάπερ καὶ τὴν Χίον
φασίν· ἐν δὲ τῇ περαίᾳ[1] τῆς Χερρονήσου πολίχνιόν ἐστι Καλλίπολις· κεῖται δ' ἐπ' ἀκτῆς,
ἐκκειμένη[2] πολὺ πρὸς τὴν Ἀσίαν κατὰ τὴν
Λαμψακηνῶν πόλιν, ὥστε τὸ δίαρμα μὴ πλέον
εἶναι τετταράκοντα σταδίων.

19. Ἐν δὲ τῷ μεταξὺ Λαμψάκου καὶ Παρίου
Παισὸς ἦν πόλις καὶ ποταμός· κατέσπασται[3] δ'
ἡ πόλις· οἱ δὲ Παισηνοὶ μετῴκησαν εἰς Λάμψακον, Μιλησίων ὄντες ἄποικοι καὶ αὐτοί, καθάπερ
καὶ οἱ Λαμψακηνοί· ὁ δὲ ποιητὴς εἴρηκεν ἀμφοτέρως, καὶ προσθεὶς τὴν πρώτην συλλαβήν,

καὶ δῆμον Ἀπαισοῦ,

καὶ ἀφελών,

ὅς ῥ' ἐνὶ Παισῷ

ναῖε πολυκτήμων.

καὶ ὁ ποταμὸς νῦν οὕτω καλεῖται. Μιλησίων δ'
εἰσὶ καὶ αἱ Κολωναὶ αἱ ὑπὲρ Λαμψάκου ἐν τῇ
μεσογαίᾳ τῆς Λαμψακηνῆς· ἄλλαι δ' εἰσὶν ἐπὶ
τῇ ἐκτὸς Ἑλλησποντίᾳ θαλάττῃ, Ἰλίου διέχουσαι
σταδίους τετταράκοντα πρὸς τοῖς ἑκατόν· ἐξ ὧν
τὸν Κύκνον φασίν. Ἀναξιμένης δὲ καὶ ἐν τῇ
Ἐρυθραίᾳ φησὶ λέγεσθαι Κολωνὰς καὶ ἐν τῇ
Φωκίδι καὶ ἐν Θετταλίᾳ· ἐν δὲ τῇ Παριανῇ ἐστιν
Ἰλιοκολώνη. ἐν δὲ τῇ Λαμψακηνῇ τόπος εὐάμ-
πελος Γεργίθιον· ἦν δὲ καὶ πόλις Γέργιθα, ἐκ
τῶν ἐν τῇ Κυμαίᾳ Γεργίθων· ἦν γὰρ κἀκεῖ πόλις

---

[1] περαίᾳ, Xylander, for στερέᾳ ; so the later editors.
[2] moz read ἐκκειμένης.
[3] κατέσπασται Foz, κατέσπαστο CDhirwx.

34

stadia distant from Abydus; and it was formerly called Pityussa, as also, it is said, was Chios. On the opposite shore of the Chersonesus is Callipolis, a small town. It is on the headland and runs far out towards Asia in the direction of the city of the Lampsaceni, so that the passage across to Asia from it is no more than forty stadia.

19. In the interval between Lampsacus and Parium lay a city and river called Paesus; but the city is in ruins. The Paeseni changed their abode to Lampsacus, they too being colonists from the Milesians, like the Lampsaceni. But the poet refers to the place in two ways, at one time adding the first syllable, "and the land of Apaesus,"[1] and at another omitting it, "a man of many possessions, who dwelt in Paesus."[2] And the river is now spelled in the latter way. Colonae,[3] which lies above Lampsacus in the interior of Lampsacenê, is also a colony of the Milesians; and there is another Colonae on the outer Hellespontine sea, which is one hundred and forty stadia distant from Ilium and is said to be the birthplace of Cycnus.[4] Anaximenes says that there are also places in the Erythraean territory and in Phocis and in Thessaly that are called Colonae. And there is an Iliocolonê in the territory of Parium. In the territory of Lampsacus is a place called Gergithium[5] which is rich in vines; and there was also a city called Gergitha from Gergithes in the territory of Cymê, for here too

---

[1] *Iliad* 2. 828.   [2] *Iliad* 5. 612.
[3] On the site of Colonae, see Leaf (*Strabo and the Troad*), p. 101.
[4] King of Colonae, slain by Achilles in the Trojan War.
[5] On Gergithium, see Leaf, p. 102.

STRABO

πληθυντικῶς καὶ θηλυκῶς λεγομένη αἱ Γέργιθες,
ὅθενπερ ὁ Γεργίθιος ἦν Κεφάλων· καὶ νῦν ἔτι
δείκνυται τόπος ἐν τῇ Κυμαίᾳ Γεργίθιον πρὸς
Λαρίσσῃ. ἐκ Παρίου μὲν οὖν ὁ γλωσσογράφος
κληθεὶς ἦν Νεοπτόλεμος μνήμης ἄξιος, ἐκ Λαμψάκου δὲ Χάρων τε ὁ συγγραφεὺς καὶ Ἀδείμαντος καὶ
Ἀναξιμένης ὁ ῥήτωρ καὶ Μητρόδωρος, ὁ τοῦ
Ἐπικούρου ἑταῖρος, καὶ αὐτὸς δ᾽ Ἐπίκουρος
τρόπον τινὰ Λαμψακηνὸς ὑπῆρξε, διατρίψας ἐν
Λαμψάκῳ καὶ φίλοις χρησάμενος τοῖς ἀρίστοις
C 590 τῶν ἐν τῇ πόλει ταύτῃ, τοῖς περὶ Ἰδομενέα καὶ
Λεοντέα. ἐντεῦθεν δὲ μετήνεγκεν Ἀγρίππας τὸν
πεπτωκότα λέοντα, Λυσίππου ἔργον· ἀνέθηκε δὲ
ἐν τῷ ἄλσει τῷ μεταξὺ τῆς λίμνης καὶ τοῦ εὐρίπου.

20. Μετὰ δὲ Λάμψακόν ἐστιν Ἄβυδος καὶ τὰ
μεταξὺ χωρία, περὶ ὧν οὕτως εἴρηκε συλλαβὼν
ὁ ποιητὴς καὶ τὴν Λαμψακηνὴν καὶ τῆς Παριανῆς
τινα (οὔπω γὰρ ἦσαν αὗται αἱ πόλεις κατὰ τὰ
Τρωικά)·

οἳ δ᾽ ἄρα Περκώτην καὶ Πράκτιον ἀμφενέμοντο,
καὶ Σηστὸν καὶ Ἄβυδον ἔχον καὶ δῖαν
Ἀρίσβην·
τῶν αὖθ᾽ Ὑρτακίδης ἦρχ᾽ Ἄσιος,

φησίν,

ὃν Ἀρίσβηθεν φέρον ἵπποι
αἴθωνες μεγάλοι ποταμοῦ ἄπο Σελλήεντος.

---

[1] Fl. in the Alexandrian period; author of works entitled
Glosses and *On Epigrams*.
[2] Early historian; author of *Persian History* and *Annals
of the Lampsaceni*.
[3] Known only as courtier of Demetrius Poliorcetes.
[4] See Frazer's note on Pausanias, 6. 18. 2.

36

there was a city called Gergithes, in the feminine plural, the birthplace of Cephalon the Gergithian. And still to-day a place called Gergithium is pointed out in the territory of Cymê near Larissa. Now Neoptolemus,[1] called the Glossographer, a notable man, was from Parium; and Charon the historian[2] and Adeimantus[3] and Anaximenes the rhetorician[4] and Metrodorus the comrade of Epicurus were from Lampsacus; and Epicurus himself was in a sense a Lampsacenian, having lived in Lampsacus and having been on intimate terms with the ablest men of that city, Idomeneus and Leonteus and their followers. It was from here that Agrippa transported the Fallen Lion, a work of Lysippus; and he dedicated it in the sacred precinct between the Lake and the Euripus.[5]

20. After Lampsacus come Abydus and the intervening places of which the poet, who comprises with them the territory of Lampsacus and part of the territory of Parium (for these two cities were not yet in existence in the Trojan times), speaks as follows: "And those who dwelt about Percotê and Practius, and held Sestus and Abydus and goodly Arisbê—these in turn were led by Asius, the son of Hyrtacus, . . . who was brought by his large sorrel horses from Arisbê, from the River Sellëeis."[6]   In

---

[5] "The Lake" seems surely to be the Stagnum Agrippae mentioned by Tacitus (*Annals* 15. 37), *i.e.* the Nemus Caesarum on the right bank of the Tiber (see A. Häbler, *Hermes* 19 (1884), p. 235). "The Stagnum Agrippae was apparently a pond constructed by Agrippa in connection with the Aqua Virgo and the canal called Euripus in the neighbourhood of the Pantheon" (C. G. Ramsay, *Annals of Tacitus*, 15. 37), or, as Leaf (*op. cit.*, p. 108) puts it, "The Euripus is the channel filled with water set up by Caesar round the arena of the Circus Maximus at Rome to protect the spectators from the wild beasts."   [6] *Iliad* 2. 835.

37

οὕτω δ' εἰπὼν ἔοικε τὸ βασίλειον ἀποφαίνειν τοῦ Ἀσίου τὴν Ἀρίσβην, ὅθεν ἥκειν αὐτόν φησιν·

δν Ἀρίσβηθεν φέρον ἵπποι ποταμοῦ ἄπο Σελλήεντος.

οὕτω δ' ἀφανῆ τὰ χωρία ταῦτά ἐστιν, ὥστε οὐδ' ὁμολογοῦσι περὶ αὐτῶν οἱ ἱστοροῦντες, πλὴν ὅτι περὶ Ἄβυδον καὶ Λάμψακόν ἐστι καὶ Πάριον, καὶ ὅτι ἡ πάλαι Περκώτη[1] μετωνομάσθη, ὁ τόπος.

21. Τῶν δὲ ποταμῶν τὸν μὲν Σελλήεντά φησιν ὁ ποιητὴς πρὸς τῇ Ἀρίσβῃ ῥεῖν, εἴπερ ὁ Ἄσιος Ἀρίσβηθέν τε ἧκε καὶ ποταμοῦ ἄπο Σελλήεντος. ὁ δὲ Πράκτιος ποταμὸς μὲν ἔστι, πόλις δ' οὐχ εὑρίσκεται, ὥς τινες ἐνόμισαν· ῥεῖ δὲ καὶ οὗτος μεταξὺ Ἀβύδου καὶ Λαμψάκου· τὸ οὖν

καὶ Πράκτιον ἀμφενέμοντο,

οὕτω δεκτέον, ὡς περὶ ποταμοῦ, καθάπερ κἀκεῖνα·

οἵ τ' ἄρα πὰρ ποταμὸν Κηφισὸν δῖον ἔναιον,

καὶ

ἀμφί τε Παρθένιον ποταμὸν κλυτὰ ἔργ' ἐνέμοντο.[2]

ἦν δὲ καὶ ἐν Λέσβῳ πόλις Ἀρίσβα, ἧς τὴν χώραν ἔχουσι Μηθυμναῖοι· ἔστι δὲ καὶ ποταμὸς Ἄρισβος ἐν Θρᾴκῃ, ὥσπερ εἴρηται, καὶ τούτου

---

[1] After Περκώτη Leaf inserts μετῳκίσθη καὶ Περκώπη (see his *Strabo on the Troad*, p. 11, footnote 3 on p. 108, and note on Percotê, p. 111). Thus, according to him, "the old Percotê was transplanted and the name of its site changed to Percopê."

speaking thus, the poet seems to set forth Arisbê, whence he says Asius came, as the royal residence of Asius: "who was brought by his horses from Arisbê, from the River Sellëeis." But these places[1] are so obscure that even investigators do not agree about them, except that they are in the neighbourhood of Abydus and Lampsacus and Parium, and that the old Percotê,[2] the site, underwent a change of name.[3]

21. Of the rivers, the Sellëeis flows near Arisbê, as the poet says, if it be true that Asius came both from Arisbê and from the Sellëeis River. The River Practius is indeed in existence, but no city of that name is to be found, as some have wrongly thought. This river also[4] flows between Abydus and Lampsacus. Accordingly, the words, "and dwelt about Practius," should be interpreted as applying to a river, as should also those other words, "and those who dwelt beside the goodly Cephisus River,"[5] and "those who had their famed estates about the Parthenius River."[6] There was also a city Arisba in Lesbos, whose territory is occupied by the Methymnaeans. And there is an Arisbus River in Thrace, as I have said before,[7] near

---

[1] i.e. Arisbê, Percotê, and the Sellëeis. Strabo himself locates the Practius (13. 1. 4, 7, 8, 21). On the sites of these places, see Leaf's *Troy*, pp. 188 ff., his note in *Jour. Hellenic Studies*, XXXVII (1917), p. 26, and his *Strabo on the Troad*, pp. 108 ff.

[2] Homer's Percotê, on the sea.   [3] See critical note.

[4] i.e. as well as the Sellëeis.   [5] *Iliad* 2. 522.

[6] *Iliad* 2. 854 (see critical note).

[7] Obviously in the lost portion of Book VII.

---

[2] Instead of ἔργ' ἐνέμοντο the Homeric MSS. have δώματ' ἔναιον, and Strabo himself so cites in 12. 3. 5. Eustathius (note on *Iliad* 2. 835) cites as in the present passage.

πλησίον οἱ Κεβρήνιοι Θρᾷκες. πολλαὶ δ' ὁμω-
νυμίαι Θραξὶ καὶ Τρωσίν, οἷον Σκαιοὶ Θρᾷκές
τινες καὶ Σκαιὸς ποταμὸς καὶ Σκαιὸν τεῖχος καὶ
ἐν Τροίᾳ Σκαιαὶ πύλαι· Ξάνθιοι Θρᾷκες, Ξάνθος
ποταμὸς ἐν Τροίᾳ· Ἄρισβος ὁ ἐμβάλλων εἰς τὸν
Ἕβρον, Ἀρίσβη ἐν Τροίᾳ· Ῥῆσος ποταμὸς ἐν
Τροίᾳ, Ῥῆσος δὲ καὶ ὁ βασιλεὺς τῶν Θρακῶν.
ἔστι δὲ καὶ τῷ Ἀσίῳ ὁμώνυμος ἕτερος παρὰ τῷ
ποιητῇ Ἄσιος,

ὃς μήτρως ἦν Ἕκτορος ἱπποδάμοιο,
αὐτοκασίγνητος Ἑκάβης, υἱὸς δὲ Δύμαντος,
ὃς Φρυγίην ναίεσκε ῥοῆς ἐπὶ Σαγγαρίοιο.

22. Ἄβυδος δὲ Μιλησίων ἐστὶ κτίσμα, ἐπιτρέψαντος Γύγου, τοῦ Λυδῶν βασιλέως· ἦν γὰρ
ἐπ' ἐκείνῳ τὰ χωρία καὶ ἡ Τρωὰς ἅπασα,
ὀνομάζεται δὲ καὶ ἀκρωτήριόν τι πρὸς Δαρδάνῳ
C 591 Γύγας· ἐπίκειται δὲ τῷ στόματι τῆς Προποντίδος
καὶ τοῦ Ἑλλησπόντου, διέχει δὲ τὸ ἴσον Λαμψάκου καὶ Ἰλίου, σταδίους περὶ ἑβδομήκοντα καὶ
ἑκατόν. ἐνταῦθα δ' ἐστὶ τὸ ἑπταστάδιον, ὅπερ
ἔζευξε Ξέρξης, τὸ διόριζον τὴν Εὐρώπην καὶ τὴν
Ἀσίαν. καλεῖται δ' ἡ ἄκρα τῆς Εὐρώπης Χερ-
ρόνησος διὰ τὸ σχῆμα, ἡ ποιοῦσα τὰ στενὰ τὰ
κατὰ τὸ ζεῦγμα· ἀντίκειται δὲ τὸ ζεῦγμα τῇ
Ἀβύδῳ. Σηστὸς δὲ ἀρίστη[1] τῶν ἐν Χερρονήσῳ
πόλεων· διὰ δὲ τὴν γειτοσύνην ὑπὸ τῷ αὐτῷ

[1] For ἀρίστη Meineke conj. κρατίστη.

---

[1] *Iliad* 16. 717.
[2] On the site of Abydus, see Leaf, *Strabo on the Troad*, p. 117.

which are situated the Thracian Cebrenians. There are many names common to the Thracians and the Trojans; for example, there are Thracians called Scaeans, and a river Scaeus, and a Scaean Wall, and at Troy the Scaean Gates. And there are Thracian Xanthians, and in Troy-land a river Xanthus. And in Troy-land there is a river Arisbus which empties into the Hebrus, as also a city Arisbê. And there was a river Rhesus in Troy-land; and there was a Rhesus who was the king of the Thracians. And there is also, of the same name as this Asius, another Asius in Homer, "who was maternal uncle to horse-taming Hector, and own brother to Hecabê, but son of Dymas, who dwelt in Phrygia by the streams of the Sangarius."[1]

22. Abydus was founded by Milesians, being founded by permission of Gyges, king of the Lydians; for this district and the whole of the Troad were under his sway; and there is a promontory named Gygas near Dardanus. Abydus lies at the mouth of the Propontis and the Hellespont; and it is equidistant from Lampsacus and Ilium, about one hundred and seventy stadia.[2] Here, separating Europe and Asia, is the Heptastadium,[3] which was bridged by Xerxes. The European promontory that forms the narrows at the place of the bridge is called the Chersonesus[4] because of its shape. And the place of the bridge lies opposite Abydus. Sestus[5] is the best of the cities in the Chersonesus; and, on account of its proximity to Abydus, it was assigned to the same governor as

[3] *i.e.* "Strait of seven stadia."
[4] *i.e.* "Land-island" or "Peninsula."
[5] On its site, see Leaf, work last cited, p. 119.

ἡγεμόνι καὶ αὕτη ἐτέτακτο οὔπω ταῖς ἠπείροις
διοριζόντων τῶν τότε τὰς ἡγεμονίας. ἡ μὲν οὖν
Ἄβυδος καὶ ἡ Σηστὸς διέχουσιν ἀλλήλων τριάκοντά που σταδίους ἐκ λιμένος εἰς λιμένα, τὸ δὲ
ζεῦγμά ἐστι μικρὸν ἀπὸ τῶν πόλεων παραλλά-
ξαντι ἐξ Ἀβύδου μὲν ὡς ἐπὶ τὴν Προποντίδα, ἐκ
δὲ Σηστοῦ εἰς τοὐναντίον· ὀνομάζεται δὲ πρὸς τῇ
Σηστῷ τόπος Ἀποβάθρα, καθ' ὃν ἐζεύγνυτο ἡ
σχεδία· ἔστι δὲ ἡ Σηστὸς ἐνδοτέρω κατὰ τὴν
Προποντίδα ὑπερδέξιος τοῦ ῥοῦ τοῦ ἐξ αὐτῆς·
διὸ καὶ εὐπετέστερον ἐκ τῆς Σηστοῦ διαίρουσι
παραλεξάμενοι[1] μικρὸν ἐπὶ τὸν τῆς Ἡροῦς
πύργον κἀκεῖθεν ἀφιέντες τὰ πλοῖα συμπράττοντος
τοῦ ῥοῦ πρὸς τὴν περαίωσιν· τοῖς δ' ἐξ Ἀβύδου
περαιουμένοις παραλεκτέον[2] ἐστὶν εἰς τἀναντία
ὀκτώ που σταδίους ἐπὶ πύργον τινὰ κατ' ἀντικρὺ
τῆς Σηστοῦ, ἔπειτα διαίρειν πλάγιον καὶ μὴ
τελέως ἐναντίον ἔχουσιν τὸν ῥοῦν. ᾤκουν δὲ τὴν
Ἄβυδον μετὰ τὰ Τρωικὰ Θρᾷκες, εἶτα Μιλήσιοι.
τῶν δὲ πόλεων ἐμπρησθεισῶν ὑπὸ Δαρείου, τοῦ
Ξέρξου πατρός, τῶν κατὰ τὴν Προποντίδα,
ἐκοινώνησε καὶ ἡ Ἄβυδος τῆς αὐτῆς συμφορᾶς.
ἐνέπρησε δὲ πυθόμενος μετὰ τὴν ἀπὸ τῶν Σκυθῶν
ἐπάνοδον, τοὺς νομάδας παρασκευάζεσθαι δια-
βαίνειν ἐπ' αὐτὸν κατὰ τιμωρίαν ὧν ἔπαθον,
δεδιὼς μὴ αἱ πόλεις πορθμεῖα παράσχοιεν τῇ
στρατιᾷ. συνέβη δὲ πρὸς ταῖς ἄλλαις μετα-
βολαῖς καὶ τῷ χρόνῳ καὶ τοῦτο αἴτιον τῆς

---

[1] παραλεξάμενοι, Kramer restores, for παραλαξάμενοι C,
παραλλαξάμενοι rw, Xylander, and other editors.
[2] παραλεκτέον, Kramer restores, for παραλλακτέον, earlier
editors.

Abydus in the times when governorships had not yet been delimited by continents. Now although Abydus and Sestus are about thirty stadia distant from one another from harbour to harbour, yet the line of the bridge across the strait is short, being drawn at an angle to that between the two cities, that is, from a point nearer than Abydus to the Propontis on the Abydus side to a point farther away from the Propontis on the Sestus side. Near Sestus is a place named Apobathra,[1] where the pontoon-bridge was attached to the shore. Sestus lies farther in towards the Propontis, farther up the stream that flows out of the Propontis. It is therefore easier to cross over from Sestus, first coasting a short distance to the Tower of Hero and then letting the ships make the passage across by the help of the current. But those who cross over from Abydus must first follow the coast in the opposite direction about eight stadia to a tower opposite Sestus, and then sail across obliquely and thus not have to meet the full force of the current. After the Trojan War Abydus was the home of Thracians, and then of Milesians. But when the cities were burned by Dareius, father of Xerxes, I mean the cities on the Propontis, Abydus shared in the same misfortune. He burned them because he had learned after his return from his attack upon the Scythians that the nomads were making preparations to cross the strait and attack him to avenge their sufferings, and was afraid that the cities would provide means for the passage of their army. And this too, in addition to the other changes and to the lapse of time, is a cause of the confusion into which the topography of

---

[1] *i.e.* "Place of Disembarkation."

43

συγχύσεως τῶν τόπων. περὶ δὲ Σηστοῦ καὶ τῆς ὅλης Χερρονήσου προείπομεν ἐν τοῖς περὶ τῆς Θρᾴκης τόποις,[1] φησὶ δὲ τὴν Σηστὸν Θεόπομπος βραχεῖαν μέν, εὐερκῆ δέ, καὶ σκέλει διπλέθρῳ συνάπτειν πρὸς τὸν λιμένα, καὶ διὰ ταῦτ' οὖν καὶ διὰ τὸν ῥοῦν κυρίαν εἶναι τῶν παρόδων.

23. Ὑπέρκειται δὲ τῆς τῶν Ἀβυδηνῶν χώρας ἐν τῇ Τρωάδι τὰ Ἄστυρα, ἃ νῦν μὲν Ἀβυδηνῶν ἐστι, κατεσκαμμένη πόλις, πρότερον δὲ ἦν καθ' αὐτά, χρυσεῖα ἔχοντα, ἃ νῦν σπάνιά ἐστιν ἐξαναλωμένα, καθάπερ τὰ ἐν τῷ Τμώλῳ τὰ περὶ τὸν Πακτωλόν. ἀπὸ Ἀβύδου δ' ἐπὶ Αἴσηπον περὶ ἑπτακοσίους φασὶ σταδίους, εὐθυπλοίᾳ δὲ ἐλάττους.

C 592   24. Ἔξω δὲ Ἀβύδου τὰ περὶ τὸ Ἴλιόν ἐστι, τά τε παράλια ἕως Λέκτου καὶ τὰ ἐν τῷ Τρωικῷ πεδίῳ καὶ τὰ παρώρεια τῆς Ἴδης τὰ ὑπὸ τῷ Αἰνείᾳ. διττῶς δὲ ταῦτ' ὀνομάζει ὁ ποιητής, τοτὲ μὲν οὕτω λέγων·

Δαρδανίων αὖτ' ἦρχεν ἐὺς παῖς Ἀγχίσαο,

Δαρδανίους καλῶν, τοτὲ δὲ Δαρδάνους,

Τρῶες καὶ Λύκιοι καὶ Δάρδανοι ἀγχιμαχηταί.

---

[1] Kramer suspects that τόποις should be ejected. Meineke conj. λόγοις, but retains τόποις in his text. Cp. *Frag.* 55*a*, Vol. III, p. 378.

---

[1] See Vol. III, *Frags.* 51 (p. 373), 55*b* (p. 379), and 51*a*, 52, and 53 (p. 375).

[2] *i.e.* about 200 feet (in breadth).

[3] According to Leaf (*l.c.*, p. 135), the *shortest* course of a vessel between Abydus and the mouth of the Aesepus measures just about 700 stadia. Hence Strabo's authorities for his statement are in error if, as usual, the *longer* voyage

the country has fallen. As for Sestus and the Chersonesus in general, I have already spoken of them in my description of the region of Thrace.[1] Theopompus says that Sestus is small but well fortified, and that it is connected with its harbour by a double wall of two plethra,[2] and that for this reason, as also on account of the current, it is mistress of the passage.

23. Above the territory of the Abydeni, in the Troad, lies Astyra. This city, which is in ruins, now belongs to the Abydeni, but in earlier times it was independent and had gold mines. These mines arc now scant, being used up, like those on Mt. Tmolus in the neighbourhood of the Pactolus River. From Abydus to the Aesepus the distance is said to be about seven hundred stadia, but less by straight sailing.[3]

24. Outside Abydus lies the territory of Ilium—the parts on the shore extending to Lectum, and the places in the Trojan Plain, and the parts on the side of Mt. Ida that were subject to Aeneias. The poet names these last parts in two ways, at one time saying as follows: "The Dardanii in turn were led by the valiant son of Anchises,"[4] calling the inhabitants "Dardanii"; and at another time, "Dardani": "The Trojans and Lycians and Dardani that fight in close combat." And it is reason-

---

is a *coasting* voyage, following the sinuosities of the gulfs, as against the *shorter*, or more direct, voyage   Leaf, however, forces the phrase "by straight sailing" to mean "a straight course wholly over the land," adding that "the meaning must be that it would be shorter if one could sail straight," and that "the expression is singularly infelicitous as applied to a journey by land in contrast to one by sea."

[4] *Iliad.* 2. 819.

εἰκὸς δ' ἐνταῦθα ἱδρῦσθαι τὸ παλαιὸν τὴν λεγομένην ὑπὸ τοῦ ποιητοῦ Δαρδανίαν·

Δάρδανον αὖ πρῶτον τέκετο νεφεληγερέτα
Ζεύς,
κτίσσε δὲ Δαρδανίην.

νῦν μὲν γὰρ οὐδ' ἴχνος πόλεως σώζεται αὐτόθι.

25. Εἰκάζει δὲ Πλάτων μετὰ τοὺς κατακλυσμοὺς τρία πολιτείας εἴδη συνίστασθαι· πρῶτον μὲν τὸ ἐπὶ τὰς ἀκρωρείας ἁπλοῦν τι καὶ ἄγριον, δεδιότων τὰ ὕδατα ἐπιπολάζοντα ἀκμὴν ἐν τοῖς πεδίοις· δεύτερον δὲ τὸ ἐν ταῖς ὑπωρείαις, θαρρούντων ἤδη κατὰ μικρόν, ἅτε δὴ καὶ τῶν πεδίων ἀρχομένων ἀναψύχεσθαι· τρίτον δὲ τὸ ἐν τοῖς πεδίοις. λέγοι δ' ἄν τις καὶ τέταρτον καὶ πέμπτον ἴσως καὶ πλείω, ὕστατον δὲ τὸ ἐν τῇ παραλίᾳ καὶ ἐν ταῖς νήσοις, λελυμένου παντὸς τοῦ τοιούτου φόβου. τὸ γὰρ μᾶλλον καὶ ἧττον θαρρεῖν πλησιάζειν τῇ θαλάττῃ πλείους ἂν ὑπογράφοι διαφορὰς πολιτειῶν καὶ ἠθῶν, καθάπερ[1] τῶν ἀγαθῶν[2] τε καὶ τῶν ἀγρίων ἔτι πως[3] ἐπὶ τὸ ἥμερον τῶν δευτέρων ὑποβεβηκότων. ἔστι δέ[4] τις διαφορὰ καὶ παρὰ τούτοις τῶν ἀγροίκων καὶ μεσαγροίκων καὶ πολιτικῶν· ἀφ' ὧν ἤδη καὶ ἐπὶ τὸ ἀστεῖον καὶ ἄριστον ἦθος ἐτελεύτησεν ἡ τῶν ὀνομάτων κατ' ὀλίγον μετά-

---

[1] καθάπερ, Xylander, for καὶ ἄπερ; so the later editors.
[2] ἀγαθῶν MSS., Leaf (op. cit. pp. 13, 140) restores, for ἁπλῶν, emendation of Groskurd accepted by other later editors. Plato (Laws 679 C) says : ἀγαθοὶ μὲν διὰ ταῦτα (i.e. the absence of riches, poverty, insolence, injustice, and envy) τε ἦσαν καὶ διὰ τὴν λεγομένην εὐήθειαν.
[3] ἔτι πως, the editors in general, for ἐστί πως moz, ἔτι πῶς

able to suppose that this was in ancient times the site
of the Dardania mentioned by the poet when he
says, "At first Dardanus was begotten by Zeus the
cloud-gatherer, and he founded Dardania";[1] for at
the present time there is not so much as a trace of
a city preserved in that territory.[2]

25. Plato[3] conjectures, however, that after the
time of the floods three kinds of civilisation were
formed: the first, that on the mountain-tops, which
was simple and wild, when men were in fear of the
waters which still deeply covered the plains; the
second, that on the foot-hills, when men were now
gradually taking courage because the plains were
beginning to be relieved of the waters; and the
third, that in the plains. One might speak equally
of a fourth and fifth, or even more, but last of all that
on the sea-coast and in the islands, when men had
been finally released from all such fear; for the
greater or less courage they took in approaching the
sea would indicate several different stages of civilisation and manners, first as in the case of the qualities of
goodness[4] and wildness, which in some way further
served as a foundation for the milder qualities in the
second stage. But in the second stage also there is
a difference to be noted, I mean between the rustic and
semi-rustic and civilised qualities; and, beginning
with these last qualities, the gradual assumption
of new names ended in the polite and highest

---

[1] *Iliad* 20. 215.
[2] On the boundaries of Dardania, see Leaf (*l.c.*, p. 137).
[3] *Laws* 677-679.   [4] See critical note.

---

other MSS.; omitted by Corais; ἤδη πως, Groskurd; ἐτέρως
Leaf.
[4] δέ, after ἔστι, Leaf omits.

ληψις, κατὰ τὴν τῶν ἠθῶν ἐπὶ τὸ κρεῖττον
μετάστασιν, παρὰ τὰς τῶν τόπων καὶ τῶν βίων
μεταβολάς. ταύτας δὴ τὰς διαφορὰς ὑπογράφειν
φησὶ τὸν ποιητὴν ὁ Πλάτων, τῆς μὲν πρώτης
πολιτείας παράδειγμα τιθέντα τὸν τῶν Κυκλώπων
βίον, αὐτοφυεῖς νεμομένων καρποὺς καὶ τὰς
ἀκρωρείας κατεχόντων ἐν σπηλαίοις τισίν·

ἀλλὰ τά γ᾽ ἄσπαρτα καὶ ἀνήροτα πάντα
    φύονται,

φησίν, αὐτοῖς·

τοῖσιν δ᾽ οὐκ ἀγοραὶ βουληφόροι, οὔτε
    θέμιστες·
ἀλλ᾽ οἵ γ᾽ ὑψηλῶν ὀρέων ναίουσι κάρηνα,
ἐν σπέσσι γλαφυροῖσι, θεμιστεύει δὲ ἕκαστος
παίδων ἠδ᾽ ἀλόχων.

τοῦ δὲ δευτέρου τὸν ἐπὶ[1] τοῦ Δαρδάνου·

κτίσσε δὲ Δαρδανίην, ἐπεὶ οὔπω Ἴλιος ἱρή
C 593 ἐν πεδίῳ πεπόλιστο, πόλις μερόπων ἀνθρώ-
    πων,
ἀλλ᾽ ἔθ᾽ ὑπωρείας ᾤκεον[2] πολυπιδάκου Ἴδης.

τοῦ δὲ τρίτου ἐπὶ τοῦ Ἴλου τὸν ἐν τοῖς πεδίοις.
τοῦτον γὰρ παραδιδόασι τοῦ Ἰλίου κτίστην, ἀφ᾽
οὗ καὶ τὴν ἐπωνυμίαν λαβεῖν τὴν πόλιν· εἰκὸς
δὲ καὶ διὰ τοῦτο ἐν μέσῳ τῷ πεδίῳ τεθάφθαι
αὐτόν, ὅτι πρῶτος ἐθάρρησεν ἐν τοῖς πεδίοις
θέσθαι τὴν κατοικίαν·

οἱ δὲ παρ᾽ Ἴλου σῆμα παλαιοῦ Δαρδανίδαο
μέσσον κὰπ πεδίον παρ᾽ ἐρινεὸν ἐσσεύοντο.

culture, in accordance with the change of manners for the better along with the changes in places of abode and in modes of life. Now these differences, according to Plato,[1] are suggested by the poet, who sets forth as an example of the first stage of civilisation the life of the Cyclopes, who lived on uncultivated fruits and occupied the mountain-tops, living in caves : "but all these things," he says, "grow unsown and unploughed" for them. . . . "And they have no assemblies for council, nor appointed laws, but they dwell on the tops of high mountains in hollow caves, and each is lawgiver to his children and his wives."[2] And as an example of the second stage, the life in the time of Dardanus, who "founded Dardania ; for not yet had sacred Ilios been builded to be a city of mortal men, but they were living on the foot-hills of many-fountained Ida."[3] And of the third stage, the life in the plains in the time of Ilus ;[4] for he is the traditional founder of Ilium, and it was from him that the city took its name. And it is reasonable to suppose, also, that he was buried in the middle of the plain for this reason—that he was the first to dare to settle in the plains : "And they sped past the tomb of ancient Ilus, son of Dardanus, through the middle of the plain past the wild fig tree."[5] Yet even Ilus did not have full

[1] *Laws* 3. 680.
[2] *Odyssey* 9. 109, 112–114 (quoted by Plato in *Laws* 3. 680).
[3] *Iliad* 20. 216 (quoted by Plato in *Laws* 3. 681).
[4] *Laws* 3. 682.   [5] *Iliad* 11. 166.

---

[1] ἐπί, Corais, for ἐκ ; so the later editors.
[2] Instead of ᾤκεον, *moz* read ἔναιον.

οὐδ᾽ οὗτος δὲ τελείως ἐθάρρησεν· οὐ γὰρ ἐνταῦθα
ἵδρυσε τὴν πόλιν, ὅπου νῦν ἐστίν, ἀλλὰ σχεδόν
τι τριάκοντα σταδίοις ἀνωτέρω πρὸς ἔω καὶ πρὸς
τὴν Ἴδην καὶ τὴν Δαρδανίαν κατὰ τὴν νῦν
καλουμένην Ἰλιέων Κώμην. οἱ δὲ νῦν Ἰλιεῖς
φιλοδοξοῦντες καὶ θέλοντες εἶναι ταύτην τὴν
παλαιὰν παρεσχήκασι λόγον τοῖς ἐκ τῆς Ὁμήρου
ποιήσεως τεκμαιρομένοις· οὐ γὰρ ἔοικεν αὕτη
εἶναι ἡ καθ᾽ Ὅμηρον. καὶ ἄλλοι δὲ ἱστοροῦσι
πλείους μεταβεβληκέναι τόπους τὴν πόλιν,
ὕστατα δ᾽ ἐνταῦθα συμμεῖναι κατὰ Κροῖσον[1]
μάλιστα. τὰς δὴ τοιαύτας μεταβάσεις εἰς τὰ
κάτω μέρη τὰς τότε συμβαινούσας ὑπολαμβάνω
καὶ βίων καὶ πολιτειῶν ὑπογράφειν διαφοράς.
ἀλλὰ ταῦτα μὲν καὶ ἄλλοτε ἐπισκεπτέον.

26. Τὴν δὲ τῶν Ἰλιέων πόλιν τῶν νῦν τέως
μὲν κώμην εἶναί φασι, τὸ ἱερὸν ἔχουσαν τῆς
Ἀθηνᾶς μικρὸν καὶ εὐτελές, Ἀλέξανδρον δὲ
ἀναβάντα μετὰ τὴν ἐπὶ Γρανίκῳ νίκην, ἀναθήμασί
τε κοσμῆσαι τὸ ἱερὸν καὶ προσαγορεῦσαι πόλιν
καὶ οἰκοδομίαις ἀναλαβεῖν προστάξαι τοῖς ἐπι-
μεληταῖς ἐλευθέραν τε κρῖναι καὶ ἄφορον, ὕστερον
δὲ μετὰ τὴν κατάλυσιν τῶν Περσῶν ἐπιστολὴν
καταπέμψαι φιλάνθρωπον, ὑπισχνούμενον πόλιν
τε ποιῆσαι μεγάλην καὶ ἱερὸν ἐπισημότατον, καὶ
ἀγῶνα ἀποδείξειν ἱερόν. μετὰ δὲ τὴν ἐκείνου

---

[1] For Κροῖσον x reads μικρόν, moz χρησμόν.

---

[1] Schliemann's excavations, however, identify Hissarlik as
the site of Homer's Troy. Hence "the site of Homer's Troy
at 'the village of Ilians' is a mere figment" (Leaf, l.c., p. 141).

courage, for he did not found the city at the place where it now is, but about thirty stadia higher up towards the east, and towards Mt. Ida and Dardania, at the place now called "Village of the Ilians."[1] But the people of the present Ilium, being fond of glory and wishing to show that their Ilium was the ancient city, have offered a troublesome argument to those who base their evidence on the poetry of Homer, for their Ilium does not appear to have been the Homeric city. Other inquirers also find that the city changed its site several times, but at last settled permanently where it now is at about the time of Croesus.[2] I take for granted, then, that such removals into the parts lower down, which took place in those times, indicate different stages in modes of life and civilisation; but this must be further investigated at another time.

26. It is said that the city of the present Ilians was for a time a mere village, having its temple of Athena, a small and cheap temple, but that when Alexander went up there after his victory at the Granicus[3] River he adorned the temple with votive offerings, gave the village the title of city, and ordered those in charge to improve it with buildings, and that he adjudged it free and exempt from tribute; and that later, after the overthrow of the Persians, he sent down a kindly letter to the place, promising to make a great city of it, and to build a magnificent sanctuary, and to proclaim sacred games.[4] But after

[2] King of Lydia, 560–546 B.C.
[3] The first of the three battles by which he overthrew the Persian empire (334 B.C.).
[4] e.g. like the Olympic Games. But his untimely death prevented the fulfilment of this promise.

τελευτὴν Λυσίμαχος μάλιστα τῆς πόλεως ἐπεμελήθη καὶ νεὼν κατεσκεύασε καὶ τεῖχος περιε-
βάλετο ὅσον τετταράκοντα σταδίων, συνῴκισέ
τε εἰς αὐτὴν τὰς κύκλῳ πόλεις ἀρχαίας ἤδη
κεκακωμένας, ὅτε καὶ Ἀλεξανδρείας ἤδη ἐπεμελήθη, συνῳκισμένης μὲν ἤδη ὑπ' Ἀντιγόνου
καὶ προσηγορευμένης Ἀντιγονίας, μεταβαλούσης
δὲ τοὔνομα, ἔδοξε γὰρ εὐσεβὲς εἶναι τοὺς Ἀλέξανδρον διαδεξαμένους ἐκείνου πρότερον κτίζειν
ἐπωνύμους πόλεις, εἶθ' ἑαυτῶν. καὶ δὴ καὶ
συνέμεινε καὶ αὔξησιν ἔσχε, νῦν δὲ καὶ Ῥωμαίων
ἀποικίαν δέδεκται καὶ ἔστι τῶν ἐλλογίμων
πόλεων.

C 594   27. Καὶ τὸ Ἴλιον δ', ὃ νῦν ἔστι, κωμόπολίς
τις ἦν, ὅτε πρῶτον Ῥωμαῖοι τῆς Ἀσίας ἐπέβησαν
καὶ ἐξέβαλον Ἀντίοχον τὸν μέγαν ἐκ τῆς ἐντὸς
τοῦ Ταύρου. φησὶ γοῦν Δημήτριος ὁ Σκήψιος,
μειράκιον ἐπιδημήσας εἰς τὴν πόλιν κατ' ἐκείνους
τοὺς καιρούς, οὕτως ὠλιγωρημένην ἰδεῖν τὴν
κατοικίαν, ὥστε μηδὲ κεραμωτὰς ἔχειν τὰς στέγας·
Ἡγησιάναξ δὲ τοὺς Γαλάτας περαιωθέντας ἐκ
τῆς Εὐρώπης ἀναβῆναι μὲν εἰς τὴν πόλιν
δεομένους ἐρύματος, παραχρῆμα δ' ἐκλιπεῖν διὰ

---

[1] Either Strabo, or his authority, Demetrius of Scepsis, or
the Greek text as it now stands, seems guilty of inconsistency
in the passage " devoted special atteṇtion to the city . . .
and then cities bearing their own." Grote (Vol. I, chapter
xv) rearranges the Greek text in the following order :
"devoted especial attention to Alexandreia" (not Ilium),
"which had indeed been founded by Antigonus and
called Antigonia, but changed its name (for it was thought to
be . . . then cities bearing their own name), and he built a

his death Lysimachus [1] devoted special attention to the city, and built a temple there and surrounded the city with a wall about forty stadia in circuit, and also incorporated into it the surrounding cities, which were now old and in bad plight. At that time he had already devoted attention to Alexandreia, which had indeed already been founded by Antigonus and called Antigonia, but had changed its name, for it was thought to be a pious thing for the successors of Alexander to found cities bearing his name before they founded cities bearing their own. And indeed the city endured and grew, and at present it not only has received a colony of Romans but is one of the notable cities of the world.

27. Also the Ilium of to-day was a kind of village-city when the Romans first set foot on Asia and expelled Antiochus the Great from the country this side of Taurus. At any rate, Demetrius of Scepsis says that, when as a lad he visited the city about that time, he found the settlement so neglected that the buildings did not so much as have tiled roofs. And Hegesianax says that when the Galatae crossed over from Europe they needed a stronghold and went up into the city for that reason, but

temple . . . forty stadia in circuit." He omits "at that time he had already devoted attention to Alexandreia," and so does Leaf (*op. cit.*, p. 142) ; but the latter, instead of rearranging the text, simply inserts " Alexandreia " after " city " in the first clause of the passage. Leaf (p. 143) adds the following important argument to those of Grote : "There is no trace whatever of any great wall at Ilium, though remains of one 40 stades in length could hardly have escaped notice. But there is at Alexandreia such a wall which is exactly the length mentioned by Strabo, and which is clearly referred to."

STRABO

τὸ ἀτείχιστον· ὕστερον δ' ἐπανόρθωσιν ἔσχε
πολλήν. εἶτ' ἐκάκωσαν αὐτὴν πάλιν οἱ μετὰ
Φιμβρίου Ῥωμαῖοι, λαβόντες ἐκ πολιορκίας ἐν
τῷ Μιθριδατικῷ πολέμῳ. συνεπέμφθη δὲ ὁ
Φιμβρίας ὑπάτῳ Οὐαλερίῳ Φλάκκῳ ταμίας,
προχειρισθέντι ἐπὶ τὸν Μιθριδάτην· καταστα-
σιάσας δὲ καὶ ἀνελὼν τὸν ὕπατον κατὰ Βιθυνίαν
αὐτὸς κατεστάθη κύριος τῆς στρατιᾶς, καὶ
προελθὼν εἰς Ἴλιον, οὐ δεχομένων αὐτὸν τῶν
Ἰλιέων, ὡς λῃστήν, βίαν τε[1] προσφέρει καὶ
ἐνδεκαταίους[2] αἱρεῖ· καυχωμένου δ', ὅτι, ἣν
Ἀγαμέμνων πόλιν δεκάτῳ ἔτει μόλις εἷλε τὸν
χιλιόναυν στόλον ἔχων καὶ τὴν σύμπασαν
Ἑλλάδα συστρατεύουσαν, ταύτην αὐτὸς ἐνδεκάτῃ
ἡμέρᾳ χειρώσαιτο, εἶπέ τις τῶν Ἰλιέων· Οὐ γὰρ
ἦν Ἕκτωρ ὁ ὑπερμαχῶν τῆς πόλεως. τοῦτον
μὲν οὖν ἐπελθὼν Σύλλας κατέλυσε, καὶ τὸν
Μιθριδάτην κατὰ συμβάσεις εἰς τὴν οἰκείαν
ἀπέπεμψε, τοὺς δ' Ἰλιέας παρεμυθήσατο πολλοῖς
ἐπανορθώμασι. καθ' ἡμᾶς μέντοι Καῖσαρ ὁ Θεὸς
πολὺ πλέον αὐτῶν προυνόησε, ζηλώσας ἅμα
καὶ Ἀλέξανδρον· ἐκεῖνος γὰρ κατὰ συγγενείας
ἀνανέωσιν ὥρμησε προνοεῖν αὐτῶν, ἅμα καὶ
φιλόμηρος ὤν. φέρεται γοῦν τις διόρθωσις τῆς
Ὁμήρου ποιήσεως, ἡ ἐκ τοῦ νάρθηκος λεγομένη,
τοῦ Ἀλεξάνδρου μετὰ τῶν περὶ Καλλισθένη καὶ
Ἀνάξαρχον ἐπελθόντος καὶ σημειωσαμένου τινά,

---

[1] βίαν τε, conj. of Casaubon, for μηχανάς τε i, μάχην rw,
ἀνάγκην x, omitted in moz, μάντι other MSS.; so Meineke.
[2] For ἐνδεκαταίους the Epit. has ἐν ἡμέραιε δεκα.

[1] i.e. in 86 B.C. by Cinna the consul, the leader of the
popular party at Rome.

54

left it at once because of its lack of walls. But later it was greatly improved. And then it was ruined again by the Romans under Fimbria, who took it by siege in the course of the Mithridatic war. Fimbria had been sent as quaestor with Valerius Flaccus the consul when the latter was appointed[1] to the command against Mithridates; but Fimbria raised a mutiny and slew the consul in the neighbourhood of Bithynia, and was himself set up as lord of the army; and when he advanced to Ilium, the Ilians would not admit him, as being a brigand, and therefore he applied force and captured the place on the eleventh day. And when he boasted that he himself had overpowered on the eleventh day the city which Agamemnon had only with difficulty captured in the tenth year, although the latter had with him on his expedition the fleet of a thousand vessels and the whole of Greece, one of the Ilians said: "Yes, for the city's champion was no Hector." Now Sulla came over and overthrew Fimbria, and on terms of agreement sent Mithridates away to his homeland, but he also consoled the Ilians by numerous improvements. In my time, however, the deified Caesar[2] was far more thoughtful of them, at the same time also emulating the example of Alexander; for Alexander set out to provide for them on the basis of a renewal of ancient kinship, and also because at the same time he was fond of Homer; at any rate, we are told of a recension of the poetry of Homer, the Recension of the Casket, as it is called, which Alexander, along with Callisthenes and Anaxarchus, perused and to a

[2] Julius Caesar.

ἔπειτα καταθέντος εἰς νάρθηκα, ὃν ηὗρεν ἐν τῇ
Περσικῇ γάζῃ, πολυτελῶς κατεσκευασμένον.
κατά τε δὴ τὸν τοῦ ποιητοῦ ζῆλον καὶ κατὰ τὴν
συγγένειαν τὴν ἀπὸ τῶν Αἰακιδῶν τῶν ἐν
Μολοττοῖς βασιλευσάντων, παρ' οἷς καὶ τὴν
Ἀνδρομάχην ἱστοροῦσι βασιλεῦσαι, τὴν Ἕκτορος
γενομένην γυναῖκα, ἐφιλοφρονεῖτο [1] πρὸς τοὺς
Ἰλιέας ὁ Ἀλέξανδρος· ὁ δὲ Καῖσαρ καὶ φιλαλέ-
ξανδρος ὢν καὶ τῆς πρὸς τοὺς Ἰλιέας συγγενείας
γνωριμώτερα [2] ἔχων τεκμήρια ἐπερρώσθη πρὸς
τὴν εὐεργεσίαν νεανικῶς· γνωριμώτερα δέ, πρῶτον
C 595 μὲν ὅτι Ῥωμαῖος· οἱ δὲ Ῥωμαῖοι τὸν [3] Αἰνείαν
ἀρχηγέτην ἡγοῦνται· ἔπειτα ὅτι Ἰούλιος ἀπὸ
Ἰούλου τινὸς τῶν προγόνων· ἐκεῖνος δ' ἀπὸ
Ἰούλου [4] τὴν προσωνυμίαν [5] ἔσχε ταύτην, τῶν
ἀπογόνων εἰς ὢν τῶν ἀπὸ Αἰνείου. χώραν τε
δὴ προσένειμεν αὐτοῖς καὶ τὴν ἐλευθερίαν καὶ
τὴν ἀλειτουργησίαν αὐτοῖς συνεφύλαξε, καὶ
μέχρι νῦν συμμένουσιν ἐν τούτοις. ὅτι δ' οὐκ
ἐνταῦθα [6] ἵδρυται τὸ παλαιὸν Ἴλιον καθ'
Ὅμηρον σκοποῦσιν, ἐκ τῶν τοιῶνδε τεκμαίρονται.
πρότερον δὲ ὑπογραπτέον τοὺς τόπους ἀπὸ τῆς
παραλίας ἀρξαμένους, ἀφ' ἧσπερ ἐλίπομεν.

---

[1] All MSS. except D*hi* read γάρ before πρός.
[2] γνωριμώτερα, Corais, for γνωριμώτατα ; so the later editors.
[3] All MSS. except *orxz* have τ' before Αἰνείαν.
[4] *ix* read Ἴλου instead of Ἰούλου.
[5] F reads προσηγορίαν instead of προσωνυμίαν.
[6] D*hi* add νῦν after ἐνταῦθα ; *h* reads ἵδρυτο, and so Corais.

---

[1] According to Plutarch (*Alexander* 8), "Alexander took
with him Aristotle's recension of the poem, called the Iliad
of the Casket, and always kept it lying beside his dagger

56

certain extent annotated, and then deposited in a
richly wrought casket which he had found amongst
the Persian treasures.[1] Accordingly, it was due both
to his zeal for the poet and to his descent from the
Aeacidae who reigned as kings of the Molossians—
where, as we are also told, Andromachê, who had
been the wife of Hector, reigned as queen—that
Alexander was kindly disposed towards the Ilians.
But Caesar, not only being fond of Alexander, but
also having better known evidences of kinship with
the Ilians, felt encouraged to bestow kindness upon
them with all the zest of youth: better known
evidences, first, because he was a Roman, and
because the Romans believe Aeneias to have been
their original founder; and secondly, because the
name Iulius was derived from that of a certain Iulus
who was one of his ancestors,[2] and this Iulus got his
appellation from the Iulus [3] who was one of the
descendants of Aeneas. Caesar therefore allotted
territory to them and also helped them to preserve
their freedom and their immunity from taxation;
and to this day they remain in possession of these
favours. But that this is not the site of the ancient
Ilium, if one considers the matter in accordance
with Homer's account, is inferred from the following considerations. But first I must give a general
description of the region in question, beginning at
that point on the coast where I left off.

---

under his pillow, as Onesicritus informs us"; and "the
casket was the most precious of the treasures of Dareius"
(*ibid.* 26).

[2] *i.e.* of the Julian gens.

[3] On "Iulus," or Ilus, see critical note.

28. Ἔστι τοίνυν μετ' Ἄβυδον ἥ τε Δαρδανὶς
ἄκρα, ἧς μικρὸν[1] πρότερον ἐμνήσθημεν, καὶ ἡ
πόλις ἡ Δάρδανος, διέχουσα τῆς Ἀβύδου
ἑβδομήκοντα σταδίους. μεταξύ τε ὁ Ῥοδίος
ἐκπίπτει ποταμός, καθ' ὃν ἐν τῇ Χερρονήσῳ τὸ
Κυνὸς σῆμά ἐστιν, ὅ φασιν Ἑκάβης εἶναι τάφον·
οἱ δὲ τὸν Ῥοδίον εἰς τὸν Αἴσηπον ἐμβάλλειν
φασίν· εἰς δ' ἐστὶ τῶν ὑπὸ τοῦ ποιητοῦ λεγομένων καὶ οὗτος·

Ῥῆσός θ' Ἑπτάπορός τε Κάρησός τε Ῥοδίος
τε.

ἡ δὲ Δάρδανος κτίσμα ἀρχαῖον, οὕτω δ' εὐκα-
ταφρόνητον, ὥστε πολλάκις οἱ βασιλεῖς οἱ μὲν
μετῴκιζον αὐτὴν εἰς Ἄβυδον, οἱ δὲ ἀνῴκιζον
πάλιν εἰς τὸ ἀρχαῖον κτίσμα. ἐνταῦθα δὲ
συνῆλθον Σύλλας τε Κορνήλιος, ὁ τῶν Ῥωμαίων
ἡγεμών, καὶ Μιθριδάτης ὁ κληθεὶς Εὐπάτωρ,
καὶ συνέβησαν πρὸς ἀλλήλους ἐπὶ καταλύσει
τοῦ πολέμου.

29. Πλησίον δ' ἐστὶ τὸ Ὀφρύνιον,[2] ἐφ' ᾧ τὸ
τοῦ Ἕκτορος ἄλσος ἐν περιφανεῖ τόπῳ· καὶ
ἐφεξῆς λίμνη[3] Πτελεώς.

30. Εἶτα Ῥοίτειον πόλις ἐπὶ λόφῳ κειμένη
καὶ τῷ Ῥοιτείῳ[4] συνεχὴς ἠιὼν ἁλιτενής,[5] ἐφ'
ᾗ μνῆμα καὶ ἱερὸν Αἴαντος καὶ ἀνδριάς, ὃν
ἄραντος Ἀντωνίου κομισθέντα εἰς Αἴγυπτον
ἀπέδωκε τοῖς Ῥοιτειεῦσι[6] πάλιν, καθάπερ καὶ

---

[1] moxz read μικρῷ instead of μικρόν.
[2] Ὀφρύνιον E and Epit., Ὀφρούνιον other MSS.
[3] λίμνη, Leaf (see his note, Troad, p. 154), following
Calvert, whom he quotes fully, emends to λιμήν.
[4] Ῥυτίῳ CFmoxz, Ῥοιτίῳ D, Ῥουτίῳ hi, Ῥουτείῳ other MSS.

28. After Abydus, then, comes the Dardanian Promontory, which I mentioned a little while ago,[1] and also the city Dardanus, which is seventy stadia distant from Abydus. Between the two places empties the Rhodius River, opposite which, in the Chersonesus, is Cynos-Sema,[2] which is said to be the tomb of Hecabê. But some say that the Rhodius empties into the Aesepus. This too is one of the rivers mentioned by the poet: " Rhesus, Heptaporus, Caresus, and Rhodius." [3] Dardanus was an ancient settlement, but it was held in such contempt that it was oftentimes transplanted by some of the kings to Abydus and then resettled again by others on the ancient site. It was here that Cornelius Sulla, the Roman commander, and Mithridates surnamed Eupator met and arranged the terms for the conclusion of the war.

29. Near by is Ophrynium, near which, in a conspicuous place, is the sacred precinct of Hector.[4] And next comes the Lake [5] of Pteleos.

30. Then come Rhoeteium, a city situated on a hill, and, adjacent to Rhoeteium, a low-lying shore, on which are a tomb and temple of Aias, and also a statue of him, which was taken up by Antony and carried off to Aegypt; but Augustus Caesar gave it back again to the Rhoeteians, just as he gave

[1] 13. 1. 11.
[2] See "Cynos-Sema" and foot-note in Vol. III, p. 377.
[3] *Iliad* 12. 20.
[4] On the site of Ophrynium, see Leaf, p. 153.
[5] Leaf, p. 154, following Calvert, emends "Lake" to " Harbour."

---

[5] Αἰάντειον, after ἁλιτενής, Jones deletes.
[6] 'Ροιτειεῦσι, the editors, for 'Ρυτιεῦσι.

ἄλλοις ἄλλους,[1] ὁ Σεβαστὸς Καῖσαρ. τὰ γὰρ
κάλλιστα ἀναθήματα ἐκ τῶν ἐπιφανεστάτων
ἱερῶν ὁ μὲν ἦρε, τῇ Αἰγυπτίᾳ χαριζόμενος, ὁ
δὲ θεοῖς ἀπέδωκε.

31. Μετὰ δὲ τὸ Ῥοίτειον[2] ἐστι τὸ Σίγειον,[3]
κατεσπασμένη πόλις, καὶ τὸ ναύσταθμον καὶ ὁ
Ἀχαιῶν λιμὴν καὶ τὸ Ἀχαϊκὸν στρατόπεδον
καὶ ἡ Στομαλίμνη καλουμένη καὶ αἱ τοῦ Σκαμάνδρου ἐκβολαί. συμπεσόντες γὰρ ὅ τε Σιμόεις
καὶ ὁ Σκάμανδρος ἐν τῷ πεδίῳ, πολλὴν κατα-
φέροντες ἰλύν, προσχοῦσι τὴν παραλίαν καὶ
τυφλὸν στόμα τε καὶ λιμνοθαλάττας καὶ ἕλη
ποιοῦσι. κατὰ δὲ τὴν Σιγειάδα[4] ἄκραν ἐστὶν
ἐν τῇ Χερρονήσῳ τὸ Πρωτεσιλάειον[5] καὶ ἡ
Ἐλεοῦσσα,[6] περὶ ὧν εἰρήκαμεν ἐν τοῖς Θρακίοις.

32. Ἔστι δὲ τὸ μῆκος τῆς παραλίας ταύτης,
ἀπὸ τοῦ Ῥοιτείου[7] μέχρι Σιγείου καὶ τοῦ
Ἀχιλλέως μνήματος εὐθυπλοούντων, ἐξήκοντα
C 596 σταδίων· ὑποπέπτωκε δὲ τῷ Ἰλίῳ πᾶσα, τῷ μὲν
νῦν κατὰ τὸν Ἀχαιῶν λιμένα ὅσον δώδεκα σταδίους διέχουσα, τῷ δὲ προτέρῳ τριάκοντα ἄλλοις
σταδίοις ἀνωτέρω κατὰ τὸ πρὸς τὴν Ἴδην μέρος.
τοῦ μὲν οὖν Ἀχιλλέως καὶ ἱερόν ἐστι καὶ μνῆμα
πρὸς τῷ Σιγείῳ, Πατρόκλου δὲ καὶ Ἀντιλόχου
μνήματα, καὶ ἐναγίζουσιν οἱ Ἰλιεῖς πᾶσι καὶ
τούτοις καὶ τῷ Αἴαντι. Ἡρακλέα δ' οὐ τιμῶσιν,

---

[1] ἄλλους, omitted by the MSS., Kramer inserts (x reads
ἄλλα); so the later editors.
[2] Ῥοίτειον, the editors, for Ῥοίτιον h, Ῥύτιον other MSS.,
except that D has οι over υ.
[3] Σίγειον E, Σίγιον other MSS.
[4] Σιγειάδα E, Σιγιάδα other MSS.

back other statues to their owners. For Antony took away the finest dedications from the most famous temples, to gratify the Egyptian woman,[1] but Augustus gave them back to the gods.

31. After Rhoeteium come Sigeium, a destroyed city, and the Naval Station and the Harbour of the Achaeans and the Achaean Camp and Stomalimnê,[2] as it is called, and the outlets of the Scamander; for after the Simoeis and the Scamander meet in the plain, they carry down great quantities of alluvium, silt up the coast, and form a blind mouth, lagoons, and marshes. Opposite the Sigeian Promontory on the Chersonesus are Eleussa[3] and the temple of Protesilaüs, both of which I have mentioned in my description of Thrace.[4]

32. The length of this coast, I mean on a straight voyage from Rhoeteium to Sigeium, and the monument of Achilles, is sixty stadia; and the whole of it lies below Ilium, not only the present Ilium, from which, at the Harbour of the Achaeans, it is about twelve stadia distant, but also the earlier Ilium, which lies thirty stadia farther inland in the direction of Mt. Ida. Now there are a temple and a monument of Achilles near Sigeium, as also monuments of Patroclus and Antilochus; and the Ilians offer sacrifices to all four heroes, both to these and to Aias. But they do not honour Heracles, giving

[1] Cleopatra.   [2] "Mouth-of-the-marsh."
[3] "Eleussa" appears to be an error for "Eleus."
[4] Book VII, *Frags.* 51, 54, 55.

[5] Πρωτεσιλάειον E, Πρωτεσίλαιον Forz, Πρωτεσιλαίων C, Πρωτεσιλέων D*hi*.
[6] Ἐλεοῦσσα, Corais emends to Ἐλαιοῦσσα.
[7] Ῥοιτίου D*h*, Ῥυτίου C, Ῥοιτείου other MSS.

αἰτιώμενοι τὴν ὑπ᾽ αὐτοῦ πόρθησιν. ἀλλ᾽ ἐκεῖνος
μέν, φαίη τις ἄν, οὕτως ἐπόρθησεν, ὥστ᾽ ἀπο-
λιπεῖν τοῖς ὕστερον ἐκπορθήσουσι κεκακωμένην
μέν, πόλιν δέ· διὸ καὶ οὕτως εἴρηκεν ὁ ποιητής·

   Ἰλίου ἐξαλάπαξε πόλιν, χήρωσε δ᾽ ἀγυιάς.

ἡ γὰρ χηρεία λειπανδρία τίς ἐστιν, οὐκ
ἀφανισμὸς τέλειος· οὗτοι δ᾽ ἠφάνισαν τελείως,
οἷς ἐναγίζειν ἀξιοῦσι καὶ τιμᾶν ὡς θεούς· εἰ μὴ
τοῦτ᾽ αἰτιάσαιντο, διότι οὗτοι μὲν δίκαιον
πόλεμον ἐξήνεγκαν, ἐκεῖνος δὲ ἄδικον, ἕνεχ᾽
ἵππων Λαομέδοντος· πρὸς τοῦτο δὲ πάλιν ἀν-
τιτίθεται μῦθος· οὐ γὰρ ἕνεκα ἵππων, ἀλλὰ
μισθοῦ ὑπὲρ τῆς Ἡσιόνης καὶ τοῦ κήτους. ἀλλ᾽
ἐάσωμεν ταῦτα· εἰς γὰρ μύθων ἀνασκευὰς
ἐκπίπτει· τάχα δὲ λανθάνουσί τινες ἡμᾶς αἰτίαι
πιστότεραι, δι᾽ ἃς τοῖς Ἰλιεῦσιν ἐπῆλθε τοὺς
μὲν τιμᾶν, τοὺς δὲ μή. ἔοικε δὲ ὁ ποιητὴς
μικρὰν ἀποφαίνειν τὴν πόλιν ἐν τῷ περὶ
Ἡρακλέους λόγῳ, εἴπερ

   ἐξ οἴης σὺν νηυσὶ καὶ ἀνδράσι παυροτέροισιν
   Ἰλίου ἐξαλάπαξε πόλιν.

καὶ φαίνεται ὁ Πρίαμος τῷ τοιούτῳ λόγῳ μέγας
ἐκ μικροῦ γεγονὼς καὶ βασιλεὺς βασιλέων, ὡς
ἔφαμεν. μικρὸν δὲ προελθοῦσιν ἀπὸ τῆς παραλίας ταύτης ἐστὶ τὸ Ἀχαίϊον, ἤδη τῆς Τενεδίων
περαίας ὕπαρχον.

---

[1] *Iliad* 5, 642.   [2] *Iliad* 5. 640.

[3] To appease the anger of Poseidon, Laomedon exposed
his daughter Hesionê on the promontory Agameia (see
Stephanus *s.v.*) to be devoured by a sea-monster. Heracles
promised to kill the monster and save Hesionê if Laomedon

as their reason his sacking of the city. But one might say that, although Heracles did sack it, yet he sacked it in such a way as still to leave it a city, even though damaged, for those who were later to sack it utterly; and for this reason the poet states it thus: "He sacked the city of Ilios and widowed her streets";[1] for "widowed" means a loss of the male population, not a complete annihilation. But the others, whom they think fit to worship with sacrifices and to honour as gods, completely annihilated the city. Perhaps they might give as their reason for this that these waged a just war, whereas Heracles waged an unjust one "on account of the horses of Laomedon."[2] But writers set over against this reason the myth that it was not on account of the horses but of the reward offered for Hesionê and the sea-monster.[3] But let us disregard these reasons, for they end merely in controversies about myths. And perhaps we fail to notice certain more credible reasons why it occurred to the Ilians to honour some and not others. And it appears that the poet, in what he says about Heracles, represents the city as small, if it be true that "with only six ships and fewer men he sacked the city of Ilium."[4] And it is clearly shown by this statement that Priam became great and king of kings from a small beginning, as I have said before.[5] Advancing a little farther along this shore, one comes to the Achaeïum, where begins the part of the mainland that belongs to Tenedos.

---

would give him his immortal horses. Laomedon agreed. Heracles fulfilled his promise, but Laomedon refused to give up the horses, and hence the war.

[4] *Iliad* 5. 641.　　　　　　[5] 12. 8. 7, 13. 1. 7.

33. Τοιούτων δὲ τῶν ἐπὶ τῇ θαλάττῃ τόπων
ὄντων, ὑπέρκειται τούτων τὸ Τρωικὸν πεδίον
μέχρι τῆς Ἴδης ἀνῆκον ἐπὶ πολλοὺς σταδίους
κατὰ τὸ πρὸς ἕω μέρος. τούτου δ᾽ ἡ μὲν
παρώρειός ἐστι στενή, τῇ μὲν ἐπὶ τὴν μεσημβρίαν
τεταμένη μέχρι τῶν κατὰ Σκῆψιν τόπων, τῇ
δ᾽ ἐπὶ τὰς ἄρκτους μέχρι τῶν κατὰ Ζέλειαν
Λυκίων. ταύτην δ᾽ ὁ ποιητὴς ὑπ᾽ Αἰνείᾳ τάττει
καὶ τοῖς Ἀντηνορίδαις, καλεῖ δὲ Δαρδανίαν.
ὑπὸ δὲ ταύτῃ Κεβρηνία, πεδιὰς ἡ πλείστη,
παράλληλός πως τῇ Δαρδανίᾳ· ἦν δὲ καὶ πόλις
ποτὲ Κεβρήνη. ὑπονοεῖ δ᾽ ὁ Δημήτριος μέχρι
δεῦρο διατείνειν τὴν περὶ τὸ Ἴλιον χώραν τὴν
ὑπὸ τῷ Ἕκτορι, ἀνήκουσαν ἀπὸ τοῦ ναυστάθμου
μέχρι Κεβρηνίας· τάφον τε γὰρ Ἀλεξάνδρου
δείκνυσθαί φησιν αὐτόθι καὶ Οἰνώνης, ἣν
ἱστοροῦσι γυναῖκα γεγονέναι τοῦ Ἀλεξάνδρου,
πρὶν Ἑλένην ἁρπάσαι· λέγειν τε τὸν ποιητὴν [1]

Κεβριόνην νόθον υἱὸν ἀγακλῆος Πριάμοιο,

C 597 ὃν εἰκὸς εἶναι ἐπώνυμον τῆς χώρας ἢ καὶ πόλεως,
ὅπερ πιθανώτερον· τὴν δὲ Κεβρηνίαν διήκειν
μέχρι τῆς Σκηψίας, ὅριον δ᾽ εἶναι τὸν Σκάμανδρον
μέσον αὐτῶν ῥέοντα· ἔχθραν δ᾽ ἀεὶ καὶ πόλεμον
εἶναι τοῖς τε Κεβρηνοῖς καὶ τοῖς Σκηψίοις, ἕως
Ἀντίγονος αὐτοὺς συνῴκισεν εἰς τὴν τότε μὲν
Ἀντιγονίαν, νῦν δὲ Ἀλεξάνδρειαν· τοὺς μὲν οὖν
Κεβρηνιέας [2] συμμεῖναι τοῖς ἄλλοις ἐν τῇ
Ἀλεξανδρείᾳ, τοὺς δὲ Σκηψίους ἐπανελθεῖν εἰς
τὴν οἰκείαν, ἐπιτρέψαντος Λυσιμάχου.

[1] λέγειν τε τὸν ποιητήν F, λέγει ὁ ποιητὴς καί x ; CDhi omit
τε, moz read τε καί.
[2] Instead of Κεβρηνιέας imoxz read Κεβρήνους.

33. Such are the places on the sea. Above these lies the Trojan Plain, which extends inland for many stadia in the direction of the east as far as Mt. Ida. The part of this plain alongside the mountain is narrow, extending on one side towards the south as far as the region of Scepsis, and on the other towards the north as far as the Lycians of Zeleia. This is the country which the poet makes subject to Aeneias and the sons of Antenor, calling it Dardania; and below this is Cebrenia, which is level for the most part and lies approximately parallel to Dardania; and in it there was once a city called Cebrenê.[1] Demetrius suspects that the territory of Ilium subject to Hector extended inland from the naval station as far as Cebrenia, for he says that the tomb of Alexander[2] is pointed out there, as also that of Oenonê, who, according to historians, had been the wife of Alexander before he carried off Helen. And, he continues, the poet mentions "Cebriones, bastard son of glorious Priam,"[3] after whom, as one may suppose, the country was named—or the city too, which is more plausible; and Cebrenia extends as far as the territory of Scepsis; and the Scamander, which flows between, is the boundary; and the Cebreni and Scepsians were always hostile to one another and at war until Antigonus settled both peoples together in Antigonia, as it was then called, or Alexandreia, as it is now called; now the Cebreni, he adds, remained with the rest in Alexandreia, but the Scepsians, by permission of Lysimachus, went back to their homeland.

[1] So the name is spelled in § 47, but "Cebren" in § 52.
[2] Paris.   [3] *Iliad* 16. 738.

34. Ἀπὸ δὲ τῆς κατὰ τούτους[1] τοὺς τόπους
Ἰδαίας ὀρεινῆς δύο φησὶν ἀγκῶνας ἐκτείνεσθαι
πρὸς θάλατταν, τὸν μὲν εὐθὺ Ῥοιτείου,[2] τὸν δὲ
Σιγείου, ποιοῦντας ἐξ ἀμφοῖν γραμμὴν ἡμικυκ-
λιώδη· τελευτᾶν δ᾽ ἐν τῷ πεδίῳ, τοσοῦτον
ἀπέχοντας τῆς θαλάττης, ὅσον τὸ νῦν Ἴλιον.
τοῦτο μὲν δὴ μεταξὺ τῆς τελευτῆς τῶν λεχθέντων
ἀγκώνων εἶναι, τὸ δὲ παλαιὸν κτίσμα μεταξὺ
τῆς ἀρχῆς· μεταλαμβάνεσθαι[3] δ᾽ ἐντὸς τό τε
Σιμοείσιον πεδίον, δι᾽ οὗ ὁ Σιμόεις φέρεται, καὶ
τὸ Σκαμάνδριον, δι᾽ οὗ Σκάμανδρος ῥεῖ. τοῦτο
δὲ καὶ ἰδίως Τρωικὸν λέγεται, καὶ τοὺς πλείστους
ἀγῶνας ὁ ποιητὴς ἐνταῦθα ἀποδίδωσι, πλατύ-
τερον γάρ ἐστι, καὶ τοὺς ὀνομαζομένους τόπους
ἐνταῦθα δεικνυμένους ὁρῶμεν, τὸν Ἐρινεόν, τὸν
τοῦ Αἰσυήτου τάφον, τὴν Βατίειαν,[4] τὸ τοῦ Ἴλου
σῆμα. οἱ δὲ ποταμοὶ ὅ τε Σκάμανδρος καὶ ὁ
Σιμόεις, ὁ μὲν τῷ Σιγείῳ πλησιάσας, ὁ δὲ
τῷ Ῥοιτείῳ, μικρὸν ἔμπροσθεν τοῦ νῦν Ἰλίου
συμβάλλουσιν, εἶτ᾽ ἐπὶ τὸ Σίγειον ἐκδιδόασι
καὶ ποιοῦσι τὴν Στομαλίμνην καλουμένην.
διείργει δ᾽ ἑκάτερον τῶν λεχθέντων πεδίων ἀπὸ
θατέρου μέγας τις αὐχὴν τῶν εἰρημένων ἀγκώνων
ἐπ᾽ εὐθείας, ἀπὸ τοῦ νῦν Ἰλίου τὴν ἀρχὴν ἔχων,
συμφυὴς αὐτῷ, τεινόμενος δ᾽ ἕως τῆς Κεβρηνίας
καὶ ἀποτελῶν τὸ Ε γράμμα πρὸς τοὺς ἑκατέρωθεν
ἀγκῶνας.

[1] τούτους, before τούς, Groskurd inserts ; so Müller-Dübner,
Meineke, and Leaf.
[2] Ῥοιτείου, the editors, for Ῥοιτίου CDF hi, Ῥυτίου other MSS.
[3] μεταλαμβάνεσθαι, all MSS. except E, which reads μετα-
λάσσασθαι, Leaf rightly restores, instead of ἀπολαμβάνεσθαι
Meineke, καταλαμβάνεσθαι Corais.

34. From the mountain range of Ida in this region,
according to Demetrius, two spurs extend to the
sea, one straight to Rhoeteium and the other
straight to Sigeium, forming together a semicircular
line, and they end in the plain at the same distance
from the sea as the present Ilium; this Ilium,
accordingly, lies between the ends of the two spurs
mentioned, whereas the old settlement lies between
their beginnings; and, he adds, the spurs include
both the Simoeisian Plain, through which the Simoeis
runs, and the Scamandrian Plain, through which the
Scamander flows.   This is called the Trojan Plain in
the special sense of the term; and here it is that
the poet represents most of the fights as taking
place, for it is wider; and here it is that we see
pointed out the places named by the poet—Erineus,[1]
the tomb of Aesyetes,[2] Batieia,[3] and the monument
of Ilus.[4]   The Scamander and Simoeis Rivers, after
running near to Sigeium and Rhoeteium respectively,
meet a little in front of the present Ilium, and then
issue towards Sigeium and form Stomalimnê,[5] as it is
called. The two plains above mentioned are separated
from each other by a great neck of land which runs
in a straight line between the aforesaid spurs, starting
from the present Ilium, with which it is connected,
and stretches as far as Cebrenia and, along with
the spurs on either side,[6] forms a complete letter Ɛ.[7]

[1] "Fig tree."   *Iliad* 6. 433.   [2] *Iliad* 2. 793.
[3] *Iliad* 2. 813.   [4] *Iliad* 10. 415.
[5] See 13. 1. 31 and foot-note.
[6] These spurs forming a semi-circular line, as stated above.
[7] *i.e.* the uncial letter written backwards (Ɔ).   See Leaf's
diagram, p. 175.

---

[4] Βατίειαν, Xylander, for Βάτειαν; so the later editors.

35. Ὑπὲρ δὲ τούτου μικρὸν ἡ τῶν Ἰλιέων κώμη ἐστίν, ἐν ᾗ νομίζεται τὸ παλαιὸν Ἴλιον ἱδρῦσθαι πρότερον, τριάκοντα σταδίους διέχον ἀπὸ τῆς νῦν πόλεως. ὑπὲρ δὲ τῆς Ἰλιέων κώμης δέκα σταδίοις ἐστὶν ἡ Καλλικολώνη, λόφος τις, παρ᾽ ὃν ὁ Σιμόεις ῥεῖ, πεντοστάδιον διέχων[1] γίνεται οὖν εὔλογον πρῶτον μὲν τὸ ἐπὶ τοῦ Ἄρεος·

ὦρτο δ᾽ Ἄρης ἑτέρωθεν ἐρεμνῇ λαίλαπι ἶσος,
ὀξὺ κατ᾽ ἀκροτάτης πόλιος Τρώεσσι κελεύων,
ἄλλοτε πὰρ Σιμόεντι θέων ἐπὶ Καλλικολώνῃ.

C 598 τῆς γὰρ μάχης ἐπὶ τῷ Σκαμανδρίῳ πεδίῳ συντελουμένης, πιθανῶς ἂν ὁ Ἄρης ἄλλοτε μὲν τὴν ἐγκέλευσιν ἀπὸ τῆς ἀκροπόλεως ποιοῖτο, ἄλλοτε δ᾽ ἐκ τῶν πλησίον τόπων τοῦ τε Σιμόεντος καὶ τῆς Καλλικολώνης, μέχρι οὗ εἰκὸς καὶ τὴν μάχην παρατετάσθαι. τετταράκοντα δὲ σταδίους διεχούσης τῆς Καλλικολώνης ἀπὸ τοῦ νῦν Ἰλίου, τί χρήσιμον ἐπὶ τοσοῦτον μεταλαμβάνεσθαι τοὺς τόπους, ἐφ᾽ ὅσον ἡ διάταξις οὐ διέτεινε; τό τε

πρὸς Θύμβρης δ᾽ ἔλαχον Λύκιοι

οἰκειότερόν ἐστι τῷ παλαιῷ κτίσματι· πλησίον γάρ ἐστι τὸ πεδίον ἡ Θύμβρα καὶ ὁ δι᾽ αὐτοῦ ῥέων ποταμὸς Θύμβριος, ἐμβάλλων εἰς τὸν Σκάμανδρον κατὰ τὸ Θυμβραίου Ἀπόλλωνος ἱερόν, τοῦ δὲ νῦν Ἰλίου καὶ πεντήκοντα σταδίους

---

[1] διέχων, Corais, from conj. of Palmer, for ἔχων; i has κύκλον after ἔχων, and so Eustathius reads (note on Iliad 20. 47, 53). The scholiast (quoted by C. Müller, Ind. Var. Lect. p. 1024) quotes Demetrius as saying that this hill is "five stadia in

35. A little above this[1] is the Village of the
Ilians, where the ancient Ilium is thought to have
been situated in earlier times, at a distance of thirty
stadia from the present city. And ten stadia above
the Village of the Ilians is Callicolonê, a hill, past
which, at a distance of five stadia, flows the Simoeis.[2]
It therefore becomes easy to understand, first, the
reference to Ares: "And over against her leaped
Ares, like unto a dreadful whirlwind, in shrill tones
cheering the Trojans from the topmost part of the
city, and now again as he sped alongside Simoeis
o'er Callicolonê"; [3] for if the battle was fought on
the Scamandrian Plain, it is plausible that Ares
should at one time shout his cheers from the acropolis
and at another from the region near the Simoeis and
Callicolonê, up to which, in all probability, the battle
would have extended. But since Callicolonê is forty
stadia distant from the present Ilium, for what
useful purpose would the poet have taken in places
so far away that the line of battle could not have
reached them? Again, the words, "And towards
Thymbra fell the lot of the Lycians," [4] are more
suitable to the ancient settlement, for the plain of
Thymbra is near it, as also the Thymbrius River,
which flows through the plain and empties into the
Scamander at the temple of the Thymbraean Apollo,
but Thymbra is actually fifty stadia distant from the

---

[1] *i.e.* a little farther inland than the country which has the
shape of the letter in question.
[2] See critical note.   [3] *Iliad* 20. 51.
[4] *Iliad* 10. 430.

---

perimeter . . ., five stadia distant from the Simoeis, and ten
stadia distant from the village of the Ilians."

διέχει. ὅ τε Ἐρινεός, τραχύς τις τόπος καὶ ἐρινεώδης, τῷ μὲν ἀρχαίῳ κτίσματι ὑποπέπτωκεν, ὥστε τὸ

> λαὸν δὲ στῆσον παρ' Ἐρινεόν, ἔνθα μάλιστα
> ἄμβατός ἐστι πόλις καὶ ἐπίδρομον ἔπλετο
>   τεῖχος

οἰκείως ἂν λέγοι[1] ἡ Ἀνδρομάχη, τῆς δὲ νῦν πόλεως πάμπολυ ἀφέστηκε.[2] καὶ ὁ Φηγὸς δὲ μικρὸν κατωτέρω ἐστὶ τοῦ Ἐρινεοῦ, ἐφ' οὗ φησὶν ὁ Ἀχιλλεύς,

>   ὄφρα δ' ἐγὼ μετ' Ἀχαιοῖσιν πολέμιζον,
> οὐκ ἐθέλεσκε μάχην ἀπὸ τείχεος ὀρνύμεν
>   Ἕκτωρ,
> ἀλλ' ὅσον ἐς Σκαιάς τε πύλας καὶ Φηγὸν
>   ἵκανεν.[3]

36. Καὶ μὴν τό γε ναύσταθμον τὸ νῦν ἔτι λεγόμενον πλησίον οὕτως ἐστὶ τῆς νῦν πόλεως, ὥστε θαυμάζειν εἰκότως ἄν τινα τῶν μὲν τῆς ἀπονοίας, τῶν δὲ τοὐναντίον τῆς ἀψυχίας· ἀπονοίας μέν, εἰ εἰς[4] τοσοῦτον χρόνον ἀτείχιστον αὐτὸ εἶχον, πλησίον οὔσης τῆς πόλεως καὶ τοσούτου πλήθους, τοῦ τ' ἐν αὐτῇ καὶ τοῦ ἐπικουρικοῦ· νεωστὶ γὰρ γεγονέναι φησὶ τὸ τεῖχος (ἢ οὐδ' ἐγένετο, ὁ δὲ πλάσας ποιητὴς ἠφάνισεν, ὡς Ἀριστοτέλης φησίν)· ἀψυχίας δέ, εἰ, γενομένου τοῦ τείχους, ἐτειχομάχουν καὶ[5] εἰσέπεσον εἰς αὐτὸ τὸ ναύσταθμον καὶ προσεμάχοντο ταῖς ναυσίν, ἀτείχιστον δὲ ἔχοντες, οὐκ ἐθάρρουν προσιόντες πολιορκεῖν, μικροῦ τοῦ

---

[1] Some of the MSS. read λέγοιτο instead of λέγοι.

present Ilium. And again, Erineus,[1] a place that is rugged and full of wild fig trees, lies at the foot of the ancient site, so that Andromachê might appropriately say, "Stay thy host beside Erineus, where best the city can be approached and the wall scaled,"[2] but Erineus stands at a considerable distance from the present Ilium. Further, a little below Erineus is Phegus,[3] in reference to which Achilles says, "But so long as I was carrying on war amid the Achaeans, Hector was unwilling to rouse battle away from the wall, but would come only as far as the Scaean Gates and Phegus."[4]

36. However, the Naval Station, still now so called, is so near the present Ilium that one might reasonably wonder at the witlessness of the Greeks and the faint-heartedness of the Trojans; witlessness, if the Greeks kept the Naval Station unwalled for so long a time, when they were near to the city and to so great a multitude, both that in the city and that of the allies; for Homer says that the wall had only recently been built (or else it was not built at all, but fabricated and then abolished by the poet, as Aristotle says); and faint-heartedness, if the Trojans, when the wall was built, could besiege it and break into the Naval Station itself and attack the ships, yet did not have the courage to march up and besiege the station when it was still unwalled and only

---

[1] See foot-note on "Erineus," § 34 above.
[2] *Iliad* 6. 433.   [3] Oak tree.   [4] *Iliad* 9. 352.

---

[2] ἀφέστηκε (the reading of Eustathius, note on *Iliad* 6. 433), Casaubon, for ἀπέοικε; so Kramer and Meineke.
[3] ἵκανεν, Xylander, for ἵκοντο; so the later editors.
[4] εἰς, Meineke omits.
[5] καί, Meineke and Leaf, from conj. of Kramer, for ὡς.

διαστήματος ὄντος· ἔστι γὰρ τὸ ναύσταθμον
πρὸς Σιγείῳ, πλησίον δὲ καὶ ὁ Σκάμανδρος
ἐκδίδωσι, διέχων τοῦ Ἰλίου σταδίους εἴκοσιν.
εἰ δὲ φήσει τις τὸν νῦν λεγόμενον Ἀχαιῶν
λιμένα εἶναι τὸ ναύσταθμον, ἐγγυτέρω τινὰ λέξει
τόπον, ὅσον δώδεκα σταδίους διεστῶτα τῆς
πόλεως, τὸ[1] ἐπὶ θαλάττῃ πεδίον συμπροστιθείς,[2]
διότι τοῦτο πᾶν πρόσχωμα[3] τῶν ποταμῶν ἐστί, τὸ
πρὸ τῆς πόλεως ἐπὶ θαλάττῃ πεδίον· ὥστε, εἰ
δωδεκαστάδιόν ἐστι νῦν τὸ μεταξύ, τότε καὶ τῷ
ἡμίσει ἔλαττον ὑπῆρχε. καὶ ἡ διήγησις δ᾽ ἡ
C 599 πρὸς τὸν Εὔμαιον ὑπὸ τοῦ Ὀδυσσέως διασκευασ-
θεῖσα μέγα ἐμφαίνει τὸ διάστημα τὸ μέχρι
τῆς πόλεως ἀπὸ τοῦ ναυστάθμου·

ὡς ὅθ᾽ ὑπὸ Τροίῃ λόχον ἤγομεν·

φησὶ γὰρ ὑποβάς·

λίην γὰρ νηῶν ἑκὰς ἤλθομεν.

ἐπί τε τὴν κατασκοπὴν πέμπονται γνωσόμενοι,
πότερον μενοῦσι παρὰ νηυσὶν ἀπόπροθεν πολὺ
ἀπεσπασμένοι τοῦ οἰκείου τείχους,

ἠὲ πόλινδε

ἂψ ἀναχωρήσουσι.

καὶ ὁ Πολυδάμας,

ἀμφὶ μάλα φράζεσθε, φίλοι· κέλομαι γὰρ
    ἔγωγε
ἄστυδε νῦν ἰέναι,

φησίν,

            ἑκὰς δ᾽ ἀπὸ τείχεός εἰμεν.

παρατίθησι δ᾽ ὁ Δημήτριος καὶ τὴν Ἀλεξανδρινὴν
Ἑστιαίαν μάρτυρα, τὴν συγγράψασαν περὶ τῆς
Ὁμήρου Ἰλιάδος, πυνθανομένην, εἰ περὶ τὴν νῦν

72

a slight distance away; for it is near Sigeium, and
the Scamander empties near it, at a distance of only
twenty stadia from Ilium. But if one shall say that
the Harbour of Achaeans, as it is now called, is the
Naval Station, he will be speaking of a place that is
still closer, only about twelve stadia distant from the
city, even if one includes the plain by the sea,
because the whole of this plain is a deposit of the
rivers—I mean the plain by the sea in front of the
city; so that, if the distance between the sea and
the city is now twelve stadia, it must have been
no more than half as great at that time. Further,
the feigned story told by Odysseus to Eumaeus
clearly indicates that the distance from the Naval
Station to the city is great, for after saying, "as
when we led our ambush[1] beneath the walls of
Troy," he adds a little below, "for we went very
far from the ships." And spies are sent forth to
find whether the Trojans will stay by the ships "far
away," far separated from their own walls, "or will
withdraw again to the city."[2] And Polydamas
says, "on both sides, friends, bethink ye well, for I,
on my own part, bid you now to go to the city;
afar from the walls are we."[3] Demetrius cites also
Hestiaea of Alexandreia as a witness, a woman who
wrote a work on Homer's *Iliad* and inquired whether

---

[1] *Odyssey* 14. 469.   [2] *Iliad* 10. 209.   [3] *Iliad* 18. 254.

---

[1] τό, before ἐπί, Groskurd inserts; so the later editors.
[2] συμπροστιθείς, Meineke, for νῦν προστιθείς; Leaf omits
ἐπὶ . . . προστιθείς; Kramer conj. οὐκ εὖ after προστιθείς.
[3] πρόσχωμα *Crwxz*, πρόχωμα other MSS.

πόλιν ὁ πόλεμος συνέστη καὶ[1] τὸ Τρωικὸν
πεδίον, ὃ μεταξὺ τῆς πόλεως καὶ τῆς θαλάττης
ὁ ποιητὴς φράζει· τὸ μὲν γὰρ πρὸ τῆς νῦν
πόλεως ὁρώμενον πρόσχωμα εἶναι τῶν ποταμῶν
ὕστερον γεγονός.

37. Ὅ τε Πολίτης,

ὃς Τρώων σκοπὸς ἷζε, ποδωκείῃσι πεποιθώς,
τύμβῳ ἐπ᾽ ἀκροτάτῳ Αἰσυήταο γέροντος,

μάταιος ἦν. καὶ γὰρ εἰ ἐπ᾽ ἀκροτάτῳ, ὅμως
ἀπὸ[2] πολὺ ἂν μείζονος ὕψους τῆς ἀκροπόλεως
ἐσκόπευεν, ἐξ ἴσου σχεδόν τι διαστήματος, μὴ
δεόμενος μηδὲν τῆς ποδωκείας τοῦ ἀσφαλοῦς
χάριν· πέντε γὰρ διέχει σταδίους ὁ νῦν δεικνύ-
μενος τοῦ Αἰσυήτου τάφος κατὰ τὴν εἰς Ἀλεξάνδρειαν ὁδόν. οὐδ᾽ ἡ τοῦ Ἕκτορος δὲ περι-
δρομὴ ἡ περὶ τὴν πόλιν ἔχει τι εὔλογον, οὐ γάρ
ἐστι περίδρομος ἡ νῦν, διὰ τὴν συνεχῆ ῥάχιν· ἡ δὲ
παλαιὰ ἔχει περιδρομήν.

38. Οὐδὲν δ᾽ ἴχνος σώζεται τῆς ἀρχαίας
πόλεως· εἰκότως· ἅτε γὰρ ἐκπεπορθημένων τῶν
κύκλῳ πόλεων, οὐ τελέως δὲ κατεσπασμένων,
ταύτης δ᾽ ἐκ βάθρων ἀνατετραμμένης, οἱ λίθοι
πάντες εἰς τὴν ἐκείνων ἀνάληψιν μετηνέχθησαν.
Ἀρχαιάνακτα γοῦν φασι τὸν Μιτυληναῖον ἐκ
τῶν ἐκεῖθεν λίθων τὸ Σίγειον τειχίσαι. τοῦτο
δὲ κατέσχον μὲν Ἀθηναῖοι, Φρύνωνα τὸν Ὀλυμ-
πιονίκην πέμψαντες, Λεσβίων ἐπιδικαζομένων
σχεδόν τι τῆς συμπάσης Τρωάδος· ὧν δὴ καὶ

[1] After καὶ Groskurd inserts ποῦ ἐστί, Kramer conj. ποῦ or
τί, Meineke indicates a lacuna, and Leaf omits altogether
τὸ Τρωικὸν πεδίον . . . ὕστερον γεγονός.

the war took place round the present Ilium and the Trojan Plain, which latter the poet places between the city and the sea; for, she says, the plain now to be seen in front of the present Ilium is a later deposit of the rivers.

37. Again, Polites, "who was wont to sit as a sentinel of the Trojans, trusting in his fleetness of foot, on the topmost part of the barrow of aged Aesyetes,"[1] was doing a foolish thing, for even though he sat on the topmost part of it, still he might have kept watch from the much greater height of the acropolis, at approximately the same distance, with no need of fleetness of foot for safety ; for the barrow of Aesyetes now pointed out is five stadia distant on the road to Alexandreia.   Neither is the "clear running space "[2] of Hector round the city easy to understand, for the present Ilium has no " clear running space," on account of the ridge that joins it.   The ancient city, however, has a " clear running space" round it.

38. But no trace of the ancient city survives ; and naturally so, for while the cities all round it were sacked, but not completely destroyed, yet that city was so utterly demolished that all the stones were taken from it to rebuild the others.   At any rate, Archaeanax of Mitylenê is said to have built a wall round Sigeium with stones taken from there.   Sigeium was seized by Athenians under Phrynon the Olympian victor, although the Lesbians laid claim to almost the whole of the Troad.   Most of the settlements in

---

[1] *Iliad* 2. 792.　　　　[2] See *Iliad* 2. 812.

---

[2] ἀπό, before πολύ, Corais inserts ; and so Meineke. Kramer and Leaf insert ἀφ᾿ before ὕψους.

κτίσματά εἰσιν αἱ πλεῖσται τῶν κατοικιῶν, αἱ
μὲν συμμένουσαι καὶ νῦν, αἱ δ' ἠφανισμέναι.
C 600 Πιττακὸς δ' ὁ Μιτυληναῖος, εἷς τῶν ἑπτὰ σοφῶν
λεγομένων, πλεύσας ἐπὶ τὸν Φρύνωνα στρατηγὸν
διεπολέμει τέως, διατιθεὶς καὶ πάσχων κακῶς,
ὅτε καὶ Ἀλκαῖός φησιν ὁ ποιητής, ἑαυτὸν ἔν
τινι ἀγῶνι κακῶς φερόμενον τὰ ὅπλα ῥίψαντα
φυγεῖν· λέγει δὲ πρός τινα κήρυκα, κελεύσας
ἀγγεῖλαι τοῖς ἐν οἴκῳ, Ἀλκαῖος σόος Ἄρει
ἔντεα δ' † οὐκυτὸν ἀληκτορὶν ἐς Γλαυκωπού ἱερὸν
ἀνεκρέμασαν Ἀττικοί,[1] ὕστερον δ' ἐκ μονομα-
χίας, προκαλεσαμένου[2] τοῦ Φρύνωνος, ἁλιευ-
τικὴν ἀναλαβὼν σκευὴν συνέδραμε, καὶ τῷ μὲν
ἀμφιβλήστρῳ περιέβαλε, τῇ τριαίνῃ δὲ καὶ τῷ
ξιφιδίῳ ἔπειρε καὶ ἀνεῖλε. μένοντος δ' ἔτι τοῦ
πολέμου, Περίανδρος διαιτητὴς αἱρεθεὶς ὑπὸ
ἀμφοῖν ἔλυσε τὸν πόλεμον.

39. Τίμαιον δὲ ψεύσασθαί φησιν ὁ Δημήτριος,
ἱστοροῦντα ἐκ τῶν λίθων τῶν ἐξ Ἰλίου Περίανδρον
ἐπιτειχίσαι[3] τὸ Ἀχίλλειον τοῖς Ἀθηναίοις, βοη-
θοῦντα τοῖς περὶ Πιττακόν· ἐπιτειχισθῆναι μὲν
γὰρ ὑπὸ τῶν Μιτυληναίων τὸν τόπον τοῦτον τῷ
Σιγείῳ, οὐ μὴν ἐκ λίθων τοιούτων, οὐδ' ὑπὸ τοῦ

[1] Meineke, following conj. of Kramer, ejects ὅτε . . .
Ἀττικοί. The passage Ἀλκαῖος . . . Ἀττικοί, from σόος to
ἀνεκρέμασαν, has been so badly mutilated by the copyists
that it is impossible to do more in a translation than to give
the general sense of it. For conjectural restorations see
Kramer, C. Müller (*Ind. Var. Lect.* p. 1025), and Bergk
(Vol. III. Frag. 32 of Alcaeus), who reads ἐνθαδ' οὐκυτὸν ἀληκτορὶν ἐς γλαυκωπὸν ἱερὸν ὃν ἐκρέμασαν Ἀττικοί. Meineke and
Leaf omit the whole passage.

[2] προκαλεσαμένου F, other MSS. προσκαλεσαμένου.

[3] ἐπιτειχίσαι, Corais, for περιτειχίσαι; so the later editors.

the Troad belong, in fact, to the Lesbians, and some
endure to this day, while others have disappeared.
Pittacus of Mitylenê, one of the Seven Wise Men,
as they are called, sailed against Phrynon the
general [1] and for a time carried on the war, but with
poor management and ill consequences. It was at
this time that the poet Alcaeus says that he himself,
being sorely pressed in a certain battle, threw away
his arms and fled. He addresses his story to a
certain herald, whom he had bidden to report to
the people at home that "Alcaeus is safe, but his
arms have been hung up as an offering to Ares by the
Attic army in the temple of Athena Glaucopis." [2] But
later, on being challenged to single combat by
Phrynon, he took up his fishing-tackle, ran to meet
him, entangled him in his fishing net, and stabbed
and slew him with trident and dagger. But since
the war still went on, Periander was chosen by both
sides as arbiter and ended it.

39. Demetrius says that Timaeus falsifies when he
informs us that Periander fortified Achilleium against
the Athenians with stones from Ilium, to help the
army of Pittacus; for this place, he says, was indeed
fortified by the Mitylenaeans against Sigeium, though
not with such stones as those, nor yet by Periander.

---

[1] The Athenian general.
[2] Only this fragment (Bergk 32) of Alcaeus' poem, ad-
dressed to Melanippus (see Herodotus 5. 95), is preserved.
But the text has been so badly mutilated by the copyists
that none of the conjectural restorations can with certainty
be adopted; and hence the translator can give only the
general sense of the passage. However, the whole reference
to Alcaeus appears to be merely a note that has crept into
the text from the margin (see critical note).

Περιάνδρου. πῶς γὰρ ἂν αἱρεθῆναι διαιτητὴν τὸν προσπολεμοῦντα; Ἀχίλλειον δ᾽ ἐστὶν ὁ τόπος, ἐν ᾧ τὸ Ἀχιλλέως μνῆμα, κατοικία μικρά. κατέσκαπται δὲ καὶ τὸ Σίγειον ὑπὸ τῶν Ἰλιέων ἀπειθοῦν· [1] ὑπ᾽ ἐκείνοις γὰρ ἦν ὕστερον ἡ παραλία πᾶσα ἡ μέχρι Δαρδάνου, καὶ νῦν ὑπ᾽ ἐκείνοις ἐστί. τὸ δὲ παλαιὸν ὑπὸ τοῖς Αἰολεῦσιν ἦν τὰ πλεῖστα, ὥστε Ἔφορος οὐκ ὀκνεῖ πᾶσαν τὴν ἀπὸ Ἀβύδου μέχρι Κύμης καλεῖν Αἰολίδα. Θουκυδίδης δέ φησιν ἀφαιρεθῆναι τὴν Τροίαν ὑπὸ Ἀθηναίων τοὺς Μιτυληναίους ἐν τῷ Πελοποννησιακῷ πολέμῳ τῷ Παχητίῳ.

40. Λέγουσι δ᾽ οἱ νῦν Ἰλιεῖς καὶ τοῦτο, ὡς οὐδὲ τελέως ἠφανίσθαι συνέβαινεν [2] τὴν πόλιν κατὰ τὴν ἅλωσιν ὑπὸ τῶν Ἀχαιῶν, οὐδ᾽ ἐξελείφθη [3] οὐδέποτε. αἱ γοῦν Λοκρίδες παρθένοι, μικρὸν ὕστερον ἀρξάμεναι, ἐπέμποντο κατ᾽ ἔτος. καὶ ταῦτα δ᾽ οὐχ Ὁμηρικά· οὔτε γὰρ τῆς Κασάνδρας φθορὰν οἶδεν Ὅμηρος, ἀλλ᾽ ὅτι μὲν παρθένος ἦν ὑπ᾽ ἐκεῖνον τὸν χρόνον λέγει·

πέφνε γὰρ Ὀθρυονῆα, Καβησόθεν ἔνδον ἐόντα,
ὅς ῥα νέον πτολέμοιο μετὰ κλέος εἰληλούθει.

[1] CDF*hirwx* read ἀπειθούντων instead of ἀπειθοῦν.
[2] *mz*, and Corais, read συνέβη instead of συνέβαινεν.
[3] ἐξελείφθη, Corais, for ἐξελήφθη CDF, ἐξηλήφθη *hi*, ἐξηλείφθη *moxz*.

[1] See 13. 1. 4.
[2] *i.e.* the campaign of Paches, the Athenian general, who in 427 B.C. captured Mitylenê (see Thucydides 3. 18–49).
[3] To appease the wrath of Athena, caused after the Trojan War by the sacrilege of Aias the Locrian in her temple (he

For how could the opponent of the Athenians have been chosen as arbiter? Achilleium is the place where stands the monument of Achilles and is only a small settlement. Sigeium, also, has been rased to the ground by the Ilians, because of its disobedience; for the whole of the coast as far as Dardanus was later subject to the Ilians and is now subject to them. In ancient times the most of it was subject to the Aeolians, so that Ephorus does not hesitate to apply the name Aeolis to the whole of the coast from Abydus to Cymê.[1] Thucydides says that Troy was taken away from the Mitylenaeans by the Athenians in the Pachetian part[2] of the Peloponnesian War.

40. The present Ilians further tell us that the city was, in fact, not completely wiped out at its capture by the Achaeans and that it was never even deserted. At any rate the Locrian maidens, beginning a little later, were sent every year.[3] But this too is non-Homeric, for Homer knows not of the violation of Cassandra, but he says that she was a maiden at about that time, "for he[4] slew Othryoneus, a sojourner in Troy from Cabesus, who had but recently come, following after the rumour of war,[5] and he

dragged Cassandra away from the altar of the Palladium), the Locrians were instructed by an oracle from Delphi to send to her temple (as temple slaves) at Ilium two maidens every year for a thousand years. It appears that the servitude of the maidens lasted for only one year, each pair being released at the end of the year when the next pair arrived, but that upon their return home they were forced to remain unmarried (see Leaf, *Annual of the British School at Athens*, XXI, pp. 148–154).

[4] Idomeneus, son of Minos and King of Crete; one of the bravest heroes of the war.

[5] Or perhaps "in quest of war's renown" (Leaf).

ἤτεε δὲ Πριάμοιο θυγατρῶν εἶδος ἀρίστην,
Κασσάνδρην, ἀνάεδνον·

βίας δὲ οὐδὲ μέμνηται, οὐδ' ὅτι ἡ φθορὰ τοῦ
Αἴαντος ἐν τῇ ναυαγίᾳ κατὰ μῆνιν Ἀθηνᾶς
συνέβη, ἢ κατὰ τοιαύτην αἰτίαν, ἀλλ' ἀπεχθα-
C 601 νόμενον μὲν τῇ Ἀθηνᾷ κατὰ τὸ κοινὸν εἴρηκεν
(ἁπάντων γὰρ εἰς τὸ ἱερὸν ἀσεβησάντων, ἅπασιν
ἐμήνιεν), ἀπολέσθαι δὲ ὑπὸ Ποσειδῶνος μεγα-
λορρημονήσαντα. τὰς δὲ Λοκρίδας πεμφθῆναι,
Περσῶν ἤδη κρατούντων, συνέβη.

41. Οὕτω μὲν δὴ λέγουσιν οἱ Ἰλιεῖς, Ὅμηρος
δὲ ῥητῶς τὸν ἀφανισμὸν τῆς πόλεως εἴρηκεν·

ἔσσεται ἦμαρ, ὅταν ποτ' ὀλώλῃ Ἴλιος ἱρή.
ἢ γὰρ[1] καὶ Πριάμοιο πόλιν διεπέρσαμεν αἰπήν
βουλῇ[2] καὶ μύθοισι.
πέρθετο δὲ Πριάμοιο πόλις δεκάτῳ ἐνιαυτῷ.

καὶ τὰ τοιαῦτα δὲ τοῦ αὐτοῦ τίθενται τεκμήρια,
οἷον, ὅτι τῆς Ἀθηνᾶς τὸ ξόανον νῦν μὲν ἑστηκὸς
ὁρᾶται, Ὅμηρος δὲ καθήμενον ἐμφαίνει· πέπλον
γὰρ κελεύει

θεῖναι Ἀθηναίης ἐπὶ γούνασιν·
ὡς καί,
μή ποτε γούνασιν οἷσιν ἐφέζεσθαι φίλον υἱόν.

βέλτιον γὰρ οὕτως, ἢ ὥς τινες δέχονται ἀντὶ τοῦ

---

[1] αὐτὰρ ἐπεί, instead of ἢ γάρ, is the reading in the *Odyssey*.
[2] The MSS., except *moz*, which omit βουλῇ καὶ μύθοισι, have εἴπερ before these words.

---

[1] *Iliad* 13. 363. Homer mentions Cassandra in only two
other places, *Iliad* 24. 699 and *Odyssey* 11. 422.

was asking Cassandra in marriage, the comeliest of
the daughters of Priam, without gifts of wooing,"[1]
and yet he does not so much as mention any violation of her or say that the destruction of Aias in
the shipwreck took place because of the wrath of
Athena or any such cause; instead, he speaks of
Aias as "hated by Athena,"[2] in accordance with her
general hatred (for since they one and all committed
sacrilege against her temple, she was angry at them
all), but says that he was destroyed by Poseidon
because of his boastful speech.[3]   But the fact is that
the Locrian maidens were first sent when the
Persians were already in power.

41. So the Ilians tell us, but Homer expressly
states that the city was wiped out: "The day shall
come when sacred Ilios shall perish";[4] and "surely
we have utterly destroyed the steep city of Priam,"[5]
"by means of counsels and persuasiveness";[6] "and
in the tenth year the city of Priam was destroyed."[7]
And other such evidences of the same thing are set
forth; for example, that the wooden image of Athena
now to be seen stands upright, whereas Homer
clearly indicates that it was sitting, for orders are
given to "put" the robe "upon Athena's knees"[8]
(compare "that never should there sit upon his
knees a dear child").[9]   For it is better to interpret
it[10] in this way than, as some do, to interpret it as

---

[2] *Odyssey* 4. 502.   [3] *Odyssey* 4. 500 ff.
[4] *Iliad* 6. 448.   [5] *Odyssey* 3. 130.
[6] This phrase is not found in the *Iliad* or *Odyssey*, but once
before (1. 2. 4) Strabo has ascribed it to Homer (see critical
note).
[7] *Iliad* 12. 15.   [8] *Iliad* 6. 92, 273.   [9] *Iliad* 9. 455.
[10] *i.e.* the Greek preposition ἐπί, which more naturally
means "upon" rather than "beside."

STRABO

παρὰ τοῖς γόνασι θεῖναι, παρατιθέντες τὸ

ἡ δ' ἧσται ἐπ' ἐσχάρῃ ἐν πυρὸς αὐγῇ

ἀντὶ τοῦ παρ' ἐσχάρῃ. τίς γὰρ ἂν νοηθείη πέπλου
ἀνάθεσις παρὰ τοῖς γόνασι; καὶ οἱ τὴν προσῳδίαν
δὲ διαστρέφοντες, γουνάσιν, ὡς θυιάσιν, ὁποτέρως
ἂν δέξωνται, ἀπεραντολογοῦσιν, εἴθ' ἱκετεύοντές
τε φρένας.[1] πολλὰ δὲ τῶν ἀρχαίων τῆς Ἀθηνᾶς
ξοάνων καθήμενα δείκνυται, καθάπερ ἐν
Φωκαίᾳ, Μασσαλίᾳ, Ῥώμῃ, Χίῳ, ἄλλαις
πλείοσιν. ὁμολογοῦσι δὲ καὶ οἱ νεώτεροι τὸν
ἀφανισμὸν τῆς πόλεως, ὧν ἐστι καὶ Λυκοῦργος
ὁ ῥήτωρ· μνησθεὶς γὰρ τῆς Ἰλιέων πόλεως
φησί· τίς οὐκ ἀκήκοεν, ὡς ἅπαξ ὑπὸ τῶν
Ἑλλήνων κατεσκάφθη, ἀοίκητον οὖσαν;
42. Εἰκάζουσι δὲ τοὺς ὕστερον ἀνακτίσαι
διανοουμένους οἰωνίσασθαι τὸν τόπον ἐκεῖνον,
εἴτε διὰ τὰς συμφοράς, εἴτε καὶ καταρασαμένου
τοῦ Ἀγαμέμνονος κατὰ παλαιὸν ἔθος (καθάπερ
καὶ ὁ Κροῖσος ἐξελὼν τὴν Σιδηνήν, εἰς ἣν ὁ
τύραννος κατέφυγε Γλαυκίας, ἀρὰς ἔθετο κατὰ
τῶν τειχιούντων πάλιν τὸν τόπον), ἐκείνου μὲν
οὖν ἀποστῆναι τοῦ χωρίου, ἕτερον δὲ τειχίσαι.
πρῶτοι μὲν οὖν Ἀστυπαλαιεῖς οἱ τὸ Ῥοίτειον
κατασχόντες συνῴκισαν πρὸς τῷ Σιμόεντι
Πόλιον, ὃ νῦν καλεῖται Πόλισμα, οὐκ ἐν εὐερκεῖ

---

[1] The words εἴθ' ἱκετεύοντές τε φρένας are unintelligible.
Meineke emends to εἴθ' ἱκετείας ἑρμηνεύοντες εἴτε φρένας;
Leaf translates (with a question mark) "whether as suppliants or mind"! Jones conj. that the words ἐπὶ (or ἐν) τῇ
τέφρᾳ ("in the ashes"), referring to ἐπ' ἐσχάρῃ, are hidden
in τε φρένας.

meaning "to put the robe 'beside' her knees," comparing the words "and she sits upon the hearth in the light of the fire," which they take to mean "beside" the hearth. For how could one conceive of the dedication of a robe "beside" the knees? Moreover, others, changing the accent on γούνασιν,[1] accenting it γουνάσιν,[2] like θυιάσιν[3] (in whichever of two ways they interpret it), talk on endlessly. . . .[4] There are to be seen many of the ancient wooden images of Athena in a sitting posture, as, for example, in Phocaea, Massalia, Rome, Chios, and several other places. Also the more recent writers agree that the city was wiped out, among whom is the orator Lycurgus,[5] who, in mentioning the city of the Ilians, says: "Who has not heard that once for all it was rased to the ground by the Greeks, and is uninhabited?"

42. It is surmised that those who later thought of refounding the city regarded that site as ill-omened, either on account of its misfortune or also because, in accordance with an ancient custom, a curse had been laid upon it by Agamemnon, just as Croesus, after he destroyed Sidenê, whither the tyrant Glaucias had fled for refuge, put a curse on any persons who should re-fortify the site; and that they therefore avoided that place and fortified another. Now the Astypalaeans who held possession of Rhoeteium were the first to settle Polium, now called Polisma, on the Simoeis River, but not on a

---

[1] "Knees."
[2] They obviously took γουνάσιν, if there ever was such a word, to mean "female suppliants."
[3] "Maenads."　　　　　[4] See critical note.
[5] *Against Leocrates*, 62.

STRABO

τόπῳ· διὸ κατεσπάσθη ταχέως. ἐπὶ δὲ τῶν
Λυδῶν ἡ νῦν ἐκτίσθη κατοικία καὶ τὸ ἱερόν· οὐ
μὴν πόλις γε ἦν, ἀλλὰ πολλοῖς χρόνοις ὕστερον,
C 602 καὶ κατ᾽ ὀλίγον, ὡς εἴρηται, τὴν αὔξησιν ἔσχεν.
Ἑλλάνικος δὲ χαριζόμενος τοῖς Ἰλιεῦσιν, οἷος
ἐκείνου θυμός,[1] συνηγορεῖ τὸ τὴν αὐτὴν εἶναι
πόλιν τὴν νῦν τῇ τότε. τὴν δὲ χώραν, ἀφανισ-
θείσης τῆς πόλεως, οἱ τὸ Σίγειον καὶ τὸ Ῥοίτειον
ἔχοντες διενείμαντο καὶ τῶν ἄλλων ὡς ἕκαστοι
τῶν πλησιοχώρων, ἀπέδοσαν δ᾽ ἀνοικισθείσης.
43. Πολυπίδακον δὲ τὴν Ἴδην ἰδίως οἴονται
λέγεσθαι διὰ τὸ πλῆθος τῶν ἐξ αὐτῆς ῥεόντων
ποταμῶν, καθ᾽ ἃ μάλιστα ἡ Δαρδανικὴ ὑποπέπτωκεν αὐτῇ καὶ μέχρι Σκήψεως καὶ τὰ περὶ
Ἴλιον. ἔμπειρος δ᾽ ὢν τῶν τόπων, ὡς ἂν
ἐπιχώριος ἀνήρ, ὁ Δημήτριος τοτὲ μὲν οὕτως
λέγει περὶ αὐτῶν· ἔστι γὰρ λόφος τις τῆς Ἴδης
Κότυλος· ὑπέρκειται δ᾽ οὗτος ἑκατόν που καὶ
εἴκοσι σταδίοις Σκήψεως, ἐξ οὗ ὅ τε Σκάμανδρος
ῥεῖ καὶ ὁ Γράνικος καὶ Αἴσηπος, οἱ μὲν πρὸς ἄρκτον
καὶ τὴν Προποντίδα, ἐκ πλειόνων πηγῶν συλλει-
βόμενοι, ὁ δὲ Σκάμανδρος ἐπὶ δύσιν ἐκ μιᾶς
πηγῆς· πᾶσαι δ᾽ ἀλλήλαις πλησιάζουσιν, ἐν
εἴκοσι σταδίων περιεχόμεναι διαστήματι· πλεῖστον δ᾽ ἀφέστηκεν ἀπὸ τῆς ἀρχῆς τὸ τοῦ Αἰσήπου
τέλος, σχεδόν τι καὶ πεντακοσίους σταδίους.
παρέχει δὲ λόγον, πῶς[2] φησιν ὁ ποιητής·

[1] θυμός, Xylander, for μῦθος; so the later editors.
[2] πῶς, Corais, for ὡς; so the later editors.

[1] i.e. of Ilium.   [2] 13. 1. 26.

well-protected site; and therefore it was soon demolished. It was in the time of the Lydians that
the present settlement[1] was founded, as also the
temple. It was not a city, however, and it was
only after many ages, and gradually, as I have said,[2]
that it increased. But Hellanicus, to gratify the
Ilians, "such is the spirit of that man,"[3] agrees with
them that the present Ilium is the same as the
ancient. When the city was wiped out, its territory
was divided up between the inhabitants of Sigeium
and Rhoeteium and several other neighbouring
peoples, but the territory was given back when the
place was refounded.

43. The epithet "many-fountained"[4] is thought
to be especially applied to Mt. Ida because of the
great number of rivers that flow from it, particularly
in those parts below it where lie the territory of
Dardanus—even as far as Scepsis—and the region of
Ilium. Demetrius, who as a native was acquainted
with the topography of the country, says in one
place as follows: There is a hill of Ida called
Cotylus; and this hill lies about one hundred and
twenty stadia above Scepsis; and from it flow the
Scamander, the Granicus, and the Aesepus, the two
latter flowing towards the north and the Propontis
and constituting a collection of streams from several
sources, while the Scamander flows towards the west
from only one source; and all the sources lie close
together, being comprised within a distance of twenty
stadia; but the end of the Aesepus stands farthest
away from its beginning, approximately five hundred
stadia. But it is a matter of argument what the poet
means when he says: "And they came to the two

---

[3] A quotation from *Iliad* 15. 94.   [4] Cf. 13. 1. 5.

κρουνὼ δ' ἵκανον καλιρρόω, ἔνθα δὲ πηγαί
δοιαὶ ἀναΐσσουσι Σκαμάνδρου δινήεντος·
ἡ μὲν γάρ θ' ὕδατι λιαρῷ ῥέει,

ὅ ἐστι θερμῷ· ἐπιφέρει δέ·

ἀμφὶ δὲ καπνὸς
γίγνεται ἐξ αὐτῆς, ὡσεὶ πυρός.
ἡ δ' ἑτέρη θέρεϊ προρέει εἰκυῖα χαλάζῃ
ἢ χιόνι ψυχρῇ.

οὔτε γὰρ θερμὰ νῦν ἐν τῷ τόπῳ εὑρίσκεται, οὔθ' ἡ
τοῦ Σκαμάνδρου πηγὴ ἐνταῦθα, ἀλλ' ἐν τῷ ὄρει·
καὶ μία, ἀλλ' οὐ δύο. τὰ μὲν οὖν θερμὰ ἐκλε-
λεῖφθαι εἰκός, τὸ δὲ ψυχρὸν κατὰ διάδοσιν [1]
ὑπεκρέον ἐκ τοῦ Σκαμάνδρου κατὰ τοῦτ' ἀνατέλ-
λειν τὸ χωρίον, ἢ καὶ διὰ τὸ πλησίον εἶναι τοῦ
Σκαμάνδρου καὶ τοῦτο τὸ ὕδωρ λέγεσθαι τοῦ
Σκαμάνδρου πηγήν· οὕτω γὰρ λέγονται πλείους
πηγαὶ τοῦ αὐτοῦ ποταμοῦ.

44. Συμπίπτει δ' εἰς αὐτὸν ὁ Ἄνδιρος ἀπὸ τῆς
Καρησηνῆς, ὀρεινῆς τινος πολλαῖς κώμαις συνοι-
κουμένης καὶ γεωργουμένης καλῶς, παρακειμένης
τῇ Δαρδανικῇ μέχρι τῶν περὶ Ζέλειαν καὶ
Πιτύειαν [2] τόπων. ὠνομάσθαι δὲ τὴν χώραν
φασὶν ἀπὸ τοῦ Καρήσου ποταμοῦ, ὃν ὠνόμακεν ὁ
ποιητής·

Ῥῆσός θ' Ἑπτάπορός τε Κάρησός τε Ῥοδίος τε.

τὴν δὲ πόλιν κατεσπάσθαι τὴν ὁμώνυμον τῷ
ποταμῷ. πάλιν δ' οὗτός φησιν· ὁ μὲν Ῥῆσος
ποταμὸς νῦν καλεῖται Ῥοείτης, εἰ μὴ ἄρα ὁ εἰς
τὸν Γράνικον ἐμβάλλων Ῥῆσός ἐστιν. Ἑπτά-

---

[1] For διάδοσιν (all MSS. and Eustathius), Corais, Meineke

fair-flowing streams, where well up the two springs of eddying Scamander; for the one flows with soft water"[1] (that is, with "hot water"), and the poet adds, "and round about a smoke arises from it as if from a blazing fire, whereas the other even in summer flows forth cold as hail or chill snow." But, in the first place, no hot waters are now to be found at the site,[2] and, secondly, the source of the Scamander is not to be found there, but in the mountain; and it has only one source, not two. It is reasonable to suppose, therefore, that the hot spring has given out, and that the cold one is evacuated from the Scamander through an underground passage and rises to the surface here, or else that because of the nearness of the Scamander this water is called a source of the Scamander; for people are wont to ascribe several sources to one and the same river in this way.

44. The Scamander is joined by the Andirus, which flows from Caresenê, a mountainous country settled with many villages and beautifully culti-vated; it extends alongside Dardania as far as the regions of Zeleia and Pityeia. It is said that the country was named after the Caresus River, which is named by the poet, " Rhesus, Heptaporus, Caresus, and Rhodius,"[3] and that the city of the same name as the river was torn down. Again, Demetrius says as follows : " The Rhesus River is now called Rhoeites, unless it be that the river which empties into the Granicus is the Rhesus. The Heptaporus,

---

[1] *Iliad* 22. 147.   [2] *i.e.* of Troy.   [3] *Iliad* 12. 20.

---

and Leaf, from conj. of Xylander, read διάδυσιν ; but the emendation is unnecessary.

[2] Πιτύειαν, Xylander, for Πιτυίαν ; so the later editors.

STRABO

πορος δέ, ὃν καὶ Πολύπορον λέγουσιν, ἑπτάκις
διαβαινόμενος ἐκ τῶν περὶ τὴν Καλὴν Πεύκην
χωρίων ἐπὶ Μελαινὰς κώμην ἰοῦσι καὶ τὸ
Ἀσκληπίειον, ἵδρυμα Λυσιμάχου. περὶ δὲ τῆς
Καλῆς Πεύκης "Ατταλος ὁ πρῶτος βασιλεύσας
οὕτως γράφει· τὴν μὲν περίμετρον εἶναί φησι
ποδῶν τεττάρων καὶ εἴκοσι, τὸ δὲ ὕψος ἀπὸ μὲν
ῥίζης ἀνιέναι[1] ἐπὶ ἑξήκοντα καὶ ἑπτὰ πόδας, εἶτ'
εἰς τρία σχιζομένην ἴσον ἀλλήλων διέχοντα, εἶτα
πάλιν συναγομένην εἰς μίαν κορυφήν, ἀποτελοῦ-
σαν τὸ[2] πᾶν ὕψος δυεῖν πλέθρων καὶ πεντεκαί-
δεκα πηχῶν· Ἀδραμυττίου δὲ διέχει πρὸς ἄρκτον
ἑκατὸν καὶ ὀγδοήκοντα σταδίους. Κάρησος δ'
ἀπὸ Μαλοῦντος ῥεῖ, τόπου τινὸς κειμένου μεταξὺ
Παλαισκήψεως καὶ Ἀχαίου τῆς Τενεδίων
περαίας· ἐμβάλλει δὲ εἰς τὸν Αἴσηπον. Ῥοδίος
δὲ ἀπὸ Κλεανδρίας καὶ Γόρδου, ἃ διέχει τῆς
Καλῆς Πεύκης ἑξήκοντα σταδίους· ἐμβάλλει δ'
εἰς τὸν Αἴνιον.[3]

45. Τοῦ δ' αὐλῶνος τοῦ περὶ τὸν Αἴσηπον ἐν
ἀριστερᾷ τῆς ῥύσεως αὐτοῦ πρῶτόν ἐστι Πολίχνα,
τειχῆρες χωρίον, εἶθ' ἡ Παλαίσκηψις, εἶτ'
Ἀλαζόνιον, τοῦτ' ἤδη πεπλασμένον πρὸς τὴν τῶν
Ἁλιζώνων ὑπόθεσιν, περὶ ὧν εἰρήκαμεν· εἶτα
Κάρησος ἐρήμη καὶ ἡ Καρησηνὴ καὶ ὁμώνυμος
ποταμός, ποιῶν καὶ αὐτὸς αὐλῶνα ἀξιόλογον,
ἐλάττω δὲ τοῦ περὶ τὸν Αἴσηπον. τὰ δ' ἑξῆς ἤδη
τὰ τῆς Ζελείας ἐστὶ πεδία καὶ ὀροπέδια καλῶς

---

[1] ἀνιέναι, Meineke and Leaf, following i, for ἐάν Dgh,
ἐὰν C, ἕως moz.
[2] Instead of τό, CDFhi read τότε.
[3] For Αἴνιον Kramer conj. Αἴσηπον.

88

also called Polyporus, is crossed seven times by one
travelling from the region of the Beautiful Pine to
the village called Melaenae and the Asclepieium
that was founded by Lysimachus. Concerning the
Beautiful Pine, King Attalus the First writes as
follows: "Its circumference is twenty-four feet;
and its trunk rises to a height of sixty-seven feet
from the root and then splits into three forks equidistant from one another, and then contracts again
into one head, thus completing a total height of two
plethra and fifteen cubits."[1] It is one hundred and
eighty stadia distant from Adramyttium, to the
north of it. The Caresus flows from Malus, a place
situated between Palaescepsis and the Achaeïum,
the part of the mainland that belongs to the Tenedians;[2] and it empties into the Aesepus. The
Rhodius flows from Cleandria and Gordus, which
are sixty stadia distant from the Beautiful Pine; and
it empties into the Aenius.[3]

45. In the dale of the Aesepus, on the left of the
stream, one comes first to Polichna, a place enclosed
by walls; and then to Palaescepsis; and then to
Alizonium (this last name having been fabricated[4]
to support the hypothesis about the Halizones,
whom I have already discussed);[5] and then to
Caresus, which is deserted, and Caresenê, and the
river of the same name,[6] which also forms a notable
dale, though smaller than that of the Aesepus;
and next follow the plains and plateaux of Zeleia,

---

[1] About 225 feet.   [2] See end of § 32.
[3] "Aenius" appears to be an error for "Aesepus," as
suggested by Kramer. See Leaf, p. 207.
[4] *i.e.* by Demetrius.   [5] 12. 3. 20-27.
[6] The Caresus, of course.

γεωργούμενα· ἐν δεξιᾷ δὲ τοῦ Αἰσήπου μεταξὺ
Πολίχνας τε καὶ Παλαισκήψεως ἡ Νέα[1] Κώμη
καὶ Ἀργυρία,[2] καὶ τοῦτο πάλιν πλάσμα[3] πρὸς
τὴν αὐτὴν ὑπόθεσιν, ὅπως σωθείη τὸ

ὅθεν ἀργύρου ἐστὶ γενέθλη.

ἡ οὖν Ἀλύβη ποῦ, ἢ Ἀλόπη ἢ ὅπως βούλονται
παρονομάζειν; ἐχρῆν γὰρ καὶ τοῦτο πλάσαι
παρατριψαμένους τὸ μέτωπον καὶ μὴ χωλὸν ἐᾶν
καὶ ἕτοιμον πρὸς ἔλεγχον ἅπαξ ἤδη ἀποτετολμη-
κότας. ταῦτα μὲν οὖν ἔνστασιν ἔχει τοιαύτην,
τἆλλα δὲ ὑπολαμβάνομεν, ἢ τά γε πλεῖστα, δεῖν
προσέχειν[4] ὡς ἀνδρὶ ἐμπείρῳ καὶ ἐντοπίῳ, φροντί-
σαντί τε τοσοῦτον περὶ τούτων, ὥστε τριάκοντα
βίβλους συγγράψαι στίχων ἐξήγησιν μικρῷ
πλειόνων ἑξήκοντα, τοῦ καταλόγου τῶν Τρώων.
φησὶ δ᾽ οὖν τὴν Παλαίσκηψιν τῆς μὲν Αἰνέας[5]
διέχειν πεντήκοντα σταδίους, τοῦ δὲ ποταμοῦ τοῦ
Αἰσήπου τριάκοντα, ἀπὸ δὲ τῆς Παλαισκήψεως
ταύτης διατεῖναι τὴν ὁμωνυμίαν καὶ εἰς ἄλλους
πλείους τόπους. ἐπάνιμεν δὲ ἐπὶ τὴν παραλίαν,
ὅθενπερ ἀπελίπομεν.

C 604   46. Ἔστι δὴ[6] μετὰ τὴν Σιγειάδα ἄκραν καὶ τὸ
Ἀχίλλειον ἡ Τενεδίων περαία, τὸ Ἀχαίιον, καὶ

---

[1] Νέα appears to be an error for Αἰνέα, and Leaf so reads.
This appears to be the same village mentioned in the same
paragraph below (Αἰνέας) and in 12. 3. 23 (Ἐνέαν Κώμην).

[2] Ἀργυρία, Corais, for ἀργυρεῖα oxz, ἀργύρια other MSS.

[3] After πλάσμα, F adds τάγματα ἀργύρια, CDhi τάγματα τὰ
ἀργύρια, τακτέον τὰ ἀργυρεῖα, x τακτέον.

[4] Professor Capps rightly suspects that αὐτῷ, or Δημητρίῳ,
has fallen out of the MSS before προσέχειν.

[5] Instead of Αἰνέας, CFh read Αἰνείας, x Νέας; Meineke
reads Νέας.

which are beautifully cultivated. On the right of the Aesepus, between Polichna and Palaescepsis, one comes to Nea[1] Comê and Argyria,[2] and this again is a name fabricated to support the same hypothesis, in order to save the words, "where is the birthplace of silver."[3] Now where is Alybê, or Alopê, or however they wish to alter the spelling of the name?[4] For having once made their bold venture, they should have rubbed their faces[5] and fabricated this name too, instead of leaving it lame and readily subject to detection. Now these things are open to objections of this kind, but, in the case of the others, or at least most of them, I take it for granted that we must give heed to him[6] as a man who was acquainted with the region and a native of it, who gave enough thought to this subject to write thirty books of commentary on a little more than sixty lines of Homer, that is, on the *Catalogue of the Trojans*.[7] He says, at any rate, that Palaescepsis is fifty stadia distant from Aenea and thirty from the Aesepus River, and that from this Palaescepsis[8] the same name was extended to several other sites. But I shall return to the coast at the point where I left off.

46. After the Sigeian Promontory and the Achilleium one comes to the Achaeïum, the part of the

---

[1] Leaf emends "Nea" ("New") to "Aenea" (see critical note).
[2] Silvertown.   [3] *Iliad* 2. 856.
[4] See 12. 3. 21.
[5] *i.e.* to make them red and thus conceal their blushes of shame.
[6] *i.e.* Demetrius of Scepsis.
[7] *Iliad* 2. 816–877.   [8] *Old Scepsis.*

---

[6] δή, Corais, for δ' ἡ ; so Meineke.

αὐτὴ ἡ Τένεδος, οὐ πλείους τῶν τετταράκοντα
σταδίων διέχουσα τῆς ἠπείρου· ἔχει δὲ τὴν
περίμετρον ὅσον ὀγδοήκοντα σταδίων καὶ πόλιν
Αἰολίδα καὶ λιμένας δύο καὶ ἱερὸν τοῦ Σμινθέως
Ἀπόλλωνος, καθάπερ καὶ ὁ ποιητὴς μαρτυρεῖ·

Τενέδοιό τε ἶφι ἀνάσσεις,

Σμινθεῦ.

περίκειται δ᾽ αὐτῇ νησία πλείω, καὶ δὴ καὶ δύο, ἃ
καλοῦσι Καλύδνας, κειμένας κατὰ τὸν ἐπὶ Λεκτὸν
πλοῦν· καὶ αὐτὴν δὲ τὴν Τένεδον Κάλυδνάν τινες
εἶπον, ἄλλοι δὲ Λεύκοφρυν.[1] μυθεύουσι δ᾽ ἐν
αὐτῇ τὰ περὶ τὸν Τέννην, ἀφ᾽ οὗ καὶ τοὔνομα τῇ
νήσῳ, καὶ τὰ περὶ τὸν Κύκνον, Θρᾷκα τὸ γένος,
πατέρα δ᾽, ὥς τινες, τοῦ Τέννου, βασιλέα δὲ
Κολωνῶν.

47. Ἦν δὲ τῷ Ἀχαιΐῳ συνεχὴς ἥ τε Λάρισα
καὶ Κολωναί, τῆς[2] Τενεδίων περαίας οὖσαι πρότερον, καὶ ἡ νῦν Χρῦσα, ἐφ᾽ ὕψους τινὸς πετρώδους
ὑπὲρ τῆς θαλάττης ἱδρυμένη, καὶ ἡ Ἀμαξιτὸς ἡ
τῷ Λεκτῷ ὑποκειμένη συνεχής· νῦν δ᾽ ἡ Ἀλεξάνδρεια συνεχής ἐστι τῷ Ἀχαιΐῳ· τὰ δὲ πολίσματα
ἐκεῖνα συνῳκισμένα τυγχάνει, καθάπερ καὶ ἄλλα
πλείω τῶν φρουρίων, εἰς τὴν Ἀλεξάνδρειαν, ὧν
καὶ Κεβρήνη καὶ Νεανδρία ἐστί, καὶ τὴν χώραν
ἔχουσιν ἐκεῖνοι· ὁ δὲ τόπος, ἐν ᾧ νῦν κεῖται ἡ
Ἀλεξάνδρεια, Σιγία ἐκαλεῖτο.

48. Ἐν δὲ τῇ Χρύσῃ ταύτῃ καὶ τὸ τοῦ

---

[1] After Λεύκοφρυν, moz add εἰσὶ δὲ καὶ ἕτερα νησία περὶ
αὐτήν.

[2] After τῆς there is a lacuna in DFh of about ten letters
followed by δίας οὖσαι κτλ. Corais writes Τενεδίας; but

mainland that belongs to the Tenedians;[1] and to
Tenedos itself, which is not more than forty stadia
distant from the mainland. It is about eighty stadia
in circumference, and has an Aeolian city and two
harbours and a temple of Sminthian Apollo, as the
poet testifies : " And dost rule mightily over Tenedos,
O Sminthian."[2] Round it lie several small islands,
in particular two, which are called the Calydnae and
are situated on the voyage to Lectum. And some
give the name Calydna to Tenedos itself, while
others call it Leucophrys. In it is laid the scene of
the myth of Tennes,[3] after whom the island was
named, as also that of Cycnus, a Thracian by birth
and, according to some, father of Tennes and king
of Colonae.[4]

47. Both Larisa and Colonae used to be adjacent
to the Achaeïum, formerly being on the part of the
mainland that belonged to the Tenedians; and then
one comes to the present Chrysa, which was founded
on a rocky height above the sea, and to Hamaxitus,
which lies below Lectum and adjacent to it. At
the present time Alexandreia is adjacent to the
Achaeïum; and those other towns, like several
others of the strongholds, have been incorporated
with Alexandreia, among them Cebrenê and
Neandria; and Alexandreia holds their territory.
But the site on which Alexandreia now lies used
to be called Sigia.

48. In this Chrysa is also the temple of Sminthian

---

[1] See end of § 32.   [2] *Iliad* 1. 38.
[3] For this myth, see Pausanias 10. 14. 1.
[4] On the myth of Cycnus, see Leaf, p. 219.

Kramer, Meineke, and Leaf write Τενεδίων περαίας, the con-
vincing conjecture of Groskurd.

Σμινθέως Ἀπόλλωνός ἐστιν ἱερὸν καὶ τὸ σύμβολον τὸ τὴν ἐτυμότητα τοῦ ὀνόματος σῶζον, ὁ
μῦς, ὑπόκειται τῷ ποδὶ τοῦ ξοάνου. Σκόπα δ᾽
ἐστὶν ἔργα[1] τοῦ Παρίου· συνοικειοῦσι δὲ καὶ τὴν
ἱστορίαν εἴτε μῦθον τούτῳ τῷ τόπῳ τὴν περὶ τῶν
μυῶν. τοῖς γὰρ ἐκ τῆς Κρήτης ἀφιγμένοις
Τεύκροις (οὓς πρῶτος παρέδωκε Καλλῖνος ὁ τῆς
ἐλεγείας ποιητής, ἠκολούθησαν δὲ πολλοί)
χρησμὸς ἦν, αὐτόθι ποιήσασθαι τὴν μονήν, ὅπου
ἂν οἱ γηγενεῖς αὐτοῖς ἐπιθῶνται· συμβῆναι δὲ
τοῦτ᾽ αὐτοῖς φασὶ περὶ Ἀμαξιτόν· νύκτωρ γὰρ
πολὺ πλῆθος ἀρουραίων μυῶν ἐξανθῆσαν διαφαγεῖν
ὅσα σκύτινα τῶν τε ὅπλων καὶ τῶν χρηστηρίων·
τοὺς δὲ αὐτόθι μεῖναι· τούτους δὲ καὶ τὴν Ἴδην
ἀπὸ τῆς ἐν Κρήτῃ προσονομάσαι.[2] Ἡρακλείδης
δ᾽ ὁ Ποντικὸς πληθύοντάς φησι τοὺς μύας περὶ
τὸ ἱερὸν νομισθῆναί τε ἱεροὺς καὶ τὸ ξόανον οὕτω
κατασκευασθῆναι βεβηκὸς ἐπὶ τῷ μυΐ. ἄλλοι δ᾽
ἐκ τῆς Ἀττικῆς ἀφῖχθαί τινα Τεῦκρόν φασιν ἐκ
δήμου Τρώων, ὃς νῦν οἱ Ξυπετεῶνες[3] λέγεται,
Τεύκρους δὲ μηδένας ἐλθεῖν ἐκ τῆς Κρήτης. τῆς
δὲ πρὸς τοὺς Ἀττικοὺς ἐπιπλοκῆς τῶν Τρώων
τιθέασι σημεῖον καὶ τὸ παρ᾽ ἀμφοτέροις Ἐρι-
χθόνιόν τινα γενέσθαι τῶν ἀρχηγετῶν.[4] λέγουσι
μὲν οὖν οὕτως οἱ νεώτεροι, τοῖς δ᾽ Ὁμήρου μᾶλλον
C 605 ἔπεσι συμφωνεῖ τὰ ἐν τῷ Θήβης πεδίῳ καὶ τῇ
αὐτόθι Χρύσῃ ἱδρυμένῃ ποτὲ δεικνύμενα ἴχνη,

---

[1] Instead of ἔργα, Eustathius reads ἔργον ; so Leaf.
[2] Instead of προσονομάσαι, moz and Eustathius read παρονο-
μάσαι ; the editors before Kramer, κατονομάσαι.
[3] οἱ Ξυπετεῶνες, Meineke, for ὀξυπετεῶν; ὁ Ξυπετεών,
Tzschucke and Corais.

94

Apollo; and the symbol which preserves the
etymology of the name,[1] I mean the mouse, lies
beneath the foot of his image. These are the works
of Scopas of Paros; and also the history, or myth,
about the mice is associated with this place: When
the Teucrians arrived from Crete (Callinus the
elegiac poet was the first to hand down an account
of these people, and many have followed him), they
had an oracle which bade them to "stay on the
spot where the earth-born should attack them";
and, he says, the attack took place round Hamaxitus,
for by night a great multitude of field-mice swarmed
out of the ground and ate up all the leather in their
arms and equipment; and the Teucrians remained
there; and it was they who gave its name to Mt. Ida,
naming it after the mountain in Crete. Heracleides
of Pontus says that the mice which swarmed round
the temple were regarded as sacred, and that for
this reason the image was designed with its foot
upon the mouse. Others say that a certain Teucer
came from the deme of Troes, now called
Xypeteones, in Attica, but that no Teucrians came
from Crete. As a further sign of the close relationship of the Trojans with the people of Attica
they record the fact that Erichthonius was one
of the original founders in both tribes. Now this
is the account of the more recent writers; but
more in agreement with Homer are the traces to be
seen in the plain of Thebê and in the Chrysa
which was once founded there, which I shall soon

[1] Sminthian means "Mouse-god."

⁴ Instead of τῶν ἀρχηγετῶν *moz* read ἀρχηγέτην.

περὶ ὧν αὐτίκα ἐροῦμεν. πολλαχοῦ δ᾽ ἐστὶ τὸ
τοῦ Σμινθέως ὄνομα· καὶ γὰρ περὶ αὐτὴν τὴν
Ἀμαξιτὸν χωρὶς τοῦ κατὰ τὸ ἱερὸν Σμινθίου δύο
τόποι καλοῦνται Σμίνθια· καὶ ἄλλοι δ᾽ ἐν τῇ
πλησίον Λαρισαίᾳ· καὶ ἐν τῇ Παριανῇ δ᾽ ἐστὶ
χωρίον τὰ Σμίνθια καλούμενον καὶ ἐν Ῥόδῳ καὶ
ἐν Λίνδῳ καὶ ἄλλοθι δὲ πολλαχοῦ·[1] καλοῦσι δὲ
νῦν τὸ ἱερὸν Σμίνθιον. χωρὶς γοῦν καὶ τὸ
Ἀλήσιον[2] πεδίον οὐ μέγα ἐντὸς[3] τοῦ Λεκτοῦ καὶ
τὸ Τραγασαῖον ἁλοπήγιον αὐτόματον τοῖς ἐτησίαις
πηγνύμενον πρὸς Ἀμαξιτᾷ. ἐπὶ δὲ τῷ Λεκτῷ
βωμὸς τῶν δώδεκα θεῶν δείκνυται, καλοῦσι δ᾽
Ἀγαμέμνονος ἵδρυμα· ἐν ἐπόψει δὲ τῷ Ἰλίῳ
ἐστὶ τὰ χωρία ταῦτα, ὡς ἐν διακοσίοις σταδίοις ἢ
μικρῷ πλείοσιν· ὡς δ᾽ αὕτως καὶ τὰ περὶ Ἄβυδον
ἐκ θατέρου μέρους, μικρὸν δ᾽ ὅμως ἐγγυτέρω ἡ
Ἄβυδος.

49. Κάμψαντι δὲ τὸ Λεκτὸν ἐλλογιμώταται
πόλεις τῶν Αἰολέων καὶ ὁ Ἀδραμυττηνὸς κόλπος
ἐκδέχεται, ἐν ᾧ τοὺς πλείους τῶν Λελέγων κατοι-
κίζων ὁ ποιητὴς φαίνεται καὶ τοὺς Κίλικας,
διττοὺς ὄντας. ἐνταῦθα δὲ καὶ ὁ τῶν Μιτυληναίων
ἐστὶν αἰγιαλός, κώμας τινὰς ἔχων τῶν[4] κατὰ τὴν
ἤπειρον τῶν Μιτυληναίων. τὸν δὲ αὐτὸν κόλπον
καὶ Ἰδαῖον λέγουσιν· ἡ γὰρ ἀπὸ τοῦ Λεκτοῦ
ῥάχις, ἀνατείνουσα πρὸς τὴν Ἴδην, ὑπέρκειται
τῶν πρώτων τοῦ κόλπου μερῶν· ἐν οἷς πρῶτον
τοὺς Λέλεγας ἱδρυμένους ὁ ποιητὴς πεποίηκεν.

[1] Leaf omits the words καλοῦσι . . . γοῦν, and indicates a lacuna.
[2] Ἀλήσιον E and the editors, Ἀλίσιον DCFhx, Ἀλύσιον moz.
[3] ἐντός, Tyrwhitt, for ἐν τοῖς ; so the later editors.
[4] τῶν, before κατά, hi, Corais and Leaf omit.

discuss. The name of Smintheus is used in many places, for in the neighbourhood of Hamaxitus itself, apart from the Sminthium at the temple, there are two places called Sminthia; and there are others in the neighbouring territory of Larisa. And also in the territory of Parium there is a place called Sminthia, as also in Rhodes and in Lindus and in many other places. And they now call the temple Sminthium. Apart, at any rate,[1] lie both the Halesian Plain, of no great size, and inland from Lectum, and the Tragasaean salt-pan near Hamaxitus, where salt is naturally caused to congeal by the Etesian winds. On Lectum is to be seen an altar of the twelve gods, said to have been founded by Agamemnon. These places are all in sight of Ilium, at a distance of about two hundred stadia or a little more; and the same is the case with the places round Abydus on the other side, although Abydus is a little closer.

49. On doubling Lectum one comes next to the most notable cities of the Aeolians, and to the Gulf of Adramyttium, on which the poet obviously places the majority of the Leleges, as also the Cilicians, who were twofold.[2] Here too is the shore-land of the Mitylenaeans, with certain villages[3] belonging to the Mitylenaeans who live on the mainland. The same gulf is also called the Idaean Gulf, for the ridge which extends from Lectum to Mt. Ida lies above the first part of the gulf, where the poet represents the Leleges as first settled.[4]

[1] The Greek for these four words seems to be corrupt.
[2] See 13. 1. 7, 60.
[3] Coryphantis and Heracleia are named in § 51.
[4] *Iliad* 10. 429.

50. Εἴρηται δὲ περὶ αὐτῶν καὶ πρότερον· καὶ νῦν δὲ προσληπτέον, ὅτι Πήδασόν τινα λέγει πόλιν αὐτῶν ὑπὸ Ἄλτῃ τεταγμένην·[1]

Ἄλτεω, ὃς Λελέγεσσι φιλοπτολέμοισιν ἀνάσσει,
Πήδασον αἰπήεσσαν ἔχων ἐπὶ Σατνιόεντι.

καὶ νῦν ὁ τόπος δείκνυται τῆς πόλεως ἔρημος. γράφουσι δέ τινες οὐκ εὖ ὑπὸ Σατνιόεντι, ὡς ὑπὸ ὄρει Σατνιόεντι κειμένης τῆς πόλεως· οὐδὲν δ᾽ ἐστὶν ὄρος ἐνταῦθα Σατνιόεις πρασαγορευόμενον, ἀλλὰ ποταμός, ἐφ᾽ ᾧ ἵδρυται ἡ πόλις· νῦν δ᾽ ἐστὶν ἐρήμη. ὀνομάζει δὲ τὸν ποταμὸν ὁ ποιη-τής·

Σάτνιον γὰρ[2] οὔτασε δουρὶ

Οἰνοπίδην,[3] ὃν ἄρα νύμφη τέκε Νηὶς ἀμύμων
Οἴνοπι[4] βουκολέοντι παρ᾽ ὄχθαις Σατνιόεντος·

καὶ πάλιν·

C 606   ναῖε δὲ Σατνιόεντος ἐϋρρείταο παρ᾽ ὄχθαις
Πήδασον αἰπεινήν.

Σατνιόεντα δ᾽ ὕστερον εἶπον, οἱ δὲ Σαφνιόεντα. ἔστι δὲ χείμαρρος μέγας· ἄξιον δὲ μνήμης πεποίη-κεν ὀνομάζων ὁ ποιητὴς αὐτόν. οὗτοι δ᾽ οἱ τόποι συνεχεῖς εἰσὶ τῇ Δαρδανίᾳ καὶ τῇ Σκηψίᾳ, ὥσπερ ἄλλη τις Δαρδανία, ταπεινοτέρα δέ.

51. Ἀσσίων δ᾽ ἐστὶ νῦν καὶ Γαργαρέων τὰ[5] ἕως τῆς κατὰ Λέσβον θαλάττης περιεχόμενα τῇ τε

---

[1] Instead of τεταγμένην, CD*hix* read τεταγμένων.
[2] γάρ, after Σάτνιον, omitted by other editors.
[3] Instead of Οἰνοπίδην, the editors before Kramer, follow-ing the MSS. of *Iliad* 14. 443, read Ἠνοπίδην.

50. But I have already discussed these matters.[1] I must now add that Homer speaks of a Pedasus, a city of the Leleges, as subject to lord Altes: "Of Altes, who is lord over the war-loving Leleges, who hold steep Pedasus on the Satnioeis."[2] And the site of the place, now deserted, is still to be seen. Some write, though wrongly, "at the foot of Satnioeis,"[3] as though the city lay at the foot of a mountain called Satnioeis; but there is no mountain here called Satnioeis, but only a river of that name, on which the city is situated; but the city is now deserted. The poet names the river, for, according to him, "he wounded Satnius with a thrust of his spear, even the son of Oenops, whom a peerless Naiad nymph bore unto Oenops, as he tended his herds by the banks of the Satnioeis";[4] and again: "And he dwelt by the banks of the fair-flowing Satnioeis in steep Pedasus."[5] And in later times it was called Satnioeis, though some called it Saphnioeis. It is only a large winter torrent, but the naming of it by the poet has made it worthy of mention. These places are continuous with Dardania and Scepsia, and are, as it were, a second Dardania, but it is lower-lying.

51. To the Assians and the Gargarians now belong all the parts as far as the sea off Lesbos that are sur-

[1] 13. 1. 7.   [2] *Iliad* 21. 86.
[3] *i.e.* ὑπό for ἐπί in the Homeric passage quoted.
[4] *Iliad* 14. 443.   [5] *Iliad* 6. 34.

---

[4] Instead of Οἴνοπι, CDF and the editors before Kramer, following *Iliad* 14. 444, read Ἤνοπι.
[5] Leaf inserts τά before ἕως.

STRABO

'Ἀντανδρίᾳ καὶ τῇ Κεβρηνίων καὶ Νεανδριέων καὶ
'Ἀμαξιτέων. τῆς μὲν γὰρ 'Ἀμαξιτοῦ Νεανδριεῖς
ὑπέρκεινται, καὶ αὐτοὶ ὄντες ἐντὸς Λεκτοῦ, μεσο-
γειότεροι δὲ [1] καὶ πλησιαίτεροι τῷ 'Ἰλίῳ· διέχουσι
γὰρ ἑκατὸν καὶ τριάκοντα σταδίους. τούτων δὲ
καθύπερθε Κεβρήνιοι, τούτων δὲ Δαρδάνιοι μέχρι
Παλαισκήψεως καὶ αὐτῆς τῆς Σκήψεως. τὴν δὲ
Ἄντανδρον 'Ἀλκαῖος μὲν καλεῖ Λελέγων πόλιν·

πρῶτα [2] μὲν Ἄντανδρος Λελέγων πόλις.

ὁ δὲ Σκήψιος ἐν ταῖς παρακειμέναις τίθησιν, ὥστ'
ἐκπίπτοι ἂν εἰς τὴν τῶν Κιλίκων· οὗτοι γάρ
εἰσι συνεχεῖς τοῖς Λέλεξι, μᾶλλόν πως τὸ νότιον
πλευρὸν τῆς Ἴδης ἀφορίζοντες· ταπεινοὶ δ' ὅμως
καὶ οὗτοι καὶ [3] τῇ παραλίᾳ συνάπτοντες μᾶλλον
τῇ κατὰ 'Ἀδραμύττιον. μετὰ γὰρ τὸ Λεκτὸν τὸ
Πολυμήδιόν ἐστι χωρίον τι ἐν τετταράκοντα
σταδίοις, εἶτ' ἐν ὀγδοήκοντα Ἄσσος,[4] μικρὸν ὑπὲρ
τῆς θαλάττης, εἶτ' ἐν ἑκατὸν καὶ τετταράκοντα

[1] δέ, Corais, for τε.
[2] For πρῶτα, Leaf, as his translation (p. 253) shows, must
have intended to read πρῶτα (πρώτη).
[3] οἱ, before τῇ, Corais rejects; so Kramer, Meineke, and
Leaf.
[4] Ἄσσος, Tzschucke, from conj. of Mannert, for ἄλσος; so
the later editors.

[1] *Frag.* 65 (Bergk). Leaf translates: "Antandros, first
city of the Leleges" (see critical note).
[2] Leaf translates: "But Demetrios puts it in the district
adjacent (to the Leleges), so that it would fall within the
territory of the Kilikes"; and in his commentary (p. 255)
he says: "As the words stand, Strabo says that 'Demetrios
places Antandros (not at Antandros but) in the neighbourhood of Antandros.' That is nonsense however we look at

rounded by the territory of Antandrus and that of
the Cebrenians and Neandrians and Hamaxitans; for
the Antandrians are situated above Hamaxitus, like
it being situated inside Lectum, though farther
inland and nearer to Ilium, for they are one hundred
and thirty stadia distant from Ilium.   Higher up
than these are the Cebrenians, and still higher up
than the latter are the Dardanians, who extend as
far as Palaescepsis and Scepsis itself.   Antandrus is
called by Alcaeus "city of the Leleges": "First,
Antandrus, city of the Leleges";[1] but it is placed
by the Scepsian among the cities adjacent to their
territory,[2] so that it would fall within the territory
of the Cilicians; for the territory of the Cilicians is
continuous with that of the Leleges, the former,
rather than the latter, marking off the southern
flank of Mt. Ida.   But still the territory of the
Cilicians also lies low and, rather than that of the
Leleges, joins the part of the coast that is near
Adramyttium.[3]   For after Lectum one comes to a
place called Polymedium, at a distance of forty stadia;
then, at a distance of eighty,[4] to Assus, slightly above
the sea; and then, at a distance of one hundred and

it."   Yet the Greek cannot mean that Demetrius transfers
Antandrus, "a fixed point," to "the adjacent district," as
Leaf interprets, but that he includes it among the cities
(ταῖς παρακειμέναις) which he enumerates as Cilician.

[3] The interpretation of the Greek for this last sentence is
somewhat doubtful.   Cf. translation and commentary of
Leaf (pp. 254–255), who regards the text as corrupt.

[4] *i.e.* eighty stadia from Polymedium, not from Lectum,
as thought by Thatcher Clark (*American Journal of
Archaeology*, 4. 291 ff., quoted by Leaf).   His interpretation,
neither accepted nor definitely rejected by Leaf (p. 257), is
not in accordance with Strabo's manner of enumerating
distances, a fact apparently overlooked by both scholars.

Γάργαρα· κεῖται δὲ τὰ Γάργαρα ἐπ' ἄκρας ποιού-
σης τὸν ἰδίως Ἀδραμυττηνὸν καλούμενον κόλπον,
λέγεται γὰρ καὶ πᾶσα ἡ ἀπὸ Λεκτοῦ μέχρι
Κανῶν παραλία τῷ αὐτῷ τούτῳ ὀνόματι, ἐν ᾧ καὶ
ὁ Ἐλαϊτικὸς περιλαμβάνεται· ἰδίως μέντοι τοῦτόν
φασιν Ἀδραμυττηνόν, τὸν κλειόμενον ὑπὸ ταύτης
τε τῆς ἄκρας, ἐφ' ᾗ τὰ Γάργαρα, καὶ τῆς Πυρρᾶς
ἄκρας προσαγορευομένης, ἐφ' ᾗ καὶ Ἀφροδίσιον
ἵδρυται. πλάτος δὲ τοῦ στόματός ἐστιν ἀπὸ τῆς
ἄκρας ἐπὶ τὴν ἄκραν δίαρμα ἑκατὸν καὶ εἴκοσι
σταδίων. ἐντὸς δὲ ἥ τε Ἄντανδρός ἐστιν, ὑπερκείμενον ἔχουσα ὄρος, ὃ καλοῦσιν Ἀλεξάνδρειαν,
ὅπου τὰς θεὰς κριθῆναί φασιν ὑπὸ τοῦ Πάριδος,
καὶ ὁ Ἀσπανεύς, τὸ ὑλοτόμιον τῆς Ἰδαίας ὕλης·
ἐνταῦθα γὰρ διατίθενται κατάγοντες τοῖς δεο-
μένοις. εἶτ' Ἄστυρα, κώμη καὶ ἄλσος τῆς
Ἀστυρηνῆς Ἀρτέμιδος ἅγιον. πλησίον δ' εὐθὺς
τὸ Ἀδραμύττιον, Ἀθηναίων ἄποικος πόλις,
ἔχουσα καὶ λιμένα καὶ ναύσταθμον· ἔξω δὲ τοῦ
C 607 κόλπου καὶ τῆς Πυρρᾶς ἄκρας ἥ τε Κισθήνη ἐστὶ
πόλις ἔρημος, ἔχουσα λιμένα. ὑπὲρ αὐτῆς ἐν τῇ
μεσογαίᾳ τό τε τοῦ χαλκοῦ μέταλλον καὶ
Περπερηνή[1] καὶ Τράριον καὶ ἄλλαι τοιαῦται
κατοικίαι. ἐν δὲ τῇ παραλίᾳ τῇ ἐφεξῆς αἱ τῶν
Μιτυληναίων κῶμαι Κορυφαντίς τε καὶ Ἡράκλεια,
καὶ μετὰ ταῦτα Ἄττεα, εἶτ' Ἀταρνεὺς καὶ
Πιτάνη καὶ αἱ τοῦ Καΐκου ἐκβολαί· ταῦτα δ'
ἤδη τοῦ Ἐλαϊτῶν κόλπου· καὶ ἔστιν ἐν τῇ

---

[1] Περπερηνή, Meineke, from conj. of Kramer, for Περπερήνα.

---

[1] See preceding foot-note.

twenty,[1] to Gargara, which lies on a promontory[2] that forms the Adramyttene Gulf, in the special sense of that term; for the whole of the coast from Lectum to Canae is also called by this same name, in which is also included the Elaïtic Gulf. In the special sense of the term, however, only that part of it is called Adramyttene which is enclosed by that promontory on which Gargara lies and the promontory called Pyrrha, on which the Aphrodisium[3] is situated. The breadth of the mouth across from promontory to promontory is a distance of one hundred and twenty stadia. Inside is Antandrus, above which lies a mountain called Alexandreia, where the Judgment of Paris is said to have taken place, as also Aspaneus, the market for the timber from Mt. Ida; for here people bring it down and sell it to those who want it. And then comes Astyra, a village with a precinct sacred to the Astyrene Artemis. And quite near Astyra is Adramyttium, a city colonised by the Athenians, which has both a harbour and a naval station. Outside the gulf and the promontory called Pyrrha lies Cisthenê, a deserted city with a harbour. Above it, in the interior, lie the copper mine and Perperenê and Trarium and other settlements like these two. On the next stretch of coast one comes to the villages of the Mitylenaeans, I mean Coryphantis and Heracleia; and after these places to Attea, and then to Atarneus and Pitanê and the outlets of the Caïcus River; and here we have already reached the Elaïtic Gulf. On the far side of the river lie

[2] So Clark; or "on a height," as Leaf translates (see his note).
[3] Temple of Aphrodite.

περαίᾳ ἡ Ἐλαία[1] καὶ ὁ λοιπὸς μέχρι Κανῶν κόλπος. λέγωμεν δὲ ἀναλαβόντες περὶ τῶν καθ' ἕκαστα πάλιν, εἴ τι παραλέλειπται μνήμης ἄξιον, καὶ πρῶτον περὶ τῆς Σκήψεως.

52. Ἔστι δ' ἡ μὲν Παλαίσκηψις ἐπάνω Κεβρῆνος κατὰ τὸ μετεωρότατον τῆς Ἴδης ἐγγὺς Πολίχνης· ἐκαλεῖτο δὲ τότε Σκῆψις, εἴτ' ἄλλως, εἴτ' ἀπὸ τοῦ περίσκεπτον εἶναι τὸν τόπον, εἰ δεῖ τὰ παρὰ τοῖς βαρβάροις ἐν τῷ τότε ὀνόματα ταῖς Ἑλληνικαῖς ἐτυμολογεῖσθαι φωναῖς· ὕστερον δὲ κατωτέρω σταδίοις[2] ἑξήκοντα εἰς τὴν νῦν Σκῆψιν μετῳκίσθησαν ὑπὸ Σκαμανδρίου τε τοῦ Ἕκτορος καὶ Ἀσκανίου τοῦ Αἰνείου παιδός· καὶ δύο γένη ταῦτα βασιλεῦσαι πολὺν χρόνον ἐν τῇ Σκήψει λέγεται· μετὰ ταῦτα δ' εἰς ὀλιγαρχίαν μετέστησαν, εἶτα Μιλήσιοι[3] συνεπολιτεύθησαν αὐτοῖς[4] καὶ δημοκρατικῶς ᾤκουν· οἱ δ' ἀπὸ τοῦ γένους οὐδὲν ἧττον ἐκαλοῦντο βασιλεῖς, ἔχοντές τινας τιμάς· εἶτ' εἰς τὴν Ἀλεξάνδρειαν συνεπόλισε τοὺς Σκηψίους Ἀντίγονος, εἶτ' ἀπέλυσε Λυσίμαχος καὶ ἐπανῆλθον εἰς τὴν οἰκείαν.

53. Οἴεται δ' ὁ Σκήψιος καὶ βασίλειον τοῦ Αἰνείου γεγονέναι τὴν Σκῆψιν, μέσην οὖσαν τῆς τε ὑπὸ τῷ Αἰνείᾳ καὶ Λυρνησσοῦ, εἰς ἣν φυγεῖν εἴρηται διωκόμενος ὑπὸ τοῦ Ἀχιλλέως· φησὶ γοῦν ὁ Ἀχιλλεύς·

---

[1] Ἐλαία, Tzschucke, from conj. of Casaubon, for Μελαία CFrxz, Μελέα D, Μελήα h, Μελία i.

[2] After σταδίοις, Leaf inserts διακοσίοις καὶ (i.e. σταδίοισσξ' instead of σταδίοισξ').

[3] Μιλήσιοι, Corais, following Ald., for Μιλήσίοις.

[4] For αὐτοῖς, moz and Corais read αὐτοί.

Elaea and the rest of the gulf as far as Canae. But let me go back and again discuss in detail the several places, if anything worthy of mention has been passed over; and first of all, Scepsis.

52. Palaescepsis lies above Cebren near the highest part of Mt. Ida, near Polichna; and it was then called Scepsis (whether for another reason or from the fact that the place is visible all round, if it is right to derive from Greek words names then used by barbarians),[1] but later the inhabitants were removed sixty stadia[2] lower down to the present Scepsis by Scamandrius the son of Hector and Ascanius the son of Aeneias; and their two families are said to have held the kingship over Scepsis for a long time. After this they changed to an oligarchy, and then Milesians settled with them as fellow-citizens;[3] and they began to live under a democracy. But the heirs of the royal family none the less continued to be called kings and retained certain prerogatives. Then the Scepsians were incorporated into Alexandreia by Antigonus; and then they were released by Lysimachus and went back to their home-land.

53. Demetrius thinks that Scepsis was also the royal residence of Aeneias, since it lies midway between the territory subject to Aeneias and Lyrnessus, to which latter he fled, according to Homer's statement, when he was being pursued by Achilles. At

---

[1] The Greek word "scepsis" means "a viewing," "an inspection."

[2] Leaf emends to "two hundred and sixty stadia" (see critical note).

[3] See 14. 1. 6.

ἢ οὐ μέμνῃ, ὅτε πέρ σε βοῶν ἄπο μοῦνον
    ἐόντα
σεῦα κατ' Ἰδαίων ὀρέων ταχέεσσι πόδεσσι,
κεῖθεν δ' ἐς Λυρνησσὸν ὑπέκφυγες· αὐτὰρ ἐγὼ
    τὴν
πέρσα, μεθορμηθείς.

οὐχ ὁμολογεῖ δὲ τῷ περὶ τῶν ἀρχηγετῶν τῆς
Σκήψεως λόγῳ τῷ λεχθέντι νῦν τὰ περὶ τοῦ
Αἰνείου θρυλούμενα. περιγενέσθαι γὰρ δὴ τοῦτόν
φασιν ἐκ τοῦ πολέμου διὰ τὴν πρὸς Πρίαμον
δυσμένειαν·

    ἀεὶ γὰρ Πριάμῳ ἐπεμήνιε δίῳ,
οὕνεκ' ἄρ' ἐσθλὸν ἐόντα μετ' ἀνδράσιν οὔ τι
    τίεσκε·

τοὺς δὲ συνάρχοντας Ἀντηνορίδας καὶ αὐτὸν τὸν
Ἀντήνορα διὰ τὴν Μενελάου παρ' αὐτῷ ξενίαν.
C 608 Σοφοκλῆς γοῦν ἐν τῇ ἁλώσει τοῦ Ἰλίου παρδαλέαν
φησὶ πρὸ τῆς θύρας τοῦ Ἀντήνορος προτεθῆναι
σύμβολον τοῦ ἀπόρθητον ἐαθῆναι τὴν οἰκίαν.
τὸν μὲν οὖν Ἀντήνορα καὶ τοὺς παῖδας μετὰ τῶν
περιγενομένων[1] Ἐνετῶν εἰς τὴν Θρᾴκην περισωθῆναι,[2] κἀκεῖθεν διαπεσεῖν εἰς τὴν λεγομένην
κατὰ τὸν Ἀδρίαν Ἐνετικήν· τὸν δὲ Αἰνείαν μετ'
Ἀγχίσου τοῦ πατρὸς καὶ τοῦ παιδὸς Ἀσκανίου
λαὸν ἀθροίσαντα πλεῦσαι, καὶ οἱ μὲν οἰκῆσαι
περὶ τὸν Μακεδονικὸν Ὄλυμπόν φασιν, οἱ δὲ
περὶ Μαντίνειαν τῆς Ἀρκαδίας κτίσαι Καπύας,
ἀπὸ Κάπυος θέμενον τοὔνομα τῷ πολίσματι, οἱ
δ' εἰς Αἴγεσταν καταραι τῆς Σικελίας σὺν Ἐλύ-

[1] περιγενουένων, Eustathius and the editors, for παραγενο-

any rate, Achilles says: "Dost thou not remember
how from the kine, when thou wast all alone, I
made thee run down the Idaean mountains with
swift feet? And thence thou didst escape to
Lyrnessus, but I rushed in pursuit of thee and
sacked it."[1] However, the oft-repeated stories of
Aeneias are not in agreement with the account
which I have just given of the founders of Scepsis.
For according to these stories he survived the war
because of his enmity to Priam: "For always he
was wroth against goodly Priam, because, although
he was brave amid warriors, Priam would not honour
him at all";[2] and his fellow-rulers, the sons of
Antenor and Antenor himself, survived because of
the hospitality shown Menelaüs at Antenor's house.
At any rate, Sophocles[3] says that at the capture of
Troy a leopard's skin was put before the doors of
Antenor as a sign that his house was to be left
unpillaged; and Antenor and his children safely
escaped to Thrace with the survivors of the Heneti,
and from there got across to the Adriatic Heneticê,[4]
as it is called, whereas Aeneias collected a host of
followers and set sail with his father Anchises and
his son Ascanius; and some say that he took up his
abode near the Macedonian Olympus, others that he
founded Capyae near Mantineia in Arcadia, deriving
the name he gave the settlement from Capys, and
others say that he landed at Aegesta in Sicily with

---

[1] *Iliad* 20. 188.   [2] *Iliad* 13. 460.
[3] *Frag.* 10 (Nauck).
[4] As distinguished from that in Paphlagonia (see 5. 1. 4).

μένων D*hi*, λεγουμένων *rwx*, . . . νομένων C; word omitted by
moz.
[2] For περισωθῆναι Corais reads περαιωθῆναι.

μῷ[1] Τρωὶ καὶ Ἔρυκα καὶ Λιλύβαιον κατασχεῖν, καὶ ποταμοὺς περὶ Αἴγεσταν προσαγορεῦσαι Σκάμανδρον καὶ Σιμόεντα· ἔνθεν δ' εἰς τὴν Λατίνην ἐλθόντα μεῖναι κατά τι λόγιον τὸ κελεῦον μένειν, ὅπου ἂν τὴν τράπεζαν καταφάγῃ· συμβῆναι δὲ τῆς Λατίνης[2] περὶ τὸ Λαουίνιον τοῦτο, ἄρτου μεγάλου τεθέντος ἀντὶ τραπέζης κατὰ ἀπορίαν[3] καὶ ἅμα ἀναλωθέντος τοῖς ἐπ' αὐτῷ κρέασιν. Ὅμηρος μέντοι συνηγορεῖν οὐδετέροις ἔοικεν, οὐδὲ τοῖς περὶ τῶν ἀρχηγετῶν τῆς Σκήψεως λεχθεῖσιν· ἐμφαίνει γὰρ μεμενηκότα τὸν Αἰνείαν ἐν τῇ Τροίᾳ καὶ διαδεδεγμένον τὴν ἀρχὴν καὶ παραδεδωκότα παισὶ παίδων τὴν διαδοχὴν αὐτῆς, ἠφανισμένου τοῦ τῶν Πριαμιδῶν γένους·

ἤδη γὰρ Πριάμου γενεὴν ἤχθηρε Κρονίων·
νῦν δὲ δὴ Αἰνείαο βίη Τρώεσσιν ἀνάξει
καὶ παίδων παῖδες, τοί κεν μετόπισθε γένωνται.

οὕτω δ' οὐδ' ἡ τοῦ Σκαμανδρίου διαδοχὴ σώζοιτ' ἄν. πολὺ δὲ μᾶλλον τοῖς ἑτέροις διαφωνεῖ τοῖς μέχρι καὶ Ἰταλίας αὐτοῦ τὴν πλάνην λέγουσι καὶ αὐτόθι ποιοῦσι τὴν καταστροφὴν τοῦ βίου. τινὲς δὲ γράφουσιν

Αἰνείαο γένος πάντεσσιν ἀνάξει,
καὶ παῖδες παίδων,

τοὺς Ῥωμαίους λέγοντες.

54. Ἐκ δὲ τῆς Σκήψεως οἵ τε Σωκρατικοὶ

---

[1] Ἐλύμῳ F, Ἐλύμνῳ other MSS.
[2] Instead of τῆς Λατίνης, D(pr. man.)ἰτιω have τοῖς Λατίνοις, moz ἐν τῇ Λατίνῃ.

Elymus the Trojan and took possession of Eryx and Lilybaeum, and gave the names Scamander and Simoeis to rivers near Aegesta, and that thence he went into the Latin country and made it his abode, in accordance with an oracle which bade him abide where he should eat up his table, and that this took place in the Latin country in the neighbourhood of Lavinium, where a large loaf of bread was put down for a table, for want of a better table, and eaten up along with the meats upon it. Homer, however, appears not to be in agreement with either of the two stories, nor yet with the above account of the founders of Scepsis; for he clearly indicates that Aeneias remained in Troy and succeeded to the empire and bequeathed the succession thereto to his sons' sons, the family of the Priamidae having been wiped out : " For already the race of Priam was hated by the son of Cronus ; and now verily the mighty Aeneias will rule over the Trojans, and his sons' sons that are hereafter to be born." [1] And in this case one cannot even save from rejection the succession of Scamandrius.[2] And Homer is in far greater disagreement with those who speak of Aeneias as having wandered even as far as Italy and make him die there. Some write, " the family of Aeneias will rule over all,[3] and his sons' sons," meaning the Romans.

54. From Scepsis came the Socratic philosophers

---

[1] *Iliad* 20. 306.
[2] The son of Hector, who, along with Ascanius, was said to have been king of Scepsis (§ 52).
[3] *i.e.* they emend "Trojans" (Τρώεσσιν) to "all" (πάντεσσιν) in the Homeric passage.

---

[3] ἀπορίαν, Casaubon, for ἀπειρίαν ; so the later editors.

γεγόνασιν Ἔραστος καὶ Κορίσκος καὶ ὁ τοῦ
Κορίσκου υἱὸς Νηλεύς, ἀνὴρ καὶ Ἀριστοτέλους
ἠκροαμένος καὶ Θεοφράστου, διαδεδεγμένος δὲ
τὴν βιβλιοθήκην τοῦ Θεοφράστου, ἐν ᾗ ἦν καὶ
ἡ τοῦ Ἀριστοτέλους· ὁ γοῦν Ἀριστοτέλης τὴν
ἑαυτοῦ Θεοφράστῳ παρέδωκεν, ᾧπερ καὶ τὴν
σχολὴν ἀπέλιπε, πρῶτος, ὧν ἴσμεν, συναγαγὼν
βιβλία καὶ διδάξας τοὺς ἐν Αἰγύπτῳ βασιλέας
C 609 βιβλιοθήκης σύνταξιν. Θεόφραστος δὲ Νηλεῖ
παρέδωκεν· ὁ δ᾿ εἰς Σκῆψιν κομίσας τοῖς μετ᾿
αὐτὸν παρέδωκεν, ἰδιώταις ἀνθρώποις, οἳ κατά-
κλειστα εἶχον τὰ βιβλία, οὐδ᾿ ἐπιμελῶς κείμενα·
ἐπειδὴ δὲ ᾔσθοντο τὴν σπουδὴν τῶν Ἀτταλικῶν
βασιλέων, ὑφ᾿ οἷς ἦν ἡ πόλις, ζητούντων βιβλία
εἰς τὴν κατασκευὴν τῆς ἐν Περγάμῳ βιβλιοθήκης,
κατὰ γῆς ἔκρυψαν ἐν διώρυγί τινι· ὑπὸ δὲ νοτίας
καὶ σητῶν κακωθέντα ὀψέ ποτε ἀπέδοντο οἱ ἀπὸ
τοῦ γένους Ἀπελλικῶντι τῷ Τηίῳ πολλῶν
ἀργυρίων τά τε Ἀριστοτέλους καὶ τὰ τοῦ
Θεοφράστου βιβλία· ἦν δὲ ὁ Ἀπελλικῶν φιλό-
βιβλος μᾶλλον ἢ φιλόσοφος· διὸ καὶ ζητῶν
ἐπανόρθωσιν τῶν διαβρωμάτων εἰς ἀντίγραφα
καινὰ μετήνεγκε τὴν γραφήν, ἀναπληρῶν οὐκ
εὖ, καὶ ἐξέδωκεν ἁμαρτάδων πλήρη τὰ βιβλία.
συνέβη δὲ τοῖς ἐκ τῶν περιπάτων τοῖς μὲν πάλαι
τοῖς μετὰ Θεόφραστον οὐκ ἔχουσιν ὅλως τὰ
βιβλία πλὴν ὀλίγων, καὶ μάλιστα τῶν ἐξω-
τερικῶν, μηδὲν ἔχειν φιλοσοφεῖν πραγματικῶς,
ἀλλὰ θέσεις ληκυθίζειν· τοῖς δ᾿ ὕστερον, ἀφ᾿
οὗ τὰ βιβλία ταῦτα προῆλθεν, ἄμεινον μὲν

---

[1] Strabo refers to Eumenes II, who reigned 197–159 B.C.

Erastus and Coriscus and Neleus the son of Coriscus,
this last a man who not only was a pupil of Aristotle
and Theophrastus, but also inherited the library of
Theophrastus, which included that of Aristotle.   At
any rate, Aristotle bequeathed his own library to
Theophrastus, to whom he also left his school; and
he is the first man, so far as I know, to have collected
books and to have taught the kings in Egypt how to
arrange a library.   Theophrastus bequeathed it to
Neleus; and Neleus took it to Scepsis and bequeathed it to his heirs, ordinary people, who kept
the books locked up and not even carefully stored.
But when they heard how zealously the Attalic
kings[1] to whom the city was subject were searching
for books to build up the library in Pergamum, they
hid their books underground in a kind of trench.
But much later, when the books had been damaged
by moisture and moths, their descendants sold them
to Apellicon[2] of Teos for a large sum of money, both
the books of Aristotle and those of Theophrastus.
But Apellicon was a bibliophile rather than a philosopher; and therefore, seeking a restoration of the
parts that had been eaten through, he made new
copies of the text, filling up the gaps incorrectly, and
published the books full of errors.   The result was
that the earlier school of Peripatetics who came after
Theophrastus had no books at all, with the exception
of only a few, mostly exoteric works, and were therefore able to philosophise about nothing in a practical
way, but only to talk bombast about commonplace
propositions, whereas the later school, from the time
the books in question appeared, though better able

[2] Died about 84 B.C.

STRABO

ἐκείνων φιλοσοφεῖν καὶ ἀριστοτελίζειν, ἀναγκά-
ζεσθαι μέντοι τὰ πολλὰ εἰκότα λέγειν διὰ τὸ
πλῆθος τῶν ἁμαρτιῶν. πολὺ δὲ εἰς τοῦτο καὶ
ἡ Ῥώμη προσελάβετο· εὐθὺς γὰρ μετὰ τὴν
Ἀπελλικῶντος τελευτὴν Σύλλας ᾖρε τὴν Ἀπελλικῶντος βιβλιοθήκην ὁ τὰς Ἀθήνας ἑλών,
δεῦρο δὲ κομισθεῖσαν Τυραννίων τε ὁ γραμματικὸς
διεχειρίσατο φιλαριστοτέλης ὤν, θεραπεύσας τὸν
ἐπὶ τῆς βιβλιοθήκης, καὶ βιβλιοπῶλαί τινες
γραφεῦσι φαύλοις χρώμενοι καὶ οὐκ ἀντι-
βάλλοντες, ὅπερ καὶ ἐπὶ τῶν ἄλλων συμβαίνει
τῶν εἰς πρᾶσιν γραφομένων βιβλίων καὶ ἐνθάδε
καὶ ἐν Ἀλεξανδρείᾳ. περὶ μὲν οὖν τούτων ἀπόχρη.

55. Ἐκ δὲ τῆς Σκήψεως καὶ ὁ Δημήτριός
ἐστιν, οὗ μεμνήμεθα πολλάκις, ὁ τὸν Τρωικὸν
διάκοσμον ἐξηγησάμενος γραμματικός, κατὰ τὸν
αὐτὸν χρόνον γεγονὼς Κράτητι καὶ Ἀριστάρχῳ·
καὶ μετὰ τοῦτο Μητρόδωρος, ἀνὴρ ἐκ τοῦ
φιλοσόφου μεταβεβληκὼς ἐπὶ τὸν πολιτικὸν
βίον καὶ ῥητορεύων τὸ πλέον ἐν τοῖς συγγράμ-
μασιν· ἐχρήσατο δὲ φράσεώς τινι χαρακτῆρι
καινῷ καὶ κατεπλήξατο[1] πολλούς· διὰ δὲ τὴν
δόξαν ἐν Χαλκηδόνι γάμου λαμπροῦ πένης ὢν
ἔτυχε καὶ ἐχρημάτιζε Χαλκηδόνιος· Μιθριδάτην
δὲ θεραπεύσας τὸν Εὐπάτορα συναπῆρεν εἰς τὸν
Πόντον ἐκείνῳ μετὰ τῆς γυναικὸς καὶ ἐτιμήθη
C 610 διαφερόντως, ταχθεὶς ἐπὶ τῆς δικαιοδοσίας, ἀφ᾽[2]
ἧς οὐκ ἦν τῷ κριθέντι ἀναβολὴ[3] τῆς δίκης ἐπὶ
τὸν βασιλέα. οὐ μέντοι διηυτύχησεν, ἀλλ᾽

[1] Instead of κατεπλήξατο, F reads κατεπλήξαντο, moxz κατέ-
πληξε (so Corais, who inserts τούς before πολλούς).

112

to philosophise and Aristotelise, were forced to call most of their statements probabilities, because of the large number of errors.[1] Rome also contributed much to this; for, immediately after the death of Apellicon, Sulla, who had captured Athens, carried off Apellicon's library to Rome, where Tyrannion the grammarian, who was fond of Aristotle, got it in his hands by paying court to the librarian, as did also certan booksellers who used bad copyists and would not collate the texts—a thing that also takes place in the case of the other books that are copied for selling, both here[2] and at Alexandria. However, this is enough about these men.

55. From Scepsis came also Demetrius, whom I often mention, the grammarian who wrote a commentary on *The Marshalling of the Trojan Forces*, and was born at about the same time as Crates and Aristarchus; and later, Metrodorus, a man who changed from his pursuit of philosophy to political life, and taught rhetoric, for the most part, in his written works; and he used a brand-new style and dazzled many. On account of his reputation he succeeded, though a poor man, in marrying brilliantly in Chalcedon; and he passed for a Chalcedonian. And having paid court to Mithridates Eupator, he with his wife sailed away with him to Pontus; and he was treated with exceptional honour, being appointed to the judgeship from which there was no appeal to the king. However, his good fortune did

---

[1] *i.e.* errors in the available texts of Aristotle.
[2] *i.e.* at Rome.

---

[2] ἀφ', Casaubon, for ἐφ'; so the later editors.
[3] ἀναβολή, Casaubon, for βουλή; so the later editors.

ἐμπεσὼν εἰς ἔχθραν ἀδικωτέρων ἀνθρώπων
ἀπέστη τοῦ βασιλέως κατὰ τὴν πρὸς Τιγράνην
τὸν Ἀρμένιον πρεσβείαν· ὁ δ᾽ ἄκοντα ἀνέπεμψεν
αὐτὸν τῷ Εὐπάτορι, φεύγοντι ἤδη τὴν προγονικήν,
κατὰ δὲ τὴν ὁδὸν κατέστρεψε τὸν βίον εἴθ᾽ ὑπὸ
τοῦ βασιλέως, εἴθ᾽ ὑπὸ νόσου· λέγεται γὰρ
ἀμφότερα. περὶ μὲν τῶν Σκηψίων ταῦτα.

56. Μετὰ δὲ Σκῆψιν Ἄνδειρα [1] καὶ Πιονίαι
καὶ ἡ Γαργαρίς. ἔστι δὲ λίθος περὶ τὰ Ἄνδειρα,
ὃς καιόμενος σίδηρος γίνεται· εἶτα μετὰ γῆς τινὸς
καμινευθεὶς ἀποστάζει ψευδάργυρον, ἣ προσλα-
βοῦσα χαλκὸν τὸ καλούμενον γίνεται κρᾶμα, ὅ
τινες ὀρείχαλκον καλοῦσι· γίνεται δὲ ψευδάργυρος
καὶ περὶ τὸν Τμῶλον. ταῦτα δ᾽ ἐστὶ τὰ χωρία,
ἃ οἱ Λέλεγες κατεῖχον· ὡς δ᾽ αὕτως καὶ τὰ περὶ
Ἄσσον.

57. Ἔστι δὲ ἡ Ἄσσος ἐρυμνὴ καὶ εὐτειχής,
ἀπὸ θαλάττης καὶ τοῦ λιμένος ὀρθίαν καὶ μακρὰν
ἀνάβασιν ἔχουσα· ὥστ᾽ ἐπ᾽ αὐτῆς οἰκείως εἰρῆσθαι
δοκεῖ τὸ τοῦ Στρατονίκου τοῦ κιθαριστοῦ·

Ἄσσον ἴθ᾽, ὥς κεν θᾶσσον ὀλέθρου πείραθ᾽
ἵκηαι.

ὁ δὲ λιμὴν χώματι κατεσκεύασται μεγάλῳ.
ἐντεῦθεν ἦν Κλεάνθης, ὁ στωικὸς φιλόσοφος ὁ
διαδεξάμενος τὴν Ζήνωνος τοῦ Κιτιέως σχολήν,
καταλιπὼν δὲ Χρυσίππῳ τῷ Σολεῖ· ἐνταῦθα δὲ
καὶ Ἀριστοτέλης διέτριψε διὰ τὴν πρὸς Ἑρμείαν
τὸν τύραννον κηδείαν. ἦν δὲ Ἑρμείας εὐνοῦχος,
τραπεζίτου τινὸς οἰκέτης· γενόμενος δ᾽ Ἀθήνησιν

---

[1] Instead of Ἄνδειρα, DEhi and Epit. read Ἄνδηρα.

not continue, but he incurred the enmity of men less just than himself and revolted from the king when he was on the embassy to Tigranes the Armenian.[1] And Tigranes sent him back against his will to Eupator, who was already in flight from his ancestral realm; but Metrodorus died on the way, whether by order of the king[2] or from disease; for both accounts are given of his death. So much for the Scepsians.

56. After Scepsis come Andeira and Pioniae and the territory of Gargara. There is a stone in the neighbourhood of Andeira which, when burned, becomes iron, and then, when heated in a furnace with a certain earth, distils mock-silver;[3] and this, with the addition of copper, makes the "mixture," as it is called, which by some is called "mountain-copper."[4] These are the places which the Leleges occupied; and the same is true of the places in the neighbourhood of Assus.

57. Assus is by nature strong and well-fortified; and the ascent to it from the sea and the harbour is very steep and long, so that the statement of Stratonicus the citharist in regard to it seems appropriate: "Go to Assus, in order that thou mayest more quickly come to the doom of death."[5] The harbour is formed by a great mole. From Assus came Cleanthes, the Stoic philosopher who succeeded Zeno of Citium as head of the school and left it to Chrysippus of Soli. Here too Aristotle tarried, because of his relationship by marriage with the tyrant Hermeias. Hermeias was a eunuch, the slave of a certain banker;[6] and on his arrival at Athens he

[1] For the story see Plutarch, *Lucullus* 22.   [2] Tigranes.
[3] *i.e.* zinc.   [4] The Latin term is *orichalcum*.
[5] A precise quotation of *Iliad* 6. 143 except that Homer's ἆσσον (("nearer")) is changed to Ἄσσον (" to Assus ").
[6] Eubulus.

ἠκροάσατο καὶ Πλάτωνος καὶ Ἀριστοτέλους·
ἐπανελθὼν δὲ τῷ δεσπότῃ συνετυράννησε, πρῶτον
ἐπιθεμένῳ τοῖς περὶ Ἀταρνέα καὶ Ἄσσον
χωρίοις· ἔπειτα διεδέξατο ἐκεῖνον, καὶ μετε-
πέμψατο τόν τε Ἀριστοτέλην καὶ Ξενοκράτην
καὶ ἐπεμελήθη αὐτῶν· τῷ δ᾽ Ἀριστοτέλει καὶ
θυγατέρα ἀδελφοῦ συνῴκισε. Μέμνων δ᾽ ὁ
Ῥόδιος ὑπηρετῶν τότε τοῖς Πέρσαις καὶ στρατη-
γῶν, προσποιησάμενος φιλίαν καλεῖ πρὸς ἑαυτὸν
ξενίας τε ἅμα[1] καὶ πραγμάτων προσποιητῶν
χάριν, συλλαβὼν δ᾽ ἀνέπεμψεν ὡς τὸν βασιλέα,
κἀκεῖ κρεμασθεὶς ἀπώλετο· οἱ φιλόσοφοι δ᾽
ἐσώθησαν, φεύγοντες τὰ χωρία, ἃ οἱ Πέρσαι
κατέσχον.

58. Φησὶ δὲ Μυρσίλος Μηθυμναίων κτίσμα
εἶναι τὴν Ἄσσον, Ἑλλάνικός τε καὶ Αἰολίδα
φησίν, ὥσπερ[2] καὶ τὰ Γάργαρα καὶ ἡ Λαμπωνία
Αἰολέων. Ἀσσίων γάρ ἐστι κτίσμα τὰ Γάργαρα,
C 611 οὐκ εὖ συνοικούμενα· ἐποίκους γὰρ οἱ βασιλεῖς
εἰσήγαγον ἐκ Μιλητουπόλεως, ἐρημώσαντες ἐκεί-
νην, ὥστε ἡμιβαρβάρους γενέσθαι φησὶ Δημήτριος
αὐτοὺς ὁ Σκήψιος ἀντὶ Αἰολέων. καθ᾽ Ὅμηρον
μέντοι ταῦτα πάντα ἦν Λελέγων, οὕς τινες μὲν
Κᾶρας ἀποφαίνουσιν, Ὅμηρος δὲ χωρίζει.

πρὸς μὲν ἁλὸς Κᾶρες καὶ Παίονες ἀγκυλότοξοι
καὶ Λέλεγες καὶ Καύκωνες.

ἕτεροι μὲν τοίνυν τῶν Καρῶν ὑπῆρξαν· ᾤκουν δὲ

---

[1] Instead of ἅμα, moz read ὀνόματι.
[2] ὥσπερ, Meineke, for ὥς τε; others omit τε.

---

[1] The historian of Methymna, who appears to have

became a pupil of both Plato and Aristotle. On his
return he shared the tyranny with his master, who
had already laid hold of the districts of Atarneus and
Assus; and then Hermeias succeeded him and sent
for both Aristotle and Xenocrates and took care of
them; and he also married his brother's daughter to
Aristotle. Memnon of Rhodes, who was at that
time serving the Persians as general, made a pre-
tence of friendship for Hermeias, and then invited
him to come for a visit, both in the name of hospitality and at the same time for pretended business
reasons; but he arrested him and sent him up to the
king, where he was put to death by hanging. But
the philosophers safely escaped by flight from the
districts above-mentioned, which were seized by the
Persians.

58. Myrsilus[1] says that Assus was founded by
the Methymnaeans; and Hellanicus too calls it an
Aeolian city, just as also Gargara and Lamponia
belonged to the Aeolians. For Gargara was founded
by the Assians; but it was not well peopled, for the
kings brought into it colonists from Miletopolis when
they devastated that city, so that instead of Aeolians,
according to Demetrius of Scepsis, the inhabitants
of Gargara became semi-barbarians. According to
Homer, however, all these places belonged to the
Leleges, who by some are represented to be Carians,
although by Homer they are mentioned apart: "Towards the sea are the Carians and the Paeonians
of the curved bow and the Leleges and the
Cauconians."[2] They were therefore a different
people from the Carians; and they lived between

flourished about 300 B.C.; only fragments of his works
remain.   [2] *Iliad* 10. 428.

μεταξὺ τῶν ὑπὸ τῷ Αἰνεία καὶ τῶν καλουμένων
ὑπὸ τοῦ ποιητοῦ Κιλίκων· ἐκπορθηθέντες δὲ ὑπὸ
τοῦ Ἀχιλλέως μετέστησαν εἰς τὴν Καρίαν, καὶ
κατέσχον τὰ περὶ τὴν νῦν Ἁλικαρνασὸν[1] χωρία.
59. Ἡ μέντοι νῦν ἐκλειφθεῖσα ὑπ' αὐτῶν πόλις
Πήδασος οὐκέτ' ἐστίν. ἐν δὲ τῇ μεσογαίᾳ τῶν
Ἁλικαρνασέων[2] τὰ Πήδασα ὑπ' αὐτῶν ὀνο-
μασθέντα ἦν πόλις, καὶ ἡ νῦν χώρα Πηδασὶς
λέγεται. φασὶ δ' ἐν αὐτῇ καὶ ὀκτὼ πόλεις
ᾠκίσθαι ὑπὸ τῶν Λελέγων πρότερον εὐανδρη-
σάντων, ὥστε καὶ τῆς Καρίας κατασχεῖν τῆς
μέχρι Μύνδου καὶ Βαργυλίων, καὶ τῆς Πισιδίας
ἀποτεμέσθαι πολλήν. ὕστερον δ' ἅμα τοῖς Καρσὶ
στρατευόμενοι κατεμερίσθησαν εἰς ὅλην τὴν
Ἑλλάδα καὶ ἠφανίσθη τὸ γένος, τῶν δ' ὀκτὼ
πόλεων τὰς ἓξ Μαύσωλος εἰς μίαν τὴν Ἁλικαρνασὸν[3] συνήγαγεν, ὡς Καλλισθένης ἱστορεῖ·
Συάγγελα[4] δὲ καὶ Μύνδον διεφύλαξε. τοῖς δὲ
Πηδασεῦσι τούτοις φησὶν Ἡρόδοτος ὅτε μέλλοι
τι ἀνεπιτήδειον[5] ἔσεσθαι καὶ τοῖς περιοίκοις, τὴν
ἱέρειαν τῆς Ἀθηνᾶς πώγωνα ἴσχειν·[6] τρὶς δὲ
συμβῆναι τοῦτο αὐτοῖς. Πήδασον[7] δὲ καὶ ἐν τῇ
νῦν Στρατονικέων πολίχνιόν ἐστιν. ἐν ὅλῃ δὲ

[1] Ἁλικαρνασόν, Dhxz, Ἁλικαρνασσόν other MSS.
[2] Ἁλικαρνασσέων CF; Ἁλικαρνασέων other MSS.
[3] Ἁλικαρνασσόν, all MSS., but see two preceding notes;
also see 8. 6. 14 (where all MSS. have Ἁλικαρνασόν) and
14. 2. 16.
[4] Συάγγελα, Kramer, for συναγέλα CDx, σὺν ἀγέλαι hmowz,
συναγελας F (Σουάγελα Tzschucke and Corais. from conj. of
Casaubon); so Müller-Dübner, Meineke, and Leaf.
[5] ἀνεπιτήδειον, Xylander, for ἐπιτήδειον; so the later
editors.
[6] ἴσχειν, Corais, for σχεῖν; so the later editors.

the people subject to Aeneias and the people whom the poet called Cilicians, but when they were pillaged by Achilles they migrated to Caria and took possession of the district round the present Halicarnassus.[1]

59. However, the city Pedasus, now abandoned by them, is no longer in existence; but in the inland territory of the Halicarnassians there used to be a city Pedasa, so named by them; and the present territory is called Pedasis. It is said that as many as eight cities were settled in this territory by the Leleges, who in earlier times were so numerous that they not only took possession of that part of Caria which extends to Myndus and Bargylia, but also cut off for themselves a large portion of Pisidia. But later, when they went out on expeditions with the Carians, they became distributed throughout the whole of Greece, and the tribe disappeared. Of the eight cities, Mausolus[2] united six into one city, Halicarnassus, as Callisthenes tells us, but kept Syangela and Myndus as they were. These are the Pedasians of whom Herodotus[3] says that when any misfortune was about to come upon them and their neighbours, the priestess of Athena would grow a beard; and that this happened to them three times. And there is also a small town called Pedasum in the present territory of Stratoniceia. And throughout the whole of Caria

---

[1] Cf. 7. 7. 2. On the variant spellings of "Halicarnas(s)us" see critical note.

[2] King of Caria 377–353 B.C. The first "Mausoleum" was so named after him.

[3] 1. 175, 8. 104.

---

[7] Instead of Πήδασον, *moz* have Πήδασος (see Stephanus, *s.v.* Πήδασα).

Καρίᾳ καὶ ἐν Μιλήτῳ[1] Λελέγων τάφοι καὶ ἐρύματα καὶ ἴχνη κατοικιῶν δείκνυται.

60. Μετὰ δὲ τοὺς Λέλεγας τὴν ἑξῆς παραλίαν ᾤκουν Κίλικες καθ᾽ Ὅμηρον, ἣν νῦν ἔχουσιν Ἀδραμυττηνοί τε καὶ Ἀταρνεῖται καὶ Πιταναῖοι μέχρι τῆς ἐκβολῆς τοῦ Καΐκου. διῄρηντο δ᾽ εἰς δύο δυναστείας οἱ Κίλικες, καθάπερ εἴπομεν, τήν τε ὑπὸ τῷ Ἠετίωνι καὶ τὴν ὑπὸ Μύνητι.

61. Τοῦ μὲν οὖν Ἠετίωνος λέγει πόλιν Θήβην·

ᾠχόμεθ᾽ ἐς Θήβην ἱερὴν πόλιν Ἠετίωνος.

τούτου δὲ καὶ τὴν Χρύσαν τὴν ἔχουσαν[2] τὸ ἱερὸν τοῦ Σμινθέως Ἀπόλλωνος ἐμφαίνει, εἴπερ ἡ Χρυσηὶς ἐκ τῆς Θήβης ἑάλω·

ᾠχόμεθα γάρ, φησίν, ἐς Θήβην,
τὴν δὲ διεπράθομέν τε καὶ ἤγομεν ἐνθάδε πάντα,
C 612 καὶ τὰ μὲν εὖ δάσσαντο μετὰ σφίσιν,
ἐκ δ᾽ ἕλον Ἀτρείδῃ Χρυσηίδα.

τοῦ δὲ Μύνητος τὴν Λυρνησσόν· ἐπειδὴ

Λυρνησσὸν διαπορθήσας καὶ τείχεα Θήβης

τόν τε Μύνητα καὶ τὸν Ἐπίστροφον ἀνεῖλεν Ἀχιλλεύς· ὥστε, ὅταν φῇ ἡ Βρισηίς,

οὐδέ μ᾽ ἔασκες, ὅτ᾽ ἄνδρ᾽ ἐμὸν ὠκὺς Ἀχιλλεὺς
ἔκτεινεν, πέρσεν δὲ πόλιν θείοιο Μύνητος,

οὐ τὴν Θήβην λέγοι ἄν (αὕτη γὰρ Ἠετίωνος), ἀλλὰ τὴν Λυρνησσόν· ἀμφότεραι δ᾽ ἦσαν ἐν τῷ κληθέντι μετὰ ταῦτα Θήβης πεδίῳ, ὃ διὰ τὴν ἀρετὴν περιμάχητον γενέσθαι φασὶ Μυσοῖς μὲν

---

[1] ἐν Μιλήτῳ, omitted by Dhi.

and in Miletus are to be seen tombs, fortifications, and traces of settlements of the Leleges.

60. After the Leleges, on the next stretch of coast, lived the Cilicians, according to Homer; I mean the stretch of coast now held by the Adramytteni and Atarneitae and Pitanaei, as far as the outlet of the Caïcus. The Cilicians, as I have said,[1] were divided into two dynasties,[2] one subject to Eëtion and one to Mynes.

61. Now Homer calls Thebê the city of Eëtion: "We went into Thebê, the sacred city of Eëtion";[3] and he clearly indicates that also Chrysa, which had the temple of Sminthian Apollo, belonged to Eëtion, if it be true that Chryseïs was taken captive at Thebê, for he says, "We went into Thebê, and laid it waste and brought hither all the spoil. And this they divided aright among themselves, but they chose out Chryseïs for the son of Atreus";[4] and that Lyrnessus belonged to Mynes, since Achilles "laid waste Lyrnessus and the walls of Thebê"[5] and slew both Mynes and Epistrophus; so that when Briseïs says, "thou wouldst not even let me,[6] when swift Achilles slew my husband and sacked the city of divine Mynes,"[7] Homer cannot mean Thebê (for this belonged to Eëtion), but Lyrnessus. Both were situated in what was afterwards called the Plain of Thebê, which, on account of its fertility, is said to have been an object of contention between the

[1] 13. 1. 7, 49.
[2] But cf. 13. 1. 70.
[3] *Iliad* 1. 366.
[4] *Iliad* 1. 366 ff.
[5] *Iliad* 2. 691.
[6] *sc.* "weep."
[7] *Iliad* 19. 295.

---

[1] τὴν ἔχουσαν, added from *moz.*

καὶ Λυδοῖς τὸ¹ πρότερον, τοῖς δ᾽ Ἕλλησιν ὕστερον
τοῖς ἐποικήσασιν ἐκ τῆς Αἰολίδος καὶ τῆς Λέσβου.
ἔχουσι δὲ νῦν Ἀδραμυττηνοὶ τὸ πλέον· ἐνταῦθα
γὰρ καὶ ἡ Θήβη καὶ ἡ Λυρνησσός, ἐρυμνὸν
χωρίον· ἔρημοι δ᾽ ἀμφότεραι· διέχουσι δὲ Ἀδραμυττίου σταδίους ἡ μὲν ἑξήκοντα, ἡ δὲ ὀγδοήκοντα
καὶ ὀκτὼ ἐπὶ θάτερα.²

62. Ἐν δὲ τῇ Ἀδραμυττηνῇ ἐστι καὶ ἡ Χρύσα
καὶ ἡ Κίλλα· πλησίον οὖν τῆς Θήβης ἔτι³ νῦν
Κίλλα τις τόπος λέγεται,⁴ ἐν ᾧ Κιλλαίου⁵ Ἀπόλ-
λωνός ἐστιν ἱερόν· παραρρεῖ δ᾽ αὐτῷ ἐξ Ἴδης
φερόμενος ὁ Κίλλαιος⁶ ποταμός· ταῦτα δ᾽ ἐστὶ
κατὰ τὴν Ἀντανδρίαν· καὶ τὸ ἐν Λέσβῳ δὲ
Κίλλαιον⁷ ἀπὸ ταύτης τῆς Κίλλης ὠνόμασται·
ἔστι δὲ καὶ Κίλλαιον ὄρος μεταξὺ Γαργάρων καὶ
Ἀντάνδρου. φησὶ δὲ Δάης ὁ Κολωναεὺς ἐν
Κολωναῖς ἱδρυθῆναι πρῶτον ὑπὸ τῶν ἐκ τῆς
Ἑλλάδος πλευσάντων Αἰολέων τὸ τοῦ Κιλλαίου
Ἀπόλλωνος ἱερόν· καὶ ἐν Χρύσῃ δὲ λέγουσι
Κίλλαιον Ἀπόλλωνα ἱδρῦσθαι, ἄδηλον, εἴτε τὸν
αὐτὸν τῷ Σμινθεῖ, εἴθ᾽ ἕτερον.

63. Ἡ δὲ Χρύσα ἐπὶ θαλάττῃ πολίχνιον ἦν
ἔχον λιμένα, πλησίον δὲ ὑπέρκειται ἡ Θήβη·
ἐνταῦθα δ᾽ ἦν καὶ τὸ ἱερὸν τοῦ Σμινθέως Ἀπόλ-

¹ τό, before πρότερον, Meineke, for τοῖς. Corais omits the
τοῖς, and so Leaf.
² Leaf omits the words καὶ ὀκτὼ ἐπὶ θάτερα (see his critical
note on text, p. 36).
³ ἔτι, Meineke, for ἔστι.
⁴ Instead of λέγεται, moz read λεγόμενος.
⁵ Κιλλαίου, Casaubon and later editors, for Κιλλεούς C,
Κιλλέους Dhrw, Κιλλεός F, Κιλλέου moxz.
⁶ Κίλλαιος, Kramer and later editors, for Κιλλεός F, Κίλλεος
other MSS.

Mysians and Lydians in earlier times, and later
between the Greeks who colonised it from Aeolis
and Lesbos. But the greater part of it is now held
by the Adramytteni, for here lie both Thebê and
Lyrnessus, the latter a natural stronghold; but both
places are deserted. From Adramyttium the former
is distant sixty stadia and the latter eighty-eight,
in opposite directions.[1]

62. In the territory of Adramyttium lie also
Chrysa and Cilla. At any rate there is still to-day
a place near Thebê called Cilla, where is a temple
of the Cillaean Apollo; and the Cillaeus River,
which runs from Mt. Ida, flows past it. These
places lie near the territory of Antandrus. The
Cillaeum in Lesbos is named after this Cilla; and
there is also a Mt. Cillaeum between Gargara and
Antandrus. Daës of Colonae says that the temple
of the Cillaean Apollo was first founded in Colonae
by the Aeolians who sailed from Greece; it is also
said that a temple of Cillaean Apollo was established
at Chrysa, though it is not clear whether he is the
same as the Sminthian Apollo or distinct from him.

63. Chrysa was a small town on the sea, with a
harbour; and near by, above it, lies Thebê. Here
too was the temple of the Sminthian Apollo; and

---

[1] The site of Thebê has been definitely identified with
that of the modern Edremid (see Leaf, p. 322). But that of
Lyrnessus is uncertain. Leaf (p. 308), regarding the text as
corrupt, reads merely "eighty" instead of "eighty-eight,"
and omits "in opposite directions" (see critical note).

---

[7] Κίλλαιον, Tzschucke and later editors, for Κιλλέου; and
so in the three subsequent instances the MSS. have ε instead
of αι.

STRABO

λωνος καὶ ἡ Χρυσηίς· ἠρήμωται δὲ νῦν τὸ χωρίον
τελέως· εἰς δὲ τὴν νῦν Χρῦσαν τὴν κατὰ Ἀμαξιτὸν
μεθίδρυται τὸ ἱερὸν τῶν Κιλίκων τῶν μὲν εἰς τὴν
Παμφυλίαν ἐκπεσόντων, τῶν δὲ εἰς Ἀμαξιτόν.
οἱ δ᾽ ἀπειρότεροι τῶν παλαιῶν ἱστοριῶν ἐνταῦθα
τὸν Χρύσην καὶ τὴν Χρυσηίδα γεγονέναι φασὶ
καὶ τὸν Ὅμηρον τούτου τοῦ τόπου μεμνῆσθαι.
ἀλλ᾽ οὔτε λιμήν ἐστιν ἐνταῦθα, ἐκεῖνος δέ φησιν·

οἱ δ᾽ ὅτε δὴ λιμένος πολυβενθέος ἐντὸς ἵκοντο.

οὔτ᾽ ἐπὶ θαλάττῃ τὸ ἱερόν ἐστιν, ἐκεῖνος δ᾽ ἐπὶ
θαλάττῃ ποιεῖ τὸ ἱερόν·

C 613
ἐκ δὲ Χρυσηὶς νηὸς βῆ ποντοπόροιο·
τὴν μὲν ἔπειτ᾽ ἐπὶ βωμὸν ἄγων πολύμητις
Ὀδυσσεὺς
πατρὶ φίλῳ ἐν χερσὶ τίθει·

οὐδὲ Θήβης πλησίον, ἐκεῖνος δὲ πλησίον· ἐκεῖθεν
γοῦν ἁλοῦσαν λέγει τὴν Χρυσηίδα. ἀλλ᾽ οὐδὲ
Κίλλα τόπος οὐδεὶς ἐν τῇ Ἀλεξανδρέων χώρᾳ
δείκνυται, οὐδὲ Κιλλαίου Ἀπόλλωνος ἱερόν· ὁ
ποιητὴς δὲ συζεύγνυσιν·

ὃς Χρύσην ἀμφιβέβηκας
Κίλλαν τε ζαθέην·

ἐν δὲ τῷ Θήβης πεδίῳ δείκνυται πλησίον· ὅ τε
πλοῦς ἀπὸ μὲν τῆς Κιλικίου Χρύσης ἐπὶ τὸ
ναύσταθμον ἑπτακοσίων που σταδίων ἐστὶν
ἡμερήσιός πως, ὅσον φαίνεται πλεύσας ὁ Ὀδυσ-
σεύς. ἐκβὰς γὰρ εὐθὺς¹ παρίστησι τὴν θυσίαν
τῷ θεῷ καὶ τῆς ἑσπέρας ἐπιλαβούσης μένει
αὐτόθι, πρωὶ δὲ ἀποπλεῖ· ἀπὸ δὲ Ἀμαξιτοῦ τὸ

124

here lived Chryseïs. But the place is now utterly deserted; and the temple was transferred to the present Chrysa near Hamaxitus when the Cilicians were driven out, partly to Pamphylia[1] and partly to Hamaxitus. Those who are less acquainted with ancient history say that it was at this Chrysa that Chryses and Chryseïs lived, and that Homer mentions this place; but, in the first place, there is no harbour here, and yet Homer says, "And when they had now arrived inside the deep harbour";[2] and, secondly, the temple is not on the sea, though Homer makes it on the sea, "and out from the seafaring ship stepped Chryseïs. Her then did Odysseus of many wiles lead to the altar, and place in the arms of her dear father";[3] neither is it near Thebê, though Homer makes it near; at any rate, he speaks of Chryseïs as having been taken captive there. Again, neither is there any place called Cilla to be seen in the territory of the Alexandreians, nor any temple of Cillaean Apollo; but the poet couples the two, "who dost stand over Chrysa and sacred Cilla."[4] But it is to be seen near by in the Plain of Thebê. And the voyage from the Cilician Chrysa to the Naval Station is about seven hundred stadia, approximately a day's voyage, such a distance, obviously, as that sailed by Odysseus;[5] for immediately upon disembarking he offered the sacrifice to the god, and since evening overtook him he remained on the spot and sailed away the next morning. But the distance from Hamaxitus is scarcely a third of that above

---

[1] Cf. 14. 4. 1.   [2] *Iliad* 1. 432.   [3] *Iliad* 1. 438.
[4] *Iliad* 1. 37.   [5] See *Iliad* 1. 430 ff.

---

[1] εὐθύς *xz*, εὐθύ other MSS.

τρίτον μόλις τοῦ λεχθέντος διαστήματός ἐστιν,
ὥστε παρῆν τῷ Ὀδυσσεῖ αὐθημερὸν ἀναπλεῖν
ἐπὶ τὸ ναύσταθμον τελέσαντι τὴν θυσίαν. ἔστι
δὲ καὶ Κίλλου μνῆμα περὶ τὸ ἱερὸν τοῦ Κιλλαίου
Ἀπόλλωνος, χῶμα μέγα· ἡνίοχον δὲ τοῦτον Πέλο-
πός φασιν ἡγησάμενον τῶν τόπων, ἀφ' οὗ ἴσως ἡ
Κιλικία ἢ ἔμπαλιν.

64. Τὰ οὖν περὶ τοὺς Τεύκρους καὶ τοὺς μύας,
ἀφ' ὧν ὁ Σμινθεύς, ἐπειδὴ σμίνθοι[1] οἱ μύες, δεῦρο
μετενεκτέον. παραμυθοῦνται δὲ τὴν ἀπὸ μικρῶν
ἐπίκλησιν τοιούτοις τισί· καὶ γὰρ ἀπὸ τῶν
παρνόπων, οὓς οἱ Οἰταῖοι[2] κόρνοπας λέγουσι,
Κορνοπίωνα[3] τιμᾶσθαι παρ' ἐκείνοις Ἡρακλέα
ἀπαλλαγῆς ἀκρίδων χάριν· Ἱποκτόνον δὲ παρ'
Ἐρυθραίοις τοῖς τὸν Μίμαντα[4] οἰκοῦσιν, ὅτι
φθαρτικὸς τῶν ἀμπελοφάγων ἰπῶν· καὶ δὴ παρ'
ἐκείνοις μόνοις τῶν Ἐρυθραίων τὸ θηρίον τοῦτο
μὴ γίνεσθαι.[5] Ῥόδιοι δὲ Ἐρυθιβίου Ἀπόλλωνος
ἔχουσιν ἐν τῇ χώρα ἱερόν, τὴν ἐρυσίβην καλοῦντες
ἐρυθίβην· παρ' Αἰολεῦσι δὲ τοῖς ἐν Ἀσίᾳ μείς
τις[6] καλεῖται Πορνοπίων, οὕτω τοὺς πάρνοπας
καλοῦντων Βοιωτῶν, καὶ θυσία συντελεῖται
Πορνοπίωνι Ἀπόλλωνι.

65. Μυσία μὲν οὖν ἐστὶν ἡ περὶ τὸ Ἀδραμύττιον, ἣν δέ ποτε ὑπὸ Λυδοῖς, καὶ νῦν Πύλαι
Λύδιαι καλοῦνται ἐν Ἀδραμυττίῳ, Λυδῶν, ὡς

---

[1] σμίνθοι, Meineke, for σμίνθιοι.
[2] Οἰταῖοι E, Ὀτέοι other MSS.
[3] E inserts τινα before τιμᾶσθαι.
[4] Μίμαντα, Corais, for Μελιοῦντα (see 14. 1. 33); so the later editors.
[5] γίνεσθαι, moz and Corais and Meineke, for γενέσθαι.
[6] μνεὶς τις EF, μύς τις Dmorz, μύσων τις hi, μιστις C.

mentioned, so that Odysseus could have completed the sacrifice and sailed back to the Naval Station on the same day. There is also a tomb of Cillus in the neighbourhood of the temple of the Cillaean Apollo, a great barrow. He is said to have been the charioteer of Pelops and to have ruled over this region; and perhaps it was after him that Cilicia was named, or vice versa.

64. Now the story of the Teucrians and the mice—whence the epithet "Sminthian,"[1] since "sminthi" means "mice"—must be transferred to this place. And writers excuse this giving of epithets from small creatures by such examples as the following: It is from locusts,[2] they say, which the Oetaeans call "cornopes," that Heracles is worshipped among the Oetaeans as "Cornopion," for ridding them of locusts; and he is worshipped among the Erythraeans who live in Mimas as "Ipoctonus,"[3] because he is the destroyer of the vine-eating *ips* ;[4] and in fact, they add, these are the only Erythraeans in whose country this creature is not to be found. And the Rhodians, who call erysibê[5] "erythibê," have a temple of Apollo "Erythibius" in their country; and among the Aeolians in Asia a certain month is called Pornopion, since the Boeotians so call the locusts, and a sacrifice is offered to Apollo Pornopion.

65. Now the territory round Adramyttium is Mysian, though it was once subject to the Lydians; and to-day there is a gate in Adramyttium which is called the Lydian Gate because, as they say, the

---

[1] *i.e.* the "Sminthian" Apollo (*Iliad* 1. 39).
[2] "Parnopes."   [3] "Ips-slayer."
[4] A kind of *cynips*.   [5] "Mildew."

φασι, τὴν πόλιν ἐκτικότων. Μυσίας δὲ Ἄστυρα τὴν πλησίον κώμην φασίν. ἦν δὲ πολίχνη ποτέ, ἐν ᾗ τὸ τῆς Ἀστυρηνῆς Ἀρτέμιδος ἱερὸν ἐν ἄλσει, προστατούμενον μετὰ ἁγιστείας ὑπ᾽ Ἀντανδρίων, οἷς μᾶλλον γειτνιᾷ· διέχει δὲ τῆς παλαιᾶς Χρύσης εἴκοσι σταδίους, καὶ αὐτῆς ἐν ἄλσει τὸ ἱερὸν ἐχούσης. αὐτοῦ δὲ καὶ ὁ Ἀχίλλειος χάραξ· ἐν δὲ τῇ μεσογαίᾳ ἀπὸ πεντήκοντα σταδίων ἐστὶν C 614 ἡ Θήβη ἔρημος,[1] ἥν φησιν ὁ ποιητὴς ὑπὸ Πλάκῳ ὑληέσσῃ· οὔτε δὲ Πλάκος ἢ Πλὰξ ἐκεῖ τι λέγεται, οὔθ᾽ ὕλη ὑπέρκειται, καίτοι πρὸς τῇ Ἴδῃ. Ἀστύρων δ᾽ ἡ Θήβη διέχει εἰς ἑβδομήκοντα σταδίους, Ἀνδείρων[2] δὲ ἑξήκοντα. πάντα δὲ ταῦτά ἐστι τὰ ὀνόματα τόπων ἐρήμων ἢ φαύλως οἰκουμένων ἢ ποταμῶν χειμάρρων· τεθρύληται δὲ διὰ τὰς παλαιὰς ἱστορίας.

66. Πόλεις δ᾽ εἰσὶν ἀξιόλογοι Ἄσσος τε καὶ Ἀδραμύττιον. ἠτύχησε δὲ τὸ Ἀδραμύττιον ἐν τῷ Μιθριδατικῷ πολέμῳ· τὴν γὰρ βουλὴν ἀπέσφαξε τῶν πολιτῶν Διόδωρος στρατηγός, χαριζόμενος τῷ βασιλεῖ, προσποιούμενος δ᾽ ἅμα τῶν τε ἐξ Ἀκαδημίας φιλοσόφων εἶναι καὶ δίκας λέγειν καὶ σοφιστεύειν τὰ ῥητορικά· καὶ δὴ καὶ συναπῆρεν εἰς τὸν Πόντον τῷ βασιλεῖ· καταλυθέντος δὲ τοῦ βασιλέως, ἔτισε δίκας τοῖς ἀδικηθεῖσιν· ἐγκλημάτων γὰρ ἐπενεχθέντων ἅμα πολλῶν, ἀπεκαρτέρησεν αἰσχρῶς, οὐ φέρων τὴν δυσφημίαν, ἐν τῇ ἡμετέρᾳ πόλει. ἀνὴρ δὲ Ἀδραμυτ-

---

[1] ἔρημος, *moz* omit.
[2] For Ἀνδείρων, DE*i* read Ἀνδήρων, in D corrected to Ἀνδίρων.

city was founded by Lydians. And they say that the neighbouring village Astyra belongs to Mysia. It was once a small town, where, in a sacred precinct, was the temple of the Astyrene Artemis, which was superintended, along with holy rites, by the Antandrians, who were its nearer neighbours. It is twenty stadia distant from the ancient Chrysa, which also had its temple in a sacred precinct. Here too was the Palisade of Achilles. And in the interior, fifty stadia away, is Thebê, now deserted, which the poet speaks of as "beneath wooded Placus";[1] but, in the first place, the name "Placus" or "Plax" is not found there at all, and, secondly, no wooded place lies above it, though it is near Mt. Ida. Thebê is as much as seventy stadia distant from Astyra and sixty from Andeira. But all these are names of deserted or scantily peopled places, or of winter torrents; and they are often mentioned only because of their ancient history.

66. Both Assus and Adramyttium are notable cities. But misfortune befell Adramyttium in the Mithridatic War, for the members of the city council were slaughtered, to please the king, by Diodorus[2] the general, who pretended at the same time to be a philosopher of the Academy, a dispenser of justice, and a teacher of rhetoric. And indeed he also joined the king on his journey to Pontus; but when the king was overthrown he paid the penalty for his misdeeds; for many charges were brought against him, all at the same time, and, being unable to bear the ignominy, he shamefully starved himself to death, in my own city. Another inhabitant of Adramyttium

---

[1] *Iliad* 6. 396.
[2] This Diodorus is otherwise unknown.

τηνὸς ῥήτωρ ἐπιφανὴς γεγένηται Ξενοκλῆς, τοῦ
μὲν ᾿Ασιανοῦ χαρακτῆρος, ἀγωνιστὴς δέ, εἴ τις
ἄλλος, καὶ εἰρηκὼς ὑπὲρ τῆς ᾿Ασίας ἐπὶ τῆς
συγκλήτου, καθ᾿ ὃν καιρὸν αἰτίαν εἶχε Μιθρι-
δατισμοῦ.

67. Πρὸς δὲ τοῖς ᾿Αστύροις λίμνη καλεῖται
Σάπρα βαραθρώδης, εἰς ῥαχιώδη τῆς θαλάττης
αἰγιαλὸν τὸ ἔκρηγμα ἔχουσα. ὑπὸ δὲ τοῖς
᾿Ανδείροις ἱερόν ἐστι Μητρὸς θεῶν ᾿Ανδειρηνῆς
ἅγιον καὶ ἄντρον ὑπόνομον μέχρι Παλαιᾶς. ἔστι
δ᾿ ἡ Παλαιὰ κατοικία τις οὕτω καλουμένη, διέχουσα τῶν ᾿Ανδείρων ἑκατὸν καὶ τριάκοντα
σταδίους· ἔδειξε δὲ τὴν ὑπονομὴν χίμαρος ἐμπεσὼν εἰς τὸ στόμα καὶ ἀνευρεθεὶς τῇ ὑστεραίᾳ
κατὰ ῎Ανδειρα[1] ὑπὸ τοῦ ποιμένος κατὰ τύχην
ἐπὶ θυσίαν ἥκοντος. ᾿Αταρνεὺς δ᾿ ἐστὶ τὸ τοῦ
῾Ερμείου[2] τυραννεῖον, εἶτα Πιτάνη, πόλις Αἰολική,
δύο ἔχουσα λιμένας, καὶ ὁ παραρρέων αὐτὴν
ποταμὸς Εὔηνος, ἐξ οὗ τὸ ὑδραγωγεῖον πεποίηται
τοῖς ᾿Αδραμυττηνοῖς. ἐκ δὲ τῆς Πιτάνης ἐστὶν
᾿Αρκεσίλαος, ὁ ἐκ τῆς ᾿Ακαδημίας, Ζήνωνος τοῦ
Κιτιέως συσχολαστὴς παρὰ Πολέμωνι. καλεῖται
δὲ καὶ ἐν τῇ Πιτάνῃ τις τόπος ἐπὶ θαλάττῃ
᾿Αταρνεὺς ὑπὸ τῇ Πιτάνῃ, κατὰ τὴν καλουμένην
νῆσον ᾿Ελεοῦσσαν.[3] φασὶ δ᾿ ἐν τῇ Πιτάνῃ τὰς
πλίνθους ἐπιπολάζειν ἐν τοῖς ὕδασι, καθάπερ καὶ
ἐν τῇ Τυρρηνίᾳ γῆ τις[4] πέπονθε· κουφοτέρα γὰρ
ἡ γῆ τοῦ ἐπισόγκου ὕδατός ἐστιν, ὥστ᾿ ἐποχεῖσθαι.

---

[1] Instead of ῎Ανδειρα, CDh read ῎Ανδιρα.
[2] ῾Ερμείου F, ῾Ερμίνου other MSS.
[3] ᾿Ελεοῦσσαν, Palmer, for ἔχουσαν; so later editors, except
Meineke and Leaf, who read ᾿Ελαιοῦσσαν.

was the famous orator Xenocles,[1] who belonged to
the Asiatic school and was as able a debater as ever
lived, having even made a speech on behalf of Asia
before the Senate,[2] at the time when Asia was accused
of Mithridatism.

67. Near Astyra is an abysmal lake called Sapra,
which has an outbreak into a reefy seashore. Below
Andeira is a temple sacred to the Andeirene Mother
of the gods, and also a cave that runs underground
as far as Palaea. Palaea is a settlement so named,[3]
at a distance of one hundred and thirty stadia from
Andeira. The underground passage became known
through the fact that a goat fell into the mouth of it
and was found on the following day near Andeira by
a shepherd who happened to have come to make sacrifice. Atarneus is the abode of the tyrant Hermeias;
and then one comes to Pitanê, an Aeolic city, which
has two harbours, and the Evenus River, which flows
past it, whence the aqueduct has been built by the
Adramytteni. From Pitanê came Arcesilaüs, of the
Academy, a fellow-student with Zeno of Citium
under Polemon. In Pitanê there is also a place on
the sea called "Atarneus below Pitanê," opposite
the island called Eleussa. It is said that in Pitanê
bricks float on water, as is also the case with a
certain earth[4] in Tyrrhenia, for the earth is lighter
than an equal bulk of water, so that it floats. And

----

[1] This Xenocles is otherwise unknown except for a reference
to him by Cicero (*Brutus* 91).
[2] The Roman Senate.   *i.e.* "*Old* Settlement."
[4] "Rotten-stone."

----

[4] γῆ τις, Corais, for νησίς; so Leaf.

STRABO

ἐν Ἰβηρίᾳ δέ φησιν ἰδεῖν Ποσειδώνιος ἔκ τινος
γῆς ἀργιλώδους, ᾗ τὰ ἀργυρώματα ἐκμάττεται,
C 615 πλίνθους πηγνυμένας καὶ ἐπιπλεούσας. μετὰ δὲ
τὴν Πιτάνην ὁ Κάϊκος εἰς τὸν Ἐλαΐτην καλούμενον
κόλπον ἐν τριάκοντα σταδίοις ἐκδίδωσιν. ἐν δὲ
τῷ πέραν τοῦ Καΐκου, δώδεκα διέχουσα τοῦ
ποταμοῦ σταδίους Ἐλαία πόλις Αἰολικὴ καὶ
αὕτη Περγαμηνῶν ἐπίνειον, ἑκατὸν καὶ εἴκοσι
σταδίους διέχουσα τοῦ Περγάμου.

68. Εἶτ᾽ ἐν ἑκατὸν σταδίοις ἡ Κάνη, τὸ ἀνταῖρον
ἀκρωτήριον τῷ Λεκτῷ καὶ ποιοῦν τὸν Ἀδραμυττηνὸν κόλπον, οὗ μέρος καὶ ὁ Ἐλαϊτικός ἐστι.
Κάναι δὲ πολίχνιον Λοκρῶν τῶν ἐκ Κύνου κατὰ
τὰ ἄκρα τῆς Λέσβου τὰ νοτιώτατα κείμενον ἐν
τῇ Καναίᾳ· αὕτη δὲ μέχρι τῶν Ἀργινουσσῶν
διῆκε καὶ τῆς ὑπερκειμένης ἄκρας, ἣν Αἰγά[1] τινες
ὀνομάζουσιν ὁμωνύμως τῷ ζῴῳ· δεῖ δὲ μακρῶς
τὴν δευτέραν συλλαβὴν ἐκφέρειν Αἰγάν,[2] ὡς
Ἀκτὰν καὶ Ἀρχάν· οὕτω γὰρ καὶ τὸ ὄρος ὅλον
ὠνομάζετο, ὃ νῦν Κάνην καὶ Κάνας λέγουσι.
κύκλῳ δὲ περὶ τὸ ὄρος πρὸς νότον μὲν καὶ δύσιν
ἡ θάλαττα, πρὸς ἕω δὲ τὸ Καΐκου πεδίον ὑπόκειται, πρὸς ἄρκτον δὲ ἡ Ἐλαῖτις· αὐτὸ δὲ καθ᾽
αὑτὸ ἱκανῶς συνέσταλται, προσνεύει δὲ ἐπὶ τὸ
Αἰγαῖον πέλαγος, ὅθεν αὐτῷ καὶ τοὔνομα· [3] ὕστε-

[1] Instead of Αἰγα, D reads Αἰγᾶ, hoz Αἶγαν, Epit. Αἴγα,
Meineke Αἰγάν.
[2] Αἰγάν Ez; so Meineke and Leaf.
[3] Leaf brackets the words ὕστερον . . . Κάναι.

[1] i.e. Αἴξ, "goat."

132

Poseidonius says that in Iberia he saw bricks moulded from a clay-like earth, with which silver is cleaned, and that they floated on water. After Pitanê one comes to the Caïcus River, which empties at a distance of thirty stadia into the Elaïtic Gulf, as it is called. On the far side of the Caïcus, twelve stadia distant from the river, is Elaea, an Aeolic city, which also is a seaport of the Pergamenians, being one hundred and twenty stadia distant from Pergamum.

68. Then, at a distance of a hundred stadia, one comes to Canê, the promontory which rises opposite Lectum and forms the Adramyttene Gulf, of which the Elaïtic Gulf is a part. Canae is a small town of Locrians from Cynus, and lies in the Canaean territory opposite the southernmost ends of Lesbos. This territory extends as far as the Arginussae Islands and the promontory above them, which some call Aega, making it the same as the word for the animal;[1] but the second syllable should be pronounced long, that is, "Aegā," like Actā and Archā, for Aega used to be the name of the whole of the mountain which is now called Canê or Canae. The mountain is surrounded on the south and west by the sea, and on the east by the plain of the Caïcus, which lies below it, and on the north by the territory of Elaea. This mountain forms a fairly compact mass off to itself, though it slopes towards the Aegaean Sea, whence it got its name.[2] Later

[2] It is not clear in the Greek whether Strabo says that the Aegean Sea got its name from Aega or vice versa. Elsewhere (8. 7. 4) he speaks of "Aegae in Boeotia, from which it is probable that the Aegean Sea got its name."

ρον δὲ αὐτὸ τὸ ἀκρωτήριον Αἰγὰ¹ κεκλῆσθαι,²
ὡς Σαπφώ φησιν,³ τὸ δὲ λοιπὸν Κάνη καὶ
Κάναι.

69. Μεταξὺ δὲ Ἐλαίας τε καὶ Πιτάνης καὶ
Ἀταρνέως καὶ Περγάμου Τευθρανία ἐστί, διέχουσα οὐδεμιᾶς αὐτῶν ὑπὲρ ἑβδομήκοντα σταδίους
ἐντὸς τοῦ Καΐκου, καὶ ὁ Τεύθρας Κιλίκων καὶ
Μυσῶν ἱστόρηται βασιλεύς. Εὐριπίδης δ' ὑπὸ
Ἀλέου⁴ φησί, τοῦ τῆς Αὔγης πατρός, εἰς λάρνακα
τὴν Αὔγην κατατεθεῖσαν ἅμα τῷ παιδὶ Τηλέφῳ
καταποντωθῆναι, φωράσαντος τὴν ἐξ Ἡρακλέους
φθοράν· Ἀθηνᾶς δὲ προνοίᾳ τὴν λάρνακα περαιω-
θεῖσαν ἐκπεσεῖν εἰς τὸ στόμα τοῦ Καΐκου, τὸν δὲ
Τεύθραντα, ἀναλαβόντα τὰ σώματα, τῇ μὲν ὡς
γαμετῇ χρήσασθαι, τῷ δ' ὡς ἑαυτοῦ παιδί. τοῦτο
μὲν οὖν μῦθος, ἄλλην δέ τινα δεῖ γεγονέναι συντυ-
χίαν, δι' ἣν ἡ τοῦ Ἀρκάδος θυγάτηρ τῷ Μυσῶν
βασιλεῖ συνῆλθε καὶ ὁ ἐξ αὐτῆς διεδέξατο τὴν
ἐκείνου βασιλείαν. πεπίστευται δ' οὖν, ὅτι καὶ
ὁ Τεύθρας καὶ ὁ Τήλεφος ἐβασίλευσαν τῆς χώρας
τῆς περὶ τὴν Τευθρανίαν καὶ τὸν Κάϊκον, ὁ δὲ
ποιητὴς ἐπὶ τοσοῦτον μέμνηται μόνον τῆς ἱστορίας
ταύτης·

ἀλλ' οἷον τὸν Τηλεφίδην κατενήρατο χαλκῷ
ἥρω' Εὐρύπυλον, πολλοὶ δ' ἀμφ' αὐτὸν ἑταῖροι
Κήτειοι κτείνοντο γυναίων εἵνεκα δώρων·

C 616 αἴνιγμα τιθεὶς ἡμῖν μᾶλλον ἢ λέγων τι σαφές.

---

¹ Αἰγά, Meineke, for Αἶγα DE, Αἰγᾶ other MSS.
² For κεκλῆσθαι Müller-Dübner write ἐκλήθη.
³ φησιν, after Σαπφώ, *moz* insert; but Meineke, following
conj. of Kramer, omits ὡς Σαπφώ.

the promontory itself was called Aega, as in Sappho,[1] but the rest was called Canê or Canae.

69. Between Elaea, Pitanê, Atarneus, and Pergamum lies Teuthrania, which is at no greater distance than seventy stadia from any of them and is this side the Caïcus River; and the story told is that Teuthras was king of the Cilicians and Mysians. Euripides[2] says that Augê, with her child Telephus, was put by Aleus, her father, into a chest and submerged in the sea when he had detected her ruin by Heracles, but that by the providence of Athena the chest was carried across the sea and cast ashore at the mouth of the Caïcus, and that Teuthras rescued the prisoners, and treated the mother as his wife and the child as his own son.[3] Now this is the myth, but there must have been some other issue of fortune through which the daughter of the Arcadian consorted with the king of the Mysians and her son succeeded to his kingdom. It is believed, at any rate, that both Teuthras and Telephus reigned as kings over the country round Teuthrania and the Caïcus, though Homer goes only so far as to mention the story thus: "But what a man was the son of Telephus, the hero Eurypylus, whom he slew with the bronze; and round him were slain many comrades, Ceteians, on account of a woman's gifts."[4] The poet thus sets before us a puzzle instead of making a clear statement; for we neither know whom we should under-

---

[1] A fragment otherwise unknown (Bergk *Frag.* 131).
[2] *Frag.* 696 (Nauck). [3] Cf. 12. 8. 2, 4. [4] *Odyssey* 11. 521.

---

[4] 'Αλέου, Xylander, for 'Αλάνου F, 'Αλαίου other MSS. ; so the later editors.

οὔτε γὰρ τοὺς Κητείους ἴσμεν, οὕστινας δέξασθαι
δεῖ, οὔτε τὸ γυναίων εἵνεκα δώρων· ἀλλὰ καὶ οἱ
γραμματικοὶ μυθάρια παραβάλλοντες εὑρεσιλο-
γοῦσι μᾶλλον ἢ λύουσι τὰ ζητούμενα.
70. Ἐάσθω δὴ ταῦτα, ἐκεῖνο δ᾽, ὅπερ ἐστὶ
μᾶλλον ἐν φανερῷ, λαβόντες λέγωμεν, ὅτι ἐν
τοῖς περὶ τὸν Κάϊκον τόποις φαίνεται βεβασι-
λευκὼς καθ᾽ Ὅμηρον ὁ Εὐρύπυλος, ὥστ᾽ ἴσως
καὶ τῶν Κιλίκων τι μέρος ἦν ὑπ᾽ αὐτῷ, καὶ οὐ
δύο δυναστεῖαι μόνον, ἀλλὰ καὶ τρεῖς ὑπῆρξαν
ἐν αὐτοῖς. τῷ δὲ λόγῳ τούτῳ συνηγορεῖ τὸ ἐν
τῇ Ἐλαΐτιδι χειμαρρῶδες ποτάμιον δείκνυσθαι
Κήτειον· ἐμπίπτει δ᾽ οὗτος εἰς ἄλλον ὅμοιον,
εἶτ᾽ ἄλλον, καταστρέφουσι δὲ εἰς τὸν Κάϊκον· ὁ
δὲ Κάϊκος οὐκ ἀπὸ τῆς Ἴδης ῥεῖ, καθάπερ εἴρηκε
Βακχυλίδης, οὐδ᾽ ὀρθῶς[1] Εὐριπίδης τὸν Μαρσύαν
φησὶ

> τὰς διωνομασμένας
> ναίειν Κελαινὰς ἐσχάτοις Ἴδης τόποις·

πολὺ γὰρ τῆς Ἴδης ἄπωθεν αἱ Κελαιναί, πολὺ
δὲ καὶ αἱ τοῦ Καΐκου πηγαί· δείκνυνται γὰρ ἐν
πεδίῳ. Τῆμνον[2] δ᾽ ἐστὶν ὄρος, ὃ διορίζει τοῦτό
τε καὶ τὸ καλούμενον Ἀπίας πεδίον, ὃ ὑπέρκειται
ἐν τῇ μεσογαίᾳ τοῦ Θήβης πεδίον· ῥεῖ δ᾽ ἐκ τοῦ
Τήμνου[3] ποταμὸς Μύσιος, ἐμβάλλων εἰς τὸν
Κάϊκον ὑπὸ ταῖς πηγαῖς αὐτοῦ, ἀφ᾽ οὗ δέχονται

---

[1] οὐδ᾽ ὀρθῶς, Jones, for οὐχ ὡς F, οὔθ᾽ other MSS.; οὔτ᾽ ὀρθῶς
conj. Meineke; Groskurd conj. οὔτ᾽ ἀληθῶς. Kramer would
omit the negative before ὡς.

[2] Τῆμνον, Xylander, for Τῆκνον.

[3] τοῦ Τήμνου, Xylander, for τοῦ Τήκνου Dhimoz, τῶν Τήκνων
CFrwx.

stand the poet to mean by the "Ceteians" nor what he means by "on account of the gifts of a woman";[1] but the grammarians too throw in petty myths, more to show their inventiveness than to solve questions.

70. However, let us dismiss these; and let us, taking that which is more obvious, say that, according to Homer, Eurypylus clearly reigned in the region of the Caïcus, so that perhaps a part of the Cilicians were subject to him, in which case there were three dynasties among them and not merely two.[2] This statement is supported by the fact that there is to be seen in the territory of Elaea a torrential stream called the Ceteius; this empties into another like it, and this again into another, and they all end in the Caïcus. But the Caïcus does not flow from Ida, as Bacchylides[3] states; neither is Euripides[4] correct in saying that Marsyas "dwells in widely-famed Celaenae, in the farthermost region of Ida"; for Celaenae is very far from Ida, and the sources of the Caïcus are also very far, for they are to be seen in a plain. Temnus is a mountain which forms the boundary between this plain and the Plain of Apia, as it is called, which lies in the interior above the Plain of Thebê. From Temnus flows a river called Mysius, which empties into the Caïcus below its sources; and it was from this fact, as some interpret

---

[1] On the variant myths of Augê and Telephus see Eustathius (note on *Od.*, *l.c.*); also Leaf's note and references (p. 340).

[2] Cf. 13. 1. 7, 67.

[3] A fragment otherwise unknown (Bergk 66).

[4] *Frag.* 1085 (Nauck).

τινες εἰπεῖν Αἰσχύλον κατὰ τὴν εἰσβολὴν τοῦ
ἐν Μυρμιδόσι προλόγου·

> ἰὼ Κάϊκε Μύσιαί τ᾽ ἐπιρροαί.

ἐγγὺς δὲ τῶν πηγῶν κώμη Γέργιθά[1] ἐστιν, εἰς
ἣν μετῴκισεν Ἄτταλος τοὺς ἐν τῇ Τρωάδι, τὸ
χωρίον ἐξελών.

II

1. Ἐπεὶ[2] δὲ τῇ παραλίᾳ τῇ ἀπὸ Λεκτοῦ μέχρι
Κανῶν ἀντιπαρατέταται νῆσος ἡ Λέσβος, λόγου
ἀξία πλείστου (περίκειται δὲ αὐτῇ καὶ νησία, τὰ
μὲν ἔξωθεν, τὰ δὲ καὶ ἐν τῷ[3] μεταξὺ αὐτῆς τε
καὶ τῆς ἠπείρου), καιρὸς ἤδη περὶ τούτων εἰπεῖν·
καὶ γὰρ ταῦτά ἐστιν Αἰολικά, σχεδὸν δέ τι καὶ
μητρόπολις ἡ Λέσβος ὑπάρχει τῶν Αἰολικῶν
πόλεων. ἀρκτέον δ᾽ ἀφ᾽ ὧνπερ καὶ τὴν παραλίαν
ἐπήλθομεν τὴν κατ᾽ αὐτήν.

2. Ἀπὸ Λεκτοῦ τοίνυν ἐπὶ Ἄσσον πλέουσιν
ἀρχὴ τῆς Λεσβίας ἐστὶ κατὰ Σίγριον τὸ πρὸς
ἄρκτον αὐτῆς ἄκρον. ἐνταῦθα δέ που καὶ
Μήθυμνα πόλις Λεσβίων ἐστὶν ἀπὸ ἑξήκοντα
σταδίων τῆς ἐκ Πολυμηδίου πρὸς τὴν Ἄσσον
παραλίας. οὔσης δὲ τῆς περιμέτρου σταδίων
χιλίων ἑκατόν, ἣν ἡ σύμπασα ἐκπληροῖ νῆσος,
τὰ καθέκαστα οὕτως ἔχει· ἀπὸ Μηθύμνης εἰς
Μαλίαν τὸ νοτιώτατον ἄκρον ἐν δεξιᾷ ἔχουσι

---

[1] Γ᾽ργιθα, Corais, for Γέργηθα.
[2] ἐπεί oz; ἐπί other MSS.
[3] τῷ, Corais, for τῇ.

the passage, that Aeschylus [1] said at the opening of
the prologue to the *Myrmidons*, "Oh! thou Caïcus
and ye Mysian in-flows." Near the sources is a
village called Gergitha, to which Attalus transferred
the Gergithians of the Troad when he had destroyed
their place.

II

1. Since Lesbos, an island worthy of a full account,
lies alongside and opposite the coast which extends
from Lectum to Canaï, and also has small islands
lying round it, some outside it and some between it
and the mainland, it is now time to describe these;
for these are Aeolian, and I might almost say that
Lesbos is the metropolis of the Aeolian cities. But
I must begin at the point whence I began to traverse
the coast that lies opposite the island.

2. Now as one sails from Lectum to Assus, the
Lesbian country begins at Sigrium, its promontory
on the north.[2] In this general neighbourhood is
also Methymna, a city of the Lesbians, sixty stadia
distant from the coast that stretches from Polymedium to Assus. But while the perimeter which
is filled out by the island as a whole is eleven
hundred stadia, the several distances are as follows:
From Methymna to Malia, the southernmost [3] promontory to one keeping the island on the right, I

---

[1] *Frag.* 143 (Nauck).
[2] But Sigrium was the westernmost promontory of the
island.
[3] More accurately, "southwesternmost."

STRABO

C 617 τὴν νῆσον, καθ᾽ ὃ αἱ Κάναι μάλιστα ἀντίκεινται τῇ νήσῳ καὶ συναπαρτίζουσι, στάδιοί εἰσι τριακόσιοι τετταράκοντα· ἐντεῦθεν δ᾽ ἐπὶ Σίγριον, ὅπερ ἐστὶ τῆς νήσου τὸ μῆκος, πεντακόσιοι ἑξήκοντα· εἶτ᾽ ἐπὶ τὴν Μήθυμναν[1] διακόσιοι δέκα. Μιτυλήνη δὲ κεῖται μεταξὺ Μηθύμνης καὶ τῆς Μαλίας ἡ μεγίστη πόλις, διέχουσα τῆς Μαλίας ἑβδομήκοντα σταδίους, τῶν δὲ Κανῶν ἑκατὸν εἴκοσιν, ὅσους καὶ τῶν Ἀργινουσσῶν, αἳ τρεῖς μέν εἰσιν οὐ μεγάλαι νῆσοι, πλησιάζουσι δὲ τῇ ἠπείρῳ, παρακείμεναι[2] ταῖς Κάναις. ἐν δὲ τῷ μεταξὺ Μιτυλήνης καὶ τῆς Μηθύμνης κατὰ κώμην τῆς Μηθυμναίας, καλουμένην Αἴγειρον, στενωτάτη ἐστὶν ἡ νῆσος, ὑπέρβασιν ἔχουσα εἰς τὸν Πυρραίων Εὔριπον σταδίων εἴκοσιν. ἵδρυται δ᾽ ἡ Πύρρα ἐν τῷ ἑσπερίῳ πλευρῷ τῆς Λέσβου, διέχουσα τῆς Μαλίας ἑκατόν. ἔχει δ᾽ ἡ Μιτυλήνη λιμένας δύο, ὧν ὁ νότιος κλειστὸς τριηρικὸς[3] ναυσὶ πεντήκοντα, ὁ δὲ βόρειος μέγας καὶ βαθύς, χώματι σκεπαζόμενος· πρόκειται δ᾽ ἀμφοῖν νησίον, μέρος τῆς πόλεως ἔχον αὐτόθι συνοικούμενον· κατεσκεύασται δὲ τοῖς πᾶσι καλῶς.

3. Ἄνδρας δ᾽ ἔσχεν ἐνδόξους, τὸ παλαιὸν μὲν Πιττακόν, ἕνα τῶν ἑπτὰ σοφῶν, καὶ τὸν ποιητὴν Ἀλκαῖον καὶ τὸν ἀδελφὸν Ἀντιμενίδαν, ὅν φησιν Ἀλκαῖος Βαβυλωνίοις συμμαχοῦντα τελέσαι

---

[1] Μήθυμναν, Kramer, for Μηθυμναίαν.
[2] δέ, after παρακείμεναι, omitted by moz and ejected by Corais and later editors.
[3] τριηρικός, Meineke, for τριήρεικαί. Wesseling conj.

mean at the point where Canae lies most directly
opposite the island and precisely corresponds with
it, the distance is three hundred and forty stadia;
thence to Sigrium, which is the length of the island,
five hundred and sixty; and then to Methymna, two
hundred and ten.[1] Mitylene, the largest city, lies
between Methymna and Malia, being seventy stadia
distant from Malia, one hundred and twenty from
Canae, and the same distance from the Arginussae,
which are three small islands lying near the mainland
alongside Canae. In the interval between Mitylene
and Methymna, in the neighbourhood of a village
called Aegeirus in the Methymnaean territory, the
island is narrowest, with a passage of only twenty
stadia over to the Euripus of the Pyrrhaeans.
Pyrrha is situated on the western side of Lesbos at
a distance of one hundred stadia from Malia. Mitylene has two harbours, of which the southern can
be closed and holds only fifty triremes, but the
northern is large and deep, and is sheltered by a
mole. Off both lies a small island, which contains
a part of the city that is settled there. And the
city is well equipped with everything.

3. Mitylene has produced famous men: in early
times, Pittacus, one of the Seven Wise Men; and
the poet Alcaeus, and his brother Antimenidas, who,
according to Alcaeus, won a great struggle when
fighting on the side of the Babylonians, and rescued

---

[1] The total, 1110, being ten more than the round number
given above.

τριηρικὸς καὶ ναύσταθμον, the complete phrase found in 14.
2. 15.

μέγαν ἆθλον καὶ ἐκ πόνων αὐτοὺς ῥύσασθαι,
κτείναντα

ἄνδρα μαχαίταν, βασιλήιον [1]
παλαστὰν [2] (ὥς φησι) ἀπολείποντα [3] μόνον
μίαν [4]
παχέων ἀπὺ πέμπων.[5]

συνήκμασε δὲ τούτοις καὶ ἡ Σαπφώ, θαυμαστόν
τι χρῆμα· οὐ γὰρ ἴσμεν ἐν τῷ τοσούτῳ χρόνῳ τῷ
μνημονευομένῳ φανεῖσάν τινα γυναῖκα ἐνάμιλλον,
οὐδὲ κατὰ μικρόν, ἐκείνῃ ποιήσεως χάριν. ἐτυ-
ραννήθη δὲ ἡ πόλις κατὰ τοὺς χρόνους τούτους
ὑπὸ πλειόνων διὰ τὰς διχοστασίας, καὶ τὰ
στασιωτικὰ καλούμενα τοῦ Ἀλκαίου ποιήματα
περὶ τούτων ἐστίν· ἐν δὲ τοῖς τυράννοις καὶ ὁ
Πιττακὸς ἐγένετο. Ἀλκαῖος μὲν οὖν ὁμοίως
ἐλοιδορεῖτο καὶ τούτῳ καὶ τοῖς ἄλλοις, Μυρσίλῳ
καὶ Μελάγχρῳ [6] καὶ τοῖς Κλεανακτίδαις καὶ
ἄλλοις τισίν, οὐδ' αὐτὸς καθαρεύων τῶν τοιούτων
νεωτερισμῶν. Πιττακὸς δ' εἰς μὲν τὴν τῶν δυνα-
στειῶν κατάλυσιν ἐχρήσατο τῇ μοναρχίᾳ καὶ
αὐτός, καταλύσας δὲ ἀπέδωκε τὴν αὐτονομίαν τῇ
πόλει. ὕστερον δ' ἐγένετο χρόνοις πολλοῖς
Διοφάνης ὁ ῥήτωρ· καθ' ἡμᾶς δὲ Ποτάμων καὶ
Λεσβοκλῆς καὶ Κριναγόρας καὶ ὁ συγγραφεὺς
Θεοφάνης. οὗτος δὲ καὶ πολιτικὸς ἀνὴρ ὑπῆρξε
καὶ Πομπηΐῳ τῷ Μάγνῳ κατέστη φίλος, μάλιστα
διὰ τὴν ἀρετὴν αὐτήν, καὶ πάσας συγκατώρθωσεν

---

[1] βασιλήιον, O. Müller (quoted by Bergk, who prefers
βασιληίων), for βασιλήων.
[2] παλαστάν DFhi and Kramer (παλάσταν Meineke) ; παλαί-
σταν other MSS.

them from their toils by killing "a warrior, the royal wrestler" (as he says), "who was but one short of five cubits in height."[1] And along with these flourished also Sappho, a marvellous woman; for in all the time of which we have record I do not know of the appearance of any woman who could rival Sappho, even in a slight degree, in the matter of poetry. The city was in those times ruled over by several tyrants because of the dissensions among the inhabitants; and these dissensions are the subject of the Stasiotic[2] poems, as they are called, of Alcaeus. And also Pittacus[3] was one of the tyrants. Now Alcaeus would rail alike at both Pittacus and the rest, Myrsilus and Melanchrus and the Cleanactidae and certain others, though even he himself was not innocent of revolutionary attempts; but even Pittacus himself used monarchy for the overthrow of the oligarchs, and then, after overthrowing them, restored to the city its independence. Diophanes the rhetorician was born much later; but Potamon, Lesbocles, Crinagoras, and Theophanes the historian in my time. Theophanes was also a statesman; and he became a friend to Pompey the Great, mostly through his very ability, and helped him to succeed in all his achievements;

---

[1] *Frag.* 33 (Bergk).   [2] Seditious.
[3] Reigned 589-579 B.C.

---

[3] ἀπολείποντα, Müller, for ἀπολιπόντα; so Kramer and Meineke.
[4] μίαν, Müller, for ἀνίαν; so Kramer and Meineke.
[5] ἀπὺ πέμπων (ἀπυπέμπων F), Müller, for ἀποπέμπων; so Kramer and Meineke.
[6] Μελάγχρῳ, Groskurd and other editors, for Μελάνδρῳ F, Μεγαλογύρῳ other MSS.

αὐτῷ τὰς πράξεις· ἀφ' ὧν τήν τε πατρίδα
ἐκόσμησε τὰ μὲν δι' ἐκείνου, τὰ δὲ δι' ἑαυτοῦ, καὶ
C 618 ἑαυτὸν πάντων τῶν Ἑλλήνων ἐπιφανέστατον
ἀνέδειξεν· υἱόν τε ἀπέλιπε Μάρκον Πομπήιον,
ὃν τῆς Ἀσίας ἐπίτροπον κατέστησέ ποτε Καῖσαρ
ὁ Σεβαστός, καὶ νῦν ἐν τοῖς πρώτοις ἐξετάζεται
τῶν Τιβερίου φίλων. Ἀθηναῖοι δ' ἐκινδύνευσαν
μὲν ἀνηκέστῳ ψόγῳ περιπεσεῖν, ψηφισάμενοι
Μιτυληναίους ἡβηδὸν ἀποσφαγῆναι, μετέγνωσαν
δέ, καὶ ἔφθη μιᾷ θᾶττον ἡμέρᾳ τὸ ψήφισμα
ἀφιγμένον ὡς τοὺς στρατηγοὺς πρὶν ἢ πρᾶξαι τὸ
προσταχθέν.

4. Ἡ δὲ Πύρρα κατέστραπται, τὸ δὲ προάστειον οἰκεῖται καὶ ἔχει λιμένα, ὅθεν εἰς Μιτυλή-
νην ὑπέρβασις σταδίων ὀγδοήκοντα. εἶτ' Ἐρε-
σός ἐστι μετὰ τὴν Πύρραν· ἵδρυται δ' ἐπὶ λόφου
καθήκει τε ἐπὶ θάλατταν· εἶτ' ἐπὶ τὸ Σίγριον
ἐντεῦθεν στάδιοι εἰκοσιοκτώ· ἐξ Ἐρεσοῦ δ'
ἦσαν Θεόφραστός τε καὶ Φανίας, οἱ ἐκ τῶν
περιπάτων φιλόσοφοι, Ἀριστοτέλους γνώριμοι.
Τύρταμος δ' ἐκαλεῖτο ἔμπροσθεν ὁ Θεόφραστος,
μετωνόμασε δ' αὐτὸν Ἀριστοτέλης Θεόφραστον,
ἅμα μὲν φεύγων τὴν τοῦ προτέρου ὀνόματος
κακοφωνίαν, ἅμα δὲ τὸν τῆς φράσεως αὐτοῦ
ζῆλον ἐπισημαινόμενος· ἅπαντας μὲν γὰρ λογίους
ἐποίησε τοὺς μαθητὰς Ἀριστοτέλης, λογιώτατον
δὲ Θεόφραστον. Ἄντισσα δ' ἐφεξῆς ἐστι τῷ
Σιγρίῳ πόλις, ἔχουσα λιμένα· ἔπειτα Μήθυμνα,
ἐντεῦθεν δ' ἦν Ἀρίων ὁ ἐπὶ τῷ δελφῖνι μυθευο-
μενος ὑπὸ τῶν περὶ Ἡρόδοτον εἰς Ταίναρον
σωθῆναι, καταποντωθεὶς ὑπὸ τῶν λῃστῶν· οὗτος
μὲν οὖν κιθαρῳδός. καὶ Τέρπανδρον δὲ τῆς αὐτῆς
144

whence he not only adorned his native land, partly through Pompey and partly through himself, but also rendered himself the most illustrious of all the Greeks. He left a son, Marcus Pompey, whom Augustus Caesar once set up as Procurator of Asia, and who is now counted among the first of the friends of Tiberius. The Athenians were in danger of suffering an irreparable disgrace when they voted that all Mitylenaeans from youth upwards should be slain, but they changed their minds and their counter-decree reached the generals only one day before the order was to be executed.

4. Pyrrha has been rased to the ground, but its suburb is inhabited and has a harbour, whence there is a passage of eighty stadia over hills to Mitylene. Then, after Pyrrha, one comes to Eressus; it is situated on a hill and extends down to the sea. Then to Sigrium, twenty-eight stadia from Eressus. Both Theophrastus and Phanias, the peripatetic philosophers, disciples of Aristotle, were from Eressus. Theophrastus was at first called Tyrtamus, but Aristotle changed his name to Theophrastus, at the same time avoiding the cacophony of his former name and signifying the fervour of his speech; for Aristotle made all his pupils eloquent, but Theophrastus most eloquent of all. Antissa, a city with a harbour, comes next in order after Sigrium. And then Methymna, whence came Arion, who, according to a myth told by Herodotus and his followers, safely escaped on a dolphin to Taenarum after being thrown into the sea by the pirates. Now Arion played, and sang to, the cithara; and Terpander,

μουσικῆς τεχνίτην γεγονέναι φασὶ καὶ τῆς αὐτῆς
νήσου, τὸν πρῶτον ἀντὶ τῆς τετραχόρδου λύρας
ἑπταχόρδῳ χρησάμενον· καθάπερ καὶ ἐν τοῖς
ἀναφερομένοις ἔπεσιν εἰς αὐτὸν λέγεται·

σοὶ δ᾽ ἡμεῖς τετράγηρυν ἀποστρέψαντες ἀοιδήν,
ἑπτατόνῳ φόρμιγγι νέους κελαδήσομεν ὕμνους.

καὶ Ἑλλάνικος δὲ Λέσβιος συγγραφεὺς καὶ
Καλλίας ὁ τὴν Σαπφὼ καὶ τὸν Ἀλκαῖον ἐξηγησάμενος.

5. Κατὰ δὲ τὸν πορθμὸν τὸν μεταξὺ τῆς
Ἀσίας καὶ τῆς Λέσβου νησία ἐστὶ περὶ εἴκοσιν,
ὡς δὲ Τιμοσθένης φησί, τεττεράκοντα· καλοῦνται
δ᾽ Ἑκατόννησοι συνθέτως, ὡς Πελοπόννησος,
κατὰ ἔθος τι τοῦ Ν γράμματος πλεονάζοντος ἐν
τοῖς τοιούτοις, ὡς Μυόννησος καὶ Προκόννησος
λέγεται καὶ Ἀλόννησος, ὥστε Ἑκατόννησοί
εἰσιν, οἷον Ἀπολλωνόννησοι, Ἕκατος γὰρ ὁ
Ἀπόλλων· παρὰ πᾶσαν γὰρ δὴ τὴν παραλίαν
ταύτην ὁ Ἀπόλλων ἐκτετίμηται μέχρι Τενέδου,
Σμινθεὺς ἢ Κιλλαῖος καλούμενος ἢ Γρυνεὺς ἤ
τινα ἄλλην ἐπωνυμίαν ἔχων. πλησίον δὲ τούτων
ἐστὶ καὶ ἡ Πορδοσελήνη,[1] πόλιν ὁμώνυμον ἔχουσα
C 619 ἐν αὐτῇ· καὶ πρὸ τῆς πόλεως ταύτης ἄλλη νῆσος[2]
μείζων αὐτῆς ὁμώνυμος, ἔρημος, ἱερὸν ἅγιον ἔχουσα
Ἀπόλλωνος.

6. Τὰς δὲ δυσφημίας τῶν ὀνομάτων φεύγοντές[3]
τινες ἐνταῦθα μὲν Ποροσελήνην δεῖν λέγειν φασί,
τὸ δ᾽ Ἀσπόρδηνον ὄρος τὸ περὶ Πέργαμον, τραχὺ

[1] Instead of Πορδοσελήνη, Dhirwxz read Παρδοσελήνη.
[2] πόλις (πόλης F) after νῆσος, Jones ejects, following conj.
of Kramer and C. Müller.

146

also, is said to have been an artist in the same music and to have been born in the same island, having been the first person to use the seven-stringed instead of the four-stringed lyre, as we are told in the verses attributed to him: " For thee I, having dismissed four-toned song, shall sing new hymns to the tune of a seven-stringed cithara."[1] Also Hellanicus the historian, and Callias, who interpreted Sappho and Alcaeus, were Lesbians.

5. In the strait between Asia and Lesbos there are about twenty small islands, but according to Timosthenes, forty. They are called Hecatonnesi, a compound name like Peloponnesus, the second letter *n* being customarily redundant in such compounds, as in the names Myonnesus, Proconnesus, and Halonnesus; and consequently we have Hecatonnesi, which means Apollonnesi, for Apollo is called Hecatus; for along the whole of this coast, as far as Tenedos, Apollo is highly honoured, being called Sminthian or Cillaean or Grynian or by some other appellation. Near these islands is Pordoselenê, which contains a city of the same name, and also, in front of this city, another island, larger and of the same name, which is uninhabited and has a temple sacred to Apollo.

6. Some writers, to avoid the indecency of the names, say that in this place we should read " Poro-selenê," and that we should call Aspordenum, the rocky and barren mountain round Pergamum, " Asporenum," and the temple of the Mother of the

---

[1] *Frag.* 5 (Bergk).

---

[3] φεύγοντες, Corais, for φυγόντες ; so the later editors.

καὶ λυπρὸν ὄν, Ἀσπόρηνον,[1] καὶ τὸ ἱερὸν τὸ
ἐνταῦθα τῆς Μητρὸς τῶν θεῶν Ἀσπορηνῆς.[2] τί οὖν
φήσομεν τὴν Πόρδαλιν καὶ τὸν Σαπέρδην καὶ τὸν
Περδίκκαν καὶ τὸ Σιμωνίδου

σὺν πορδακοῖσιν ἐκπεσόντες εἵμασιν[3]

ἀντὶ τοῦ διαβρόχοις, καὶ ἐν τῇ ἀρχαίᾳ που
κωμῳδίᾳ

πορδακὸν τὸ χωρίον,

τὸ λίμναζον; διέχει δ' ἡ Λέσβος τὸ ἴσον ἀπὸ
τῆς Τενέδου καὶ Λήμνου καὶ Χίου σχεδόν τι τῶν
πεντακοσίων ἐνδοτέρω σταδίων.

III

1. Τοιαύτης δὲ τῆς πρὸς τοὺς Τρῶας οἰκειό-
τητος ὑπαρχούσης τοῖς τε Λέλεξι καὶ τοῖς Κίλιξι,
ζητοῦσιν αἰτίαν, δι' ἣν οὐ συγκαταλέγονται καὶ
οὗτοι ἐν τῷ καταλόγῳ. εἰκὸς δὲ διὰ τὴν τῶν
ἡγεμόνων διαφθορὰν καὶ τὴν τῶν πόλεων
ἐκπόρθησιν ὀλίγους ὑπολειφθέντας τοὺς Κίλικας
ὑπὸ τῷ Ἕκτορι τάττεσθαι· ὅ τε γὰρ Ἠετίων
καὶ οἱ παῖδες αὐτοῦ λέγονται πρὸ τοῦ καταλόγου
διαφθαρῆναι·

ἤτοι μὲν πατέρ' ἀμὸν[4] ἀπέκτανε δῖος Ἀχιλλεύς,
ἐκ δὲ πόλιν πέρσεν Κιλίκων,
Θήβην ὑψίπυλον.

---

[1] Instead of Ἀσπόρηνον, F reads Ἀσπρόκνον, oz Ἀσπόρινον.
[2] Ἀσπορινῆς oz.

gods there the temple of the "Asporene" mother.[1]
What, then, shall we say of Pordalis and Saperdes
and Perdiccas, and of the phrase of Simonides,
"banished, 'pordacian' clothes and all," instead of
"wet" clothes, and, somewhere in the early comedy,
"the place is 'pordacian,'" that is, the place that
is "marshy"? Lesbos is equidistant from Tenedos
and Lemnos and Chios, one might say rather less
than five hundred stadia.

III

1. Since the Leleges and the Cilicians were so
closely related to the Trojans, people inquire for the
reason why they are not included with the Trojans
in the *Catalogue*. But it is reasonable to suppose
that because of the loss of their leaders and the
sacking of their cities the few Cilicians that were
left were placed under the command of Hector,
for both Eëtion and his sons are said to have
been slain before the *Catalogue*: [2] "Verily my father
was slain by the goodly Achilles, who utterly sacked
the city of Cilicians, Thebê of the lofty gates.

---

[1] *i.e.* they avoid "pord," which, as also "perd," is the
stem of an indecent Greek word.

[2] *i.e.* before the marshalling of the troops as described in
the *Catalogue*.

---

[3] εἵμασιν, Tyrwhitt, for ἵμασιν ; so the later editors.

[4] ἁμόν, Xylander, for ἐμόν ; so the later editors.

οἳ δέ μοι ἑπτὰ κασίγνητοι ἔσαν ἐν μεγάροισιν,
οἱ μὲν πάντες ἰῷ κίον ἤματι Ἄϊδος εἴσω·
πάντας γὰρ κατέπεφνε ποδάρκης δῖος Ἀχιλλεύς.

ὡς δ᾽ αὔτως καὶ οἱ ὑπὸ Μύνητι τούς τε ἡγεμόνας
ἀποβεβλήκασι καὶ τὴν πόλιν·

καδ᾽ δὲ Μύνητ᾽ ἔβαλε καὶ Ἐπίστροφον,
πέρσεν δὲ πόλιν θείοιο Μύνητος.

τοὺς δὲ Λέλεγας τοῖς μὲν ἀγῶσι παρόντας ποιεῖ,
ὅταν οὕτω λέγῃ·
πρὸς μὲν ἁλὸς Κᾶρες καὶ Παίονες ἀγκυλότοξοι
καὶ Λέλεγες καὶ Καύκωνες·

καὶ πάλιν·

Σάτνιον οὔτασε δουρὶ
Οἰνοπίδην, ὃν ἄρα νύμφη τέκε Νηὶς ἀμύμων
Οἴνοπι βουκολέοντι παρ᾽ ὄχθας Σατνιόεντος.

οὐ γὰρ οὕτως ἐξελελοίπεσαν τελέως, ὥστε μὴ
καὶ καθ᾽ αὑτοὺς ἔχειν τι σύστημα, ἅτε τοῦ
βασιλέως αὐτῶν ἔτι περιόντος,

Ἄλτεω, ὃς Λελέγεσσι φιλοπτολέμοισιν ἀνάσσει,

καὶ τῆς πόλεως οὐ τελέως ἠφανισμένης· ἐπιφέρει
γὰρ

Πήδασον αἰπήεσσαν ἔχων ἐπὶ[1] Σατνιόεντι.

C 620 ἐν μέντοι τῷ καταλόγῳ παραλέλοιπεν αὐτούς,
οὐχ ἱκανὸν ἡγούμενος τὸ σύστημα, ὥστ᾽ ἐν
καταλόγῳ τάττεσθαι, ἢ καὶ[2] ὑπὸ τῷ Ἕκτορι καὶ
τούτους συγκαταλέγων, οὕτως ὄντας οἰκείους.
ὁ γὰρ Λυκάων φησίν, ἀδελφὸς ὢν Ἕκτορος·

And the seven brothers of mine in our halls, all these on the same day[1] went inside the home of Hades, for all were slain by swift-footed, goodly Achilles."[2]   And so, in the same way, those subject to Mynes lost both their leaders and their city: "And he laid low Mynes and Epistrophus, and sacked the city of godlike Mynes."[3]   But he makes the Leleges present at the battles when he says as follows: "Towards the sea are situated the Carians and the Paeonians, with curved bows, and the Leleges and Caucones."[4]   And again, "he pierced with his spear Satnius, son of Oenops, whom a noble Naiad nymph bore to Oenops, as he tended his herds beside the banks of the Satnioeis";[5] for they had not so completely disappeared that they did not have a separate organisation of their own, since their king still survived, "of Altes, who is lord over the war-loving Leleges,"[6] and since their city had not been utterly wiped out, for the poet adds, "who holds steep Pedasus on the Satnioeis."[7] However, the poet has omitted them in the *Catalogue*, not considering their organisation sufficient to have a place in it, or else including them under the command of Hector because they were so closely related;

---

[1] *i.e.* with Eëtion.   [2] *Iliad* 6. 414.
[3] *Iliad* 2. 692, 19. 296.   [4] *Iliad* 10. 428.
[5] *Iliad* 14. 443.   [6] *Iliad* 21. 86.   [7] *Iliad* 21. 87.

---

[1] ἐπί, Corais, for ὑπό.
[2] καί, before ὑπό, omitted by C.

μινυνθάδιον δέ με μήτηρ
γείνατο Λαοθόη, θυγάτηρ Ἄλταο γέροντος,
Ἄλτεω, ὃς Λελέγεσσι φιλοπτολέμοισιν ἀνάσσει.

ταῦτα μὲν οὖν τοιαύτην τινὰ ἔχει τὴν εἰκοτο-
λογίαν.

2. Εἰκοτολογεῖν δ' ἐστί, κἂν εἴ τις τὸν ἀκριβῆ
ζητεῖ κατὰ τὸν ποιητὴν ὅρον, μέχρι τίνος οἱ
Κίλικες διέτεινον καὶ οἱ Πελασγοὶ καὶ ἔτι οἱ
μεταξὺ τούτων Κήτειοι λεγόμενοι οἱ ὑπὸ τῷ
Εὐρυπύλῳ. περὶ μὲν οὖν τῶν Κιλίκων καὶ τῶν
ὑπ' Εὐρυπύλῳ τὰ ἐνόντα εἴρηται, καὶ διότι ἐπὶ[1] τὰ
περὶ τὸν Κάϊκον μάλιστα περατοῦνται. τοὺς δὲ
Πελασγοὺς εὔλογον τούτοις ἐφεξῆς τιθέναι ἔκ τε
τῶν ὑφ' Ὁμήρου λεγομένων καὶ ἐκ τῆς ἄλλης
ἱστορίας. ὁ μὲν γὰρ οὕτω φησίν·

Ἱππόθοος δ' ἄγε φῦλα Πελασγῶν ἐγχεσι-
μώρων,
τῶν, οἳ Λάρισαν ἐριβώλακα ναιετάασκον·
τῶν ἦρχ' Ἱππόθοός τε Πύλαιός τ' ὄζος Ἄρηος,
υἷε δύω Λήθοιο Πελασγοῦ Τευταμίδαο.

ἐξ ὧν πλῆθός τε ἐμφαίνει ἀξιόλογον τὸ τῶν
Πελασγῶν (οὐ γὰρ φῦλον, ἀλλὰ φῦλα ἔφη) καὶ
τὴν οἴκησιν ἐν Λαρίσῃ φράζει. πολλαὶ μὲν οὖν
αἱ Λάρισαι, δεῖ δὲ τῶν ἐγγύς τινα δέξασθαι,
μάλιστα δ' ἂν τὴν περὶ Κύμην ὑπολάβοι τις
ὀρθῶς· τριῶν γὰρ οὐσῶν, ἡ μὲν καθ' Ἁμαξιτὸν ἐν
ὄψει τελέως ἐστὶ τῷ Ἰλίῳ, καὶ ἐγγὺς σφόδρα ἐν
διακοσίοις που σταδίοις, ὥστ' οὐκ ἂν λέγοιτο

---

[1] ἐπί, Meineke inserts.

for Lycaon, who was a brother of Hector, says, " to a short span of life my mother, daughter of the old man Altes, bore me—Altes who is lord over the war-loving Leleges." [1]   Such, then, are the probabilities in this matter.

2. And it is also a matter of reasoning from probabilities if one inquires as to the exact bounds to which the poet means that the Cilicians extended, and the Pelasgians, and also the Ceteians, as they are called, under the command of Eurypylus, who lived between those two peoples.   Now as for the Cilicians and the peoples under the command of Eurypylus, all has been said about them that can be said, and that their country is in a general way bounded by the region of the Caïcus River.   As for the Pelasgians, it is reasonable, both from the words of Homer and from history in general, to place them next in order after these peoples; for Homer says as follows : " And Hippothoüs led the tribes of the Pelasgians that rage with the spear, them that dwelt in fertile Larisa ; these were ruled by Hippothoüs and Pylaeus, scion of Ares, the two sons of Pelasgian Lethus, son of Teutamus." [2]   By these words he clearly indicates that the number of Pelasgians was considerable, for he says " tribes," not " tribe ; " and he also specifies their abode as " in Larisa."   Now there are many Larisas, but we must interpret him as meaning one of those that were near ; and best of all one might rightly assume the one in the neighbourhood of Cymê ; for of the three Larisas the one near Hamaxitus was in plain sight of Ilium and very near it, within a distance of two hundred stadia, and therefore it could not be said with plausibility that

[1] *Iliad* 21. 84.   [2] *Iliad* 2. 840.

πιθανῶς ὁ Ἱππόθοος πεσεῖν ἐν τῷ ὑπὲρ Πατρόκλου ἀγῶνι

τὴλ' ἀπὸ Λαρίσης,

ταύτης γε, ἀλλὰ μᾶλλον τῆς περὶ Κύμην· χίλιοι
γάρ που στάδιοι μεταξύ· τρίτη δ' ἐστὶ Λάρισα,
κώμη τῆς Ἐφεσίας ἐν τῷ Καϋστρίῳ πεδίῳ, ἥν
φασι πόλιν ὑπάρξαι πρότερον, ἔχουσαν καὶ ἱερὸν
Ἀπόλλωνος Λαρισηνοῦ, πλησιάζουσαν τῷ Τμώλῳ
μᾶλλον ἢ τῇ Ἐφέσῳ· ταύτης γὰρ ἑκατὸν καὶ
ὀγδοήκοντα διέχει σταδίους, ὥστε ὑπὸ τοῖς
Μήοσιν ἄν τις τάττοι ταύτην. Ἐφέσιοι δ'
αὐξηθέντες ὕστερον πολλὴν τῆς τῶν Μηόνων,
οὓς νῦν Λυδούς φαμεν, ἀπετέμοντο, ὥστ' οὐδ'
αὕτη ἂν ἡ τῶν Πελασγῶν Λάρισα εἴη, ἀλλ'
ἐκείνη μᾶλλον. καὶ γὰρ τῆς μὲν ἐν τῇ Καϋστριανῇ
Λαρίσης οὐδὲν ἔχομεν τεκμήριον ἰσχυρόν, ὡς ἦν
ἤδη τότε· οὐδὲ γὰρ τῆς Ἐφέσου· τῆς δὲ περὶ τὴν
C 621 Κύμην μαρτύριόν ἐστι πᾶσα ἡ Αἰολικὴ ἱστορία,
μικρὸν ὕστερον τῶν Τρωικῶν γενομένη.

3. Φασὶ γὰρ τοὺς ἐκ τοῦ Φρικίου [1] τοῦ ὑπὲρ
Θερμοπυλῶν Λοκρικοῦ ὄρους ὁρμηθέντας καταραι
μὲν εἰς τὸν τόπον, ὅπου νῦν ἡ Κύμη ἐστί,
καταλαβόντας δὲ τοὺς Πελασγοὺς κεκακωμένους
ὑπὸ τοῦ Τρωικοῦ πολέμου, κατέχοντας δ' ὅμως
ἔτι τὴν Λάρισαν διέχουσαν τῆς Κύμης ὅσον
ἑβδομήκοντα σταδίους, ἐπιτειχίσαι αὐτοῖς τὸ νῦν
ἔτι λεγόμενον Νέον τεῖχος ἀπὸ τριάκοντα σταδίων
τῆς Λαρίσης, ἑλόντας [2] δὲ κτίσαι τὴν Κύμην καὶ
τοὺς περιγενομένους ἀνθρώπους ἐκεῖσε ἀνοικίσαι·

---

[1] ἐκ τοῦ Φρικίου, Tyrwhitt, for ἐν τῷ Φρικίῳ; so the later
editors.

Hippothoüs fell in the fight over Patroclus "far away from" this "Larisa," but rather from the Larisa near Cymê, for the distance between the two is about a thousand stadia. The third Larisa is a village in the territory of Ephesus in the Caÿster Plain; it is said to have been a city in earlier times, containing a temple of Larisaean Apollo and being situated closer to Mt. Tmolus than to Ephesus. It is one hundred and eighty stadia distant from Ephesus, and might therefore be placed under the Maeonians. But the Ephesians, having grown in power, later cut off for themselves much of the territory of the Maeonians, whom we now call Lydians, so that this could not be the Larisa of the Pelasgians either, but rather the one near Cymê. In fact we have no strong evidence that the Larisa in the Caÿster Plain was already in existence at that time, for we have no such evidence as to Ephesus either; but all Aeolian history, which arose but shortly after the Trojan times, bears testimony to the existence of the Larisa near Cymê.

3. For it is said that the people who set out from Phricium, the Locrian mountain above Thermopylae, put in at the place where Cymê now is, and finding the Pelasgians in bad plight because of the Trojan War, though still in possession of Larisa, which was about seventy stadia distant from Cymê, built on their frontier what is still to-day called Neon Teichos,[1] thirty stadia from Larisa, and that, having captured Larisa, they founded Cymê and settled there the survivors. And Cymê is called Cymê

[1] "New wall."

___

[2] ἐλόντας, Corais, Kramer, and Meineke, for ἐλθόντας; ἀνελθόντας Groskurd.

ἀπὸ δὲ τοῦ Λοκρικοῦ ὄρους τήν τε Κύμην
Φρικωνίδα καλοῦσιν, ὁμοίως δὲ καὶ τὴν Λάρισαν·
ἐρήμη δ᾽ ἐστὶ νῦν. ὅτι δ᾽ οἱ Πελασγοὶ μέγα ἦν
ἔθνος, καὶ ἐκ τῆς ἄλλης ἱστορίας οὕτως ἐκμαρτυ-
ρεῖσθαί[1] φασι· Μενεκράτης γοῦν ὁ Ἐλαΐτης ἐν
τοῖς περὶ κτίσεων φησὶ τὴν παραλίαν τὴν νῦν
Ἰωνικὴν πᾶσαν, ἀπὸ Μυκάλης ἀρξαμένην, ὑπὸ
Πελασγῶν οἰκεῖσθαι πρότερον καὶ τὰς πλησίον
νήσους. Λέσβιοι δ᾽ ὑπὸ Πυλαίῳ τετάχθαι λέγουσι σφᾶς, τῷ ὑπὸ τοῦ ποιητοῦ λεγομένῳ τῶν
Πελασγῶν ἄρχοντι, ἀφ᾽ οὗ καὶ τὸ παρ᾽ αὐτοῖς
ὄρος ἔτι Πύλαιον καλεῖσθαι. καὶ Χῖοι δὲ οἰκιστὰς
ἑαυτῶν Πελασγούς φασι τοὺς ἐκ τῆς Θετταλίας.
πολύπλανον δὲ καὶ ταχὺ τὸ ἔθνος πρὸς ἀπαναστάσεις,[2] ηὐξήθη τε ἐπὶ πολὺ καὶ ἀθρόαν
ἔλαβε τὴν ἔκλειψιν, καὶ μάλιστα κατὰ τὴν
τῶν Αἰολέων καὶ τῶν Ἰώνων περαίωσιν εἰς τὴν
Ἀσίαν.

4. Ἴδιον δέ τι τοῖς Λαρισαίοις συνέβη τοῖς
τε Καϋστριανοῖς[3] καὶ τοῖς Φρικωνεῦσι καὶ τρίτοις
τοῖς ἐν Θετταλίᾳ· ἅπαντες γὰρ ποταμόχωστον
τὴν χώραν ἔσχον, οἱ μὲν ὑπὸ τοῦ Καΰστρου, οἱ
δ᾽ ὑπὸ τοῦ Ἕρμου, οἱ δ᾽ ὑπὸ τοῦ Πηνειοῦ. ἐν
δὲ τῇ Φρικωνίδι Λαρίσῃ τετιμῆσθαι λέγεται
Πίασος, ὅν φασιν ἄρχοντα Πελασγῶν ἐρασθῆναι
τῆς θυγατρὸς Λαρίσης, βιασάμενον δ᾽ αὐτὴν
τῖσαι τῆς ὕβρεως δίκην· ἐγκύψαντα γὰρ εἰς
πίθον οἴνου καταμαθοῦσαν τῶν σκελῶν λαβο-
μένην ἐξᾶραι καὶ καθεῖναι αὐτὸν εἰς τὸν πίθον.
τὰ μὲν οὖν ἀρχαῖα τοιαῦτα.

---

[1] Dhi read τοῦτο ἐκμαρτυρῆσαι.
[2] ἀπαναστάσεις, Corais, for ἐπαναστάσεις.

Phriconis after the Locrian mountain; and likewise
Larisa is called Larisa Phriconis; but Larisa is now
deserted. That the Pelasgians were a great tribe is
said also to be the testimony of history in general:
Menecrates of Elaea, at any rate, in his work *On the
Founding of Cities,* says that the whole of what is now
the Ionian coast, beginning at Mycalê, as also the
neighbouring islands, were in earlier times inhabited
by Pelasgians. But the Lesbians say that their
people were placed under the command of Pylaeus,
the man whom the poet calls the ruler of the
Pelasgians,[1] and that it is from him that the mountain
in their country is still called Pylaeus. The Chians,
also, say that the Pelasgians from Thessaly were
their founders. But the Pelasgian race, ever
wandering and quick to migrate, greatly increased
and then rapidly disappeared, particularly at the time
of the migration of the Aeolians and Ionians to Asia.

4. A peculiar thing happened in the case of the
Larisaeans, I mean the Caÿstrian and the Phryconian
Larisaeans and, third, those in Thessaly: they all
held land that was deposited by rivers, by the
Caÿster and by the Hermus and by the Peneius. It
is at the Phryconian Larisa that Piasus is said to
have been honoured, who, they say, was ruler of the
Pelasgians and fell in love with his daughter Larisa,
and, having violated her, paid the penalty for the
outrage; for, observing him leaning over a cask of
wine, they say, she seized him by the legs, raised
him, and plunged him into the cask. Such are the
ancient accounts.

[1] *Iliad* 2. 842.

[3] Instead of Καῦστριανοῖς, CDE*himoz* read Καῦστρηνοῖς, F*x*
Καυστρινοῖς.

STRABO

5. Ταῖς δὲ νῦν Αἰολικαῖς πόλεσιν ἔτι καὶ τὰς Αἰγὰς¹ προσληπτέον καὶ τὴν Τῆμνον, ὅθεν ἦν Ἑρμαγόρας ὁ τὰς ῥητορικὰς τέχνας συγγράψας· ἵδρυνται δ' αἱ πόλεις αὗται κατὰ τὴν ὀρεινὴν τὴν ὑπερκειμένην τῆς τε Κυμαίας καὶ τῆς Φωκαέων καὶ Σμυρναίων γῆς, παρ' ἣν ὁ Ἕρμος ῥεῖ. οὐκ ἄπωθεν δὲ τούτων τῶν πόλεων οὐδ' ἡ Μαγνησία ἐστὶν ἡ ὑπὸ Σιπύλῳ, ἐλευθέρα πόλις ὑπὸ Ῥωμαίων κεκριμένη. καὶ ταύτην δ' ἐκάκωσαν οἱ νεωστὶ γενόμενοι σεισμοί. εἰς δὲ

C 622 τἀναντία τὰ ἐπὶ τὸν Κάϊκον νεύοντα ἀπὸ Λαρίσης μὲν διαβάντι τὸν Ἕρμον εἰς Κύμην ἑβδομήκοντα στάδιοι, ἐντεῦθεν δ' εἰς Μύριναν τετταράκοντα στάδιοι, τὸ δ' ἴσον ἐντεῦθεν εἰς Γρύνιον, κἀκεῖθεν εἰς Ἐλαίαν· ὡς δ' Ἀρτεμίδωρος, ἀπὸ τῆς Κύμης εἰσὶν Ἄδαι, εἶτ' ἄκρα μετὰ τετταράκοντα σταδίους, ἣν καλοῦσιν Ὕδραν, ἡ ποιοῦσα τὸν κόλπον τὸν Ἐλαϊτικὸν πρὸς τὴν ἀπεναντίον ἄκραν Ἁρματοῦντα. τοῦ μὲν οὖν στόματος τὸ πλάτος περὶ ὀγδοήκοντα σταδίους ἐστίν, ἐγκολπίζοντι δὲ Μύρινα ἐν ἑξήκοντα σταδίοις, Αἰολὶς πόλις ἔχουσα λιμένα, εἶτ' Ἀχαιῶν λιμήν, ὅπου οἱ βωμοὶ τῶν δώδεκα θεῶν, εἶτα πολίχνιον Γρύνιον καὶ ἱερὸν Ἀπόλλωνος καὶ μαντεῖον ἀρχαῖον καὶ νεὼς πολυτελὴς λίθου λευκοῦ, στάδιοι δ' ἐπ' αὐτὴν τετταράκοντα· εἶθ' ἑβδομήκοντα εἰς Ἐλαίαν, λιμένα ἔχουσαν καὶ ναύσταθμον τῶν Ἀτταλικῶν βασιλέων, Μενεσθέως κτίσμα καὶ τῶν σὺν αὐτῷ Ἀθηναίων τῶν συστρατευσάντων ἐπὶ Ἴλιον. τὰ δ' ἑξῆς εἴρηται τὰ περὶ Πιτάνην καὶ Ἀταρνέα καὶ τἆλλα τὰ ταύτῃ.

158

5. To the present Aeolian cities we must add
Aegae, and also Temnus, the birthplace of Hermagoras, who wrote *The Art of Rhetoric*. These cities
are situated in the mountainous country that lies
above the territory of Cymê and that of the Phocians
and that of the Smyrnaeans, along which flows the
Hermus. Neither is Magnesia, which is situated
below Mt. Sipylus and has been adjudged a free
city by the Romans, far from these cities. This city
too has been damaged by the recent earthquakes.
To the opposite parts, which incline towards the
Caïcus, from Larisa across the Hermus to Cymê, the
distance is seventy stadia; thence to Myrina, forty
stadia; thence to Grynium, the same; and from
there to Elaea. But, according to Artemidorus, one
goes from Cymê to Adae, and then, forty stadia
distant, to a promontory called Hydra, which with
the opposite promontory Harmatus forms the Elaïtic
Gulf. Now the width of the mouth of this gulf is
about eighty stadia, but, including the sinuosities of
the gulf, Myrina, an Aeolian city with a harbour, is at
a distance of sixty stadia; and then one comes to the
Harbour of the Achaeans, where are the altars of
the twelve gods; and then to a town Grynium and
an altar of Apollo and an ancient oracle and a costly
shrine of white marble, to which the distance is forty
stadia; and then seventy stadia to Elaea, with
harbour and naval station belonging to the Attalic
kings, which was founded by Menestheus and the
Athenians who took the expedition with him to
Ilium. I have already spoken of the places that
come next, those about Pitanê and Atarneus and
the others in that region.

---

[1] Αἰγᾶς Dh.

6. Μεγίστη δέ ἐστι τῶν Αἰολικῶν καὶ ἀρίστη Κύμη καὶ σχεδὸν μητρόπολις αὕτη τε καὶ ἡ Λέσβος τῶν ἄλλων πόλεων, περὶ τριάκοντά που τὸν ἀριθμόν, ὧν ἐκλελοίπασιν οὐκ ὀλίγαι. σκώπτεται δ᾿ εἰς ἀναισθησίαν ἡ Κύμη κατὰ τοιαύτην τινά, ὥς φασιν ἔνιοι, δόξαν, ὅτι τριακοσίοις ἔτεσιν ὕστερον τῆς κτίσεως ἀπέδοντο τοῦ λιμένος τὰ τέλη, πρότερον δ᾿ οὐκ ἐκαρποῦτο τὴν πρόσοδον ταύτην ὁ δῆμος· κατέσχεν οὖν δόξα, ὡς ὀψὲ ᾐσθημένων, ὅτι ἐπὶ θαλάττῃ πόλιν οἰκοῖεν. ἔστι δὲ καὶ ἄλλος λόγος, ὅτι δανεισά- μενοι χρήματα δημοσίᾳ τὰς στοὰς ὑπέθεντο, εἶτ᾿ οὐκ ἀποδιδόντες κατὰ τὴν ὡρισμένην ἡμέραν εἴργοντο τῶν περιπάτων· ὅτε μέντοι ὄμβρος εἴη, κατ᾿ αἰδῶ τινὰ κηρύττοιεν οἱ δανεισταί, κελεύοντες ὑπὸ τὰς στοὰς ὑπέρχεσθαι· τοῦ δὴ κήρυκος οὕτω φθεγγομένου "ὑπὸ τὰς στοὰς ὑπέλθετε," ἐκπεσεῖν λόγον, ὡς Κυμαίων οὐκ αἰσθανομένων, ὡς ἐν τοῖς ὄμβροις ὑπὸ τὰς στοὰς ὑπελθετέον, ἂν μὴ σημάνῃ τις αὐτοῖς διὰ κηρύγματος. ἀνὴρ δ᾿ ἄξιος μνήμης ἐκ τῆσδε τῆς πόλεως ἀναντιλέκτως μέν ἐστιν Ἔφορος, τῶν Ἰσοκράτους γνωρίμων τοῦ ῥήτορος, ὁ τὴν ἱστορίαν συγγράψας καὶ τὰ περὶ τῶν εὑρημάτων· καὶ ἔτι πρότερος τούτου Ἡσίοδος ὁ ποιητής· αὐτὸς γὰρ εἴρηκεν, ὅτι ὁ πατὴρ αὐτοῦ Δῖος μετῴκησεν εἰς Βοιωτούς, Κύμην Αἰολίδα προλιπών·

νάσσατο δ᾿ ἄγχ᾿ Ἑλικῶνος ὀϊζυρῇ ἐνὶ κώμῃ
Ἄσκρῃ, χεῖμα κακῇ, θέρει ἀργαλέῃ, οὐδέ ποτ᾿
ἐσθλῇ.

C 623 Ὅμηρος δ᾿ οὐχ ὁμολογουμένως· πολλοὶ γὰρ

6. The largest and best of the Aeolian cities is Cymê; and this with Lesbos might be called the metropolis of the rest of the cities, about thirty in number, of which not a few have disappeared. Cymê is ridiculed for its stupidity, owing to the repute, as some say, that not until three hundred years after the founding of the city did they sell the tolls of the harbour, and that before this time the people did not reap this revenue. They got the reputation, therefore, of being a people who learned late that they were living in a city by the sea. There is also another report of them, that, having borrowed money in the name of the state, they pledged their porticoes as security, and then, failing to pay the money on the appointed day, were prohibited from walking in them; when it rained, however, their creditors, through a kind of shame, would bid them through a herald to go under the porticoes; so the herald would cry out the words, "Go under the porticoes," but the report went abroad that the Cymaeans did not understand that they were to go under the porticoes when it rained unless they were given notice by the herald. Ephorus, a man indisputably noteworthy, a disciple of Isocrates the orator, and the author of the *History* and of the work on *Inventions*, was from this city; and so was Hesiod the poet, still earlier than Ephorus, for Hesiod himself states that his father Dius left Aeolian Cymê and migrated to Boeotia: "And he settled near Helicon in a wretched village, Ascrê, which is bad in winter, oppressive in summer, and pleasant at no time."[1] But it is not agreed that Homer was from Cymê, for

---

[1] *Works and Days*, 639-40 (quoted also in 9. 2. 25).

ἀμφισβητοῦσιν αὐτοῦ. τὸ δ' ὄνομα ἀπὸ Ἀμα-
ζόνος τῇ πόλει τεθεῖσθαι, καθάπερ καὶ τῇ
Μυρίνῃ ἀπὸ τῆς ἐν τῷ Τρωικῷ πεδίῳ κειμένης
ὑπὸ τῇ Βατιείᾳ·

τὴν ἤτοι ἄνδρες Βατίειαν κικλήσκουσιν,
ἀθάνατοι δέ τε σῆμα πολυσκάρθμοιο Μυρίνης.

σκώπτεται δὲ καὶ ὁ Ἔφορος, διότι τῆς πατρίδος
ἔργα οὐκ ἔχων φράζειν ἐν τῇ διαριθμήσει τῶν
ἄλλων πράξεων, οὐ μὴν οὐδ'[1] ἀμνημόνευτον αὐτὴν
εἶναι θέλων, οὕτως ἐπιφωνεῖ· "Κατὰ δὲ τὸν
αὐτὸν καιρὸν Κυμαῖοι τὰς ἡσυχίας ἦγον." ἐπεὶ
δὲ διεληλύθαμεν τὴν Τρωικὴν ἅμα καὶ τὴν
Αἰολικὴν παραλίαν, ἐφεξῆς ἂν εἴη τὴν μεσόγαιαν
ἐπιδραμεῖν μέχρι τοῦ Ταύρου, φυλάσσοντας τὴν
αὐτὴν τῆς ἐφόδου τάξιν.

IV

1. Ἔχει δέ τινα ἡγεμονίαν πρὸς τοὺς τόπους
τούτους τὸ Πέργαμον, ἐπιφανὴς πόλις καὶ πολὺν
συνευτυχήσασα χρόνον τοῖς Ἀτταλικοῖς βασι-
λεῦσι· καὶ δὴ καὶ ἐντεῦθεν ἀρκτέον τῆς ἑξῆς
περιοδείας, καὶ πρῶτον περὶ τῶν βασιλέων,
ὁπόθεν ὡρμήθησαν καὶ εἰς ἃ κατέστρεψαν, ἐν
βραχέσι δηλωτέον. ἦν μὲν δὴ τὸ Πέργαμον
Λυσιμάχου γαζοφυλάκιον τοῦ Ἀγαθοκλέους, ἑνὸς
τῶν Ἀλεξάνδρου διαδόχων, αὐτὴν τὴν ἄκραν τοῦ
ὄρους συνοικουμένην ἔχον· ἔστι δὲ στροβιλοειδὲς
τὸ ὄρος εἰς ὀξεῖαν κορυφὴν ἀπολῆγον. ἐπεπίσ-
τευτο δὲ τὴν φυλακὴν τοῦ ἐρύματος τούτου καὶ
τῶν χρημάτων (ἦν δὲ τάλαντα ἐννακισχίλια)

many peoples lay claim to him. It is agreed, however, that the name of the city was derived from an
Amazon, as was Myrina from the Amazon who lies
in the Trojan plain below Batieia, "which verily
men call Batieia, but the immortals the tomb of
much-bounding Myrina."[1] Ephorus, too, is ridiculed
because, though unable to tell of deeds of his native
land in his enumeration of the other achievements in
history, and yet unwilling that it should be unmen-
tioned, he exclaims as follows: "At about the same
time the Cymaeans were at peace."

Since I have traversed at the same time the Trojan
and Aeolian coasts, it would be next in order to treat
cursorily the interior as far as the Taurus, observing
the same order of approach.

IV

1. A kind of hegemony is held over these places
by Pergamum, which is a famous city and for a long
time prospered along with the Attalic kings; indeed
I must begin my next description here, and first I
must show briefly the origin of the kings and the
end to which they came. Now Pergamum was a
treasure-hold of Lysimachus, the son of Agathocles,
who was one of the successors of Alexander, and its
people are settled on the very summit of the
mountain; the mountain is cone-like and ends in a
sharp peak. The custody of this stronghold and the
treasure, which amounted to nine thousand talents,

---

[1] Also quoted in 12. 8. 6.

---

[1] All MSS. except Fi insert ἂν after οὐδ'.

Φιλέταιρος, ἀνὴρ Τιανός,[1] θλιβίας ἐκ παιδός.
συνέβη γὰρ ἔν τινι ταφῇ θέας οὔσης καὶ πολλῶν
παρόντων, ἀποληφθεῖσαν ἐν τῷ ὄχλῳ τὴν κομί-
ζουσαν τροφὸν τὸν Φιλέταιρον ἔτι νήπιον συν-
θλιβῆναι μέχρι τοσοῦδε, ὥστε πηρωθῆναι τὸν
παῖδα. ἦν μὲν δὴ εὐνοῦχος, τραφεὶς δὲ καλῶς
ἐφάνη τῆς πίστεως ταύτης ἄξιος. τέως μὲν οὖν
εὔνους διέμεινε[2] τῷ Λυσιμάχῳ, διενεχθεὶς δὲ
πρὸς Ἀρσινόην τὴν γυναῖκα αὐτοῦ διαβάλλου-
σαν αὐτὸν ἀπέστησε τὸ χωρίον καὶ πρὸς τοὺς
καιροὺς ἐπολιτεύετο, ὁρῶν ἐπιτηδείους πρὸς νεω-
τερισμόν· ὅ τε γὰρ Λυσίμαχος κακοῖς οἰκείοις
περιπεσὼν ἠναγκάσθη τὸν υἱὸν ἀνελεῖν Ἀγα-
θοκλέα, Σέλευκός τε ἐπελθὼν[3] ὁ Νικάτωρ ἐκεῖνόν
τε κατέλυσε καὶ αὐτὸς κατελύθη, δολοφονηθεὶς
ὑπὸ Πτολεμαίου τοῦ Κεραυνοῦ. τοιούτων δὲ
θορύβων ὄντων, διεγένετο μένων ἐπὶ τοῦ ἐρύματος
ὁ εὐνοῦχος καὶ πολιτευόμενος δι᾽[4] ὑποσχέσεων
καὶ τῆς ἄλλης θεραπείας ἀεὶ πρὸς τὸν ἰσχύοντα
καὶ ἐγγὺς παρόντα· διετέλεσε γοῦν ἔτη εἴκοσι
κύριος ὢν τοῦ φρουρίου καὶ τῶν χρημάτων.

C 624   2. Ἦσαν δ᾽ αὐτῷ δύο ἀδελφοί, πρεσβύτερος
μὲν Εὐμένης, νεώτερος δ᾽ Ἄτταλος· ἐκ μὲν οὖν
τοῦ Εὐμένους ἐγένετο ὁμώνυμος τῷ πατρὶ Εὐμένης,
ὅσπερ καὶ διεδέξατο τὸ Πέργαμον, καὶ ἦν ἤδη
δυνάστης τῶν κύκλῳ χωρίων, ὥστε καὶ περὶ
Σάρδεις ἐνίκησε μάχῃ συμβαλὼν Ἀντίοχον
τὸν Σελεύκου· δύο δὲ καὶ εἴκοσιν ἄρξας ἔτη
τελευτᾷ τὸν βίον. ἐκ δὲ Ἀττάλου καὶ Ἀν-

---

[1] Τιαννός C, Τυανός x, Τυανεύς moz.
[2] Instead of διέμεινε, CDxz and Corais read διέμενε.
[3] ἐπανελθών moz, instead of ἐπελθών.

was entrusted to Philetaerus of Tieium, who was a eunuch from boyhood; for it came to pass at a certain burial, when a spectacle was being given at which many people were present, that the nurse who was carrying Philetaerus, still an infant, was caught in the crowd and pressed so hard that the child was incapacitated. He was a eunuch, therefore, but he was well trained and proved worthy of this trust. Now for a time he continued loyal to Lysimachus, but he had differences with Arsinoê, the wife of Lysimachus, who slandered him, and so he caused Pergamum to revolt, and governed it to suit the occasion, since he saw that it was ripe for a change; for Lysimachus, beset with domestic troubles, was forced to slay his son Agathocles, and Seleucus Nicator invaded his country and overthrew him, and then he himself was overthrown and treacherously murdered by Ptolemy Ceraunus. During these disorders the eunuch continued to be in charge of the fortress and to manage things through promises and courtesies in general, always catering to any man who was powerful or near at hand. At any rate, he continued lord of the stronghold and the treasure for twenty years.

2. He had two brothers, the elder of whom was Eumenes, the younger Attalus. Eumenes had a son of the same name, who succeeded to the rule of Pergamum, and was by this time sovereign of the places round about, so that he even joined battle with Antiochus the son of Seleucus near Sardeis and conquered him. He died after a reign of twenty-two years.[1] Attalus, the son of Attalus and Antiochis,

---

[1] 263–241 b.c.

---

⁴ μεθ' *moz*, instead of δι'.

τιοχίδος, τῆς Ἀχαιοῦ, γεγονὼς Ἄτταλος διεδέξατο τὴν ἀρχήν, καὶ ἀνηγορεύθη βασιλεὺς πρῶτος, νικήσας Γαλάτας μάχῃ μεγάλῃ. οὗτος δὲ καὶ Ῥωμαίοις κατέστη φίλος καὶ συνεπολέμησε πρὸς Φίλιππον μετὰ τοῦ Ῥοδίων ναυτικοῦ· γηραιὸς δὲ ἐτελεύτα,¹ βασιλεύσας ἔτη τρία καὶ τεττα-ράκοντα, κατέλιπε δὲ τέτταρας υἱοὺς ἐξ Ἀπολ-λωνίδος Κυζικηνῆς γυναικός, Εὐμένη, Ἄτταλον, Φιλέταιρον, Ἀθήναιον. οἱ μὲν οὖν νεώτεροι διε-τέλεσαν ἰδιῶται, τῶν δ’ ἄλλων ὁ πρεσβύτερος Εὐμένης ἐβασίλευσε· συνεπολέμησε δὲ οὗτος Ῥωμαίοις πρός τε Ἀντίοχον τὸν μέγαν καὶ πρὸς Περσέα, καὶ ἔλαβε παρὰ τῶν Ῥωμαίων ἅπασαν τὴν ὑπ’ Ἀντιόχῳ τὴν ἐντὸς τοῦ Ταύρου. πρό-τερον δ’ ἦν τὰ περὶ Πέργαμον οὐ πολλὰ χωρία μέχρι τῆς θαλάττης τῆς κατὰ τὸν Ἐλαΐτην κόλπον καὶ τὸν Ἀδραμυττηνόν. κατεσκεύασε δ’ οὗτος τὴν πόλιν καὶ τὸ Νικηφόριον ἄλσει κατεφύτευσε, καὶ ἀναθήματα καὶ βιβλιοθήκας καὶ τὴν ἐπὶ τοσόνδε κατοικίαν τοῦ Περγάμου τὴν νῦν οὖσαν ἐκεῖνος προσεφιλοκάλησε· βασι-λεύσας δὲ² ἔτη τετταράκοντα καὶ ἐννέα ἀπέλιπεν υἱῷ τὴν ἀρχὴν Ἀττάλῳ, γεγονότι ἐκ Στρατονίκης τῆς Ἀριαράθου θυγατρὸς τοῦ Καππαδόκων βασιλέως. ἐπίτροπον δὲ κατέστησε καὶ τοῦ παιδὸς νέου τελέως ὄντος καὶ τῆς ἀρχῆς τὸν ἀδελφὸν Ἄτταλον. ἐν δὲ καὶ εἴκοσιν ἔτη βασι-λεύσας γέρων οὗτος τελευτᾷ, κατορθώσας πολλά·

¹ ἐτελεύτησε moz, instead of ἐτελεύτα.
² δέ, before ἔτη, inserted by x; moz have τε.

¹ 241–197 B.C.

daughter of Achaeus, succeeded to the throne and was the first to be proclaimed king, after conquering the Galatians in a great battle. Attalus not only became a friend of the Romans but also fought on their side against Philip along with the fleet of the Rhodians. He died in old age, having reigned as king forty-three years;[1] and he left four sons by Apollonis, a woman from Cyzicus, Eumenes, Attalus, Philetaerus, and Athenaeus. Now the two younger sons remained private citizens, but Eumenes, the elder of the other two, reigned as king. Eumenes fought on the side of the Romans against Antiochus the Great and against Perseus, and he received from the Romans all the country this side the Taurus that had been subject to Antiochus. But before that time the territory of Pergamum did not include many places that extended as far as the sea at the Elaïtic and Adramyttene Gulfs. He built up the city and planted Nicephorium with a grove, and the other elder brother,[2] from love of splendour, added sacred buildings and libraries and raised the settlement of Pergamum to what it now is. After a reign of forty-nine years[3] Eumenes left his empire to Attalus, his son by Stratonicê, the daughter of Ariathres, king of the Cappadocians. He appointed his brother Attalus[4] as guardian both of his son, who was extremely young, and of the empire. After a reign of twenty-one years,[5] his brother died an old man, having won success in many undertakings; for

[2] Others make ἐκεῖνος refer to Eumenes, but the present translator must make it refer to Attalus, unless the text is corrupt.

[3] But he died in 159 B.C. (see Pauly-Wissowa, s.v. "Eumenes," p. 1103), thus having reigned 197–159 B.C.

[4] Attalus Philadelphus.   [5] 159–138 B.C.

καὶ γὰρ Δημήτριον τὸν Σελεύκου συγκατεπολέ-
μησεν Ἀλεξάνδρῳ τῷ Ἀντιόχου καὶ συνεμάχησε
Ῥωμαίοις ἐπὶ τὸν Ψευδοφίλιππον, ἐχειρώσατο
δὲ καὶ Διήγυλιν τὸν Καινῶν¹ βασιλέα στρα-
τεύσας εἰς τὴν Θρᾴκην, ἀνεῖλε δὲ καὶ Προυσίαν,
ἐπισυστήσας αὐτῷ Νικομήδη τὸν υἱόν, κατέλιπε
δὲ² τὴν ἀρχὴν τῷ ἐπιτροπευθέντι Ἀττάλῳ·
βασιλεύσας δὲ οὗτος ἔτη πέντε καὶ κληθεὶς
Φιλομήτωρ ἐτελεύτα νόσῳ τὸν βίον, κατέλιπε
δὲ κληρονόμους Ῥωμαίους· οἱ δ' ἐπαρχίαν ἀπέ-
δειξαν τὴν χώραν, Ἀσίαν προσαγορεύσαντες,
ὁμώνυμον τῇ ἠπείρῳ. παραρρεῖ δ' ὁ Κάϊκος τὸ
Πέργαμον, διὰ τοῦ Καΐκου πεδίου προσαγορευο-
μένου σφόδρα εὐδαίμονα γῆν διεξιών, σχεδὸν δέ
τι καὶ τὴν ἀρίστην τῆς Μυσίας.

C 625   3. Ἄνδρες δ' ἐγένοντο ἐλλόγιμοι καθ' ἡμᾶς
Περγαμηνοί, Μιθριδάτης τε Μηνοδότου υἱὸς καὶ
Ἀδοβογίωνος, ὃς³ τοῦ τετραρχικοῦ τῶν Γαλατῶν
γένους ἦν, ἣν⁴ καὶ⁵ παλλακεῦσαι τῷ βασιλεῖ
Μιθριδάτῃ φασίν· ὅθεν καὶ τοὔνομα τῷ παιδὶ
θέσθαι τοὺς ἐπιτηδείους, προσποιησμένους ἐκ
τοῦ βασιλέως αὐτὸν γεγονέναι. οὗτος γοῦν
Καίσαρι τῷ Θεῷ γενόμενος φίλος εἰς τοσόνδε
προῆλθε τιμῆς, ὥστε καὶ τετράρχης ἀπεδείχθη
ἀπὸ⁶ τοῦ μητρῴου γένους καὶ βασιλεὺς ἄλλων
τε καὶ τοῦ Βοσπόρου· κατελύθη δ' ὑπὸ Ἀσάν-
δρου⁷ τοῦ καὶ Φαρνάκην ἀνελόντος τὸν βασιλέα
καὶ κατασχόντος τὸν Βόσπορον. οὗτός τε δὴ

---

¹ Καινῶν, Tzschucke, for ἐκείνων CDhimoriwxz, ἐκεῖνον F,
καινόν Epit.; so the later editors.
² The MSS., except Fz, have καί after δέ.
³ Ἀδοβογίωνος, ὅς, the editors, for Ἀδοβογίων, ὅς.

example, he helped Alexander, the son of Antiochus,
to defeat in war Demetrius, the son of Seleucus,
and he fought on the side of the Romans against
the Pseudo-Philip, and in an expedition against
Thrace he defeated Diegylis the king of the Caeni,
and he slew Prusias, having incited his son Nicomedes
against him, and he left his empire, under a guardian,
to Attalus. Attalus, surnamed Philometor, reigned
five years,[1] died of disease, and left the Romans his
heirs. The Romans proclaimed the country a
province, calling it Asia, by the same name as the
continent. The Caïcus flows past Pergamum, through
the Caïcus Plain, as it is called, traversing land that
is very fertile and about the best in Mysia.

3. Pergamenians have become famous in my time:
Mithridates the son of Menodotus and of Adobogion.
Menodotus was of the family of the tetrarchs of the
Galatians, and Adobogion, it is said, was also the
concubine of King Mithridates,[2] and for this reason
her relatives gave to the child the name of
Mithridates, pretending that he was the son of the
king. At any rate, he became a friend to the deified
Caesar and reached so great preferment with him
that he was appointed tetrarch from his mother's
family and king both of the Bosporus and other
territories. He was overthrown by Asander, who
not only slew King Pharnaces but also took possession of the Bosporus. Mithridates, then, has been

---

[1] 138-133 B.C.   [2] Mithridates the Great.

---

[4] ἤν, inserted by the editors.
[5] ὅν, before παλλακεῦσαι, ejected by the editors.
[6] ἀπό, Casaubon inserts ; so the later editors.
[7] Ἀσάνδρου, Casaubon, for Λυσάνδρου ; so the later editors.

169

ὀνόματος ἠξίωται μεγάλου, καὶ Ἀπολλόδωρος ὁ
ῥήτωρ ὁ τὰς τέχνας συγγράψας καὶ τὴν Ἀπολ-
λοδώρειον αἵρεσιν παραγαγών, ἥτις ποτ' ἐστί·
πολλὰ γὰρ ἐπεκράτει, μείζονα δὲ ἢ καθ' ἡμᾶς
ἔχοντα τὴν κρίσιν, ὧν ἐστι καὶ ἡ Ἀπολλοδώρειος
αἵρεσις καὶ ἡ Θεοδώρειος. μάλιστα δὲ ἐξῆρε
τὸν Ἀπολλόδωρον ἡ τοῦ Καίσαρος φιλία τοῦ
Σεβαστοῦ, διδάσκαλον τῶν λόγων γενόμενον·
μαθητὴν δ' ἔσχεν ἀξιόλογον Διονύσιον τὸν
ἐπικληθέντα Ἀττικόν, πολίτην αὐτοῦ, καὶ γὰρ
σοφιστὴς ἦν ἱκανὸς καὶ συγγραφεὺς καὶ
λογογράφος.

4. Προϊόντι δ' ἀπὸ τοῦ πεδίου καὶ τῆς πόλεως
ἐπὶ μὲν τὰ πρὸς ἕω μέρη πόλις ἐστὶν Ἀπολλωνία,
μετεώροις ἐπικειμένη τόποις· ἐπὶ δὲ τὸν νότον
ὀρεινὴ ῥάχις ἐστίν, ἣν ὑπερβᾶσι καὶ βαδίζουσιν
ἐπὶ Σάρδεων πόλις ἐστὶν ἐν ἀριστερᾷ Θυάτειρα,
κατοικία Μακεδόνων, ἣν Μυσῶν ἐσχάτην τινές
φασιν. ἐν δεξιᾷ δ' Ἀπολλωνίς, διέχουσα Περγάμου τριακοσίους σταδίους, τοὺς δὲ ἴσους καὶ τῶν
Σάρδεων, ἐπώνυμος δ' ἐστὶ τῆς Κυζικηνῆς Ἀπολ-
λωνίδος· εἶτ' ἐκδέχεται τὸ Ἕρμου πεδίον καὶ
Σάρδεις· τὰ δὲ προσάρκτια τῷ Περγάμῳ τὰ
πλεῖστα ὑπὸ Μυσῶν ἔχεται τὰ ἐν δεξιᾷ τῶν
Ἀβαειτῶν[1] λεγομένων, οἷς συνάπτει ἡ Ἐπί-
κτητος μέχρι Βιθυνίας.

5. Αἱ δὲ Σάρδεις πόλις ἐστὶ μεγάλη, νεωτέρα
μὲν τῶν Τρωικῶν, ἀρχαία δ' ὅμως, ἄκραν ἔχουσα
εὐερκῆ· βασίλειον δ' ὑπῆρξε τῶν Λυδῶν, οὓς ὁ

---

[1] Ἀβαειτῶν, Kramer, from conj. of Kiepert, for Ἀβλιτῶν E,
Ἀβλίτων other MSS.

thought worthy of a great name, as has also
Apollodorus the rhetorician, who wrote the work
on *Rhetoric* and was the leader of the Apollodoreian
sect, whatever in the world it is; for numerous
philosophies were prevalent, but to pass judgment
upon them is beyond my power, and among these
are the sects of Apollodorus and Theodorus. But
the friendship of Caesar Augustus has most of all
exalted Apollodorus, who was his teacher in the art
of speech. And Apollodorus had a notable pupil in
Dionysius, surnamed Atticus, his fellow-citizen, for he
was an able sophist and historian and speech-writer.

4. As one proceeds from the plain and the city
towards the east, one comes to a city called
Apollonia, which lies on an elevated site, and also,
towards the south, to a mountain range, on crossing
which, on the road to Sardeis, one comes to
Thyateira, on the left-hand side, a settlement of
the Macedonians, which by some is called the
farthermost city of the Mysians. On the right is
Apollonis, which is three hundred stadia distant
from Pergamum, and the same distance from Sardeis, and it is named after the Cyzicene Apollonis.
Next one comes to the plain of Hermus and to
Sardeis. The country to the north of Pergamum is
held for the most part by the Mysians, I mean the
country on the right of the Abaeïtae, as they are
called, on the borders of which is the Epictetus [1] as
far as Bithynia.

5. Sardeis is a great city, and, though of later
date than the Trojan times, is nevertheless old, and
has a strong citadel. It was the royal city of the
Lydians, whom the poet calls Meïonians; and later

[1] Phrygia Epictetus (see 12. 3. 7, 12. 4. 1, and 12. 4. 5).

ποιητὴς καλεῖ Μήονας, οἱ δ᾽ ὕστερον Μαίονας,
οἱ μὲν τοὺς αὐτοὺς τοῖς Λυδοῖς, οἱ δ᾽ ἑτέρους
ἀποφαίνοντες, τοὺς δ᾽ αὐτοὺς ἄμεινόν ἐστι λέγειν.
ὑπέρκειται δὲ τῶν Σάρδεων ὁ Τμῶλος, εὔδαιμον
ὄρος, ἐν τῇ ἀκρωρείᾳ σκοπὴν ἔχον, ἐξέδραν
λευκοῦ λίθου, Περσῶν ἔργον, ἀφ᾽ οὗ κατοπτεύεται
τὰ κύκλῳ πεδία, καὶ μάλιστα τὸ Καϋστριανόν·
περιοικοῦσι δὲ Λυδοὶ καὶ Μυσοὶ καὶ Μακεδόνες.
ῥεῖ δ᾽ ὁ Πακτωλὸς ἀπὸ τοῦ Τμώλου, καταφέρων
τὸ παλαιὸν ψῆγμα χρυσοῦ πολύ, ἀφ᾽ οὗ τὸν
C 626 Κροίσου λεγόμενον πλοῦτον καὶ τῶν προγόνων
αὐτοῦ διονομασθῆναί φασι· νῦν δ᾽ ἐκλέλοιπε
τὸ ψῆγμα. καταφέρεται δ᾽ ὁ Πακτωλὸς εἰς
τὸν Ἕρμον, εἰς ὃν καὶ ὁ Ὕλλος ἐμβάλλει,
Φρύγιος νυνὶ καλούμενος· συμπεσόντες δ᾽ οἱ
τρεῖς καὶ ἄλλοι ἀσημότεροι σὺν αὐτοῖς εἰς
τὴν κατὰ Φωκαίαν ἐκδιδόασι θάλατταν, ὡς
Ἡρόδοτός φησιν. ἄρχεται δ᾽ ἐκ Μυσίας ὁ
Ἕρμος, ἐξ ὄρους ἱεροῦ τῆς Δινδυμήνης, καὶ διὰ
τῆς Κατακεκαυμένης εἰς τὴν Σαρδιανὴν φέρεται καὶ τὰ[1] συνεχῆ πεδία, ὡς εἴρηται, μέχρι
τῆς θαλάττης. ὑπόκειται δὲ τῇ πόλει τό τε
Σαρδιανὸν πεδίον καὶ τὸ τοῦ Κύρου[2] καὶ τὸ τοῦ
Ἕρμου καὶ τὸ Καϋστριανόν, συνεχῆ τε ὄντα
καὶ πάντων ἄριστα πεδίων. ἐν δὲ σταδίοις
τετταράκοντα ἀπὸ τῆς πόλεώς ἐστιν ἡ Γυγαία
μὲν ὑπὸ τοῦ ποιητοῦ λεγομένη, Κολόη δ᾽ ὕστερον
μετονομασθεῖσα, ὅπου τὸ ἱερὸν τῆς Κολοηνῆς
Ἀρτέμιδος, μεγάλην ἁγιστείαν ἔχον. φασὶ δ᾽

[1] καὶ τά Eix, κατά CFw, κατὰ τά Dhmoz.
[2] Κύρου (see Κύρου πεδίον, 13. 4. 13), Tzschucke, for κόρου;
Καῖκου, Corais.

writers call them Maeonians, some identifying them
with the Lydians and others representing them as
different, but it is better to call them the same
people. Above Sardeis is situated Mt. Tmolus, a
blest mountain, with a look-out on its summit, an
arcade of white marble, a work of the Persians,
whence there is a view of the plains below all round,
particularly the Caÿster Plain. And round it dwell
Lydians and Mysians and Macedonians. The Pactolus River flows from Mt. Tmolus; in early times a
large quantity of gold-dust was brought down in
it, whence, it is said, arose the fame of the riches of
Croesus and his forefathers. But the gold-dust
has given out. The Pactolus runs down into the
Hermus, into which also the Hyllus, now called
the Phrygius, empties. These three, and other less
significant rivers with them, meet and empty into
the sea near Phocaea, as Herodotus says.[1] The
Hermus rises in Mysia, in the sacred mountain
Dindymenê, and flows through the Catacecaumene
country into the territory of Sardeis and the contiguous plains, as I have already said,[2] to the sea.
Below the city lie the plain of Sardeis and that
of the Cyrus and that of the Hermus and that
of the Caÿster, which are contiguous to one another
and are the best of all plains. Within forty stadia
from the city one comes to Gygaea,[3] which is
mentioned by the poet, the name of which was
later changed to Coloê, where is the temple of
Coloënian Artemis, which is characterised by great
holiness. They say that at the festivals here the

[1] 1. 80.   [2] Cf. 13. 1. 2.
[3] *Lake* Gygaea, *Iliad* 2. 865.

ἐνταῦθα χορεύειν τοὺς καλάθους[1] κατὰ τὰς
ἑορτάς, οὐκ οἶδ᾽ ὅπως ποτὲ παραδοξολογοῦντες
μᾶλλον ἢ ἀληθεύοντες.

6. Κειμένων δ᾽ οὕτω πως τῶν ἐπῶν παρ᾽
Ὁμήρῳ·

Μῄοσιν αὖ Μέσθλης τε καὶ Ἄντιφος ἡγησάσθην,
υἷε Ταλαιμένεος,[2] τὼ Γυγαίη τέκε λίμνη,
οἳ καὶ Μῄονας ἦγον ὑπὸ Τμώλῳ γεγαῶτας,
προσγράφουσί τινες τοῦτο τέταρτον ἔπος·

Τμώλῳ ὑπὸ νιφόεντι, Ὕδης[3] ἐν πίονι δήμῳ.

οὐδεμία δ᾽ εὑρίσκεται Ὕδη ἐν τοῖς Λυδοῖς. οἱ δὲ
καὶ τὸν Τυχίον ἐνθένδε ποιοῦσιν, ὅν φησιν ὁ
ποιητής·

σκυτοτόμων ὄχ᾽ ἄριστος Ὕδη[4] ἔνι,

προστιθέασι δὲ καί, διότι δρυμώδης ὁ τόπος καὶ
κεραυνόβολος, καὶ ὅτι ἐνταῦθα οἱ Ἄριμοι· καὶ
γὰρ τῷ[5]

εἰν Ἀρίμοις, ὅθι φασὶ Τυφωέος ἔμμεναι εὐνάς

ἐπεισφέρουσι

χώρῳ ἐνὶ δρυόεντι, Ὕδης ἐν πίονι δήμῳ.

ἄλλοι δ᾽ ἐν Κιλικίᾳ, τινὲς δ᾽ ἐν Συρίᾳ πλάττουσι
τὸν μῦθον τοῦτον, οἱ δ᾽ ἐν Πιθηκούσσαις, οἳ καὶ
τοὺς πιθήκους φασὶ παρὰ τοῖς Τυρρηνοῖς ἀρίμους
καλεῖσθαι· οἱ δὲ τὰς Σάρδεις Ὕδην ὀνομάζουσιν,
οἱ δὲ τὴν ἀκρόπολιν αὐτῆς. πιθανωτάτους δ᾽ ὁ

---

[1] Instead of καλάθους, *rw* read καθόλου; *mz*, Ald., and
Casaubon πιθήκους; Lobeck conj. πιθάκνας and certain others
καλάμους.

baskets dance,[1] though I do not know why in the world they talk marvels rather than tell the truth.

6. The verses of Homer are about as follows: "Mnesthles and Antiphus, the two sons of Talaemenes, whose mother was Lake Gygaea, who led also the Meïonians, who were born at the foot of Tmolus";[2] but some add the following fourth verse: "At the foot of snowy Tmolus, in the fertile land of Hydê." But there is no Hydê to be found in the country of the Lydians. Some also put Tychius there, of whom the poet says, "far the best of workers in hide, who lived in Hydê."[3] And they add that the place is woody and subject to strokes of lightning, and that the Arimi live there, for after Homer's verse, "in the land of the Arimi where men say is the couch of Typhon,"[4] they insert the words, "in a wooded place, in the fertile land of Hydê." But others lay the scene of this myth in Cilicia, and some lay it in Syria, and still others in the Pithecussae Islands, who say that among the Tyrrhenians "pitheci"[5] are called "arimi." Some call Sardeis Hydê, while others call its acropolis Hydê. But

---

[1] Thought to be the baskets carried on the heads of maidens at festivals.

[2] *Iliad* 2. 864.

[3] *Iliad* 7. 221.

[4] *Iliad* 2. 783.

[5] *i.e.* monkeys.

---

[2] Ταλαιμένεος, Corais, for Παλαιμένεος D*hriw*, Πυλαιμένεος CEF*xz*.

[3] Ὕδης E*moz*, Ὕλης CDF*hirwx*. Thus the MSS. vary in the following Ὕδη.

[4] Instead of Ὕδη, *h*(by corr.)*orx* read Ὕλη.

[5] τῷ E (so Meineke); οὕτως other MSS.

Σκήψιος ἡγεῖται τοὺς ἐν τῇ Κατακεκαυμένῃ τῆς Μυσίας τοὺς Ἀρίμους τιθέντας. Πίνδαρος δὲ συνοικειοῖ τοῖς ἐν τῇ Κιλικίᾳ τὰ ἐν Πιθηκούσσαις, ἅπερ ἐστὶ πρὸ τῆς Κυμαίας, καὶ τὰ ἐν Σικελίᾳ· καὶ γὰρ τῇ Αἴτνῃ φησὶν ὑποκεῖσθαι τὸν Τυφῶνα·

τόν ποτε
Κιλίκιον θρέψεν πολυώνυμον ἄντρον· νῦν γε μὰν

C 627 ταί θ᾽ [1] ὑπὲρ Κύμας ἁλιερκέες ὄχθαι
Σικελία τ᾽ αὐτοῦ πιέζει στέρνα λαχνάεντα.[2]

καὶ πάλιν·

κείνῳ μὲν Αἴτνα δεσμὸς ὑπερφίαλος ἀμφίκειται.

καὶ πάλιν·

ἀλλ᾽ οἶος ἄπλατον κεράϊζε θεῶν
Τυφῶνα πεντηκοντακέφαλον [3] ἀνάγκᾳ Ζεὺς πατὴρ
ἐν Ἀρίμοις ποτέ.

οἱ δὲ τοὺς Σύρους Ἀρίμους [4] δέχονται, οὓς νῦν Ἀραμαίους λέγουσι, τοὺς δὲ Κίλικας τοὺς ἐν Τροίᾳ μεταναστάντας εἰς Συρίαν ἀνῳκισμένους, ἀποτεμέσθαι παρὰ τῶν Σύρων τὴν νῦν λεγομένην Κιλικίαν. Καλλισθένης δ᾽ ἐγγὺς τοῦ Καλυκάδνου καὶ τῆς Σαρπηδόνος ἄκρας παρ᾽ αὐτὸ τὸ Κωρύκιον ἄντρον εἶναι τοὺς Ἀρίμους, ἀφ᾽ ὧν τὰ ἐγγὺς ὄρη λέγεσθαι Ἄριμα.

7. Περίκειται δὲ τῇ λίμνῃ τῇ Κολόῃ τὰ μνήματα τῶν βασιλέων. πρὸς δὲ ταῖς Σάρδεσίν ἐστι τὸ τοῦ Ἀλυάττου ἐπὶ κρηπῖδος ὑψηλῆς

the Scepsian [1] thinks that those writers are most plausible who place the Arimi in the Catacecaumene country in Mysia. But Pindar associates the Pithecussae which lie off the Cymaean territory, as also the territory in Sicily, with the territory in Cilicia, for he says that Typhon lies beneath Aetna : " Once he dwelt in a far-famed Cilician cavern ; now, however, his shaggy breast is o'er-pressed by the sea-girt shores above Cymae and by Sicily." [2] And again, "round about him lies Aetna with her haughty fetters," and again, " but it was father Zeus that once amongst the Arimi, by necessity, alone of the gods, smote monstrous Typhon of the fifty heads." [3] But some understand that the Syrians are Arimi, who are now called the Arimaeans, and that the Cilicians in Troy, forced to migrate, settled again in Syria and cut off for themselves from Syria what is now called Cilicia. Callisthenes says that the Arimi, after whom the neighbouring mountains are called Arima, are situated near Mt. Calycadnus and the promontory of Sarpedon near the Corycian cave itself.

7. Near Lake Coloê are the monuments of the kings. At Sardeis is the great mound, on a lofty base, of Alyattes, built, as Herodotus [4] says, by the

---

[1] Demetrius of Scepsis.
[3] *Frag.* 93 (Bergk).

[2] *Pythian Odes*, 1. 31.
[4] 1. 93.

---

[1] Instead of μὰν ταί θ', CDF*h* have μαντευθ'.

[2] λαχνάεντα, the editors, for λαχνήεντα.

[3] For πεντηκοντακέφαλον, Bergk, following Hermann and Boeckh, reads ἑκατοντακάρανον (see Pindar, *Pyth.* 8. 16 and *Ol.* 4. 7). Meineke emends to πεντηκοντακάρανον.

[4] Ἀρίμους, Casaubon, for Ἀράμους.

STRABO

χῶμα μέγα, ἐργασθέν, ὥς φησιν Ἡρόδοτος, ὑπὸ τοῦ πλήθους τῆς πόλεως, οὗ τὸ πλεῖστον ἔργον αἱ παιδίσκαι συνετέλεσαν· λέγει δ' ἐκεῖνος καὶ πορνεύεσθαι πάσας, τινὲς δὲ καὶ πόρνης μνῆμα λέγουσι τὸν τάφον. χειροποίητον δὲ τὴν λίμνην ἔνιοι ἱστοροῦσι τὴν Κολόην πρὸς τὰς ἐκδοχὰς τῶν πλημμυρίδων, αἳ συμβαίνουσι τῶν ποταμῶν πληρουμένων. Ὕπαιπα δὲ πόλις ἐστὶ καταβαίνουσιν ἀπὸ τοῦ Τμώλου πρὸς τὸ τοῦ Καΰστρου πεδίον.

8. Φησὶ δὲ Καλλισθένης ἁλῶναι τὰς Σάρδεις ὑπὸ Κιμμερίων πρῶτον, εἶθ' ὑπὸ Τρηρῶν καὶ Λυκίων, ὅπερ καὶ Καλλῖνον δηλοῦν, τὸν τῆς ἐλεγείας ποιητήν, ὕστατα δὲ τὴν ἐπὶ Κύρου καὶ Κροίσου γενέσθαι ἅλωσιν. λέγοντος δὲ τοῦ Καλλίνου τὴν ἔφοδον τῶν Κιμμερίων ἐπὶ τοὺς Ἠσιονῆας γεγονέναι, καθ' ἣν αἱ Σάρδεις ἑάλωσαν, εἰκάζουσιν οἱ περὶ τὸν Σκήψιον ἰαστὶ λέγεσθαι Ἠσιονεῖς τοὺς Ἀσιονεῖς· τάχα γὰρ ἡ Μηονία, φησίν, Ἀσία ἐλέγετο, καθ' ὃ καὶ Ὅμηρος εἴρηκεν·

Ἀσίῳ ἐν λειμῶνι Καϋστρίου ἀμφὶ ῥέεθρα.

ἀναληφθεῖσα δ' ἀξιολόγως ὕστερον διὰ τὴν ἀρετὴν τῆς χώρας ἡ πόλις καὶ οὐδεμιᾶς λειπομένη τῶν ἀστυγειτόνων, νεωστὶ ὑπὸ σεισμῶν ἀπέβαλε πολλὴν τῆς κατοικίας. ἡ δὲ τοῦ Τιβερίου πρόνοια, τοῦ καθ' ἡμᾶς ἡγεμόνος, καὶ ταύτην καὶ τῶν ἄλλων συχνὰς ἀνέλαβε ταῖς εὐεργεσίαις, ὅσαι περὶ τὸν αὐτὸν καιρὸν ἐκοινώνησαν τοῦ αὐτοῦ πάθους.

9. Ἄνδρες δ' ἀξιόλογοι γεγόνασι τοῦ αὐτοῦ γένους Διόδωροι δύο οἱ ῥήτορες, ὧν ὁ πρεσβύτερος

C 628

178

common people of the city, most of the work on which was done by prostitutes; and he says that all women of that country prostituted themselves; and some call the tomb of Alyattes a monument of prostitution. Some report that Lake Coloê is an artificial lake, made to receive the overflows which take place when the rivers are full. Hypaepa is a city which one comes to on the descent from Mt. Tmolus to the Caÿster Plain.

8. Callisthenes says that Sardeis was captured first by the Cimmerians, and then by the Treres and the Lycians, as is set forth by Callinus the elegiac poet, and lastly in the time of Cyrus and Croesus. But when Callinus says that the incursion of the Cimmerians was against the Esioneis, at the time of which Sardeis was captured, the Scepsian[1] and his followers surmise that the Asioneis were by Callinus called the Esioneis, in the Ionic dialect; for perhaps Meïonia, he says, was called Asia, and accordingly Homer likewise says, "on the Asian mead about the streams of the Caÿster." The city was later restored in a notable way because of the fertility of its territory, and was inferior to none of its neighbours, though recently it has lost many of its buildings through earthquakes. However, the forethought of Tiberius, our present ruler, has, by his beneficence, restored not only this city but many others—I mean all the cities that shared in the same misfortune at about the same time.

9. Notable men of the same family were born at Sardeis: the two Diodoruses, the orators, of whom

---

[1] Again Demetrius of Scepsis.

ἐκαλεῖτο Ζωνᾶς, ἀνὴρ πολλοὺς ἀγῶνας ἠγωνισμένος ὑπὲρ τῆς Ἀσίας, κατὰ δὲ τὴν Μιθριδάτου τοῦ βασιλέως ἔφοδον αἰτίαν ἐσχηκώς, ὡς ἀφιστὰς παρ᾽ αὑτοῦ[1] τὰς πόλεις, ἀπελύσατο τὰς διαβολὰς ἀπολογησάμενος· τοῦ δὲ νεωτέρου φίλου ἡμῖν γενομένου καὶ ἱστορικὰ συγγράμματά ἐστι καὶ μέλη καὶ ἄλλα ποιήματα, τὴν ἀρχαίαν γραφὴν ἐπιφαίνοντα ἱκανῶς. Ξάνθος δὲ ὁ παλαιὸς συγγραφεὺς Λυδὸς μὲν λέγεται, εἰ δὲ ἐκ Σάρδεων, οὐκ ἴσμεν.

10. Μετὰ δὲ Λυδούς εἰσιν οἱ Μυσοὶ καὶ πόλις Φιλαδέλφεια σεισμῶν πλήρης. οὐ γὰρ διαλείπουσιν οἱ τοῖχοι διιστάμενοι, καὶ ἄλλοτ᾽ ἄλλο μέρος τῆς πόλεως κακοπαθοῦν· οἰκοῦσιν οὖν ὀλίγοι διὰ τοῦτο τὴν πόλιν, οἱ δὲ πολλοὶ καταβιοῦσιν ἐν τῇ χώρᾳ γεωργοῦντες, ἔχοντες εὐδαίμονα γῆν· ἀλλὰ καὶ τῶν ὀλίγων θαυμάζειν ἐστίν, ὅτι οὕτω φιλοχωροῦσιν, ἐπισφαλεῖς τὰς οἰκήσεις ἔχοντες· ἔτι δ᾽ ἄν τις μᾶλλον θαυμάσειε τῶν κτισάντων αὐτήν.

11. Μετὰ δὲ ταῦτ᾽ ἐστὶν ἡ Κατακεκαυμένη λεγομένη χώρα μῆκος μὲν καὶ πεντακοσίων σταδίων, πλάτος δὲ τετρακοσίων, εἴτε Μυσίαν χρὴ καλεῖν, εἴτε Μῃονίαν (λέγεται γὰρ ἀμφοτέρως), ἅπασα ἄδενδρος πλὴν ἀμπέλου τὸν Κατακεκαυμενίτην φερούσης οἶνον, οὐδενὸς τῶν ἐλλογίμων ἀρετῇ λειπόμενον. ἔστι δὲ ἡ ἐπιφάνεια τεφρώδης τῶν πεδίων, ἡ δ᾽ ὀρεινὴ καὶ πετρώδης μέλαινα, ὡς ἂν

---

[1] παρ᾽ αὑτοῦ, Xylander changes from a position between τὰς and πόλεις; so the later editors.

---

[1] i.e. "burnt" country, situated about the upper course

the elder was called Zonas, a man who many times pleaded the cause of Asia; and at the time of the attack of King Mithridates, he was accused of trying to cause the cities to revolt from him, but in his defence he acquitted himself of the slander. The younger Diodorus, who was a friend of mine, is the author, not only of historical treatises, but also of melic and other poems, which display full well the ancient style of writing. Xanthus, the ancient historian, is indeed called a Lydian, but whether or not he was from Sardeis I do not know.

10. After the Lydians come the Mysians; and the city Philadelphia, ever subject to earthquakes. Incessantly the walls of the houses are cracked, different parts of the city being thus affected at different times. For this reason but few people live in the city, and most of them spend their lives as farmers in the country, since they have a fertile soil. Yet one may be surprised at the few, that they are so fond of the place when their dwellings are so insecure; and one might marvel still more at those who founded the city.

11. After this region one comes to the Catacecaumene country,[1] as it is called, which has a length of five hundred stadia and a breadth of four hundred, whether it should be called Mysia or Meïonia (for both names are used); the whole of it is without trees except the vine that produces the Catacecaumenite wine, which in quality is inferior to none of the notable wines. The surface of the plains are covered with ashes, and the mountainous and rocky country

of the Hermus and its tributaries. Hamilton (*Researches*, II, p. 136), quoted by Tozer (*Selections*, p. 289), confirms Strabo's account.

ἐξ ἐπικαύσεως. εἰκάζουσι μὲν οὖν τινὲς ἐκ κεραυνοβολιῶν καὶ πρηστήρων συμβῆναι τοῦτο, καὶ οὐκ ὀκνοῦσι τὰ περὶ τὸν Τυφῶνα ἐνταῦθα μυθολογεῖν. Ξάνθος δὲ καὶ Ἀριμοῦν τινά λέγει τῶν τόπων τούτων βασιλέα. οὐκ εὔλογον δὲ ὑπὸ τοιούτων παθῶν τὴν τοσαύτην χώραν ἐμπρησθῆναι ἀθρόως, ἀλλὰ μᾶλλον ὑπὸ γηγενοῦς πυρός, ἐκλιπεῖν δὲ νῦν τὰς πηγάς· δείκνυνται δὲ καὶ βόθροι τρεῖς, οὓς φύσας καλοῦσιν, ὅσον τεττα- ράκοντα ἀλλήλων διεστῶτες σταδίους· ὑπέρκειν- ται δὲ λόφοι τραχεῖς, οὓς εἰκὸς ἐκ τῶν ἀναφυση- θέντων σεσωρεῦσθαι μύδρων. τὸ δ' εὐάμπελον τὴν τοιαύτην ὑπάρχειν γῆν, λάβοι τις ἂν καὶ ἐκ τῆς Καταναίας[1] τῆς χωσθείσης τῇ σποδῷ καὶ νῦν ἀποδιδούσης οἶνον δαψιλῆ καὶ καλόν. ἀστειζό- μενοι δέ τινες, εἰκότως πυριγενῆ τὸν Διόνυσον λέγεσθαί φασιν, ἐκ τῶν τοιούτων χωρίων τεκμαι- ρόμενοι.

12. Τὰ δ' ἑξῆς ἐπὶ τὰ νότια μέρη τοῖς τόποις τούτοις ἐμπλοκὰς ἔχει μέχρι πρὸς τὸν Ταῦρον, ὥστε καὶ τὰ Φρύγια καὶ τὰ Καρικὰ καὶ τὰ Λύδια καὶ ἔτι τὰ τῶν Μυσῶν δυσδιάκριτα εἶναι, παρα- πίπτοντα εἰς ἄλληλα· εἰς δὲ τὴν σύγχυσιν ταύτην οὐ μικρὰ συλλαμβάνει τὸ τοὺς Ῥωμαίους μὴ κατὰ φῦλα διελεῖν αὐτούς, ἀλλὰ ἕτερον τρόπον διατάξαι τὰς διοικήσεις, ἐν αἷς τὰς ἀγοραίους ποιοῦνται καὶ τὰς δικαιοδοσίας. ὁ μέν γε Τμῶλος ἱκανῶς συνῆκται[2] καὶ περιγραφὴν ἔχει μετρίαν, ἐν αὐτοῖς ἀφοριζόμενος τοῖς Λυδίοις μέρεσιν, ἡ δὲ

---

[1] Καταναίας, Xylander, for Καταναίας.
[2] συνῆκται E, συνῆπται other MSS.

---

[1] "Fire-born."

is black, as though from conflagration. Now some conjecture that this resulted from thunderbolts and from fiery subterranean outbursts, and they do not hesitate to lay there the scene of the mythical story of Typhon; and Xanthus adds that a certain Arimus was king of this region; but it is not reasonable to suppose that all that country was burnt all at once by reason of such disturbances, but rather by reason of an earth-born fire, the sources of which have now been exhausted. Three pits are to be seen there, which are called "bellows," and they are about forty stadia distant from each other. Above them lie rugged hills, which are reasonably supposed to have been heaped up by the hot masses blown forth from the earth. That such soil should be well adapted to the vine one might assume from the land of Catana, which was heaped with ashes and now produces excellent wine in great plenty. Some writers, judging from places like this, wittily remark that there is good reason for calling Dionysus "Pyrigenes." [1]

12. The parts situated next to this region towards the south as far as the Taurus are so inwoven with one another that the Phrygian and the Carian and the Lydian parts, as also those of the Mysians, since they merge into one another, are hard to distinguish. To this confusion no little has been contributed by the fact that the Romans did not divide them according to tribes, but in another way organised their jurisdictions, within which they hold their popular assemblies and their courts. Mt. Tmolus is a quite contracted mass of mountain and has only a moderate circumference, its limits lying within the territory of the Lydians themselves; but the Mesogis extends

STRABO

Μεσωγὶς [1] εἰς τὸ ἀντικείμενον μέρος διατείνει μέχρι
Μυκάλης, ἀπὸ Κελαινῶν ἀρξάμενον, ὥς φησι
Θεόπομπος· ὥστε τὰ μὲν αὐτοῦ Φρύγες κατέ-
χουσι, τὰ πρὸς ταῖς Κελαιναῖς καὶ τῇ Ἀπαμείᾳ,
C 629 τὰ δὲ Μυσοὶ καὶ Λυδοί, τὰ δὲ Κᾶρες καὶ Ἴωνες.
οὕτω δὲ καὶ οἱ ποταμοί, καὶ μάλιστα ὁ Μαίανδρος,
τὰ μὲν διορίζοντες τῶν ἐθνῶν, δι' ὧν δὲ μέσοι
φερόμενοι, δύσληπτον ποιοῦσι τἀκριβές· καὶ περὶ
τῶν πεδίων δὲ τῶν ἐφ' ἑκάτερα τῆς τε ὀρεινῆς καὶ
τῆς ποταμίας ὁ αὐτὸς λόγος. οὐδ' [2] ἡμῖν ἴσως ἐπὶ
τοσοῦτον φροντιστέον, ὡς ἀναγκαῖον [3] χωρομετ-
ροῦσιν, ἀλλὰ τοσοῦτον μόνον ὑπογραπτέον,[4] ὅσον
καὶ οἱ πρὸ ἡμῶν παραδεδώκασι.

13. Τῷ δὴ Καϋστριανῷ πεδίῳ μεταξὺ πίπτοντι
τῆς τε Μεσωγίδος [5] καὶ τοῦ Τμώλου, συνεχές ἐστι
πρὸς ἔω τὸ Κιλβιανὸν πεδίον, πολύ τε καὶ συνοι-
κούμενον εὖ καὶ χώραν ἔχον σπουδαίαν· εἶτα τὸ
Ὑρκάνιον πεδίον, Περσῶν ἐπονομασάντων καὶ
ἐποίκους ἀγαγόντων ἐκεῖθεν (ὁμοίως δὲ καὶ τὸ
Κύρου πεδίον [6] Πέρσαι κατωνόμασαν)· εἶτα τὸ
Πελτινὸν πεδίον, ἤδη Φρύγιον, καὶ τὸ Κιλλάνιον
καὶ τὸ Ταβηνόν, ἔχοντα [7] πολίχνας μιξοφρυγίους,
ἐχούσας τι καὶ Πισιδικόν, ἀφ' ὧν αὐτὰ κατωνο-
μάσθη.

14. Ὑπερβάλλουσι δὲ τὴν Μεσωγίδα τὴν
μεταξὺ Καρῶν τε καὶ τῆς Νυσαΐδος, ἥ ἐστι χώρα

[1] Μεσωγίς, Palmer, μεσόγαιος F, μεσόγειος other MSS.
[2] οὐδ', Meineke, for οὔθ'.
[3] ἀναγκαῖον, Kramer, for ἄρα κενῇ, all MSS. except F, which
has ἀναγκαῖον κενῇ.
[4] Instead of ὑπογραπτέον, Dhi have περιγραπτέον.
[5] Μεσωγίδος, Casaubon, for μεσογειώτιδος; so the later
editors.

184

in the opposite direction as far as Mycalê, beginning at Celaenae, according to Theopompus. And therefore some parts of it are occupied by the Phrygians, I mean the parts near Celaenae and Apameia, and other parts by Mysians and Lydians, and other parts by Carians and Ionians. So, also, the rivers, particularly the Maeander, form the boundary between some of the tribes, but in cases where they flow through the middle of countries they make accurate distinction difficult. And the same is to be said of the plains that are situated on either side of the mountainous territory and of the river-land. Neither should I, perhaps, attend to such matters as closely as a surveyor must, but sketch them only so far as they have been transmitted by my predecessors.

13. Contiguous on the east to the Caÿster Plain, which lies between the Mesogis and the Tmolus, is the Cilbian Plain. It is extensive and well settled and has a fertile soil. Then comes the Hyrcanian Plain, a name given it by the Persians, who brought Hyrcanian colonists there (the Plain of Cyrus, likewise, was given its name by the Persians). Then come the Peltine Plain (we are now in Phrygian territory) and the Cillanian and the Tabene Plains, which have towns with a mixed population of Phrygians, these towns also containing a Pisidian element; and it is after these that the plains themselves were named.

14. When one crosses over the Mesogis, between the Carians and the territory of Nysa, which latter is

---

⁶ ὅ, after πεδίον, the editors eject.

⁷ ἔχοντα, Corais and Meineke, for ἔχοντας *Dh*, ἔχον τάς other MSS.

κατὰ τὸ τοῦ Μαιάνδρου πέραν μέχρι τῆς Κιβυ-
ράτιδος καὶ τῆς Καβαλίδος, πόλεις[1] εἰσί, πρὸς
μὲν τῇ Μεσωγίδι καταντικρὺ Λαοδικείας Ἱερά-
πολις, ὅπου τὰ θερμὰ ὕδατα καὶ τὸ Πλουτώνιον,
ἄμφω παραδοξολογίαν τινὰ ἔχοντα. τὸ μὲν γὰρ
ὕδωρ οὕτω ῥᾳδίως εἰς πῶρον μεταβάλλει πηττό-
μενον, ὥστ' ὀχετοὺς ἐπάγοντες φραγμοὺς ἀπεργά-
ζονται μονολίθους, τὸ δὲ Πλουτώνιον ὑπ' ὀφρύι
μικρᾷ τῆς ὑπερκειμένης ὀρεινῆς στόμιόν ἐστι
σύμμετρον, ὅσον ἄνθρωπον δέξασθαι δυνάμενον,
βεβάθυται δ' ἐπὶ πολύ· πρόκειται δὲ τούτου
δρυφάκτωμα τετράγωνον, ὅσον ἡμιπλέθρου τὴν
περίμετρον· τοῦτο δὲ πλῆρές ἐστιν ὁμιχλώδους
παχείας ἀχλύος, ὥστε μόγις τοὔδαφος καθορᾶν.
τοῖς μὲν οὖν κύκλῳ πλησιάζουσι πρὸς τὸν δρύ-
φακτον ἄλυπός ἐστιν ὁ ἀήρ, καθαρεύων ἐκείνης
C 630   τῆς ἀχλύος ἐν ταῖς νηνεμίαις· συμμένει γὰρ ἐντὸς
τοῦ περιβόλου· τῷ δ' εἴσω παριόντι ζῴῳ θάνατος
παραχρῆμα ἀπαντᾷ· ταῦροι γοῦν εἰσαχθέντες
πίπτουσι καὶ ἐξέλκονται νεκροί, ἡμεῖς δὲ στρουθία
ἐπέμψαμεν καὶ ἔπεσεν εὐθὺς ἐκπνεύσαντα· οἱ δ'
ἀπόκοποι Γάλλοι παρίασιν ἀπαθεῖς, ὥστε καὶ
μέχρι τοῦ στομίου πλησιάζειν καὶ ἐγκύπτειν καὶ
καταδύνειν μέχρι ποσοῦ συνέχοντας ὡς ἐπὶ τὸ
πολὺ τὸ πνεῦμα (ἑωρῶμεν γὰρ ἐκ τῆς ὄψεως
ὡς ἂν πνιγώδους τινὸς πάθους ἔμφασιν), εἴτε

---

[1] δ', after πόλεις, omitted by x and the later editors.

---

[1] On the "Plutonia," see Vol. II, p. 442, footnote 1.
[2] "The road overlooks many green spots, once vineyards
and gardens, separated by partitions of the same material"

a country on the far side of the Maeander extending
to Cibyratis and Cabalis, one comes to certain cities.
First, near the Mesogis, opposite Laodiceia, to
Hierapolis, where are the hot springs and the
Plutonium,[1] both of which have something marvellous about them ; for the water of the springs
so easily congeals and changes into stone that people
conduct streams of it through ditches and thus
make stone fences[2] consisting of single stones, while
the Plutonium, below a small brow of the mountainous country that lies above it, is an opening
of only moderate size, large enough to admit a
man, but it reaches a considerable depth, and it is
enclosed by a quadrilateral handrail, about half a
plethrum in circumference, and this space is full of
a vapour so misty and dense that one can scarcely
see the ground. Now to those who approach the
handrail anywhere round the enclosure the air is
harmless, since the outside is free from that vapour
in calm weather, for the vapour then stays inside
the enclosure, but any animal that passes inside
meets instant death. At any rate. bulls that are
led into it fall and are dragged out dead ; and I
threw in sparrows and they immediately breathed
their last and fell. But the Galli,[3] who are eunuchs,
pass inside with such impunity that they even
approach the opening, bend over it, and descend
into it to a certain depth, though they hold their
breath as much as they can (for I could see in their
countenances an indication of a kind of suffocating
attack, as it were),—whether this immunity belongs

(Chandler, *Travels in Asia Minor*, I. p. 288), quoted by Tozer
(*op. cit.*, p. 290).
    [3] Priests of Cybelê.

STRABO

πάντων οὕτω πεπηρωμένων τοῦτο, εἴτε μόνον
τῶν περὶ τὸ ἱερόν, καὶ εἴτε θείᾳ προνοίᾳ,
καθάπερ ἐπὶ τῶν ἐνθουσιασμῶν εἰκός, εἴτε ἀντιδό-
τοις τισὶ δυνάμεσι τούτου[1] συμβαίνοντος. τὸ δὲ
τῆς ἀπολιθώσεως καὶ ἐπὶ τῶν ἐν Λαοδικείᾳ ποταμῶν φασὶ συμβαίνειν, καίπερ ὄντων ποτίμων.
ἔστι δὲ καὶ πρὸς βαφὴν ἐρίων θαυμαστῶς σύμμετρον τὸ κατὰ τὴν Ἱεράπολιν ὕδωρ, ὥστε τὰ ἐκ
τῶν ῥιζῶν βαπτόμενα ἐνάμιλλα εἶναι τοῖς[2] ἐκ
τῆς κόκκου καὶ τοῖς ἁλουργέσιν· οὕτω δ' ἐστὶν
ἄφθονον τὸ πλῆθος τοῦ ὕδατος, ὥστε ἡ πόλις
μεστὴ τῶν αὐτομάτων βαλανείων ἐστί.

15. Μετὰ δὲ τὴν Ἱεράπολιν τὰ πέραν τοῦ
Μαιάνδρου, τὰ μὲν[3] περὶ Λαοδίκειαν καὶ Ἀφρο-
δισιάδα καὶ τὰ μέχρι Καρούρων εἴρηται. τὰ δ'
ἐξῆς ἐστι τὰ μὲν πρὸς δύσιν, ἡ τῶν Ἀντιοχέων
πόλις τῶν ἐπὶ Μαιάνδρῳ, τῆς Καρίας ἤδη· τὰ δὲ
πρὸς νότον ἡ Κίβυρά ἐστιν ἡ μεγάλη καὶ ἡ Σίνδα
καὶ ἡ Καβαλὶς[4] μέχρι τοῦ Ταύρου καὶ τῆς Λυκίας.
ἡ μὲν οὖν Ἀντιόχεια μετρία πόλις ἐστὶν ἐπ' αὐτῷ
κειμένη τῷ Μαιάνδρῳ κατὰ τὸ πρὸς τῇ Φρυγίᾳ
μέρος, ἐπέζευκται δὲ γέφυρα· χώραν δ' ἔχει
πολλὴν ἐφ' ἑκάτερα τοῦ ποταμοῦ, πᾶσαν εὐδαίμονα, πλείστην δὲ φέρει τὴν καλουμένην Ἀντιο-
χικὴν ἰσχάδα, τὴν δὲ αὐτὴν καὶ τρίφυλλον
ὀνομάζουσιν· εὔσειστος δὲ καὶ οὗτός ἐστιν ὁ
τόπος. σοφιστὴς δὲ παρὰ τούτοις ἔνδοξος γεγένη-

[1] Instead of τούτου, Dhi and Corais read οὕτω.
[2] τοῖς Fxz, ταῖς other MSS.
[3] After μέν, E and Meineke read οὖν.
[4] Καβαλίς, the editors, for Καβαλαῖς, all MSS. except Dh, which read Καβαλλαῖς.

188

to all who are maimed in this way or only to those
round the temple, or whether it is because of divine
providence, as would be likely in the case of divine
obsessions, or whether it is the result of certain
physical powers that are antidotes against the
vapour. The changing of water into stone is said
also to be the case with the rivers in Laodiceia,
although their water is potable. The water at
Hierapolis is remarkably adapted also to the dyeing
of wool, so that wool dyed with the roots[1] rivals
that dyed with the coccus[2] or with the marine
purple.[3] And the supply of water is so abundant
that the city is full of natural baths.

15. After Hierapolis one comes to the parts on
the far side of the Maeander; I have already described[4] those round Laodiceia and Aphrodisias and
those extending as far as Carura. The next thereafter are the parts towards the west, I mean the
city of the Antiocheians on the Maeander, where
one finds himself already in Caria, and also the parts
towards the south, I mean Greater Cibyra and Sinda
and Cabalis, extending as far as the Taurus and
Lycia. Now Antiocheia is a city of moderate size,
and is situated on the Maeander itself in the region
that lies near Phrygia, and there is a bridge over
the river. Antiocheia has considerable territory on
each side of the river, which is everywhere fertile,
and it produces in greatest quantities the " Anti-
ocheian " dried fig, as it is called, though they also
name the same fig " three-leaved." This region, too,
is much subject to earthquakes. Among these people

---

[1] Madder-root.   [2] Kermes-berries.
[3] Using this particular water, of course.
[4] 12. 8. 13, 16, 17.

ται Διοτρέφης, οὗ διήκουσεν ῾Υβρέας, ὁ καθ᾽
ἡμᾶς γενόμενος μέγιστος ῥήτωρ.

16. Σολύμους δ᾽ εἶναί φασι τοὺς Καβαλεῖς·[1]
τῆς γοῦν Τερμησσέων[2] ἄκρας ὁ ὑπερκείμενος
λόφος καλεῖται Σόλυμος, καὶ αὐτοὶ δὲ οἱ Τερμησσεῖς[3] Σόλυμοι καλοῦνται. πλησίον δ᾽ ἐστὶ καὶ
ὁ Βελλεροφόντου χάραξ καὶ ὁ Πεισάνδρου τάφος
τοῦ υἱοῦ, πεσόντος ἐν τῇ πρὸς Σολύμους μάχῃ.
ταῦτα δὲ καὶ τοῖς[4] ὑπὸ τοῦ ποιητοῦ λεγομένοις
ὁμολογεῖται· περὶ μὲν γὰρ τοῦ Βελλεροφόντου
φησὶν οὕτως·

δεύτερον αὖ Σολύμοισι μαχέσσατο κυδαλίμοισι·

περὶ δὲ τοῦ παιδὸς αὐτοῦ·

C 631 Πείσανδρον[5] δέ οἱ υἱὸν ῎Αρης ἆτος πολέμοιο
μαρνάμενον Σολύμοισι κατέκτανεν.

ἡ δὲ Τερμησσός ἐστι Πισιδικὴ πόλις ἡ μάλιστα
καὶ ἔγγιστα ὑπερκειμένη τῆς Κιβύρας.

17. Λέγονται δὲ ἀπόγονοι Λυδῶν οἱ Κιβυρᾶται
τῶν κατασχόντων τὴν Καβαλίδα,[6] ὕστερον δὲ
Πισιδῶν τῶν ὁμόρων οἰκισάντων[7] καὶ μετακτι-
σάντων εἰς ἕτερον τόπον εὐερκέστατον ἐν κύκλῳ
σταδίων περὶ ἑκατόν. ηὐξήθη δὲ διὰ τὴν εὐνομίαν,
καὶ αἱ κῶμαι παρεξέτειναν ἀπὸ Πισιδίας καὶ τῆς
ὁμόρου Μιλυάδος[8] ἕως Λυκίας καὶ τῆς ῾Ροδίων

---

[1] Καβαλεῖς x, Καβαλλεῖς other MSS.
[2] Τερμησσέων, Corais, for Τερμησέως CDF moxz, Τελμήσσεως
rw, Τελμισσέων E.
[3] Instead of Τερμησσεῖς, CDFhx read Τελμησεῖς, rw Τελμησ-
σεῖς, Ei Τελμισεῖς.
[4] δὲ καὶ τοῖς, Corais, for δ᾽ ἑκάστοις CDFhirw, δ᾽ ἑκάστοις
τοῖς x, δ᾽ ἕκαστα τοῖς, δὲ τοῖς moz.

arose a famous sophist, Diotrephes, whose complete
course was taken by Hybreas, who became the greatest
orator of my time.

16. The Cabaleis are said to be the Solymi; at
any rate, the hill that lies above the fortress of the
Termessians is called Solymus, and the Termessians
themselves are called Solymi. Near by is the
Palisade of Bellerophon, and also the tomb of his
son Peisander, who fell in the battle against the
Solymi. This account agrees also with the words of
the poet, for he says of Bellerophon, "next he
fought with the glorious Solymi," [1] and of his son,
"and Peisander [2] his son was slain by Ares, insatiate
of war, when he was fighting with the Solymi." [3]
Termessus is a Pisidian city, which lies directly
above Cibyra and very near it.

17. It is said that the Cibyratae are descendants
of the Lydians who took possession of Cabalis, and
later of the neighbouring Pisidians, who settled
there and transferred the city to another site, a
site very strongly fortified and about one hundred
stadia in circuit. It grew strong through its good
laws; and its villages extended alongside it from
Pisidia and the neighbouring Milyas as far as Lycia
and the Peraea [4] of the Rhodians. Three bordering

[1] *Iliad* 6. 184.
[2] The Homeric text reads "Isander" (see 12. 8. 5).
[3] *Iliad* 6. 203.   [4] Mainland territory.

---

[5] Instead of Πείσανδρον, E reads Πίσανδρον. The Homeric
text has Ἴσανδρον.
[6] Καβαλίδα, the editors, for Καβαλλίδα.
[7] DF*horz* read οἰκησάντων.
[8] Μιλυάδος, Tzschucke, for Μυλίαδος.

περαίας· προσγενομένων δὲ τριῶν πόλεων ὁμόρων,
Βουβῶνος,[1] Βαλβούρων, Οἰνοάνδων,[2] τετράπολις
τὸ σύστημα ἐκλήθη, μίαν ἑκάστης ψῆφον ἐχούσης, δύο δὲ τῆς Κιβύρας· ἔστελλε γὰρ αὕτη
πεζῶν μὲν τρεῖς μυριάδας, ἱππέας δὲ δισχιλίους·
ἐτυραννεῖτο δ' ἀεί, σωφρόνως δ' ὅμως· ἐπὶ Μοα-
γέτου δ' ἡ τυραννὶς τέλος ἔσχε, καταλύσαντος
αὐτὴν Μουρηνᾶ καὶ Λυκίοις προσορίσαντος τὰ
Βάλβουρα καὶ τὴν Βουβῶνα· οὐδὲν δ' ἧττον ἐν
ταῖς μεγίσταις ἐξετάζεται διοικήσεσι τῆς Ἀσίας
ἡ Κιβυρατική. τέτταρσι δὲ γλώτταις ἐχρῶντο
οἱ Κιβυρᾶται, τῇ Πισιδικῇ, τῇ Σολύμων, τῇ
Ἑλληνίδι, τῇ Λυδῶν· τῆς Λυδῶν[3] δὲ οὐδ' ἴχνος
ἐστὶν ἐν Λυδίᾳ. ἴδιον δ' ἐστὶν ἐν Κιβύρᾳ τὸ τὸν
σίδηρον τορεύεσθαι ῥᾳδίως. Μιλύα[4] δ' ἐστὶν
ἡ ἀπὸ τῶν κατὰ Τερμησσὸν στενῶν καὶ τῆς εἰς
τὸ ἐντὸς τοῦ Ταύρου ὑπερθέσεως δι' αὐτῶν ἐπὶ
Ἴσινδα παρατείνουσα ὀρεινὴ μέχρι Σαγαλασσοῦ
καὶ τῆς Ἀπαμέων χώρας.

---

[1] Βουβῶνος, Tzschucke, for Βουβούνων C, Βουβώνων other MSS.

[2] Οἰνοάνδων, Tzschucke, for Οἰνοάνδρου.

[3] τῆς Λυδῶν, Müller-Dübner insert ; νῦν ί, ταύτης certain editors.

cities were added to it, Bubon, Balbura, and
Oenoanda, and the union was called Tetrapolis,
each of the three having one vote, but Cibyra two;
for Cibyra could send forth thirty thousand foot-
soldiers and two thousand horse. It was always
ruled by tyrants; but still they ruled it with
moderation. However, the tyranny ended in the
time of Moagetes, when Murena overthrew it and
included Balbura and Bubon within the territory of
the Lycians. But none the less the jurisdiction of
Cibyra is rated among the greatest in Asia. The
Cibyratae used four languages, the Pisidian, that of
the Solymi, Greek, and that of the Lydians;[1] but
there is not even a trace of the language of the
Lydians in Lydia. The easy embossing of iron is
a peculiar thing at Cibyra. Milya is the mountain-
range extending from the narrows at Termessus and
from the pass that leads over through them to the
region inside the Taurus towards Isinda, as far as
Sagalassus and the country of the Apameians.

---

[1] See A. H. Sayce, *Anatolian Studies presented to Sir
William Mitchell Ramsay*, p. 396.

---

⁴ Instead of Μιλύα, DE read Μυλία, *oz* Μιλία.

BOOK XIV

Ι

C 632 1. Λοιπὸν δ᾽ ἐστὶν εἰπεῖν περὶ Ἰώνων καὶ
Καρῶν καὶ τῆς ἔξω τοῦ Ταύρου παραλίας, ἣν
ἔχουσι Λύκιοί τε καὶ Πάμφυλοι[1] καὶ Κίλικες·
οὕτω γὰρ ἂν ἔχοι τέλος ἡ πᾶσα τῆς χερρονήσου
περιήγησις, ἧς ἰσθμὸν ἔφαμεν τὴν ὑπέρβασιν τὴν
ἐκ τῆς Ποντικῆς θαλάττης ἐπὶ τὴν Ἰσσικήν.
2. Ἔστι δὲ τῆς Ἰωνίας ὁ μὲν περίπλους ὁ
παρὰ γῆν σταδίων που τρισχιλίων τετρακοσίων
τριάκοντα διὰ τοὺς κόλπους καὶ διὰ τὸ χερ-
ρονησίζειν ἐπὶ πλεῖον τὴν χώραν, τὸ δ᾽ ἐπ᾽
εὐθείας μῆκος οὐ πολύ. αὐτὸ οὖν τὸ ἐξ Ἐφέσου
μέχρι Σμύρνης ὁδὸς μέν ἐστιν ἐπ᾽ εὐθείας τριακόσιοι εἴκοσι στάδιοι· εἰς γὰρ Μητρόπολιν ἑκατὸν
καὶ εἴκοσι στάδιοι, οἱ λοιποὶ δὲ εἰς Σμύρναν,
περίπλους δὲ μικρὸν ἀπολείπων τῶν δισχιλίων
καὶ διακοσίων. ἔστι δ᾽ οὖν ἀπὸ τοῦ Ποσειδίου
τοῦ Μιλησίων καὶ τῶν Καρικῶν ὅρων[2] μέχρι
Φωκαίας καὶ τοῦ Ἕρμου τὸ πέρας τῆς Ἰωνικῆς
παραλίας.
3. Ταύτης δέ φησι Φερεκύδης Μίλητον μὲν καὶ
Μυοῦντα καὶ τὰ περὶ Μυκάλην καὶ Ἔφεσον

[1] Πάμφυλοι DF ; Παμφύλιοι other MSS.
[2] ὅρων, Groskurd, for ὀρῶν ; so the later editors.

---

[1] For map of Asia Minor, see Vol. V (at end).

BOOK XIV

I

1.[1] IT remains for me to speak of the Ionians and the Carians and the seaboard outside the Taurus, which last is occupied by Lycians, Pamphylians, and Cilicians; for in this way I can finish my entire description of the peninsula, the isthmus of which, as I was saying,[2] is the road which leads over from the Pontic Sea to the Issic Sea.

2. The coasting voyage round Ionia is about three thousand four hundred and thirty stadia, this distance being so great because of the gulfs and the fact that the country forms a peninsula of unusual extent; but the distance in a straight line across the isthmus is not great. For instance, merely the distance from Ephesus to Smyrna is a journey, in a straight line, of three hundred and twenty stadia, for the distance to Metropolis is one hundred and twenty stadia and the remainder to Smyrna, whereas the coasting voyage is but slightly short of two thousand two hundred. Be that as it may, the bounds of the Ionian coast extend from the Poseidium of the Milesians, and from the Carian frontiers, as far as Phocaea and the Hermus River, which latter is the limit of the Ionian seaboard.

3. Pherecydes says concerning this seaboard that Miletus and Myus and the parts round Mycalê and

[2] 12. 1. 3.

Κᾶρας ἔχειν πρότερον, τὴν δ' ἑξῆς παραλίαν
μέχρι Φωκαίας καὶ Χίου καὶ Σάμου,[1] ἧς Ἀγκαῖος
ἦρχε, Λέλεγας· ἐκβληθῆναι δ' ἀμφοτέρους ὑπὸ
τῶν Ἰώνων, καὶ εἰς τὰ λοιπὰ μέρη τῆς Καρίας
ἐκπεσεῖν. ἄρξαι δέ φησιν Ἄνδροκλον τῆς τῶν
Ἰώνων ἀποικίας, ὕστερον τῆς Αἰολικῆς, υἱὸν
γνήσιον Κόδρου τοῦ Ἀθηνῶν βασιλέως, γενέσθαι
C 633 δὲ τοῦτον Ἐφέσου κτίστην· διόπερ τὸ βασίλειον
τῶν Ἰώνων ἐκεῖ συστῆναί φασι· καὶ ἔτι νῦν οἱ
ἐκ τοῦ γένους ὀνομάζονται βασιλεῖς, ἔχοντές τινας
τιμάς, προεδρίαν τε ἐν ἀγῶσι καὶ πορφύραν ἐπίσημον τοῦ βασιλικοῦ γένους, σκίπωνα ἀντὶ σκήπ-
τρου, καὶ τὰ ἱερὰ τῆς Ἐλευσινίας Δήμητρος. καὶ
Μίλητον δ' ἔκτισεν Νηλεὺς ἐκ Πύλου τὸ γένος
ὤν· οἵ τε Μεσσήνιοι καὶ οἱ Πύλιοι συγγένειάν
τινα προσποιοῦνται, καθ' ἣν καὶ Μεσσήνιον τὸν
Νέστορα οἱ νεώτεροί φασι ποιηταί, καὶ τοῖς περὶ
Μέλανθον τὸν Κόδρου πατέρα πολλοὺς καὶ τῶν
Πυλίων συνεξᾶραί φασιν εἰς τὰς Ἀθήνας· τοῦτον
δὴ πάντα τὸν λαὸν μετὰ τῶν Ἰώνων κοινῇ στεῖλαι
τὴν ἀποικίαν. τοῦ δὲ Νηλέως ἐπὶ τῷ Ποσειδίῳ
βωμὸς ἵδρυμα δείκνυται. Κυδρῆλος δὲ νόθος
υἱὸς Κόδρου Μυοῦντα κτίζει· Ἀνδρόπομπος δὲ
Λέβεδον, καταλαβόμενος τόπον τινὰ Ἄρτιν·
Κολοφῶνα δ' Ἀνδραίμων[2] Πύλιος, ὥς φησι καὶ
Μίμνερμος ἐν Ναννοῖ· Πριήνην δ' Αἴπυτος ὁ
Νηλέως, εἶθ' ὕστερον Φιλώτας ἐκ Θηβῶν λαὸν
ἀγαγών· Τέῳ δὲ Ἀθάμας μὲν πρότερον, διόπερ
Ἀθαμαντίδα καλεῖ αὐτὴν Ἀνακρέων, κατὰ δὲ

---

[1] For Χίον and Σάμον Kramer conj. Χίον and Σάμον.
[2] Ἀνδρεμών CFsxz.

[1] A fragment (Bergk 10) otherwise unknown.

Ephesus were in earlier times occupied by Carians, and that the coast next thereafter, as far as Phocaea and Chios and Samos, which were ruled by Ancaeus, was occupied by Leleges, but that both were driven out by the Ionians and took refuge in the remaining parts of Caria. He says that Androclus, legitimate son of Codrus the king of Athens, was the leader of the Ionian colonisation, which was later than the Aeolian, and that he became the founder of Ephesus; and for this reason, it is said, the royal seat of the Ionians was established there. And still now the descendants of his family are called kings; and they have certain honours, I mean the privilege of front seats at the games and of wearing purple robes as insignia of royal descent, and staff instead of sceptre, and of the superintendence of the sacrifices in honour of the Eleusinian Demeter. Miletus was founded by Neleus, a Pylian by birth. The Messenians and the Pylians pretend a kind of kinship with one another, according to which the more recent poets call Nestor a Messenian; and they say that many of the Pylians accompanied Melanthus, father of Codrus, and his followers to Athens, and that, accordingly, all this people sent forth the colonising expedition in common with the Ionians. There is an altar, erected by Neleus, to be seen on the Poseidium. Myus was founded by Cydrelus, bastard son of Codrus; Lebedus by Andropompus, who seized a place called Artis; Colophon by Andraemon a Pylian, according to Mimnermus in his *Nanno*;[1] Prienê by Aepytus the son of Neleus, and then later by Philotas, who brought a colony from Thebes; Teos, at first by Athamas, for which reason it is by Anacreon called Athamantis, and at

199

τὴν Ἰωνικὴν ἀποικίαν Ναῦκλος υἱὸς Κόδρου νόθος, καὶ μετὰ τοῦτον Ἄποικος[1] καὶ Δάμασος Ἀθηναῖοι καὶ Γέρης[2] ἐκ Βοιωτῶν· Ἐρυθρὰς δὲ Κνῶπος, καὶ οὗτος υἱὸς Κόδρου νόθος· Φωκαίαν δ᾽ οἱ μετὰ Φιλογένους Ἀθηναῖοι· Κλαζομενὰς δὲ Πάραλος· Χίον δὲ Ἐγέρτιος, σύμμικτον ἐπαγόμενος πλῆθος· Σάμον δὲ Τεμβρίων,[3] εἶθ᾽ ὕστερον Προκλῆς.[4]

4. Αὗται μὲν δώδεκα Ἰωνικαὶ πόλεις, προσελήφθη δὲ χρόνοις ὕστερον καὶ Σμύρνα, εἰς τὸ Ἰωνικὸν ἐναγαγόντων Ἐφεσίων· ἦσαν γὰρ αὐτοῖς σύνοικοι τὸ παλαιόν, ἡνίκα καὶ Σμύρνα ἐκαλεῖτο ἡ Ἔφεσος· καὶ Καλλῖνός που οὕτως ὠνόμακεν αὐτήν, Σμυρναίους τοὺς Ἐφεσίους καλῶν ἐν τῷ πρὸς τὸν Δία λόγῳ·

Σμυρναίους δ᾽ ἐλέησον·

καὶ πάλιν·

μνῆσαι δ᾽ εἴκοτέ τοι μηρία καλὰ βοῶν
Σμυρναῖοι κατέκηαν.[5]

Σμύρνα δ᾽ ἦν Ἀμαζὼν ἡ κατασχοῦσα τὴν Ἔφεσον, ἀφ᾽ ἧς τοὔνομα καὶ τοῖς ἀνθρώποις καὶ τῇ πόλει, ὡς καὶ ἀπὸ Σισύρβης Σισυρβῖταί τινες τῶν Ἐφεσίων ἐλέγοντο· καὶ τόπος δέ τις τῆς Ἐφέσου Σμύρνα ἐκαλεῖτο, ὡς δηλοῖ Ἱππῶναξ·

ᾤκει δ᾽ ὄπισθε τῆς πόλιος ἐν Σμύρνῃ
μεταξὺ Τρηχείης τε καὶ Λεπρῆς ἀκτῆς.

ἐκαλεῖτο γὰρ Λεπρὴ μὲν ἀκτὴ ὁ Πριὼν ὁ ὑπερκείμενος τῆς νῦν πόλεως, ἔχων μέρος τοῦ τείχους αὐτῆς· τὰ γοῦν ὄπισθεν τοῦ Πριῶνος κτήματα

[1] Ἄποικος, Tzschucke, for Ποίκης F, Πύκνης x, Ποίκνης other MSS.

the time of the Ionian colonisation by Nauclus, bastard son of Codrus, and after him by Apoecus and Damasus, who were Athenians, and Geres, a Boeotian; Erythrae by Cnopus, he too a bastard son of Codrus; Phocaea by the Athenians under Philogenes; Clazomenae by Paralus; Chios by Egertius, who brought with him a mixed crowd; Samos by Tembrion, and then later by Procles.

4. These are the twelve Ionian cities,[1] but at a later time Smyrna was added, being induced by the Ephesians to join the Ionian League; for the Ephesians were fellow-inhabitants of the Smyrnaeans in ancient times, when Ephesus was also called Smyrna. And Callinus somewhere so names it, when he calls the Ephesians Smyrnaeans in the prayer to Zeus, "and pity the Smyrnaeans"; and again, "remember, if ever the Smyrnaeans burnt up beautiful thighs of oxen in sacrifice to thee."[2] Smyrna was an Amazon who took possession of Ephesus; and hence the name both of the inhabitants and of the city, just as certain of the Ephesians were called Sisyrbitae after Sisyrbê. Also a certain place belonging to Ephesus was called Smyrna, as Hipponax plainly indicates: "He lived behind the city in Smyrna between Tracheia and Lepra Actê";[3] for the name Lepra Actê was given to Mt. Prion, which lies above the present city and has on it a part of the city's wall. At any rate, the possessions behind Prion

---

[1] 8. 7. 1.   [2] *Frag.* 2 (Bergk).   [3] *Frag.* 44 (Bergk).

---

[2] Γέρης, the editors, for γὰρ ἦν.
[3] Τεμβρίων, the editors, for Τημβρίων.
[4] Instead of Προκλῆς, *moxz* read Πατροκλῆς (cp. *Etym. Mag.* s.v.).
[5] Σμυρναῖοι κατέκηαν, Jones inserts, from conj. of Corais.

C 634 ἔτι νυνὶ λέγεται ἐν τῇ Ὀπισθολεπρίᾳ· Τραχεῖα
δ' ἐκαλεῖτο ἡ περὶ τὸν Κορησσὸν παρώρειος. ἡ
δὲ πόλις ἦν τὸ παλαιὸν περὶ τὸ Ἀθήναιον τὸ
νῦν ἔξω τῆς πόλεως ὂν κατὰ τὴν καλουμένην
Ὑπέλαιον, ὥστε ἡ Σμύρνα ἦν κατὰ τὸ νῦν γυμνάσιον ὄπισθεν μὲν τῆς νῦν[1] πόλεως, μεταξὺ
δὲ Τρηχείης τε καὶ Λεπρῆς[2] ἀκτῆς. ἀπελθόντες
δὲ παρὰ τῶν Ἐφεσίων οἱ Σμυρναῖοι στρατεύουσιν
ἐπὶ τὸν τόπον, ἐν ᾧ νῦν ἐστιν ἡ Σμύρνα, Λελέγων
κατεχόντων· ἐκβαλόντες δ' αὐτοὺς ἔκτισαν τὴν
παλαιὰν Σμύρναν, διέχουσαν τῆς νῦν περὶ εἴκοσι
σταδίους. ὕστερον δὲ ὑπὸ Αἰολέων ἐκπεσόντες
κατέφυγον εἰς Κολοφῶνα, καὶ μετὰ τῶν ἐνθένδε
ἐπιόντες τὴν σφετέραν ἀπέλαβον· καθάπερ καὶ
Μίμνερμος ἐν τῇ Ναννοῖ φράζει, μνησθεὶς τῆς
Σμύρνης, ὅτι περιμάχητος ἀεί·

ἡμεῖς αἰπὺ[3] Πύλου[4] Νηλήιον ἄστυ λιπόντες
ἱμερτὴν Ἀσίην νηυσὶν ἀφικόμεθα.
ἐς δ' ἐρατὴν[5] Κολοφῶνα βίην ὑπέροπλον
ἔχοντες
ἑζόμεθ' ἀργαλέης ὕβριος ἡγεμόνες.
κεῖθεν δ' Ἀστήεντος[6] ἀπορνύμενοι ποταμοῖο
θεῶν βουλῇ Σμύρναν εἵλομεν[7] Αἰολίδα.

ταῦτα μὲν περὶ τούτων· ἐφοδευτέον δὲ πάλιν τὰ
καθ' ἕκαστα, τὴν ἀρχὴν ἀπὸ τῶν ἡγεμονικωτέρων

---

[1] Instead of νῦν, F reads ποτε; whence Kramer conj.
ποτε and Meineke reads τότε.

[2] Λεπρῆς, the editors, for Λεπρίης.

[3] Instead of αἰπύ, F reads ἐπεί; τε, after αἰπύ, the editors
since Hopper omit, except Meineke, who writes ἡμεῖς δηὖτε
for αἰπύ τε.

[4] Πύλου Bergk, for Πύλον, which latter Meineke retains.

are still now referred to as in the "opistholeprian"
territory,[1] and the country alongside the mountain
round Coressus was called "Tracheia."[2] The city
was in ancient times round the Athenaeum, which
is now outside the city near the Hypelaeus,[3] as it
is called; so that Smyrna was near the present
gymnasium, behind the present city, but between
Tracheia and Lepra Actê. On departing from the
Ephesians, the Smyrnaeans marched to the place
where Smyrna now is, which was in the possession
of the Leleges, and, having driven them out, they
founded the ancient Smyrna, which is about twenty
stadia distant from the present Smyrna. But later,
being driven out by the Aeolians, they fled for
refuge to Colophon, and then with the Colophonians
returned to their own land and took it back, as
Mimnermus tells us in his *Nanno,* after recalling that
Smyrna was always an object of contention : " After
we left Pylus, the steep city of Neleus, we came by
ship to lovely Asia, and with our overweening might
settled in beloved Colophon, taking the initiative in
grievous insolence. And from there, setting out from
the Astëeis River, by the will of the gods we took
Aeolian Smyrna."[4] So much, then, on this subject.
But I must again go over the several parts in detail,

---

[1] *i.e.* in the territory "behind Lepra."
[2] *i.e.* "Rugged" country.
[3] A fountain. [4] *Frag.* 9 (Bergk).

---

[5] ἐρατήν, Wyttenbach, for ἄρα τήν ; so the editors.
[6] δ' Ἀστήεντος is doubtful (see C. Müller, *Ind. Var. Lect.*
p. 1028) ; CFoz read διαστήεντος ; the editors before Kramer,
δ' Ἀστύεντος.
[7] εἵλομεν, Clavier, for εἵδομεν ; so the editors.

τόπων ποιησαμένους, ἐφ᾽[1] ὧνπερ καὶ πρῶτον αἱ κτίσεις ἐγένοντο, λέγω δὲ τῶν περὶ Μίλητον καὶ Ἔφεσον· αὗται γὰρ ἄρισται πόλεις καὶ ἐνδοξόταται.

5. Μετὰ δὲ τὸ Ποσείδιον τὸ Μιλησίων ἑξῆς ἐστὶ τὸ μαντεῖον τοῦ Διδυμέως Ἀπόλλωνος τὸ ἐν Βραγχίδαις, ἀναβάντι ὅσον ὀκτωκαίδεκα σταδίους· ἐνεπρήσθη δ᾽ ὑπὸ Ξέρξου, καθάπερ καὶ τὰ ἄλλα ἱερὰ πλὴν τοῦ ἐν Ἐφέσῳ· οἱ δὲ Βραγχίδαι τοὺς θησαυροὺς τοῦ θεοῦ παραδόντες τῷ Πέρσῃ φεύγοντι συναπῆραν, τοῦ μὴ τῖσαι δίκας τῆς ἱεροσυλίας καὶ τῆς προδοσίας. ὕστερον δ᾽ οἱ Μιλήσιοι μέγιστον νεὼν τῶν πάντων κατεσκεύασαν, διέμεινε δὲ χωρὶς ὀροφῆς διὰ τὸ μέγεθος· κώμης γοῦν κατοικίαν ὁ τοῦ σηκοῦ περίβολος δέδεκται καὶ ἄλσος ἐντός τε καὶ ἐκτὸς πολυτελές· ἄλλοι δὲ σηκοὶ τὸ μαντεῖον καὶ τὰ ἱερὰ συνέχουσιν· ἐνταῦθα δὲ μυθεύεται τὰ περὶ τὸν Βράγχον καὶ τὸν ἔρωτα τοῦ Ἀπόλλωνος· κεκόσμηται δ᾽ ἀναθήμασι τῶν ἀρχαίων τεχνῶν πολυτελέστατα· ἐντεῦθεν δ᾽ ἐπὶ τὴν πόλιν οὐ πολλὴ ὁδός ἐστιν, οὐδὲ πλοῦς.

6. Φησὶ δ᾽ Ἔφορος τὸ πρῶτον κτίσμα εἶναι Κρητικόν, ὑπὲρ τῆς θαλάττης τετειχισμένον, ὅπου νῦν ἡ πάλαι Μίλητός ἐστι, Σαρπηδόνος ἐκ Μιλήτου τῆς Κρητικῆς ἀγαγόντος οἰκήτορας καὶ C 635 θεμένου τοὔνομα τῇ πόλει τῆς ἐκεῖ πόλεως ἐπώνυμον, κατεχόντων πρότερον Λελέγων τὸν τόπον· τοὺς δὲ περὶ Νηλέα ὕστερον τὴν νῦν τειχίσαι πόλιν. ἔχει δὲ τέτταρας λιμένας ἡ νῦν, ὧν ἕνα καὶ στόλῳ ἱκανόν. πολλὰ δὲ τῆς πόλεως ἔργα

___
[1] ἐφ᾽, Corais, for ἀφ᾽.

beginning with the principal places, those where the foundings first took place, I mean those round Miletus and Ephesus; for these are the best and most famous cities.

5. Next after the Poseidium of the Milesians, eighteen stadia inland, is the oracle of Apollo Didymeus among the Branchidae.[1] It was set on fire by Xerxes, as were also the other temples, except that at Ephesus. The Branchidae gave over the treasures of the god to the Persian king, and accompanied him in his flight in order to escape punishment for the robbing and the betrayal of the temple. But later the Milesians erected the largest temple in the world, though on account of its size it remained without a roof. At any rate, the circuit of the sacred enclosure holds a village settlement; and there is a magnificent sacred grove both inside and outside the enclosure; and other sacred enclosures contain the oracle and the shrines. Here is laid the scene of the myth of Branchus and the love of Apollo. The temple is adorned with costliest offerings consisting of early works of art. Thence to the city is no long journey, by land or by sea.

6. Ephorus says: Miletus was first founded and fortified above the sea by the Cretans, where the Miletus of olden times is now situated, being settled by Sarpedon, who brought colonists from the Cretan Miletus and named the city after that Miletus, the place formerly being in the possession of the Leleges; but later Neleus and his followers fortified the present city. The present city has four harbours, one of which is large enough for a fleet. Many are

[1] *i.e.* at Didyma. On this temple see Herod. 1. 46, 5. 36, 6. 19.

ταύτης, μέγιστον δὲ τὸ πλῆθος τῶν ἀποικιῶν·[1]
ὅ τε γὰρ Εὔξεινος πόντος ὑπὸ τούτων συνῴκισται
πᾶς καὶ ἡ Προποντὶς καὶ ἄλλοι πλείους τόποι.
᾿Αναξιμένης γοῦν ὁ Λαμψακηνὸς οὕτω φησίν, ὅτι
καὶ ῎Ικαρον τὴν νῆσον καὶ Λέρον Μιλήσιοι συνῴκισαν καὶ περὶ ῾Ελλήσποντον ἐν μὲν τῇ Χερρονήσῳ Λίμνας, ἐν δὲ τῇ ᾿Ασίᾳ ῎Αβυδον, ῎Αρισβαν,
Παισόν· ἐν δὲ τῇ Κυζικηνῶν νήσῳ ᾿Αρτάκην,
Κύζικον· ἐν δὲ τῇ μεσογαίᾳ τῆς Τρῳάδος Σκῆψιν·
ἡμεῖς δ᾿ ἐν τοῖς καθ᾿ ἕκαστα λέγομεν καὶ τὰς
ἄλλας τὰς ὑπὸ τούτου παραλελειμμένας. Οὔλιον
δ᾿ ᾿Απόλλωνα καλοῦσί τινα καὶ Μιλήσιοι καὶ
Δήλιοι, οἷον ὑγιαστικὸν καὶ παιωνικόν· τὸ γὰρ
οὔλειν ὑγιαίνειν, ἀφ᾿ οὗ καὶ τὸ οὐλὴ καὶ τὸ

οὐλέ τε καὶ μέγα[2] χαῖρε·

ἰατικὸς γὰρ ὁ ᾿Απόλλων· καὶ ἡ ῎Αρτεμις ἀπὸ τοῦ
ἀρτεμέας ποιεῖν· καὶ ὁ ῞Ηλιος δὲ καὶ ἡ Σελήνη
συνοικειοῦνται τούτοις, ὅτι τῆς περὶ τοὺς ἀέρας
εὐκρασίας αἴτιοι· καὶ τὰ λοιμικὰ δὲ πάθη καὶ
τοὺς αὐτομάτους θανάτους τούτοις ἀνάπτουσι τοῖς
θεοῖς.

7. ῎Ανδρες δ᾿ ἄξιοι μνήμης ἐγένοντο ἐν τῇ
Μιλήτῳ Θαλῆς τε, εἷς τῶν ἑπτὰ σοφῶν, ὁ πρῶτος
φυσιολογίας ἄρξας ἐν τοῖς ῞Ελλησι καὶ μαθη-
ματικῆς, καὶ ὁ τούτου μαθητὴς ᾿Αναξίμανδρος
καὶ ὁ τούτου πάλιν ᾿Αναξιμένης, ἔτι δ᾿ ῾Εκαταῖος
ὁ τὴν ἱστορίαν συντάξας, καθ᾿ ἡμᾶς δὲ Αἰσχίνης

---

[1] ἀποικιῶν, x and the editors, instead of ἀποίκων.
[2] The Homeric text has μάλα instead of μέγα.

---

[1] i.e. a "healed wound"; also a "scar."
[2] i.e. "safe and sound."   ε The Sun-god.

the achievements of this city, but the greatest is the number of its colonisations; for the Euxine Pontus has been colonised everywhere by these people, as also the Propontis and several other regions. At any rate, Anaximenes of Lampsacus says that the Milesians colonised the islands Icaros and Leros; and, near the Hellespont, Limnae in the Chersonesus, as also Abydus and Arisba and Paesus in Asia; and Artacê and Cyzicus in the island of the Cyziceni; and Scepsis in the interior of the Troad. I, however, in my detailed description speak of the other cities, which have been omitted by him. Both Milesians and Delians invoke an Apollo "Ulius," that is, as god of "health and healing," for the verb "ulein" means "to be healthy"; whence the noun "ulê"[1] and the salutation, "Both health and great joy to thee"; for Apollo is the god of healing. And Artemis has her name from the fact that she makes people "Artemeas."[2] And both Helius[3] and Selenê[4] are closely associated with these, since they are the causes of the temperature of the air. And both pestilential diseases and sudden deaths are imputed to these gods.

7. Notable men were born at Miletus: Thales, one of the Seven Wise Men, the first to begin the science of natural philosophy[5] and mathematics among the Greeks, and his pupil Anaximander, and again the pupil of the latter, Anaximenes, and also Hecataeus, the author of the *History*, and, in my time, Aeschines the orator, who remained in exile

---

[4] The Moon-goddess.
[5] Literally "physiology," which again shows the perversion of Greek scientific names in English (cf. Vol. I, p. 27, footnote 2).

ὁ ῥήτωρ, ὃς ἐν φυγῇ διετέλεσε, παρρησιασάμενος πέρα τοῦ μετρίου πρὸς Πομπήιον Μάγνον. ἠτύχησε δ᾽ ἡ πόλις, ἀποκλείσασα Ἀλέξανδρον καὶ βίᾳ ληφθεῖσα, καθάπερ καὶ Ἁλικαρνασός· ἔτι δὲ πρότερον ὑπὸ Περσῶν· καί φησί γε Καλλισθένης, ὑπ᾽ Ἀθηναίων χιλίαις δραχμαῖς ζημιωθῆναι Φρύνιχον τὸν τραγικόν, διότι δρᾶμα ἐποίησε Μιλήτου ἅλωσιν ὑπὸ Δαρείου. πρόκειται δ᾽ ἡ Λάδη νῆσος πλησίον καὶ τὰ[1] περὶ τὰς Τραγαίας νησία, ὑφόρμους ἔχοντα λῃσταῖς.

8. Ἑξῆς δ᾽ ἐστὶν ὁ Λατμικὸς[2] κόλπος, ἐν ᾧ Ἡράκλεια ἡ ὑπὸ Λάτμῳ λεγομένη, πολίχνιον ὕφορμον ἔχον· ἐκαλεῖτο δὲ πρότερον Λάτμος ὁμωνύμως τῷ ὑπερκειμένῳ ὄρει, ὅπερ Ἑκαταῖος μὲν ἐμφαίνει τὸ αὐτὸ εἶναι νομίζων τῷ ὑπὸ τοῦ ποιητοῦ Φθειρῶν ὄρει λεγομένῳ (ὑπὲρ γὰρ τῆς Λάτμου φησὶ τὸ Φθειρῶν ὄρος κεῖσθαι), τινὲς
C 636 δὲ τὸ Γρίον φασίν, ὡς ἂν παράλληλον τῷ Λάτμῳ ἀνῆκον ἀπὸ τῆς Μιλησίας πρὸς ἕω διὰ τῆς Καρίας μέχρι Εὐρώμου καὶ Χαλκητόρων· ὑπέρκειται δὲ ταύτης ἐν ὕψει.[3] μικρὸν δ᾽ ἄπωθεν διαβάντι ποταμίσκον πρὸς τῷ Λάτμῳ δείκνυται τάφος Ἐνδυμίωνος ἔν τινι σπηλαίῳ· εἶτα ἀφ᾽ Ἡρακλείας ἐπὶ Πύρραν πολίχνην πλοῦς ἑκατόν που σταδίων.

9. Μικρὸν δὲ πλέον τὸ ἀπὸ Μιλήτου εἰς Ἡράκλειαν ἐγκολπίζοντι, εὐθυπλοίᾳ δ᾽ εἰς Πύρ-

[1] τά, omitted by MSS. except E.
[2] Λατμικός, Xylander, for Λητομηκός F, Λατομμικός s, Λατομικός other MSS.
[3] For ὕψει Groskurd conj. ὄψει, and Meineke so reads.

to the end, since he spoke freely, beyond moderation, before Pompey the Great. But the city was unfortunate, since it shut its gates against Alexander and was taken by force, as was also the case with Halicarnassus; and also, before that time, it was taken by the Persians. And Callisthenes says that Phrynichus the tragic poet was fined a thousand drachmas by the Athenians because he wrote a play entitled *The Capture of Miletus by Dareius.* The island Ladê lies close in front of Miletus, as do also the isles in the neighbourhood of the Tragaeae, which afford anchorage for pirates.

8. Next comes the Latmian Gulf, on which is situated "Heracleia below Latmus," as it is called, a small town that has an anchoring-place. It was at first called Latmus, the same name as the mountain that lies above it, which Hecataeus indicates, in his opinion, to be the same as that which by the poet is called "the mountain of the Phtheires"[1] (for he says that the mountain of the Phtheires lies above Latmus), though some say that it is Mt. Grium, which is approximately parallel to Latmus and extends inland from Milesia towards the east through Caria to Euromus and Chalcetores.[2] This mountain lies above Heracleia, and at a high elevation.[3] At a slight distance away from it, after one has crossed a little river near Latmus, there is to be seen the sepulchre of Endymion, in a cave. Then from Heracleia to Pyrrha, a small town, there is a voyage of about one hundred stadia.

9. But the voyage from Miletus to Heracleia, including the sinuosities of the gulfs, is a little more

[1] *Iliad* 2. 868.   [2] See 14. 2. 22.
[3] Or rather, perhaps, "and in sight of it" (see critical note).

ραν ἐκ Μιλήτου τριάκοντα· τοσαύτην ἔχει μακροπορίαν ὁ παρὰ γῆν πλοῦς. ἀνάγκη δ᾽ ἐπὶ τῶν ἐνδόξων τόπων ὑπομένειν τὸ περισκελὲς τῆς τοιαύτης γεωγραφίας.

10. Ἐκ δὲ Πύρρας ἐπὶ τὴν ἐκβολὴν τοῦ Μαιάνδρου πεντήκοντα· τεναγώδης δ᾽ ὁ τόπος καὶ ἐλώδης· ἀναπλεύσαντι δ᾽ ὑπηρετικοῖς σκάφεσι τριάκοντα σταδίους πόλις Μυοῦς, μία τῶν Ἰάδων τῶν δώδεκα, ἡ νῦν δι᾽ ὀλιγανδρίαν Μιλησίοις συμπεπόλισται. ταύτην ὄψον λέγεται Θεμιστοκλεῖ δοῦναι Ξέρξης, ἄρτον δὲ Μαγνησίαν, οἶνον δὲ Λάμψακον.

11. Ἔνθεν ἐν σταδίοις τέτταρσι κώμη Καρικὴ Θυμβρία, παρ᾽ ἣν Ἄορνόν ἐστι σπήλαιον ἱερόν, Χαρώνιον λεγόμενον ὀλεθρίους ἔχον ἀποφοράς. ὑπέρκειται δὲ Μαγνησία ἡ πρὸς Μαιάνδρῳ, Μαγνήτων ἀποικία τῶν ἐν Θετταλίᾳ καὶ Κρητῶν, περὶ ἧς αὐτίκα ἐροῦμεν.

12. Μετὰ δὲ τὰς ἐκβολὰς τοῦ Μαιάνδρου ὁ κατὰ Πριήνην ἐστὶν αἰγιαλός, ὑπὲρ αὐτοῦ δ᾽ ἡ Πριήνη καὶ Μυκάλη τὸ ὄρος, εὔθηρον καὶ εὔδενδρον. ἐπίκειται δὲ τῇ Σαμίᾳ καὶ ποιεῖ πρὸς αὐτὴν ἐπέκεινα τῆς Τρωγιλίου καλουμένης ἄκρας ὅσον ἑπταστάδιον πορθμόν. λέγεται δ᾽ ὑπό τινων ἡ Πριήνη Κάδμη, ἐπειδὴ Φιλώτας ὁ ἐπικτίσας αὐτὴν Βοιώτιος ὑπῆρχεν· ἐκ Πριήνης δ᾽ ἦν Βίας, εἷς τῶν ἑπτὰ σοφῶν, περὶ οὗ φησιν οὕτως Ἱππῶναξ·

καὶ δικάσσασθαι Βίαντος τοῦ Πριηνέως κρέσσων.

than one hundred stadia, though that from Miletus to Pyrrha, in a straight course, is only thirty—so much longer is the journey along the coast. But in the case of famous places my reader must needs endure the dry part of such geography as this.

10. The voyage from Pyrrha to the outlet of the Maeander River is fifty stadia, a place which consists of shallows and marshes; and, going inland in rowboats thirty stadia, one comes to the city Myus, one of the twelve Ionian cities, which, on account of its sparse population, has now been incorporated into Miletus. Xerxes is said to have given this city to Themistocles to supply him with fish, Magnesia to supply him with bread, and Lampsacus with wine.

11. Thence, within four stadia, one comes to a village, the Carian Thymbria, near which is Aornum, a sacred cave, which is called Charonium, since it emits deadly vapours. Above it lies Magnesia on the Maeander, a colony of the Magnesians of Thessaly and the Cretans, of which I shall soon speak.[1]

12. After the outlets of the Maeander comes the shore of Prienê, above which lies Prienê, and also the mountain Mycalê, which is well supplied with wild animals and with trees. This mountain lies above the Samian territory[2] and forms with it, on the far side of the promontory called Trogilian, a strait about seven stadia in width. Prienê is by some writers called Cadmê, since Philotas, who founded it, was a Boeotian. Bias, one of the Seven Wise Men, was a native of Prienê, of whom Hipponax says "stronger in the pleading of his cases than Bias of Prienê."[3]

---

[1] §§ 39-40 following.   [2] The isle of Samos.
[3] *Frag.* 79 ι Bergk).

13. Τῆς δὲ Τρωγιλίου πρόκειται νησίον ὁμώ-
νυμον· ἐντεῦθεν δὲ τὸ ἐγγυτάτω δίαρμά ἐστιν
ἐπὶ Σούνιον σταδίων χιλίων ἑξακοσίων, κατ᾽
ἀρχὰς μὲν Σάμον ἐν δεξιᾷ ἔχοντι καὶ Ἰκαρίαν
καὶ Κορσίας,¹ τοὺς δὲ Μελαντίους ² σκοπέλους
ἐξ εὐωνύμων, τὸ λοιπὸν δὲ διὰ μέσων τῶν
Κυκλάδων νήσων. καὶ αὐτὴ δ᾽ ἡ Τρωγίλιος
ἄκρα πρόπους τις τῆς Μυκάλης ἐστί. τῇ
Μυκάλῃ δ᾽ ὄρος ἄλλο πρόσκειται τῆς Ἐφεσίας
Πακτύης· καὶ ἡ Μεσωγὶς δὲ εἰς αὐτὴν κατα-
στρέφει.

14. Ἀπὸ δὲ τῆς Τρωγιλίου στάδιοι τετταράκοντα εἰς τὴν Σάμον· βλέπει δὲ πρὸς νότον
καὶ αὐτὴ καὶ ὁ λιμήν, ἔχων ναύσταθμον. ἔστι
C 637 δ᾽ αὐτῆς ἐν ἐπιπέδῳ τὸ πλέον, ὑπὸ τῆς θαλάττης
κλυζόμενον, μέρος δέ τι καὶ εἰς τὸ ὄρος ἀνέχει
τὸ ὑπερκείμενον. ἐν δεξιᾷ μὲν οὖν προσπλέουσι
πρὸς τὴν πόλιν ἐστὶ τὸ Ποσείδιον, ἄκρα ἡ
ποιοῦσα πρὸς τὴν Μυκάλην τὸν ἑπταστάδιον
πορθμόν, ἔχει δὲ νεὼν Ποσειδῶνος· πρόκειται
δ᾽ αὐτοῦ νησίδιον ἡ Ναρθηκίς· ἐπ᾽ ἀριστερᾷ δὲ
τὸ προάστειον τὸ πρὸς τῷ Ἡραίῳ καὶ ὁ Ἴμβρασος
ποταμὸς καὶ τὸ Ἡραῖον, ἀρχαῖον ἱερὸν καὶ νεὼς
μέγας, ὃς νῦν πινακοθήκη ἐστί· χωρὶς δὲ τοῦ
πλήθους τῶν ἐνταῦθα κειμένων πινάκων ἄλλαι
πινακοθῆκαι καὶ ναΐσκοι τινές εἰσι πλήρεις τῶν
ἀρχαίων τεχνῶν· τό τε ὕπαιθρον ὁμοίως μεστὸν
ἀνδριάντων ἐστὶ τῶν ἀρίστων· ὧν τρία Μύρωνος
ἔργα κολοσσικὰ ἱδρυμένα ἐπὶ μιᾶς βάσεως, ἃ

¹ Καρσίας F ; Tzschucke emends to Κορασσίας.
² Μελαντίους, Tzschucke, from conj. of Voss, for Μελαν-
θίους ; so the later editors.

13. Off the Trogilian promontory lies an isle of the same name. Thence the nearest passage across to Sunium is one thousand six hundred stadia; on the voyage one has at first Samos and Icaria and Corsia on the right, and the Melantian rocks on the left; and the remainder of the voyage is through the midst of the Cyclades islands. The Trogilian promontory itself is a kind of spur of Mt. Mycalê. Close to Mycalê lies another mountain, in the Ephesian territory, I mean Mt. Pactyes, in which the Mesogis terminates.

14. The distance from the Trogilian promontory to Samos[1] is forty stadia. Samos faces the south, both it and its harbour, which latter has a naval station. The greater part of it is on level ground, being washed by the sea, but a part of it reaches up into the mountain that lies above it. Now on the right, as one sails towards the city, is the Poseidium, a promontory which with Mt. Mycalê forms the seven-stadia strait; and it has a temple of Poseidon; and in front of it lies an isle called Narthecis; and on the left is the suburb near the Heraeum, and also the Imbrasus River, and the Heraeum, which consists of an ancient temple and a great shrine, which latter is now a repository of tablets.[2] Apart from the number of the tablets placed there, there are other repositories of votive tablets and some small chapels full of ancient works of art. And the temple, which is open to the sky, is likewise full of most excellent statues. Of these, three of colossal size, the work of Myron, stood upon one base; Antony

---

[1] *i.e.* the *city* Samos.
[2] Whether maps or paintings, or both, the translator does not know.

ἦρε μὲν Ἀντώνιος, ἀνέθηκε δὲ πάλιν ὁ Σεβαστὸς
Καῖσαρ εἰς τὴν αὐτὴν βάσιν τὰ δύο, τὴν Ἀθηνᾶν
καὶ τὸν Ἡρακλέα, τὸν δὲ Δία εἰς τὸ Καπετώλιον
μετήνεγκε, κατασκευάσας αὐτῷ ναΐσκον.

15. Περίπλους δ᾽ ἐστὶ τῆς Σαμίων νήσου
σταδίων ἑξακοσίων. ἐκαλεῖτο δὲ Παρθενία
πρότερον οἰκούντων Καρῶν, εἶτα Ἀνθεμοῦς,[1]
εἶτα Μελάμφυλλος,[2] εἶτα Σάμος, εἴτ᾽ ἀπό τινος
ἐπιχωρίου ἥρωος, εἴτ᾽ ἐξ Ἰθάκης καὶ Κεφαλληνίας
ἀποικήσαντος.[3] καλεῖται μὲν οὖν καὶ ἄκρα τις
Ἄμπελος βλέπουσά πως πρὸς τὸ τῆς Ἰκαρίας
Δρέπανον, ἀλλὰ καὶ τὸ ὄρος ἅπαν, ὃ ποιεῖ τὴν
ὅλην νῆσον ὀρεινήν, ὁμωνύμως λέγεται· ἔστι δ᾽
οὐκ εὔοινος, καίπερ εὐοινουσῶν τῶν κύκλῳ νήσων,
καὶ τῆς ἠπείρου σχεδόν τι τῆς προσεχοῦς πάσης
τοὺς ἀρίστους ἐκφερούσης οἴνους, οἷον Χίου καὶ
Λέσβου καὶ Κῶ.[4] καὶ μὴν καὶ ὁ Ἐφέσιος καὶ Μη-
τροπολίτης ἀγαθοί, ἥ τε Μεσωγὶς καὶ ὁ Τμῶλος
καὶ ἡ Κατακεκαυμένη καὶ Κνίδος καὶ Σμύρνα
καὶ ἄλλοι ἀσημότεροι τόποι διαφόρως χρηστοι-
νοῦσιν ἢ πρὸς ἀπόλαυσιν ἢ πρὸς διαίτας ἰατρι-
κάς. περὶ μὲν οὖν[5] οἴνους οὐ πάνυ εὐτυχεῖ
Σάμος, τὰ δ᾽ ἄλλα εὐδαίμων, ὡς δῆλον ἔκ τε τοῦ
περιμάχητον γενέσθαι καὶ ἐκ τοῦ τοὺς ἐπαινοῦντας
μὴ ὀκνεῖν ἐφαρμόττειν αὐτῇ τὴν λέγουσαν παροιμίαν, ὅτι φέρει καὶ ὀρνίθων γάλα, καθάπερ

---

[1] For Ἀνθεμοῦς, Corais, following Eustathius (note on
Dionys. 533), reads Ἀνθεμίς. By some writers the name is
spelled Ἀνθεμοῦσα.

[2] Μελάμφυλλος, Meineke, for Μελάμφυλος.

[3] ἀποικήσαντος F, ἀποικίσαντος other MSS.

[4] οἷον . . . Κῶ, Meineke ejects.

took these statues away,[1] but Augustus Caesar restored two of them, those of Athena and Heracles, to the same base, although he transferred the Zeus to the Capitolium, having erected there a small chapel for that statue.

15. The voyage round the island of the Samians is six hundred stadia. In earlier times, when it was inhabited by Carians, it was called Parthenia, then Anthemus, then Melamphyllus, and then Samos, whether after some native hero or after someone who colonised it from Ithaca and Cephallenia.[2] Now in Samos there is a promontory approximately facing Drepanum in Icaria which is called Ampelus, but the entire mountain which makes the whole of the island mountainous is called by the same name. The island does not produce good wine, although good wine is produced by the islands all round, and although most of the whole of the adjacent mainland produces the best of wines, for example, Chios and Lesbos and Cos. And indeed the Ephesian and Metropolitan wines are good; and Mt. Mesogis and Mt. Tmolus and the Catacecaumene country and Cnidos and Smyrna and other less significant places produce exceptionally good wine, whether for enjoyment or medicinal purposes. Now Samos is not altogether fortunate in regard to wines, but in all other respects it is a blest country, as is clear from the fact that it became an object of contention in war, and also from the fact that those who praise it do not hesitate to apply to it the proverb, that "it

---

[1] See 13. 1. 30.   [2] See 10. 2. 17.

---

[5] οὖν, before οἴνους, Meineke inserts.

που καὶ Μένανδρος ἔφη.[1] τοῦτο δὲ καὶ τῶν
τυραννίδων αἴτιον αὐτῇ κατέστη, καὶ τῆς πρὸς
Ἀθηναίους ἔχθρας.

16 Αἱ μὲν οὖν τυραννίδες ἤκμασαν κατὰ
Πολυκράτη μάλιστα καὶ τὸν ἀδελφὸν αὐτοῦ
Συλοσῶντα· ἦν δ' ὁ μὲν καὶ τύχῃ καὶ δυνάμει
λαμπρός, ὥστε καὶ θαλαττοκρατῆσαι· τῆς δ'
C 638 εὐτυχίας αὐτοῦ σημεῖον τιθέασιν, ὅτι ῥίψαντος
εἰς τὴν θάλατταν ἐπίτηδες τὸν δακτύλιον λίθου
καὶ γλύμματος πολυτελοῦς, ἀνήνεγκε μικρὸν
ὕστερον τῶν ἁλιέων τις τὸν καταπιόντα ἰχθὺν
αὐτόν· ἀνατμηθέντος δ' εὑρέθη ὁ δακτύλιος·
πυθόμενον δὲ τοῦτο τὸν Αἰγυπτίων βασιλέα
φασὶ μαντικῶς πως ἀποφθέγξασθαι, ὡς ἐν
βραχεῖ καταστρέψει τὸν βίον εἰς οὐκ εὐτυχὲς
τέλος ὁ τοσοῦτον ἐξηρμένος ταῖς εὐπραγίαις· καὶ
δὴ καὶ συμβῆναι τοῦτο· ληφθέντα γὰρ ἐξ
ἀπάτης ὑπὸ τοῦ σατράπου τῶν Περσῶν κρε-
μασθῆναι. τούτῳ συνεβίωσεν Ἀνακρέων ὁ
μελοποιός· καὶ δὴ καὶ πᾶσα ἡ ποίησις πλήρης
ἐστὶ τῆς περὶ αὐτοῦ μνήμης. ἐπὶ τούτου δὲ
καὶ Πυθαγόραν ἱστοροῦσιν ἰδόντα φυομένην τὴν
τυραννίδα ἐκλιπεῖν τὴν πόλιν καὶ ἀπελθεῖν εἰς
Αἴγυπτον καὶ Βαβυλῶνα φιλομαθείας χάριν·
ἐπανιόντα δ' ἐκεῖθεν, ὁρῶντα ἔτι συμμένουσαν
τὴν τυραννίδα, πλεύσαντα εἰς Ἰταλίαν ἐκεῖ
διατελέσαι τὸν βίον. περὶ Πολυκράτους μὲν
ταῦτα.

17. Συλοσῶν δ' ἀπελείφθη μὲν ἰδιώτης ὑπὸ τοῦ
ἀδελφοῦ, Δαρείῳ δὲ τῷ Ὑστάσπεω χαρισάμενος

---

[1] καθάπερ . . . ἔφη, Meineke ejects.

produces even birds' milk," as Menander somewhere says. This was also the cause of the establishment of the tyrannies there, and of their enmity against the Athenians.

16. Now the tyrannies reached their greatest height in the time of Polycrates and his brother Syloson. Polycrates was such a brilliant man, both in his good fortune and in his natural ability, that he gained supremacy over the sea; and it is set down,[1] as a sign of his good fortune, that he purposely flung into the sea his ring, a ring of very costly stone and engraving, and that a little later one of the fishermen brought him the very fish that swallowed it; and that when the fish was cut open the ring was found; and that on learning this the king of the Egyptians, it is said, declared in a kind of prophetic way that any man who had been exalted so highly in welfare would shortly come to no happy end of life; and indeed this is what happened, for he was captured by treachery by the satrap of the Persians and hanged. Anacreon the melic poet lived in companionship with Polycrates; and indeed the whole of his poetry is full of his praises. It was in his time, as we are told, that Pythagoras, seeing that the tyranny was growing in power, left the city and went off to Egypt and Babylon, to satisfy his fondness for learning; but when he came back and saw that the tyranny still endured, he set sail for Italy and lived there to the end of his life. So much for Polycrates.

17. Syloson was left a private citizen by his brother, but to gratify Dareius, the son of Hystas-

---

[1] See Herodotus, 3. 40–43, and 120, 125.

ἐσθῆτα, ἧς ἐπεθύμησεν ἐκεῖνος φοροῦντα ἰδών,
οὔπω δ' ἐβασίλευε τότε, βασιλεύσαντος ἀντέλαβε
δῶρον τὴν τυραννίδα. πικρῶς δ' ἦρξεν, ὥστε
καὶ ἐλειπάνδρησεν ἡ πόλις· κἀκεῖθεν ἐκπεσεῖν
συνέβη τὴν παροιμίαν·

ἔκητι Συλοσῶντος εὐρυχωρίη.

18. Ἀθηναῖοι δὲ πρότερον μὲν πέμψαντες
στρατηγὸν Περικλέα καὶ σὺν αὐτῷ Σοφοκλέα
τὸν ποιητὴν πολιορκίᾳ κακῶς διέθηκαν ἀπει-
θοῦντας τοὺς Σαμίους, ὕστερον δὲ καὶ κληρού-
χους ἔπεμψαν δισχιλίους ἐξ ἑαυτῶν, ὧν ἦν καὶ
Νεοκλῆς, ὁ Ἐπικούρου τοῦ φιλοσόφου πατήρ,
γραμματοδιδάσκαλος, ὥς φασι· καὶ δὴ καὶ
τραφῆναί φασιν ἐνθάδε καὶ ἐν Τέῳ, καὶ ἐφη-
βεῦσαι Ἀθήνησι· γενέσθαι δ' αὐτῷ συνέφηβον
Μένανδρον τὸν κωμικόν· Σάμιος δ' ἦν καὶ
Κρεώφυλος, ὅν φασι δεξάμενον ξενίᾳ ποτὲ
Ὅμηρον, λαβεῖν δῶρον τὴν ἐπιγραφὴν τοῦ ποιή-
ματος, ὃ καλοῦσιν Οἰχαλίας ἅλωσιν. Καλλί-
μαχος δὲ τοὐναντίον ἐμφαίνει δι' ἐπιγράμματός
τινος, ὡς ἐκείνου μὲν ποιήσαντος, λεγομένου δ'
Ὁμήρου διὰ τὴν λεγομένην ξενίαν·

τοῦ Σαμίου πόνος εἰμί, δόμῳ ποτὲ θεῖον
Ὅμηρον
δεξαμένου· κλείω[1] δ' Εὔρυτον, ὅσσ' ἔπαθεν,
καὶ ξανθὴν Ἰόλειαν· Ὁμήρειον δὲ καλεῦμαι
γράμμα· Κρεωφύλῳ, Ζεῦ φίλε, τοῦτο μέγα.

C 639 τινὲς δὲ διδάσκαλον Ὁμήρου τοῦτόν φασιν, οἱ
δ' οὐ τοῦτον, ἀλλ' Ἀριστέαν τὸν Προκοννήσιον.

---

[1] κλείω, Meineke, for καίω; κλαίω Tzschucke.

pes, he gave him a robe which Dareius desired
when he saw him wearing it; and Dareius at that
time was not yet king, but when Dareius became
king, Syloson received as a return-gift the tyranny of
Samos. But he ruled so harshly that the city became
depopulated; and thence arose the proverb, "by the
will of Syloson there is plenty of room."

18. The Athenians at first sent Pericles as general
and with him Sophocles the poet, who by a siege
put the disobedient Samians in bad plight; but
later they sent two thousand allottees from their
own people, among whom was Neocles, the father
of Epicurus the philosopher, a schoolmaster as they
call him. And indeed it is said that Epicurus grew
up here and in Teos, and that he became an
ephebus[1] at Athens, and that Menander the comic
poet became an ephebus at the same time. Creophylus, also, was a Samian, who, it is said, once
entertained Homer and received as a gift from him
the inscription of the poem called *The Capture of
Oechalia*. But Callimachus clearly indicates the contrary in an epigram of his, meaning that Creophylus
composed the poem, but that it was ascribed to
Homer because of the story of the hospitality shown
him: "I am the toil of the Samian, who once
entertained in his house the divine Homer. I
bemoan Eurytus, for all that he suffered, and golden-
haired Ioleia. I am called Homer's writing. For
Creophylus, dear Zeus, this is a great achievement."
Some call Creophylus Homer's teacher, while others
say that it was not Creophylus, but Aristeas the
Proconnesian, who was his teacher.

---

[1] *i.e.* at eighteen years of age underwent a "scrutiny" and
was registered as an Athenian citizen.

19. Παράκειται δὲ τῇ Σάμῳ νῆσος Ἰκαρία, ἀφ' ἧς τὸ Ἰκάριον πέλαγος. αὕτη δ' ἐπώνυμός ἐστιν Ἰκάρου, παιδὸς τοῦ Δαιδάλου, ὅν φασι τῷ πατρὶ κοινωνήσαντα τῆς φυγῆς, ἡνίκα ἀμφότεροι πτερωθέντες ἀπῆραν ἐκ Κρήτης, πεσεῖν ἐνθάδε, μὴ κρατήσαντα τοῦ δρόμου· μετεωρισθέντι γὰρ πρὸς τὸν ἥλιον ἐπὶ πλέον περιρρυῆναι τὰ πτερά, τακέντος τοῦ κηροῦ.[1] τριακοσίων δ' ἐστὶ τὴν περίμετρον σταδίων ἡ νῆσος ἅπασα καὶ ἀλίμενος, πλὴν ὑφόρμων, ὧν ὁ κάλλιστος Ἰστοὶ λέγονται· ἄκρα δ' ἐστὶν ἀνατείνουσα πρὸς ζέφυρον. ἔστι δὲ καὶ Ἀρτέμιδος ἱερόν, καλούμενον Ταυροπόλιον, ἐν τῇ νήσῳ καὶ πολισμάτιον Οἰνόη, καὶ ἄλλο Δράκανον, ὁμώνυμον τῇ ἄκρᾳ, ἐφ' ᾗ ἵδρυται, πρόσορμον ἔχον· ἡ δὲ ἄκρα διέχει τῆς Σαμίων ἄκρας, τῆς Κανθαρίου καλουμένης, ὀγδοήκοντα σταδίους, ὅπερ ἐστὶν ἐλάχιστον δίαρμα τὸ μεταξύ. νυνὶ μέντοι λειπανδροῦσαν Σάμιοι νέμονται τὰ πολλὰ βοσκημάτων χάριν.

20. Μετὰ δὲ τὸν Σάμιον πορθμὸν τὸν πρὸς Μυκάλῃ πλέουσιν εἰς Ἔφεσον ἐν δεξιᾷ ἐστιν ἡ Ἐφεσίων παραλία· μέρος δέ τι ἔχουσιν αὐτῆς καὶ οἱ Σάμιοι. πρῶτον δ' ἐστὶν ἐν τῇ παραλίᾳ τὸ Πανιώνιον, τρισὶ σταδίοις ὑπερκείμενον τῆς θαλάττης, ὅπου τὰ Πανιώνια, κοινὴ πανήγυρις τῶν Ἰώνων, συντελεῖται τῷ Ἑλικωνίῳ Ποσειδῶνι καὶ θυσία· ἱερῶνται δὲ Πριηνεῖς· εἴρηται δὲ περὶ αὐτῶν ἐν τοῖς Πελοποννησιακοῖς. εἶτα Νεάπολις, ἣ πρότερον μὲν ἦν Ἐφεσίων, νῦν δὲ

---

[1] i.e. the wax which joined the wings to his body.

19. Alongside Samos lies the island Icaria, whence was derived the name of the Icarian Sea. This island is named after Icarus the son of Daedalus, who, it is said, having joined his father in flight, both being furnished with wings, flew away from Crete and fell here, having lost control of their course; for, they add, on rising too close to the sun, his wings slipped off, since the wax[1] melted. The whole island is three hundred stadia in perimeter; it has no harbours, but only places of anchorage, the best of which is called Histi.[2] It has a promontory which extends towards the west. There is also on the island a temple of Artemis, called Tauropolium; and a small town Oenoê; and another small town Dracanum, bearing the same name as the promontory on which it is situated and having near by a place of anchorage. The promontory is eighty stadia distant from the promontory of the Samians called Cantharius, which is the shortest distance between the two. At the present time, however, it has but few inhabitants left, and is used by Samians mostly for the grazing of cattle.

20. After the Samian strait, near Mt. Mycalê, as one sails to Ephesus, one comes, on the right, to the seaboard of the Ephesians; and a part of this seaboard is held by the Samians. First on the seaboard is the Panionium, lying three stadia above the sea where the Pan-Ionia, a common festival of the Ionians, are held, and where sacrifices are performed in honour of the Heliconian Poseidon; and Prienians serve as priests at this sacrifice, but I have spoken of them in my account of the Peloponnesus.[3] Then comes Neapolis, which in earlier times belonged to

---

[1] *i.e.* Masts.   [2] 8. 7. 2.

STRABO

Σαμίων, διαλλαξαμένων πρὸς τὸ Μαραθήσιον,
τὸ ἐγγυτέρω πρὸς τὸ ἀπωτέρω· εἶτα Πύγελα
πολίχνιον, ἱερὸν ἔχον Ἀρτέμιδος Μουνυχίας,
ἵδρυμα Ἀγαμέμνονος, οἰκούμενον ὑπὸ μέρους τῶν
ἐκείνου λαῶν· πυγαλγέας[1] γάρ τινάς φασι[2] καὶ
γενέσθαι καὶ κληθῆναι, κάμνοντας δ' ὑπὸ τοῦ
πάθους καταμεῖναι, καὶ τυχεῖν οἰκείου τοῦδε
τοῦ ὀνόματος τὸν τόπον. εἶτα λιμὴν Πάνορμος
καλούμενος, ἔχων ἱερὸν τῆς Ἐφεσίας Ἀρτέμιδος·
εἶθ' ἡ πόλις. ἐν δὲ τῇ αὐτῇ παραλίᾳ μικρὸν
ὑπὲρ τῆς θαλάττης ἐστὶ καὶ ἡ Ὀρτυγία, δια-
πρεπὲς ἄλσος παντοδαπῆς ὕλης, κυπαρίττου
δὲ τῆς πλείστης. διαρρεῖ δὲ ὁ Κέγχριος
ποταμός, οὗ φασὶ νίψασθαι τὴν Λητὼ μετὰ
τὰς ὠδῖνας. ἐνταῦθα γὰρ μυθεύουσι τὴν λοχείαν
καὶ τὴν τροφὸν τὴν Ὀρτυγίαν καὶ τὸ ἄδυτον,
ἐν ᾧ ἡ λοχεία, καὶ τὴν πλησίον ἐλαίαν,
ᾗ πρῶτον ἐπαναπαύσασθαί φασι τὴν θεὸν
C 640 ἀπολυθεῖσαν τῶν ὠδίνων. ὑπέρκειται δὲ τοῦ
ἄλσους ὄρος ὁ Σολμισσός, ὅπου στάντας φασὶ
τοὺς Κουρῆτας τῷ ψόφῳ τῶν ὅπλων ἐκπλῆξαι
τὴν Ἥραν ζηλοτύπως ἐφεδρεύουσαν, καὶ λαθεῖν
συμπράξαντας τὴν λοχείαν τῇ Λητοῖ. ὄντων δ'
ἐν τῷ τόπῳ πλειόνων ναῶν, τῶν μὲν ἀρχαίων,
τῶν δ' ὕστερον γενομένων, ἐν μὲν τοῖς ἀρχαίοις
ἀρχαῖά ἐστι ξόανα, ἐν δὲ τοῖς ὕστερον Σκόπα
ἔργα·[3] ἡ μὲν Λητὼ σκῆπτρον ἔχουσα, ἡ δ'
Ὀρτυγία παρέστηκεν ἑκατέρᾳ τῇ χειρὶ παιδίον

[1] πυγαλγέας, Corais, for πυγαλλίας Coxz, πυγαλίας other
MSS.; πυγαλγίας Meineke.
[2] φασι, Jones inserts.
[3] Instead of Σκόπα ἔργα, F has σκολιὰ σκόπ' ἔργα; other
MSS. σκολιὰ ἔργα, except v which has Σκόπα in the margin.
222

the Ephesians, but now belongs to the Samians, who gave in exchange for it Marathesium, the more distant for the nearer place. Then comes Pygela, a small town, with a temple of Artemis Munychia, founded by Agamemnon and inhabited by a part of his troops; for it is said that some of his soldiers became afflicted with a disease of the buttocks[1] and were called "diseased-buttocks," and that, being afflicted with this disease, they stayed there, and that the place thus received this appropriate name. Then comes the harbour called Panormus, with a temple of the Ephesian Artemis; and then the city Ephesus. On the same coast, slightly above the sea, is also Ortygia, which is a magnificent grove of all kinds of trees, of the cypress most of all. It is traversed by the Cenchrius River, where Leto is said to have bathed herself after her travail.[2] For here is the mythical scene of the birth, and of the nurse Ortygia, and of the holy place where the birth took place, and of the olive tree near by, where the goddess is said first to have taken a rest after she was relieved from her travail. Above the grove lies **Mt.** Solmissus, where, it is said, the Curetes stationed themselves, and with the din of their arms frightened Hera out of her wits when she was jealously spying on Leto, and when they helped Leto to conceal from Hera the birth of her children. There are several temples in the place, some ancient and others built in later times; and in the ancient temples are many ancient wooden images, but in those of later times there are works of Scopas; for example, Leto holding a sceptre and Ortygia standing beside her with a

---

[1] In Greek, with "pygalgia."
[2] Referring, of course, to the birth of Apollo and Artemis.

ἔχουσα. πανήγυρις δ' ἐνταῦθα συντελεῖται κατ'
ἔτος, ἔθει δέ τινι οἱ νέοι φιλοκαλοῦσι, μάλιστα
περὶ τὰς ἐνταῦθα εὐωχίας λαμπρυνόμενοι· τότε
δὲ καὶ τῶν Κουρήτων ἀρχεῖον συνάγει συμπόσια,
καί τινας μυστικὰς θυσίας ἐπιτελεῖ.

21. Τὴν δὲ πόλιν ᾤκουν μὲν Κᾶρές τε καὶ
Λέλεγες, ἐκβαλὼν δ' ὁ Ἄνδροκλος τοὺς πλείστους ᾤκισεν ἐκ τῶν συνελθόντων αὐτῷ περὶ τὸ
Ἀθήναιον καὶ τὴν Ὑπέλαιον, προσπεριλαβὼν
καὶ τῆς περὶ τὸν Κορησσὸν παρωρείας. μέχρι
μὲν δὴ τῶν κατὰ Κροῖσον οὕτως ᾤκεῖτο, ὕστερον
δ' ἀπὸ τῆς παρωρείου καταβάντες, περὶ τὸ νῦν
ἱερὸν ᾤκησαν μέχρι Ἀλεξάνδρου. Λυσίμαχος
δὲ τὴν νῦν πόλιν τειχίσας, ἀηδῶς τῶν ἀνθρώπων
μεθισταμένων, τηρήσας καταρράκτην ὄμβρον
συνήργησε καὶ αὐτὸς καὶ τοὺς ῥινούχους ἐνέ-
φραξεν, ὥστε κατακλύσαι τὴν πόλιν· οἱ δὲ
μετέστησαν ἄσμενοι. ἐκάλεσε δ' Ἀρσινόην ἀπὸ
τῆς γυναικὸς τὴν πόλιν, ἐπεκράτησε μέντοι τὸ
ἀρχαῖον ὄνομα. ἦν δὲ γερουσία καταγραφομένη,
τούτοις δὲ συνῇεσαν οἱ ἐπίκλητοι καλούμενοι καὶ
διῴκουν πάντα.

22. Τὸν δὲ νεὼν τῆς Ἀρτέμιδος πρῶτος[1] μὲν
Χερσίφρων ἠρχιτεκτόνησεν, εἶτ' ἄλλος[2] ἐποίησε
μείζω· ὡς δὲ τοῦτον Ἡρόστρατός τις ἐνέπρησεν,
ἄλλον ἀμείνω κατεσκεύασαν συνενέγκαντες τὸν
τῶν γυναικῶν κόσμον καὶ τὰς ἰδίας οὐσίας,
διαθέμενοι δὲ καὶ τοὺς προτέρους κίονας· τούτων
δὲ μαρτύριά ἐστι τὰ γενηθέντα τότε ψηφίσματα,

---

[1] πρῶτον F.   [2] ἄλλος, Xylander, for ἄλλον.

---

[1] Men specially summoned, privy-councillors.

child in each arm. A general festival is held there annually; and by a certain custom the youths vie for honour, particularly in the splendour of their banquets there. At that time, also, a special college of the Curetes holds symposiums and performs certain mystic sacrifices.

21. The city of Ephesus was inhabited both by Carians and by Leleges, but Androclus drove them out and settled the most of those who had come with him round the Athenaeum and the Hypelaeus, though he also included a part of the country situated on the slopes of Mt. Coressus. Now Ephesus was thus inhabited until the time of Croesus, but later the people came down from the mountain-side and abode round the present temple until the time of Alexander. Lysimachus built a wall round the present city, but the people were not agreeably disposed to change their abodes to it; and therefore he waited for a downpour of rain and himself took advantage of it and blocked the sewers so as to inundate the city; and the inhabitants were then glad to make the change. He named the city after his wife Arsinoê; the old name, however, prevailed. There was a senate, which was conscripted; and with these were associated the Epicleti,[1] as they were called, who administered all the affairs of the city.

22. As for the temple of Artemis, its first architect was Chersiphron; and then another man made it larger. But when it was set on fire by a certain Herostratus, the citizens erected another and better one, having collected the ornaments of the women and their own individual belongings, and having sold also the pillars of the former temple. Testimony is borne to these facts by the decrees that were made

ἅπερ ἀγνοοῦντά φησιν ὁ Ἀρτεμίδωρος τὸν
Ταυρομενίτην Τίμαιον, καὶ ἄλλως βάσκανον
ὄντα καὶ συκοφάντην (διὸ καὶ Ἐπιτίμαιον[1]
κληθῆναι), λέγειν, ὡς ἐκ τῶν Περσικῶν παρα-
καταθηκῶν ἐποιήσαντο τοῦ ἱεροῦ τὴν ἐπισκευήν·
οὔτε δὲ ὑπάρξαι παρακαταθήκας τότε, εἴ τε
ὑπῆρξαν, συνεμπεπρῆσθαι ἂν[2] τῷ ναῷ· μετὰ δὲ
τὴν ἔμπρησιν τῆς ὀροφῆς ἠφανισμένης, ἐν
ὑπαίθρῳ τῷ σηκῷ τίνα ἂν ἐθελῆσαι παρακατα-
θήκην κειμένην ἔχειν; Ἀλέξανδρον δὴ τοῖς
C 641 Ἐφεσίοις ὑποσχέσθαι τὰ γεγονότα καὶ τὰ μέλ-
λοντα ἀναλώματα, ἐφ' ᾧ τε τὴν ἐπιγραφὴν
αὐτὸν ἔχειν, τοὺς δὲ μὴ ἐθελῆσαι, πολὺ μᾶλλον
οὐκ ἂν ἐθελήσαντας ἐξ ἱεροσυλίας καὶ ἀποστε-
ρήσεως φιλοδοξεῖν· ἐπαινεῖ τε τὸν εἰπόντα τῶν
Ἐφεσίων πρὸς τὸν βασιλέα, ὡς οὐ πρέποι θεῷ
θεοῖς ἀναθήματα κατασκευάζειν.

23. Μετὰ δὲ τὴν τοῦ νεὼ συντέλειαν, ὅν φησιν
εἶναι Χειροκράτους[3] ἔργον (τοῦ δ' αὐτοῦ καὶ τὴν
Ἀλεξανδρείας κτίσιν· τὸν δ' αὐτὸν ὑποσχέσθαι
Ἀλεξάνδρῳ τὸν Ἄθω διασκευάσειν εἰς αὐτόν,
ὡσανεὶ ἐκ πρόχου τινὸς εἰς φιάλην καταχέοντα
σπονδήν, ποιήσοντα πόλεις δύο, τὴν μὲν ἐκ
δεξιῶν τοῦ ὄρους, τὴν δ' ἐν ἀριστερᾷ, ἀπὸ δὲ
τῆς ἑτέρας εἰς τὴν ἑτέραν ῥέοντα ποταμόν).

---

[1] Ἐπιτίμαιον, F; ἐπιτίμιον other MSS.
[2] ἂν, Jones inserts.
[3] Instead of Χειροκράτους, w has Δεινοκράτους, which is apparently correct; and so read Corais and Meineke.

---

[1] Calumniator.

at that time. Artemidorus says: Timaeus of Tauro-
menium, being ignorant of these decrees and being
anyway an envious and slanderous fellow (for which
reason he was also called Epitimaeus),[1] says that
they exacted means for the restoration of the temple
from the treasures deposited in their care by the
Persians; but there were no treasures on deposit in
their care at that time, and, even if there had been,
they would have been burned along with the temple;
and after the fire, when the roof was destroyed, who
could have wished to keep deposits of treasure lying
in a sacred enclosure that was open to the sky?
Now Alexander, Artemidorus adds, promised the
Ephesians to pay all expenses, both past and future,
on condition that he should have the credit therefor
on the inscription, but they were unwilling, just as
they would have been far more unwilling to acquire
glory by sacrilege and a spoliation of the temple.[2]
And Artemidorus praises the Ephesian who said to
the king[3] that it was inappropriate for a god to
dedicate offerings to gods.

23. After the completion of the temple, which,
he says, was the work of Cheirocrates[4] (the same
man who built Alexandreia and the same man who
proposed to Alexander to fashion Mt. Athos into
his likeness, representing him as pouring a libation
from a kind of ewer into a broad bowl, and to make
two cities, one on the right of the mountain and the
other on the left, and a river flowing from one to

[2] Referring, of course, to the charge that they took the
Persian treasures.
[3] Alexander.
[4] Apparently an error for "Deinocrates," a Macedonian
architect (cf. Vitruvius 1. 1. 4).

μετὰ δ᾽ οὖν τὸν νεὼν τὸ τῶν ἄλλων ἀναθημάτων
πλῆθος εὑρέσθαι τῇ ἐκτιμήσει τῶν δημιουργῶν,
τὸν δὲ δὴ βωμὸν εἶναι τῶν Πραξιτέλους ἔργων
ἅπαντα σχεδόν τι πλήρη. ἡμῖν δ᾽ ἐδείκνυτο καὶ
τῶν Θράσωνός τινα, οὗπερ καὶ τὸ Ἑκατήσιόν
ἐστι καὶ ἡ κηρίνη[1] Πηνελόπη καὶ ἡ πρεσβῦτις
ἡ Εὐρύκλεια. ἱερέας δ᾽ εὐνούχους εἶχον, οὓς
ἐκάλουν Μεγαβύζους, καὶ ἀλλαχόθεν μετιόντες
ἀεί τινας ἀξίους τῆς τοιαύτης προστασίας, καὶ
ἦγον ἐν τιμῇ μεγάλῃ· συνιερᾶσθαι δὲ τούτοις
ἐχρῆν παρθένους. νυνὶ δὲ τὰ μὲν φυλάττεται
τῶν νομίμων, τὰ δ᾽ ἧττον, ἄσυλον δὲ μένει τὸ
ἱερὸν καὶ νῦν καὶ πρότερον· τῆς δ᾽ ἀσυλίας τοὺς
ὅρους ἀλλαγῆναι συνέβη πολλάκις, Ἀλεξάνδρου
μὲν ἐπὶ στάδιον ἐκτείναντος, Μιθριδάτου δὲ
τόξευμα ἀφέντος ἀπὸ τῆς γωνίας τοῦ κεράμου
καὶ δόξαντος ὑπερβαλέσθαι μικρὰ τὸ στάδιον,
Ἀντωνίου δὲ διπλασιάσαντος τοῦτο[2] καὶ συμ-
περιλαβόντος τῇ ἀσυλίᾳ μέρος τι τῆς πόλεως·
ἐφάνη δὲ τοῦτο βλαβερὸν καὶ ἐπὶ τοῖς κακούρ-
γοις ποιοῦν τὴν πόλιν, ὥστ᾽ ἠκύρωσεν ὁ Σεβαστὸς
Καῖσαρ.

24. Ἔχει δ᾽ ἡ πόλις καὶ νεώρια καὶ λιμένα·
βραχύστομον δ᾽ ἐποίησαν οἱ ἀρχιτέκτονες, συν-
εξαπατηθέντες τῷ κελεύσαντι βασιλεῖ. οὗτος δ᾽
ἦν Ἄτταλος ὁ Φιλάδελφος· οἰηθεὶς γὰρ οὗτος

[1] κηρίνη F (and Meineke) ; κρήνη other MSS.
[2] διπλασιάσαντος τοῦτο CF, πλησιάσαντας τούτῳ other MSS.

[1] Artemidorus means, of course, that the *local* artists were
actuated by piety and patriotism.

the other)—after the completion of the temple, he
says, the great number of dedications in general
were secured by means of the high honour they
paid their artists,[1] but the whole of the altar
was filled, one might say, with the works of
Praxiteles. They showed me also some of the works
of Thrason, who made the chapel of Hecatê, the
waxen image of Penelopê, and the old woman
Eurycleia. They had eunuchs as priests, whom
they called Megabyzi. And they were always
in quest of persons from other places who were
worthy of this preferment, and they held them in
great honour. And it was obligatory for maidens
to serve as colleagues with them in their priestly
office. But though at the present some of their
usages are being preserved, yet others are not; but
the temple remains a place of refuge, the same as
in earlier times, although the limits of the refuge
have often been changed; for example, when Alexander extended them for a stadium, and when Mithridates shot an arrow from the corner of the roof
and thought it went a little farther than a stadium,
and when Antony doubled this distance and included
within the refuge a part of the city. But this
extension of the refuge proved harmful, and put the
city in the power of criminals; and it was therefore
nullified by Augustus Caesar.

24. The city has both an arsenal and a harbour.
The mouth of the harbour was made narrower by
the engineers,[2] but they, along with the king who
ordered it, were deceived as to the result, I mean
Attalus Philadelphus; for he thought that the

---

[1] Literally, "architects."

STRABO

βαθὺν τὸν εἴσπλουν ὁλκάσι μεγάλαις ἔσεσθαι
καὶ αὐτὸν τὸν λιμένα, τεναγώδη ὄντα πρότερον
διὰ τὰς ἐκ τοῦ Καΰστρου προσχώσεις,[1] ἐὰν
παραβληθῇ χῶμα τῷ στόματι, πλατεῖ τελέως
ὄντι, ἐκέλευσε γενέσθαι τὸ χῶμα. συνέβη δὲ
τοὐναντίον· ἐντὸς γὰρ ἡ χοῦς εἰργομένη τεναγίζειν
μᾶλλον ἐποίησε τὸν λιμένα σύμπαντα μέχρι τοῦ
στόματος· πρότερον δ' ἱκανῶς αἱ πλημμυρίδες
καὶ ἡ παλίρροια τοῦ πελάγους ἀφῄρει τὴν χοῦν
καὶ ἀνέσπα πρὸς τὸ ἐκτός. ὁ μὲν οὖν λιμὴν
τοιοῦτος· ἡ δὲ πόλις τῇ πρὸς τὰ ἄλλα εὐκαιρίᾳ
τῶν τόπων αὔξεται καθ' ἑκάστην ἡμέραν, ἐμπόριον οὖσα μέγιστον τῶν κατὰ τὴν Ἀσίαν τὴν
C 642 ἐντὸς τοῦ Ταύρου.

25. Ἄνδρες δ' ἀξιόλογοι γεγόνασιν ἐν αὐτῇ τῶν
μὲν παλαιῶν Ἡράκλειτός τε ὁ σκοτεινὸς καλούμενος καὶ Ἑρμόδωρος, περὶ οὗ ὁ αὐτὸς οὗτός φησιν·
Ἄξιον Ἐφεσίοις ἡβηδὸν ἀπάγξασθαι, οἵτινες
Ἑρμόδωρον ἄνδρα ἑωυτῶν ὀνήιστον ἐξέβαλον,
φάντες, Ἡμέων μηδεὶς ὀνήιστος ἔστω, εἰ δὲ μή,
ἄλλῃ τε καὶ μετ' ἄλλων· δοκεῖ δ' οὗτος ὁ ἀνὴρ
νόμους τινὰς Ῥωμαίοις συγγράψαι. καὶ Ἱπ-
πῶναξ δ' ἐστὶν ὁ ποιητὴς ἐξ Ἐφέσου καὶ
Παρράσιος ὁ ζωγράφος καὶ Ἀπελλῆς, τῶν δὲ
νεωτέρων Ἀλέξανδρος ῥήτωρ ὁ Λύχνος προσαγορευθείς, ὃς καὶ ἐπολιτεύσατο καὶ συνέγραψεν
ἱστορίαν καὶ ἔπη κατέλιπεν, ἐν οἷς τά τε
οὐράνια διατίθεται καὶ τὰς ἠπείρους γεωγραφεῖ,
καθ' ἑκάστην ἐκδοὺς ποίημα.[2]

26. Μετὰ δὲ τὴν ἐκβολὴν τοῦ Καΰστρου

---

[1] προσχώσεις Emo, προχώσεις other MSS. and Meineke.

230

entrance would be deep enough for large merchant vessels—as also the harbour itself, which formerly had shallow places because of the silt deposited by the Caÿster River—if a mole were thrown up at the mouth, which was very wide, and therefore ordered that the mole should be built. But the result was the opposite, for the silt, thus hemmed in, made the whole of the harbour, as far as the mouth, more shallow. Before this time the ebb and flow of the tides would carry away the silt and draw it to the sea outside. Such, then, is the harbour; and the city, because of its advantageous situation in other respects, grows daily, and is the largest emporium in Asia this side the Taurus.

25. Notable men have been born in this city: in ancient times, Heracleitus the Obscure, as he is called; and Hermodorus, concerning whom Heracleitus himself says: "It were right for the Ephesians from youth upwards to be hanged, who banished their most useful man, saying: 'Let no man of us be most useful; otherwise, let him be elsewhere and with other people.'" Hermodorus is reputed to have written certain laws for the Romans. And Hipponax the poet was from Ephesus; and so were Parrhasius the painter and Apelles, and more recently Alexander the orator, surnamed Lychnus,[1] who was a statesman, and wrote history, and left behind him poems in which he describes the position of the heavenly bodies and gives a geographic description of the continents, each forming the subject of a poem.

26. After the outlet of the Caÿster River comes

[1] i.e. Lamp.

---

[2] ποίημα F, ποιήματα other MSS.

STRABO

λίμνη ἐστὶν ἐκ τοῦ πελάγους ἀναχεομένη,
καλεῖται δὲ Σελινουσία, καὶ ἐφεξῆς ἄλλη σύρ-
ρους αὐτῇ, μεγάλας ἔχουσαι προσόδους· ἃς οἱ
βασιλεῖς μέν, ἱερὰς οὔσας, ἀφείλοντο τὴν θεόν,
Ῥωμαῖοι δ' ἀπέδοσαν· πάλιν δ' οἱ δημοσιῶναι
βιασάμενοι περιέστησαν εἰς ἑαυτοὺς τὰ τέλη,
πρεσβεύσας δὲ ὁ Ἀρτεμίδωρος, ὥς φησι, τάς
τε λίμνας ἀπέλαβε τῇ θεῷ, καὶ τὴν Ἡρακλεῶτιν
ἀφισταμένην ἐξενίκησε, κριθεὶς ἐν Ῥώμῃ· ἀντὶ
δὲ τούτων εἰκόνα χρυσῆν ἀνέστησεν ἡ πόλις
ἐν τῷ ἱερῷ. τῆς δὲ λίμνης ἐν τῷ κοιλοτάτῳ
βασιλέως ἐστὶν ἱερόν· φασὶ δ' Ἀγαμέμνονος
ἵδρυμα.

27. Εἶτα τὸ Γαλλήσιον ὄρος καὶ ἡ Κολοφών,
πόλις Ἰωνική, καὶ τὸ πρὸ αὐτῆς ἄλσος τοῦ
Κλαρίου Ἀπόλλωνος, ἐν ᾧ καὶ μαντεῖον ἦν ποτε
παλαιόν. λέγεται δὲ Κάλχας ὁ μάντις μετ'
Ἀμφιλόχου τοῦ Ἀμφιαράου κατὰ τὴν ἐκ Τροίας
ἐπάνοδον πεζῇ δεῦρο ἀφικέσθαι, περιτυχὼν δ'
ἑαυτοῦ κρείττονι μάντει κατὰ τὴν Κλάρον,
Μόψῳ τῷ Μαντοῦς τῆς Τειρεσίου θυγατρός,
διὰ λύπην ἀποθανεῖν. Ἡσίοδος μὲν οὖν οὕτω
πως διασκευάζει τὸν μῦθον· προτεῖναι γάρ τι
τοιοῦτο τῷ Μόψῳ τὸν Κάλχαντα·

θαῦμά μ' ἔχει κατὰ θυμόν, ὅσους ἐρινεὸς
ὀλύνθους[1]

οὗτος ἔχει, μικρός περ ἐών· εἴποις ἂν ἀριθμόν ;
τὸν δ' ἀποκρίνασθαι·

μύριοι εἰσιν ἀριθμόν, ἀτὰρ μέτρον γε μέδιμνος·

---

[1] ὅσους ἐρινεὸς ὀλύνθους, Tzschucke and later editors, for
ἐρινεὸς ὅσους ὀλύνθους.

232

a lake that runs inland from the sea, called Seli-
nusia; and next comes another lake that is confluent
with it, both affording great revenues. Of these
revenues, though sacred, the kings deprived the
goddess, but the Romans gave them back; and
again the tax-gatherers forcibly converted the tolls
to their own use; but when Artemidorus was sent
on an embassy, as he says, he got the lakes back
for the goddess, and he also won the decision over
Heracleotis, which was in revolt,[1] his case being
decided at Rome; and in return for this the city
erected in the temple a golden image of him. In
the innermost recess of the lake there is a temple
of a king, which is said to have been built by
Agamemnon.

27. Then one comes to the mountain Gallesius,
and to Colophon, an Ionian city, and to the sacred
precinct of Apollo Clarius, where there was once an
ancient oracle. The story is told that Calchas the
prophet, with Amphilochus the son of Amphiaräus,
went there on foot on his return from Troy, and
that having met near Clarus a prophet superior to
himself, Mopsus, the son of Manto, the daughter of
Teiresias, he died of grief. Now Hesiod [2] revises
the myth as follows, making Calchas propound to
Mopsus this question: "I am amazed in my heart at
all these figs on this wild fig tree, small though it
is; can you tell me the number?" And he makes
Mopsus reply: "They are ten thousand in number,
and their measure is a medimnus; [3] but there is one

---

[1] *i.e.* from Ephesus.
[2] *Frag.* 160 (Rzach).
[3] About a bushel and a half.

εἰς δὲ περισσεύει, τὸν ἐπενθέμεν[1] οὔ κε δύναιο.
ὣς φάτο· καὶ σφιν ἀριθμὸς ἐτήτυμος εἴδετο
μέτρου.
καὶ τότε δὴ Κάλχανθ᾽ ὕπνος θανάτοιο κάλυψε.

C 643 Φερεκύδης δέ φησιν ὗν προβαλεῖν ἔγκυον τὸν
Κάλχαντα, πόσους ἔχει χοίρους, τὸν δ᾽ εἰπεῖν,
ὅτι τρεῖς, ὧν ἕνα θῆλυν· ἀληθεύσαντος δ᾽, ἀποθανεῖν ὑπὸ λύπης. οἱ δὲ τὸν μὲν Κάλχαντα
προβαλεῖν τὴν ὗν φασί, τὸν δὲ τὸν ἐρινεόν, καὶ
τὸν μὲν εἰπεῖν τἀληθές, τὸν δὲ μή, ἀποθανεῖν
δὲ ὑπὸ λύπης καὶ κατά τι λόγιον. λέγει δ᾽
αὐτὸ Σοφοκλῆς ἐν Ἑλένης ἀπαιτήσει, ὡς εἱμαρ-
μένον εἴη ἀποθανεῖν, ὅταν κρείττονι ἑαυτοῦ
μάντει περιτύχῃ· οὗτος δὲ καὶ εἰς Κιλικίαν
μεταφέρει τὴν ἔριν καὶ τὸν θάνατον τοῦ Κάλχαντος. τὰ μὲν παλαιὰ τοιαῦτα.

28. Ἐκτήσαντο δέ ποτε καὶ ναυτικὴν ἀξιόλογον δύναμιν Κολοφώνιοι καὶ ἱππικήν, ἐν ᾗ
τοσοῦτον διέφερον τῶν ἄλλων, ὥσθ᾽, ὅπου ποτὲ
ἐν τοῖς δυσκαταλύτοις πολέμοις τὸ ἱππικὸν τῶν
Κολοφωνίων ἐπικουρήσειε, λύεσθαι τὸν πόλεμον·
ἀφ᾽ οὗ καὶ τὴν παροιμίαν ἐκδοθῆναι τὴν λέγουσαν, τὸν Κολοφῶνα ἐπέθηκεν, ὅταν τέλος
ἐπιτεθῇ βέβαιον τῷ πράγματι. ἄνδρες δ᾽ ἐγένοντο Κολοφώνιοι τῶν μνημονευομένων Μίμνερμος, αὐλητὴς ἅμα καὶ ποιητὴς ἐλεγείας, καὶ
Ξενοφάνης ὁ φυσικός, ὁ τοὺς σίλλους ποιήσας
διὰ ποιημάτων· λέγει δὲ Πίνδαρος καὶ Πολύ-
μναστόν τινα τῶν περὶ τὴν μουσικὴν ἐλλογίμων·

---

[1] ἐπενθέμεν, Spohn, for ἐπελθέμεν; so the later editors.

over, which you cannot put in the measure."[1]
"Thus he spake," Hesiod adds, "and the number
the measure could hold proved true. And then the
eyes of Calchas were closed by the sleep of death."
But Pherecydes says that the question propounded
by Calchas was in regard to a pregnant sow, how
many pigs she carried, and that Mopsus said, "three,
one of which is a female," and that when Mopsus
proved to have spoken the truth, Calchas died of
grief. Some say that Calchas propounded the question
in regard to the sow, but that Mopsus propounded
the question in regard to the wild fig tree, and that
the latter spoke the truth but that the former did not,
and died of grief, and in accordance with a certain
oracle. Sophocles tells the oracle in his *Reclaiming
of Helen*, that Calchas was destined to die when he
met a prophet superior to himself, but he transfers
the scene of the rivalry and of the death of Calchas
to Cilicia. Such are the ancient stories.

28. The Colophonians once possessed notable naval
and cavalry forces, in which latter they were so far
superior to the others that wherever in wars that
were hard to bring to an end, the cavalry of the
Colophonians served as ally, the war came to an
end; whence arose the proverb, "he put Colophon
to it," which is quoted when a sure end is put to
any affair. Native Colophonians, among those of
whom we have record, were: Mimnermus, who was
both a flute-player and elegiac poet; Xenophanes,
the natural philosopher, who composed the "Silli"[2]
in verse; and Pindar[3] speaks also of a certain

---

[1] *i.e.* the measure would hold only 999 of these figs.
[2] Satires. or lampoons, attacking Homer and Hesiod.
[3] *Frag.* 188 (Bergk).

φθέγμα μὲν πάγκοινον ἔγνωκας Πολυμνάστου
Κολοφωνίου ἀνδρός·

καὶ "Ομηρον δέ τινες ἐντεῦθεν εἶναί φασιν.
εὐθυπλοίᾳ μὲν οὖν ἑβδομήκοντα στάδιοί εἰσιν
ἐξ 'Εφέσου, ἐγκολπίζοντι δὲ ἑκατὸν καὶ εἴκοσι.

29 Μετὰ δὲ Κολοφῶνα ὄρος Κοράκιον καὶ
νησίον ἱερὸν 'Αρτέμιδος, εἰς ὃ διανηχομένας
τίκτειν τὰς ἐλάφους πεπιστεύκασιν. εἶτα Λέ-
βεδος, διέχουσα Κολοφῶνος ἑκατὸν καὶ εἴκοσι·
ἐνταῦθα τῶν περὶ τὸν Διόνυσον τεχνιτῶν ἡ
σύνοδος καὶ κατοικία τῶν ἐν 'Ιωνίᾳ μέχρι
'Ελλησπόντου, ἐν ᾗ πανήγυρίς τε καὶ ἀγῶνες
κατ' ἔτος συντελοῦνται τῷ Διονύσῳ. ἐν Τέῳ
δὲ ᾤκουν πρότερον τῇ ἐφεξῆς πόλει τῶν 'Ιώνων·
ἐμπεσούσης δὲ στάσεως, εἰς "Εφεσον κατέφυγον.
'Αττάλου δ' εἰς Μυόννησον αὐτοὺς καταστήσαντος
μεταξὺ Τέω καὶ Λεβέδου, πρεσβεύονται Τήιοι
δεόμενοι 'Ρωμαίων, μὴ περιιδεῖν ἐπιτειχιζομένην
σφίσι τὴν Μυόννησον, οἱ δὲ μετέστησαν εἰς
Λέβεδον, δεξαμένων τῶν Λεβεδίων ἀσμένως διὰ
τὴν κατέχουσαν αὐτοὺς ὀλιγανδρίαν. καὶ Τέως
δὲ Λεβέδου διέχει ἑκατὸν εἴκοσι, μεταξὺ δὲ
νῆσος 'Ασπίς, οἱ δ' 'Αρκόννησον καλοῦσι· καὶ
ἡ Μυόννησος δὲ ἐφ' ὕψους χερρονησίζοντος
κατοικεῖται.

C 644　30. Καὶ ἡ Τέως δὲ ἐπὶ χερρονήσῳ ἵδρυται,
λιμένα ἔχουσα· ἐνθένδ' ἐστὶν 'Ανακρέων ὁ
μελοποιός, ἐφ' οὗ Τήιοι, τὴν πόλιν ἐκλιπόντες,
εἰς "Αβδηρα ἀπῴκησαν, Θρακίαν πόλιν, οὐ
φέροντες τὴν τῶν Περσῶν ὕβριν, ἀφ' οὗ καὶ
τοῦτ' εἴρηται·

Polymnastus as one of the famous musicians: "Thou knowest the voice, common to all, of Polymnastus the Colophonian." And some say that Homer was from there. On a straight voyage it is seventy stadia from Ephesus, but if one includes the sinuosities of the gulfs it is one hundred and twenty.

29. After Colophon one comes to the mountain Coracius and to an isle sacred to Artemis, whither deer, it has been believed, swim across and give birth to their young. Then comes Lebedus, which is one hundred and twenty stadia distant from Colophon. This is the meeting-place and settlement of all the Dionysiac artists in Ionia as far as the Hellespont; and this is the place where both games and a general festal assembly are held every year in honour of Dionysus. They formerly lived in Teos, the city of the Ionians that comes next after Colophon, but when the sedition broke out they fled for refuge to Ephesus. And when Attalus settled them in Myonnesus between Teos and Lebedus the Tëians sent an embassy to beg of the Romans not to permit Myonnesus to be fortified against them; and they migrated to Lebedus, whose inhabitants gladly received them because of the dearth of population by which they were then afflicted. Teos, also, is one hundred and twenty stadia distant from Lebedus; and in the intervening distance there is an island Aspis, by some called Arconnesus. And Myonnesus is settled on a height that forms a peninsula.

30. Teos also is situated on a peninsula; and it has a harbour. Anacreon the melic poet was from Teos; in whose time the Tëians abandoned their city and migrated to Abdera, a Thracian city, being unable to bear the insolence of the Persians; and

Ἄβδηρα, καλὴ Τηίων ἀποικία.

πάλιν δ᾽ ἐπανῆλθόν τινες αὐτῶν χρόνῳ ὕστερον·
εἴρηται δὲ καὶ περὶ Ἀπελλικῶντος, ὅτι Τήιος
ἦν κἀκεῖνος· γέγονε δὲ καὶ συγγραφεὺς Ἑκαταῖος
ἐκ τῆς αὐτῆς πόλεως. ἔστι καὶ ἄλλος λιμὴν ὁ
πρόσβορρος ἀπὸ τριάκοντα σταδίων τῆς πόλεως,
Γερραιίδαι.

31. Εἶτα Χαλκιδεῖς καὶ[1] ὁ τῆς Χερρονήσου
ἰσθμὸς τῆς Τηίων καὶ Ἐρυθραίων· ἐντὸς μὲν
οὖν τοῦ ἰσθμοῦ οἰκοῦσιν οὗτοι, ἐπ᾽ αὐτῷ δὲ τῷ
ἰσθμῷ Τήιοι καὶ Κλαζομένιοι· τὸ μὲν γὰρ νότιον
τοῦ ἰσθμοῦ πλευρὸν ἔχουσι Τήιοι, τοὺς Χαλκι-
δέας, τὸ δὲ πρόσβορρον Κλαζομένιοι, καθ᾽ ὃ
συνάπτουσι τῇ Ἐρυθραίᾳ. κεῖται δ᾽ Ὑπόκρημ-
νος ὁ τόπος ἐπὶ τῇ ἀρχῇ τοῦ ἰσθμοῦ, ἐντὸς
μὲν ἀπολαμβάνων τὴν Ἐρυθραίαν, ἐκτὸς[2] δὲ
τὴν τῶν Κλαζομενίων. ὑπέρκειται δὲ τῶν
Χαλκιδέων ἄλσος καθιερωμένον Ἀλεξάνδρῳ τῷ
Φιλίππου, καὶ ἀγὼν ὑπὸ[3] τοῦ κοινοῦ τῶν
Ἰώνων Ἀλεξάνδρεια καταγγέλλεται, συντελού-
μενος ἐνταῦθα. ἡ δ᾽ ὑπέρβασις τοῦ ἰσθμοῦ τοῦ
ἀπὸ τοῦ Ἀλεξανδρείου καὶ τῶν Χαλκιδέων μέχρι
τοῦ Ὑποκρήμνου πεντήκοντά εἰσι στάδιοι, ὁ δὲ
περίπλους πλείους ἢ χίλιοι. κατὰ μέσον δέ που
τὸν περίπλουν αἱ Ἐρυθραί, πόλις Ἰωνική, λιμένα ἔχουσα, καὶ νησῖδας προκειμένας τέτταρας
Ἵππους καλουμένας.

32. Πρὶν δ᾽ ἐλθεῖν ἐπὶ τὰς Ἐρυθράς, πρῶτον
μὲν Ἔραι πολίχνιόν ἐστι Τηίων· εἶτα Κώρυκος,

---

[1] καί, the editors insert.   [2] ἐκτός E, ἐντός other MSS.
[3] ὑπό, Corais, for ἀπό.

hence the verse in reference to Abdera. "Abdera, beautiful colony of the Tëians." But some of them returned again in later times. As I have already said,[1] Apellicon also was a Tëian; and Hecataeus the historian was from the same city. And there is also another harbour to the north, thirty stadia distant from the city, called Gerrhaeïdae.

31. Then one comes to Chalcideis, and to the isthmus of the Chersonesus, belonging to the Tëians and Erythraeans. Now the latter people live this side the isthmus, but the Tëians and Clazomenians live on the isthmus itself; for the southern side of the isthmus, I mean the Chalcideis, is occupied by Tëians, but the northern by Clazomenians, where their territory joins the Erythraean. At the beginning of the isthmus lies the place called Hypocremnus, which lies between the Erythraean territory this side the isthmus and that of the Clazomenians on the other side. Above the Chalcideis is situated a sacred precinct consecrated to Alexander the son of Philip; and games, called the Alexandreia, are proclaimed by the general assembly of the Ionians and are celebrated there. The passage across the isthmus from the sacred precinct of Alexander and from the Chalcideis to Hypocremnus is fifty stadia, but the voyage round by sea is more than one thousand. Somewhere about the middle of the circuit is Erythrae, an Ionian city, which has a harbour, and also four isles lying off it, called Hippi.[2]

32. Before coming to Erythrae, one comes first to a small town Erae belonging to the Tëians; and then

---

[1] 13. 1. 54.   [2] i.e. Horses.

STRABO

ὄρος ὑψηλόν, καὶ λιμὴν ὑπ᾽ αὐτῷ Κασύστης καὶ ἄλλος Ἐρυθρᾶς λιμὴν καλούμενος καὶ ἐφεξῆς πλείους ἕτεροι. φασὶ δὲ τὸν παράπλουν τοῦ Κωρύκου πάντα ληστήριον ὑπάρξαι τῶν Κωρυκαίων καλουμένων, εὑρομένων τρόπον καινὸν τῆς ἐπιβουλῆς τῶν πλοϊζομένων· κατεσπαρμένους γὰρ ἐν τοῖς λιμέσι τοῖς καθορμιζομένοις ἐμπόροις προσφοιτᾶν καὶ ὠτακουστεῖν, τί φέροιεν καὶ ποῦ πλέοιεν, εἶτα συνελθόντας ἀναχθεῖσι τοῖς ἀνθρώποις ἐπιτίθεσθαι καὶ καθαρπάζειν· ἀφ᾽ οὗ δὴ πάντα τὸν πολυπράγμονα καὶ κατακούειν ἐπιχειροῦντα τῶν λάθρα καὶ ἐν ἀπορρήτῳ διαλεγομένων Κωρυκαῖον καλοῦμεν, καὶ ἐν παροιμίᾳ φαμέν·

τοῦ δ᾽ ἄρ᾽[1] ὁ Κωρυκαῖος ἠκροάζετο,

ὅταν δοκῇ τις πράττειν δι᾽ ἀπορρήτων ἢ λαλεῖν, μὴ λανθάνῃ δὲ διὰ τοὺς κατασκοποῦντας καὶ φιλοπευστοῦντας τὰ μὴ προσήκοντα.

33. Μετὰ δὲ Κώρυκον Ἀλόννησος νησίον· C 645 εἶτα τὸ Ἄργεννον, ἄκρα τῆς Ἐρυθραίας πλησιάζουσα μάλιστα τῷ Χίων Ποσειδίῳ, ποιοῦντι πορθμὸν ὅσον ἑξήκοντα σταδίων. μεταξὺ δὲ τῶν Ἐρυθρῶν καὶ τοῦ Ὑποκρήμνου Μίμας ἐστὶν ὄρος ὑψηλόν, εὔθηρον, πολύδενδρον· εἶτα κώμη Κυβελία καὶ ἄκρα Μέλαινα καλουμένη, μύλων ἔχουσα λατόμιον.

34. Ἐκ δ᾽ Ἐρυθρῶν Σίβυλλά ἐστιν, ἔνθους καὶ μαντικὴ γυνὴ τῶν ἀρχαίων τις· κατ᾽ Ἀλέξανδρον δὲ ἄλλη ἦν τὸν αὐτὸν τρόπον μαντική,

---

[1] ἄρ᾽, Jones, from conj. of Professor Capps, for ἄρ᾽.

240

to Corycus, a high mountain, and to a harbour at the foot of it, Casystes, and to another harbour called Erythras, and to several others in order thereafter. The waters along the coast of Mt. Corycus, they say, were everywhere the haunt of pirates, the Corycaeans, as they are called, who had found a new way of attacking vessels; for, they say, the Corycaeans would scatter themselves among the harbours, follow up the merchants whose vessels lay at anchor in them, and overhear what cargoes they had aboard and whither they were bound, and then come together and attack the merchants after they had put to sea and plunder their vessels; and hence it is that we call every person who is a busybody and tries to overhear private and secret conversations a Corycaean; and that we say in a proverb: "Well then, the Corycaean was listening to this," when one thinks that he is doing or saying something in secret, but fails to keep it hidden because of persons who spy on him and are eager to learn what does not concern them.

33. After Mt. Corycus one comes to Halonnesos, a small island. Then to Argennum, a promontory of the Erythraean territory; it is very close to the Poseidium of the Chians, which latter forms a strait about sixty stadia in width. Between Erythrae and Hypocremnus lies Mimas, a lofty mountain, which is well supplied with game and well wooded. Then one comes to a village Cybelia, and to a promontory Melaena, as it is called, which has a millstone quarry.

34. Erythrae was the native city of Sibylla, a woman who was divinely inspired and had the gift of prophecy, one of the ancients. And in the time of Alexander there was another woman who likewise

καλουμένη Ἀθηναΐς, ἐκ τῆς αὐτῆς πόλεως· καὶ
καθ᾽ ἡμᾶς Ἡρακλείδης Ἡροφίλειος[1] ἰατρός,
συσχολαστὴς Ἀπολλωνίου τοῦ Μυός.

35. Ἡ δὲ Χίος τὸν μὲν περίπλουν ἐστὶ σταδίων
ἐννακοσίων παρὰ γῆν φερομένῳ, πόλιν δ᾽ ἔχει
εὐλίμενον καὶ ναύσταθμον ναυσὶν ὀγδοήκοντα.
ἐν δὲ τῷ περίπλῳ δεξιὰν τὴν νῆσον ἔχοντι ἀπὸ
τῆς πόλεως πρῶτον μέν ἐστι τὸ Ποσείδιον, εἶτα
Φάναι, λιμὴν βαθύς, καὶ νεὼς Ἀπόλλωνος καὶ
ἄλσος φοινίκων· εἶτα Νότιον, ὕφορμος αἰγιαλός·
εἶτα Λάιους, καὶ οὗτος ὕφορμος αἰγιαλός, ὅθεν
εἰς τὴν πόλιν ἑξήκοντα σταδίων ἰσθμός· περίπλους δὲ τριακοσίων ἑξήκοντα, ὃν ἐπήλθομεν.
εἶτα Μέλαινα ἄκρα, καθ᾽ ἣν τὰ Ψύρα, νῆσος ἀπὸ
πεντήκοντα σταδίων τῆς ἄκρας, ὑψηλή, πόλιν
ὁμώνυμον ἔχουσα· κύκλος δὲ τῆς νήσου τετταράκοντα στάδιοι. εἶθ᾽ ἡ Ἀριουσία χώρα τραχεῖα
καὶ ἀλίμενος, σταδίων ὅσον τριάκοντα,[2] οἶνον
ἄριστον φέρουσα τῶν Ἑλληνικῶν. εἶτα τὸ
Πελιναῖον ὄρος ὑψηλότατον τῶν ἐν τῇ νήσῳ.
ἔχει δ᾽ ἡ νῆσος καὶ λατόμιον μαρμάρου λίθου.
ἄνδρες δὲ Χῖοι γεγόνασιν ἐλλόγιμοι Ἴων τε ὁ
τραγικὸς καὶ Θεόπομπος ὁ συγγραφεὺς καὶ
Θεόκριτος ὁ σοφιστής· οὗτοι δὲ καὶ ἀντεπολι-
τεύσαντο ἀλλήλοις. ἀμφισβητοῦσι δὲ καὶ
Ὁμήρου Χῖοι, μαρτύριον μέγα[3] τοὺς Ὁμηρίδας
καλουμένους ἀπὸ τοῦ ἐκείνου γένους προχειριζό-
μενοι, ὧν καὶ Πίνδαρος μέμνηται·

[1] Ἡροφίλειος, Tzschucke, for Ἡρόϐιλος.
[2] τριάκοντα, Kramer, following Stephanus, for τριακοσίων;
so Meineke.
[3] μέγα, Meineke, for μετά; μὲν moxx, κατά w; word omitted
in E.

242

had the gift of prophecy; she was called Athenaïs, and was a native of the same city. And, in my time, Heracleides the Herophileian physician, fellow-pupil of Apollonius Mys,[1] was born there.

35. As for Chios, the voyage round it along the coast is nine hundred stadia; and it has a city with a good port and with a naval station for eighty ships. On making the voyage round it from the city, with the island on the right, one comes first to the Poseidium. Then to Phanae, a deep harbour, and to a temple of Apollo and a grove of palm trees. Then to Notium, a shore suited to the anchoring of vessels. Then to Laïus, this too a shore suited to the anchoring of vessels; whence to the city there is an isthmus of sixty stadia, but the voyage round, which I have just now described, is three hundred and sixty stadia. Then to Melaena, a promontory, opposite to which lies Psyra, an island fifty stadia distant from the promontory, lofty, and having a city of the same name. The circuit of the island is forty stadia. Then one comes to Ariusia, a rugged and harbourless country, about thirty stadia in extent, which produces the best of the Grecian wines. Then to Pelinaeus, the highest mountain in the island. And the island also has a marble quarry. Famous natives of Chios are: Ion the tragic poet, and Theopompus the historian, and Theocritus the sophist. The two latter were political opponents of one another. The Chians also claim Homer, setting forth as strong testimony that the men called Homeridae were descendants of Homer's family; these are mentioned by Pindar:[2]

[1] Mus, *i.e.* Mouse.   [2] *Nemean Odes* 2. 1.

ὅθεν περ καὶ Ὁμηρίδαι
ῥαπτῶν ἐπέων τὰ πόλλ' ἀοιδοί.

ἐκέκτηντο δὲ καὶ ναυτικόν ποτε Χῖοι, καὶ
ἀνθήπτοντο τῆς κατὰ θάλατταν ἀρχῆς καὶ
ἐλευθερίας. ἐκ Χίου δ' ἐς Λέσβον νότῳ τετρα-
κόσιοί που στάδιοι.

36. Ἐκ δὲ τοῦ Ὑποκρήμνου [1] Χύτριόν ἐστι
τόπος, ὅπου πρότερον ἵδρυντο Κλαζομεναί· εἶθ'
ἡ νῦν πόλις, νησία ἔχουσα προκείμενα ὀκτὼ
γεωργούμενα. Κλαζομένιος δ' ἦν ἀνὴρ ἐπιφανὴς
Ἀναξαγόρας ὁ φυσικός, Ἀναξιμένους ὁμιλητὴς
τοῦ Μιλησίου· διήκουσαν δὲ τούτου Ἀρχέλαος
ὁ φυσικὸς καὶ Εὐριπίδης ὁ ποιητής. εἶθ' ἱερὸν
Ἀπόλλωνος καὶ θερμὰ ὕδατα καὶ ὁ Σμυρναίων
κόλπος καὶ ἡ πόλις.

C 646   37. Ἑξῆς δὲ ἄλλος κόλπος, ἐν ᾧ ἡ παλαιὰ
Σμύρνα ἀπὸ εἴκοσι σταδίων τῆς νῦν. Λυδῶν δὲ
κατασπασάντων τὴν Σμύρναν, περὶ τετρακόσια
ἔτη διετέλεσεν οἰκουμένη κωμηδόν· εἶτα ἀνήγειρεν
αὐτὴν Ἀντίγονος, καὶ μετὰ ταῦτα Λυσίμαχος,
καὶ νῦν ἐστι καλλίστη τῶν πασῶν, μέρος μέν
τι ἔχουσα ἐπ' ὄρει τετειχισμένον, τὸ δὲ πλέον
ἐν πεδίῳ πρὸς τῷ λιμένι καὶ πρὸς τῷ Μητρῴῳ
καὶ πρὸς γυμνασίῳ. ἔστι δ' ἡ ῥυμοτομία
διάφορος ἐπ' εὐθειῶν εἰς δύναμιν καὶ αἱ ὁδοὶ
λιθόστρωτοι στοαί τε μεγάλαι τετράγωνοι, ἐπί-
πεδοί τε καὶ ὑπερῷοι· ἔστι δὲ καὶ βιβλιοθήκη
καὶ τὸ Ὁμήρειον, στοὰ τετράγωνος, ἔχουσα νεὼν
Ὁμήρου καὶ ξόανον· μεταποιοῦνται γὰρ καὶ οὗτοι

---

[1] Ὑποκρήμνου F, Ἀποκρήμνου other MSS.; but cp. Ὑποκρήμνου
in 14. 1. 33.

"Whence also the Homeridae, singers of deftly woven lays, most often . . . ." The Chians at one time possessed also a fleet, and attained to liberty and to maritime empire. The distance from Chios to Lesbos, sailing southwards, is about four hundred stadia.

36. After Hypocremnus one comes to Chytrium, the site on which Clazomenae was situated in earlier times. Then to the present Clazomenae, with eight small islands lying off it that are under cultivation. Anaxagoras, the natural philosopher, an illustrious man and associate of Anaximenes the Milesian, was a Clazomenian. And Archeläus the natural philosopher and Euripides the poet took his entire course. Then to a temple of Apollo and to hot springs, and to the gulf and the city of the Smyrnaeans.

37. Next one comes to another gulf, on which is the old Smyrna, twenty stadia distant from the present Smyrna. After Smyrna had been rased by the Lydians, its inhabitants continued for about four hundred years to live in villages. Then they were reassembled into a city by Antigonus, and afterwards by Lysimachus, and their city is now the most beautiful of all; a part of it is on a mountain and walled, but the greater part of it is in the plain near the harbour and near the Metröum and near the gymnasium. The division into streets is exceptionally good, in straight lines as far as possible; and the streets are paved with stone; and there are large quadrangular porticoes, with both lower and upper stories. There is also a library; and the Homereium, a quadrangular portico containing a shrine and wooden statue[1] of Homer; for the

---

[1] The primary meaning of the Greek word here used for "statue," *xoanon*, is "a prehistoric statue *carved* of wood."

διαφερόντως τοῦ ποιητοῦ, καὶ δὴ καὶ νόμισμά τι χαλκοῦν παρ' αὐτοῖς Ὁμήρειον λέγεται. ῥεῖ δὲ πλησίον τοῦ τείχους ὁ Μέλης ποταμός. ἔστι δὲ πρὸς τῇ ἄλλῃ κατασκευῇ τῆς πόλεως καὶ λιμὴν κλειστός. ἐν δ' ἐλάττωμα τῶν ἀρχιτεκτόνων οὐ μικρόν, ὅτι τὰς ὁδοὺς στορνύντες,[1] ὑπορρύσεις οὐκ ἔδωκαν αὐταῖς, ἀλλ' ἐπιπολάζει τὰ σκύβαλα, καὶ μάλιστα ἐν τοῖς ὄμβροις ἐπαφιεμένων τῶν ἀποσκευῶν.[2] ἐνταῦθα Δολοβέλλας Τρεβώνιον ἐκπολιορκήσας ἀνεῖλεν, ἕνα τῶν δολοφονησάντων Καίσαρα τὸν Θεόν, καὶ τῆς πόλεως παρέλυσε πολλὰ μέρη.

38. Μετὰ δὲ Σμύρναν αἱ Λεῦκαι πολίχνιον, ὃ ἀπέστησεν Ἀριστόνικος μετὰ τὴν Ἀττάλου τοῦ Φιλομήτορος τελευτήν, δοκῶν τοῦ γένους εἶναι τοῦ τῶν βασιλέων καὶ διανοούμενος εἰς ἑαυτὸν ποιεῖσθαι τὴν ἀρχήν· ἐντεῦθεν μὲν οὖν ἐξέπεσεν, ἡττηθεὶς ναυμαχίᾳ περὶ τὴν Κυμαίαν ὑπὸ Ἐφεσίων, εἰς δὲ τὴν μεσόγαιαν ἀνιὼν ἤθροισε διὰ ταχέων πλῆθος ἀπόρων τε ἀνθρώπων καὶ δούλων ἐπ' ἐλευθερίᾳ κατακεκλημένων, οὓς Ἡλιοπολίτας ἐκάλεσε. πρῶτον μὲν οὖν παρεισέπεσεν εἰς Θυάτειρα, εἶτ' Ἀπολλωνίδα ἔσχεν, εἶτ' ἄλλων ἐφίετο φρουρίων· οὐ πολὺν δὲ διεγένετο χρόνον, ἀλλ' εὐθὺς αἵ τε πόλεις ἔπεμψαν πλῆθος, καὶ Νικομήδης ὁ Βιθυνὸς ἐπεκούρησε καὶ οἱ τῶν Καππαδόκων βασιλεῖς. ἔπειτα πρέσβεις Ῥωμαίων πέντε ἧκον, καὶ μετὰ ταῦτα

---

[1] στορνύντες Meineke, for στρωννύντες E, στορνήντες F, στοοέννυντες other MSS.

[2] ἀποσκευῶν, Corais, for παρασκευῶν.

Smyrnaeans also lay especial claim to the poet; and indeed a bronze coin of theirs is called Homereium. The River Meles flows near the walls; and, in addition to the rest of the city's equipment, there is also a harbour that can be closed. But there is one error, not a small one, in the work of the engineers, that when they paved the streets they did not give them underground drainage; instead, filth covers the surface, and particularly during rains, when the cast-off filth is discharged upon the streets. It was here that Dolabella captured by siege, and slew, Trebonius, one of the men who treacherously murdered the deified Caesar; and he set free[1] many parts of the city.

38. After Smyrna one comes to Leucae, a small town, which after the death of Attalus Philometor[2] was caused to revolt by Aristonicus, who was reputed to belong to the royal family and intended to usurp the kingdom. Now he was banished from Smyrna, after being defeated in a naval battle near the Cymaean territory by the Ephesians, but he went up into the interior and quickly assembled a large number of resourceless people, and also of slaves, invited with a promise of freedom, whom he called Heliopolitae.[3] Now he first fell upon Thyateira unexpectedly, and then got possession of Apollonis, and then set his efforts against other fortresses. But he did not last long; the cities immediately sent a large number of troops against him, and they were assisted by Nicomedes the Bithynian and by the kings of the Cappadocians. Then came five Roman

---

[1] Others translate the verb "destroyed," or the like, but cf. its use in 8. 6. 14 and Herodotus 1. 149.

[2] See 13. 4. 2.   [3] Citizens of the city of Helius (Sun-god).

στρατιὰ¹ καὶ ὕπατος Πόπλιος Κράσσος, καὶ
μετὰ ταῦτα Μάρκος Περπέρνας, ὃς καὶ κατέλυσε
τὸν πόλεμον, ζωγρίᾳ λαβὼν τὸν Ἀριστόνικον καὶ
ἀναπέμψας εἰς Ῥώμην. ἐκεῖνος μὲν οὖν ἐν τῷ
δεσμωτηρίῳ κατέστρεψε τὸν βίον, Περπέρναν δὲ
νόσος διέφθειρε, Κράσσος δὲ περὶ Λεύκας, ἐπιθε-
μένων τινῶν, ἔπεσεν ἐν μάχῃ. Μάνιος δ᾽ Ἀκύλ-
λιος, ἐπελθὼν ὕπατος μετὰ δέκα πρεσβευτῶν,
διέταξε τὴν ἐπαρχίαν εἰς τὸ νῦν ἔτι συμμένον
C 647 τῆς πολιτείας σχῆμα. μετὰ δὲ Λεύκας Φώκαια
ἐν κόλπῳ· περὶ δὲ ταύτης εἰρήκαμεν ἐν τῷ περὶ
Μασσαλίας λόγῳ. εἶθ᾽ οἱ ὅροι τῶν Ἰώνων καὶ
τῶν Αἰολέων· εἴρηται δὲ καὶ περὶ τούτων. ἐν
δὲ τῇ μεσογαίᾳ τῆς Ἰωνικῆς παραλίας λοιπά
ἐστι τὰ περὶ τὴν ὁδὸν τὴν ἐξ Ἐφέσου μέχρι
Ἀντιοχείας καὶ τοῦ Μαιάνδρου. ἔστι δὲ καὶ
τὰ χωρία ταῦτα Λυδοῖς καὶ Καρσὶν ἐπίμικτα καὶ
τοῖς Ἕλλησι.

39. Πρώτη δ᾽ ἐστὶν ἐξ Ἐφέσου Μαγνησία,
πόλις Αἰολίς, λεγομένη δὲ ἐπὶ Μαιάνδρῳ· πλησίον
γὰρ αὐτοῦ ἵδρυται· πολὺ δὲ πλησιαίτερον ὁ
Ληθαῖος, ἐμβάλλων εἰς τὸν Μαίανδρον, τὴν δ᾽
ἀρχὴν ἔχων ἀπὸ Πακτύου² τοῦ τῶν Ἐφεσίων
ὄρους· ἕτερος δ᾽ ἐστὶ Ληθαῖος ὁ ἐν Γορτύνῃ καὶ
ὁ περὶ Τρίκκην, ἐφ᾽ ᾧ ὁ Ἀσκληπιὸς γεννηθῆναι
λέγεται, καὶ ἔτι ἐν τοῖς Ἑσπερίταις Λίβυσι.
κεῖται δ᾽ ἐν πεδίῳ πρὸς ὄρει καλουμένῳ Θώρακι
ἡ πόλις, ἐφ᾽ ᾧ σταυρωθῆναί φασι Δαφίταν τὸν
γραμματικόν, λοιδορήσαντα τοὺς βασιλέας διὰ
διστίχου.³

---

¹ στρατιά, Corais, for στρατεία.
² Πακτύου, Xylander, for Πακτίου.

248

ambassadors, and after that an army under Publius
Crassus the consul,[1] and after that Marcus Perpernas,
who brought the war to an end, having captured
Aristonicus alive and sent him to Rome. Now
Aristonicus ended his life in prison; Perpernas died
of disease; and Crassus, attacked by certain people
in the neighbourhood of Leucae, fell in battle. And
Manius Aquillius came over as consul[2] with ten
lieutenants and organised the province into the form
of government that still now endures. After Leucae
one comes to Phocaea, on a gulf, concerning which
I have already spoken in my account of Massalia.
Then to the boundaries of the Ionians and the
Aeolians; but I have already spoken of these. In
the interior above the Ionian seaboard there remain
to be described the places in the neighbourhood of
the road that leads from Ephesus to Antiocheia and
the Maeander River. These places are occupied by
Lydians and Carians mixed with Greeks.

39. The first city one comes to after Ephesus is
Magnesia, which is an Aeolian city and is called
"Magnesia on the Maeander," for it is situated near
that river. But it is much nearer the Lethaeus
River, which empties into the Maeander and has its
beginning in Mt. Pactyes, the mountain in the
territory of the Ephesians. There is another Lethaeus
in Gortyna, and another near Triccê, where Asclepius
is said to have been born, and still another in the
country of the Western Libyans. And the city lies
in the plain near the mountain called Thorax, on
which Daphitas the grammarian is said to have been
crucified, because he reviled the kings in a distich:[3]

---

[1] 131 B.C.   [2] 129 B.C.

[3] διστίχου F, στίχου other MSS.

πορφύρεοι μώλωπες, ἀπορρινήματα γάζης
Λυσιμάχου, Λυδῶν ἄρχετε καὶ Φρυγίης.

καὶ λόγιον δ' ἐκπεσεῖν αὐτῷ λέγεται, φυλάττεσθαι
τὸν Θώρακα.

40. Δοκοῦσι δ' εἶναι Μάγνητες Δελφῶν ἀπόγονοι, τῶν ἐποικησάντων τὰ Δίδυμα ὄρη ἐν
Θετταλίᾳ, περὶ ὧν φησὶν Ἡσίοδος·

ἢ οἵη Διδύμους ἱεροὺς ναίουσα κολωνούς,
Δωτίῳ ἐν πεδίῳ πολυβότρυος ἀντ' Ἀμύροιο,
νίψατο Βοιβιάδος λίμνης πόδα παρθένος ἀδμής.

ἐνταῦθα δ' ἦν καὶ τὸ τῆς Δινδυμήνης ἱερόν,
Μητρὸς θεῶν· ἱεράσασθαι¹ δ' αὐτοῦ τὴν Θεμι-
στοκλέους γυναῖκα, οἱ δὲ θυγατέρα παραδιδόασι·
νῦν δ' οὐκ ἔστι τὸ ἱερὸν διὰ τὸ τὴν πόλιν εἰς
ἄλλον μετῳκίσθαι τόπον· ἐν δὲ τῇ νῦν πόλει τὸ
τῆς Λευκοφρυήνης ἱερόν ἐστιν Ἀρτέμιδος, ὃ τῷ
μὲν μεγέθει τοῦ ναοῦ καὶ τῷ πλήθει τῶν ἀναθημάτων λείπεται τοῦ ἐν Ἐφέσῳ, τῇ δ' εὐρυθμίᾳ
καὶ τῇ τέχνῃ τῇ περὶ τὴν κατασκευὴν τοῦ σηκοῦ
πολὺ διαφέρει· καὶ τῷ μεγέθει ὑπεραίρει πάντας
τοὺς ἐν Ἀσίᾳ πλὴν δυεῖν, τοῦ ἐν Ἐφέσῳ καὶ
τοῦ ἐν Διδύμοις. καὶ τὸ παλαιὸν δὲ συνέβη
τοῖς Μάγνησιν ὑπὸ Τρηρῶν ἄρδην ἀναιρεθῆναι,
Κιμμερικοῦ ἔθνους, εὐτυχήσαντας² πολὺν χρόνον·
τῷ δ' ἑξῆς ἔτει Μιλησίους κατασχεῖν τὸν τόπον.
Καλλῖνος μὲν οὖν ὡς εὐτυχούντων ἔτι τῶν
Μαγνήτων μέμνηται καὶ κατορθούντων ἐν τῷ
πρὸς τοὺς Ἐφεσίους πολέμῳ, Ἀρχίλοχος δὲ ἤδη
φαίνεται γνωρίζων τὴν γενομένην αὐτοῖς συμφο-
ράν·

"Purpled with stripes, mere filings of the treasure of Lysimachus, ye rule the Lydians and Phrygia." It is said that an oracle was given out that Daphitas should be on his guard against Thorax.

40. The Magnetans are thought to be descendants of Delphians who settled in the Didyman hills, in Thessaly, concerning whom Hesiod says: "Or as the unwedded virgin who, dwelling on the holy Didyman hills, in the Dotian Plain, in front of Amyrus, bathed her foot in Lake Boebeïs." [1] Here was also the temple of Dindymenê, Mother of the gods. According to tradition, the wife of Themistocles, some say his daughter, served as a priestess there. But the temple is not now in existence, because the city has been transferred to another site. In the present city is the temple of Artemis Leucophryenê, which in the size of its shrine and in the number of its votive offerings is inferior to the temple at Ephesus, but in the harmony and skill shown in the structure of the sacred enclosure is far superior to it. And in size it surpasses all the sacred enclosures in Asia except two, that at Ephesus and that at Didymi. In ancient times, also, it came to pass that the Magnetans were utterly destroyed by the Treres, a Cimmerian tribe, although they had for a long time been a prosperous people, but the Milesians took possession of the place in the following year. Now Callinus mentions the Magnetans as still being a prosperous people and as being successful in their war against the Ephesians, but Archilochus is obviously already aware of the

---

[1] Also quoted in 9. 5. 22.

---

[1] ἱεράσασθαι Dh, ἱερᾶσθαι other MSS.
[2] εὐτυχήσαντας F, εὐτυχήσαντος other MSS.

STRABO

κλαίειν τὰ Θασίων,[1] οὐ[2] τὰ Μαγνήτων κακά·

C 648 ἐξ οὗ καὶ αὐτὸν νεώτερον εἶναι τοῦ Καλλίνου τεκμαίρεσθαι πάρεστιν. ἄλλης δέ τινος ἐφόδου τῶν Κιμμερίων μέμνηται πρεσβυτέρας ὁ Καλλῖνος, ἐπὰν φῇ·

νῦν δ' ἐπὶ Κιμμερίων στρατὸς ἔρχεται ὀβρι-
μοεργῶν·

ἐν ᾗ τὴν Σάρδεων ἅλωσιν δηλοῖ.

41. Ἄνδρες δ' ἐγένοντο γνώριμοι Μάγνητες Ἡγησίας τε ὁ ῥήτωρ, ὃς ἦρξε μάλιστα τοῦ Ἀσιανοῦ λεγομένου ζήλου, παραφθείρας τὸ καθεστηκὸς ἔθος τὸ Ἀττικόν, καὶ Σῖμος[3] ὁ μελοποιός, παραφθείρας καὶ αὐτὸς τὴν τῶν προτέρων μελοποιῶν ἀγωγὴν καὶ τὴν Σιμῳδίαν εἰσαγαγών, καθάπερ ἔτι μᾶλλον Λυσιῳδοὶ καὶ Μαγῳδοί, καὶ Κλεόμαχος ὁ πύκτης, ὃς εἰς ἔρωτα ἐμπεσὼν κιναίδου τινὸς καὶ παιδίσκης ὑπὸ τῷ[4] κιναίδῳ τρεφομένης ἀπεμιμήσατο τὴν ἀγωγὴν τῶν παρὰ τοῖς κιναίδοις διαλέκτων καὶ τῆς ἠθοποιίας· ἦρξε δὲ Σωτάδης μὲν πρῶτος τοῦ κιναιδολογεῖν, ἔπειτα Ἀλέξανδρος ὁ Αἰτωλός· ἀλλ' οὗτοι μὲν ἐν ψιλῷ λόγῳ, μετὰ μέλους δὲ Λῦσις, καὶ ἔτι πρότερος τούτου ὁ Σῖμος. Ἀναξήνορα δὲ τὸν κιθαρῳδὸν ἐξῆρε μὲν καὶ τὰ θέατρα, ἀλλ' ὅτι[5] μάλιστα Ἀντώνιος, ὅς[6] γε καὶ τεττάρων πόλεων ἀπέδειξε φορολόγον, στρατιώτας αὐτῷ συστήσας. καὶ ἡ

---

[1] τὰ Θασίων, Tyrwhitt, for θάσ(σ)ων; so Tzschucke and Corais.
[2] οὐ, Tzschucke and Corais, for οὗ.
[3] Σῖμος, Tzschucke, for Σίμων; so Meineke.
[4] τῷ, Corais inserts; so Meineke.

misfortune that befell them: "to bewail the woes of the Thasians, not those of the Magnetans";[1] whence one may judge that he was more recent than Callinus. And Callinus recalls another, and earlier, invasion of the Cimmerians when he says: "And now the army of the Cimmerians, mighty in deeds, advanceth,"[2] in which he plainly indicates the capture of Sardeis.

41. Well-known natives of Magnesia are: Hegesias the orator, who, more than any other, initiated the Asiatic style, as it is called, whereby he corrupted the established Attic custom; and Simus the melic poet, he too a man who corrupted the style handed down by the earlier melic poets and introduced the Simoedia,[3] just as that style was corrupted still more by the Lysioedi and the Magoedi, and by Cleomachus the pugilist, who, having fallen in love with a certain cinaedus[4] and with a young female slave who was kept as a prostitute by the cinaedus, imitated the style of dialects and mannerisms that was in vogue among the cinaedi. Sotades was the first man to write the talk of the cinaedi; and then Alexander the Aetolian. But though these two men imitated that talk in mere speech, Lysis accompanied it with song; and so did Simus, who was still earlier than he. As for Anaxenor, the citharoede,[5] the theatres exalted him, but Antony exalted him all he possibly could, since he even appointed him exactor of tribute from four cities, giving him a body-guard of soldiers.

---

[1] *Frag.* 20 (Bergk).   [2] *Frag.* 3 (Bergk).
[3] A loose song.   [4] An obscene talker.
[5] One who played the cithara and sang to its accompaniment (cf. 9. 3. 10 and note on "the citharoedes").

---

[5] ὅτι, Meineke, for ἔτι.   [6] ὅς, Kramer, for ὅν.

πατρὶς δ' ἱκανῶς αὐτὸν ηὔξησε, πορφύραν ἐνδύ-
σασα, ἱερωμένον[1] τοῦ Σωσιπόλιδος Διός, καθάπερ καὶ ἡ γραπτὴ εἰκὼν ἐμφανίζει ἡ ἐν τῇ ἀγορᾷ.
ἔστι δὲ καὶ χαλκῆ.εἰκὼν ἐν τῷ θεάτρῳ, ἐπιγραφὴν
ἔχουσα·

  ἤτοι μὲν τόδε καλὸν ἀκουέμεν ἐστὶν ἀοιδοῦ
  τοιοῦδ', οἷος ὅδ' ἐστί, θεοῖς ἐναλίγκιος αὐδή.

οὐ στοχασάμενος δὲ ὁ ἐπιγράψας τὸ τελευταῖον
γράμμα τοῦ δευτέρου ἔπους παρέλιπε, τοῦ πλά-
τους τῆς βάσεως μὴ συνεξαρκοῦντος· ὥστε τῆς
πόλεως ἀμαθίαν καταγινώσκειν παρέσχε διὰ τὴν
ἀμφιβολίαν τὴν περὶ[2] τὴν γραφήν, εἴτε τὴν
ὀνομαστικὴν δέχοιτο πτῶσιν τῆς ἐσχάτης προση-
γορίας, εἴτε τὴν δοτικήν· πολλοὶ γὰρ χωρὶς τοῦ ι
γράφουσι τὰς δοτικὰς καὶ ἐκβάλλουσι δὲ[3] τὸ
ἔθος φυσικὴν αἰτίαν οὐκ ἔχον.

42. Μετὰ δὲ Μαγνησίαν ἡ ἐπὶ Τράλλεις ἐστὶν
ὁδὸς ἐν ἀριστερᾷ μὲν τὴν Μεσωγίδα ἔχουσιν,
ἐν αὐτῇ δὲ τῇ ὁδῷ καὶ ἐν δεξιᾷ τὸ Μαιάνδρου
πεδίον, Λυδῶν ἅμα καὶ Καρῶν νεμομένων καὶ
Ἰώνων, Μιλησίων τε καὶ Μυησίων, ἔτι δὲ Αἰολέων
τῶν ἐν Μαγνησίᾳ· ὁ δ' αὐτὸς τρόπος[4] τῆς το-
ποθεσίας καὶ μέχρι Νύσης καὶ Ἀντιοχείας.
ἵδρυται δ' ἡ μὲν τῶν Τραλλιανῶν πόλις ἐπὶ
τραπεζίου τινός, ἄκραν ἔχοντος ἐρυμνήν· καὶ τὰ
C 649 κύκλῳ δ' ἱκανῶς εὐερκῆ· συνοικεῖται δὲ καλῶς,
εἴ τις ἄλλη τῶν κατὰ τὴν Ἀσίαν, ὑπὸ εὐπόρων
ἀνθρώπων, καὶ ἀεί τινες ἐξ αὐτῆς εἰσὶν οἱ
πρωτεύοντες κατὰ τὴν ἐπαρχίαν, οὓς Ἀσιάρχας

---

[1] Instead of ἱερωμένον, CDmoz have ἱερωμένην.
[2] περί, Kramer, for παρά.

Further, his native land greatly increased his honours, having clad him in purple as consecrated to Zeus Sosipolis,[1] as is plainly indicated in his painted image in the market-place. And there is also a bronze statue of him in the theatre, with the inscription, " Surely this is a beautiful thing, to listen to a singer such as this man is, like unto the gods in voice."[2] But the engraver, missing his guess, left out the last letter of the second verse, the base of the statue not being wide enough for its inclusion ; so that he laid the city open to the charge of ignorance, because of the ambiguity of the writing, as to whether the last word should be taken as in the nominative case or in the dative ;[3] for many write the dative case without the iota, and even reject the ordinary usage as being without natural cause.

42. After Magnesia comes the road to Tralleis, with Mt. Mesogis on the left, and, at the road itself and on the right, the plain of the Maeander River, which is occupied by Lydians and Carians, and by Ionians, both Milesians and Myesians, and also by the Aeolians of Magnesia. And the same kind of topographical account applies as far as Nysa and Antiocheia. The city of the Tralleians is situated upon a trapezium-shaped site, with a height fortified by nature ; and the places all round are well defended. And it is as well peopled as any other city in Asia by people of means ; and always some of its men hold the chief places in the province, being called Asiarchs.

---

[1] City-Saviour. [2] *Odyssey* 9. 3.
[3] *i.e.* as ΑΥΔΗ or ΑΥΔΗΙ.

---

[3] δέ, Meineke, for γε ; Corais τε.
[4] καί, after τρόπος, omitted by *moxz.*

καλοῦσιν· ὧν Πυθόδωρός τε ἦν, ἀνὴρ Νυσαεὺς
τὸ ἐξ ἀρχῆς, ἐκεῖσε δὲ μεταβεβηκὼς διὰ τὴν
ἐπιφάνειαν, καὶ ἐν τῇ πρὸς Πομπήιον φιλίᾳ
διαπρέπων μετ᾽ ὀλίγων· περιεβέβλητο δὲ καὶ
οὐσίαν βασιλικὴν πλειόνων ἢ δισχιλίων ταλάντων, ἣν ὑπὸ Καίσαρος τοῦ Θεοῦ πραθεῖσαν
διὰ τὴν πρὸς Πομπήιον φιλίαν ἐξωνησάμενος οὐχ
ἥττω τοῖς παισὶ κατέλιπε· τούτου δ᾽ ἐστὶ θυγάτηρ
Πυθοδωρίς, ἡ νῦν βασιλεύουσα ἐν τῷ Πόντῳ,
περὶ ἧς εἰρήκαμεν. οὗτος δὴ καθ᾽ ἡμᾶς ἤκμασε
καὶ Μηνόδωρος, ἀνὴρ λόγιος καὶ ἄλλως σεμνὸς
καὶ βαρύς, ἔχων τὴν ἱερωσύνην τοῦ Διὸς τοῦ
Λαρισαίου· κατεστασιάσθη δ᾽ ὑπὸ τῶν Δομετίου
τοῦ Ἀηνοβάρβου φίλων, καὶ ἀνεῖλεν αὐτὸν
ἐκεῖνος, ὡς ἀφιστάντα τὸ ναυτικόν, πιστεύσας
τοῖς ἐνδειξαμένοις. ἐγένοντο δὲ καὶ ῥήτορες
ἐπιφανεῖς Διονυσοκλῆς τε καὶ μετὰ ταῦτα Δάμασος ὁ Σκόμβρος. κτίσμα δέ φασιν εἶναι τὰς
Τράλλεις Ἀργείων καί τινων Θρακῶν Τραλλίων,
ἀφ᾽ ὧν τοὔνομα. τυραννηθῆναι δ᾽ ὀλίγον συνέ-
πεσε χρόνον τὴν πόλιν ὑπὸ τῶν Κρατίππου
παίδων κατὰ τὰ Μιθριδατικά.

43. Νῦσα δ᾽ ἵδρυται πρὸς τῇ Μεσωγίδι τὸ
πλέον τῷ ὄρει προσανακεκλιμένη, ἔστι δ᾽ ὥσπερ
δίπολις, διαιρεῖ γὰρ αὐτὴν χαράδρα τις, ποιοῦσα
φάραγγα, ἧς τὸ μὲν γέφυραν ἐπικειμένην ἔχει,
συνάπτουσαν τὰς δύο πόλεις, τὸ δ᾽ ἀμφιθεάτρῳ
κεκόσμηται, κρυπτὴν ἔχοντι τὴν ὑπόρρυσιν τῶν
χαραδρωδῶν ὑδάτων· τῷ δὲ θεάτρῳ δύο ἄκραι,
ὧν τῇ μὲν ὑπόκειται τὸ γυμνάσιον τῶν νέων,

---

[1] 12. 3. 29, 31, 37.

Among these was Pythodorus, originally a native of
Nysa, but he changed his abode to Tralleis because
of its celebrity; and with only a few others he stood
out conspicuously as a friend of Pompey. And he
came into possession of the wealth of a king, worth
more than two thousand talents, which, though
sold by the deified Caesar, was redeemed by him
through his friendship with Pompey and was left by
him unimpaired to his children. He was the father
of Pythodoris, the present queen in Pontus, of whom
I have already spoken.[1] Pythodorus, then, flourished
in my time, as also Menodorus, a man of learning,
and otherwise august and grave, who held the
priesthood of Zeus Larisaeus. But he was overthrown by a counter-party friendly to Dometius
Ahenobarbus; and Dometius, relying on his in-
formers, slew him, as guilty of causing the fleet to
revolt. Here were born famous orators: Dionysocles
and afterwards Damasus Scombrus. Tralleis is said
to have been founded by Argives and by certain
Tralleian Thracians, and hence the name. And the
city was ruled for a short time by tyrants, the
sons of Cratippus, at the time of the Mithridatic
war.

43. Nysa is situated near Mt. Mesogis, for the
most part lying upon its slopes; and it is a double
city, so to speak, for it is divided by a torrential
stream that forms a gorge, which at one place
has a bridge over it, joining the two cities, and at
another is adorned with an amphitheatre, with a
hidden underground passage for the torrential waters.
Near the theatre are two heights, below one of
which is the gymnasium of youths; and below the
other is the market-place and the gymnasium for

τῇ δ' ἀγορᾷ καὶ τὸ γεροντικόν· πρὸς δὲ νότον
ὑποπέπτωκε τῇ πόλει τὸ πεδίον, καθάπερ καὶ
ταῖς Τράλλεσιν.

44. Ἐν δὲ τῇ ὁδῷ τῇ μεταξὺ τῶν Τράλλεων
καὶ τῆς Νύσης, κώμη τῶν Νυσαέων ἐστὶν οὐκ
ἄπωθεν τῆς πόλεως Ἀχάρακα, ἐν ᾗ τὸ Πλουτώνιον, ἔχον καὶ ἄλσος πολυτελὲς καὶ νεὼν
Πλούτωνός τε καὶ Κόρης,[1] καὶ τὸ Χαρώνιον,
ἄντρον ὑπερκείμενον τοῦ ἄλσους θαυμαστὸν τῇ
φύσει· λέγουσι γὰρ δὴ καὶ τοὺς νοσώδεις καὶ
προσέχοντας ταῖς τῶν θεῶν τούτων θεραπείαις
φοιτᾶν ἐκεῖσε καὶ διαιτᾶσθαι ἐν τῇ κώμῃ πλησίον
τοῦ ἄντρου παρὰ τοῖς ἐμπείροις τῶν ἱερέων, οἳ
ἐγκοιμῶνταί τε ὑπὲρ αὐτῶν καὶ διατάττουσιν
ἐκ τῶν ὀνείρων τὰς θεραπείας. οὗτοι δ' εἰσὶ καὶ
οἱ ἐγκαλοῦντες τὴν τῶν θεῶν ἰατρείαν· ἄγουσι δὲ
πολλάκις εἰς τὸ ἄντρον καὶ ἱδρύουσι μένοντας
καθ' ἡσυχίαν ἐκεῖ, καθάπερ ἐν φωλεῷ σιτίων
C 650 χωρὶς ἐπὶ πλείους ἡμέρας. ἔστι δ' ὅτε καὶ
ἰδίοις ἐνυπνίοις οἱ νοσηλευόμενοι προσέχουσι,
μυσταγωγοῖς δ' ὅμως καὶ συμβούλοις ἐκείνοις
χρῶνται, ὡς ἂν ἱερεῦσι· τοῖς δ' ἄλλοις ἄδυτός
ἐστιν ὁ τόπος καὶ ὀλέθριος. πανήγυρις δ' ἐν
τοῖς Ἀχαράκοις συντελεῖται κατ' ἔτος, καὶ τότε
μάλιστα ὁρᾶν ἔστι καὶ ἀκούειν περὶ τῶν τοσούτων[2] τοὺς πανηγυρίζοντας· τότε δὲ καὶ περὶ
τὴν μεσημβρίαν ὑπολαβόντες ταῦρον οἱ ἐκ τοῦ
γυμνασίου νέοι καὶ ἔφηβοι, γυμνοὶ λίπ' ἀληλιμμένοι,[3] μετὰ σπουδῆς ἀνακομίζουσιν εἰς τὸ ἄντρον·
ἀφεθεὶς δέ, μικρὸν προελθὼν πίπτει καὶ ἔκπνους
γίνεται.

[1] Κόρης, second hand in C, for Ἥρας elsewhere.

older persons. The plain lies to the south of the city, as it does to the south of Tralleis.

44. On the road between the Tralleis and Nysa is a village of the Nysaeans, not far from the city, Acharaca, where is the Plutonium, with a costly sacred precinct and a shrine of Pluto and Corê, and also the Charonium, a cave that lies above the sacred precinct, by nature wonderful; for they say that those who are diseased and give heed to the cures prescribed by these gods resort thither and live in the village near the cave among experienced priests, who on their behalf sleep in the cave and through dreams prescribe the cures. These are also the men who invoke the healing power of the gods. And they often bring the sick into the cave and leave them there, to remain in quiet, like animals in their lurking-holes, without food for many days. And sometimes the sick give heed also to their own dreams, but still they use those other men, as priests, to initiate them into the mysteries and to counsel them. To all others the place is forbidden and deadly. A festival is celebrated every year at Acharaca; and at that time in particular those who celebrate the festival can see and hear concerning all these things; and at the festival, too, about noon, the boys and young men of the gymnasium, nude and anointed with oil, take up a bull and with haste carry him up into the cave; and, when let loose, the bull goes forward a short distance, falls, and breathes out his life.

---

² τοσούτων is emended by Corais and Meineke to νοσούντων.

³ λίπ' ἀληλιμμένοι, Meineke, for ἀπαληλιμμένοι.

45. Ἀπὸ δὲ τριάκοντα σταδίων τῆς Νύσης ὑπερβᾶσι Τμῶλον καὶ[1] τὸ ὄρος τὴν Μεσωγίδα ἐπὶ τὰ πρὸς τὸν νότον μέρη καλεῖται τόπος Λειμών, εἰς ὃν ἐξοδεύουσι πανηγυριοῦντες Νυσαεῖς τε καὶ οἱ κύκλῳ πάντες· οὐ πόρρω δὲ τούτου στόμιόν ἐστιν ἱερὸν τῶν αὐτῶν θεῶν, ὅ φασι καθήκειν μέχρι τῶν Ἀχαράκων. τοῦτον δὲ τὸν λειμῶνα ὀνομάζειν τὸν ποιητήν φασιν, ὅταν φῇ,

Ἀσίῳ ἐν λειμῶνι,
δεικνύντες Καϋστρίου καὶ Ἀσίου τινὸς ἡρῷον καὶ τὸν Κάϋστρον πλησίον ἀπορρέοντα.

46. Ἱστοροῦσι δὲ τρεῖς ἀδελφούς, Ἀθύμβρόν τε καὶ Ἀθύμβραδον καὶ Ὕδρηλον, ἐλθόντας ἐκ Λακεδαίμονος, τὰς ἐπωνύμους αὐτῶν κτίσαι πόλεις, λειπανδρῆσαι δ᾽ ὕστερον, ἐξ ἐκείνων δὲ συνοικισθῆναι τὴν Νῦσαν· καὶ νῦν Ἀθύμβρον ἀρχηγέτην νομίζουσιν οἱ Νυσαεῖς.

47. Περίκεινται δὲ ἀξιόλογοι κατοικίαι πέραν τοῦ Μαιάνδρου, Κοσκίνια καὶ Ὀρθωσία· ἐντὸς δὲ Βρίουλα, Μάσταυρα, Ἀχάρακα, καὶ ὑπὲρ τῆς πόλεως ἐν τῷ ὄρει τὰ Ἄρομα[2] (συστέλλοντες τὸ ῥῶ γράμμα)·[3] ὅθεν ἄριστος Μεσωγίτης οἶνος ὁ Ἀρομεύς.

[1] καί, before τὸ ὄρος, Jones inserts. E reads τὸ ὄρος καὶ τὴν Μεσωγίδα.

[2] Ἄρομα, Corais. for Ἀρώματα CDF (the o being above ω in D), Ἀρόματα E h i m o z.

[3] The words in parenthesis are probably a gloss, and are ejected by Meineke.

---

[1] The text, which seems to be corrupt, is recast and emended by Groskurd to read, "having crossed the Mesogis

45. Thirty stadia from Nysa, after one crosses over Mt. Tmolus and the mountain called Mesogis, towards the region to the south of the Mesogis,[1] there is a place called Leimon,[2] whither the Nysaeans and all the people about go to celebrate their festivals. And not far from Leimon is an entrance into the earth sacred to the same gods, which is said to extend down as far as Acharaca. The poet is said to name this meadow when he says, "On the Asian meadow"; and they point out a hero-temple of Caÿster and a certain Asius, and the Caÿster River that streams forth near by.

46. The story is told that three brothers, Athymbrus and Athymbradus and Hydrelus, who came from Lacedaemon, founded the three cities which were named after them, but that the cities later became scantily populated, and that the city Nysa was founded by their inhabitants; but that Athymbrus is now regarded by Nysaeans as their original founder.

47. Near Nysa, on the far side of the Maeander River, are situated noteworthy settlements; I mean Coscinia and Orthosia; and this side the river, Briula, Mastaura and Acharaca, and above the city, on the mountain, Aroma (in which the letter *rho*[3] is short), whence comes the best Mesogitan wine, I mean the Aromian.

---

towards the region to the south of Tmolus." But the simple rectification of the text made by the present translator solves the difficulty quite as well (see critical note).

[2] *i.e.* meadow.

[3] Apparently an error for "in which name the letter *omega* is shortened to *omicron* (cp. the well-known Greek word Arōma, which may mean either "spice" or "arable land.")

48. Ἄνδρες δὲ γεγόνασιν ἔνδοξοι Νυσαεῖς
Ἀπολλώνιός τε ὁ Στωικὸς φιλόσοφος, τῶν
Παναιτίου γνωρίμων ἄριστος, καὶ Μενεκράτης,
Ἀριστάρχου μαθητής, καὶ Ἀριστόδημος, ἐκείνου
υἱός, οὗ διηκούσαμεν ἡμεῖς ἐσχατόγηρω νέοι
παντελῶς ἐν τῇ Νύσῃ· καὶ Σώστρατος δέ, ὁ
ἀδελφὸς τοῦ Ἀριστοδήμου, καὶ ἄλλος Ἀριστόδημος, ἀνεψιὸς αὐτοῦ, ὁ παιδεύσας Μάγνον Πομπήιον, ἀξιόλογοι γεγόνασι γραμματικοί· ὁ δ᾽
ἡμέτερος καὶ ἐρρητόρευε, καὶ ἐν τῇ Ῥόδῳ καὶ ἐν
τῇ πατρίδι δύο σχολὰς συνεῖχε, πρωὶ μὲν τὴν
ῥητορικήν, δείλης δὲ τὴν γραμματικὴν σχολήν·
ἐν δὲ τῇ Ῥώμῃ τῶν Μάγνου παίδων ἐπιστατῶν
ἠρκεῖτο τῇ γραμματικῇ σχολῇ.

II

1. Τὰ δὲ πέραν ἤδη τοῦ Μαιάνδρου, τὰ λειπό-
C 651 μενα τῆς περιοδείας, πάντ᾽ ἐστὶ Καρικά, οὐκέτι
τοῖς Λυδοῖς ἐπιμεμιγμένων ἐνταῦθα τῶν Καρῶν,
ἀλλ᾽ ἤδη καθ᾽ αὑτοὺς ὄντων, πλὴν εἴ τι Μιλήσιοι
καὶ Μυήσιοι τῆς παραλίας ἀποτέτμηνται. ἀρχὴ
μὲν οὖν τῆς παραλίας ἐστὶν ἡ τῶν Ῥοδίων περαία
πρὸς θαλάττης, τέλος δὲ τὸ Ποσείδιον τῶν
Μιλησίων· ἐν δὲ τῇ μεσογαίᾳ τὰ ἄκρα τοῦ
Ταύρου μέχρι Μαιάνδρου. λέγουσι γὰρ ἀρχὴν
εἶναι τοῦ Ταύρου τὰ ὑπερκείμενα ὄρη τῶν Χελιδονίων καλουμένων νήσων, αἵπερ ἐν μεθορίῳ τῆς
Παμφυλίας καὶ τῆς Λυκίας πρόκεινται· ἐντεῦθεν
γὰρ ἐξαίρεται πρὸς ὕψος ὁ Ταῦρος· τὸ δ᾽ ἀληθὲς καὶ

---

[1] For map of Asia Minor, see Vol. V. (at end).

48. Famous men born at Nysa are: Apollonius the Stoic philosopher, best of the disciples of Panaetius; and Menecrates, pupil of Aristarchus; and Aristodemus, his son, whose entire course, in his extreme old age, I in my youth took at Nysa; and Sostratus, the brother of Aristodemus, and another Aristodemus, his cousin, who trained Pompey the Great, proved themselves notable grammarians. But my teacher also taught rhetoric and had two schools, both in Rhodes and in his native land, teaching rhetoric in the morning and grammar in the evening; at Rome, however, when he was in charge of the children of Pompey the Great, he was content with the teaching of grammar.

II

1. Coming now to the far side of the Maeander,[1] the parts that remain to be described are all Carian, since here the Lydians are no longer intermingled with the Carians, and the latter occupy all the country by themselves, except that a segment of the seaboard is occupied by Milesians and Myesians. Now the beginning of the seaboard is the Peraea[2] of the Rhodians on the sea, and the end of it is the Poseidium of the Milesians; but in the interior are the extremities of the Taurus, extending as far as the Maeander River. For it is said that the mountains situated above the Chelidonian islands, as they are called, which islands lie off the confines of Pamphylia and Lycia, form the beginning of the Taurus, for thence the Taurus rises to a height;

[2] Mainland territory.

τὴν Λυκίαν ἅπασαν ὀρεινὴ ῥάχις τοῦ Ταύρου διείργει πρὸς τὰ ἐκτὸς καὶ τὸ νότιον μέρος ἀπὸ τῶν
Κιβυρατικῶν μέχρι τῆς περαίας τῶν Ῥοδίων.
κἀνταῦθα δ᾽ ἐστὶ συνεχὴς ὀρεινή, πολὺ μέντοι
ταπεινοτέρα, καὶ οὐκέτι τοῦ Ταύρου νομίζεται,
οὐδὲ τὰ μὲν ἐκτὸς αὐτοῦ, τὰ δ᾽ ἐντός, διὰ τὸ
σποράδας εἶναι τὰς ἐξοχὰς καὶ τὰς εἰσοχὰς
ἐπίσης εἰς[1] τε πλάτος καὶ μῆκος τῆς χώρας
ἁπάσης καὶ μηδὲν ἔχειν ὅμοιον διατειχίσματι.
ἔστι δ᾽ ἅπας μὲν ὁ περίπλους κατακολπίζοντι
σταδίων τετρακισχιλίων ἐννακοσίων, αὐτὸς δὲ
ὁ τῆς περαίας τῶν Ῥοδίων ἐγγὺς χιλίων καὶ
πεντακοσίων.

2. Ἀρχὴ δὲ τὰ Δαίδαλα, τῆς Ῥοδίας χωρίον,
πέρας δὲ τὸ καλούμενον ὄρος Φοῖνιξ, καὶ τοῦτο
τῆς Ῥοδίας. πρόκειται δ᾽ Ἐλαιοῦσσα[2] νῆσος
διέχουσα τῆς Ῥόδου σταδίους ἑκατὸν εἴκοσι.
μεταξὺ δὲ πρῶτον μὲν ἀπὸ Δαιδάλων πλέουσιν
ἐπὶ τὴν δύσιν ἐπ᾽ εὐθείας τῇ ἐκ Κιλικίας καὶ
Παμφυλίας καὶ Λυκίας παραλίᾳ κόλπος ἐστὶν εὐλίμενος, Γλαῦκος καλούμενος, εἶτα τὸ Ἀρτεμίσιον
ἄκρα καὶ ἱερόν, εἶτα τὸ Λητῷον ἄλσος· ὑπὲρ
αὐτοῦ δὲ καὶ τῆς θαλάττης ἐν ἑξήκοντα σταδίοις
Κάλυνδα[3] πόλις· εἶτα Καῦνος καὶ ποταμὸς
πλησίον Κάλβις βαθύς, ἔχων εἰσαγωγήν, καὶ
μεταξὺ Πίσιλις.

3. Ἔχει δ᾽ ἡ πόλις νεώρια καὶ λιμένα κλειστόν·
ὑπέρκειται δὲ τῆς πόλεως ἐν ὕψει φρούριον

---

[1] εἰς, Kramer inserts ; so the later editors.
[2] Ἐλαιοῦσσα, Tzschucke, for Ἐλεοῦσσα; so Corais and
Meineke.
[3] Κάλυνδα, Casaubon, for Κάλυμνα; so the later editors.

but the truth is that the whole of Lycia, towards
the parts outside and on its southern side, is separated by a mountainous ridge of the Taurus from the
country of the Cibyrans as far as the Peraea of the
Rhodians. From here the ridge continues, but is
much lower and is no longer regarded as a part of the
Taurus; neither are the parts outside the Taurus and
this side of it so regarded, because of the fact that
the eminences and depressions are scattered equally
throughout the breadth and the length of the whole
country, and present nothing like a wall of partition.
The whole of the voyage round the coast, following
the sinuosities of the gulfs, is four thousand nine
hundred stadia, and merely that round the Peraea
of the Rhodians is close to fifteen hundred.

2. The Peraea of the Rhodians begins with
Daedala, a place in the Rhodian territory, but ends
with Mt. Phoenix, as it is called, which is also in the
Rhodian territory. Off the Peraea lies the island
Elaeussa, distant one hundred and twenty stadia from
Rhodes. Between the two, as one sails towards the
west from Daedala in a straight line with the coast
of Cilicia and Pamphylia and Lycia, one comes to a
gulf called Glaucus, which has good harbours; then
to the Artemisium, a promontory and temple; then
to the sacred precinct of Leto, above which, and
above the sea, at a distance of sixty stadia, lies
Calynda, a city; then to Caunus and to the Calbis, a
river near Caunus, which is deep and affords passage
for merchant vessels; and between the two lies
Pisilis.

3. The city[1] has dockyards, and a harbour that
can be closed. Above the city, on a height, lies

---

[1] Caunus.

STRABO

Ἴμβρος. τῆς δὲ χώρας εὐδαίμονος οὔσης, ἡ πόλις τοῦ θέρους ὁμολογεῖται παρὰ πάντων εἶναι δυσάερος καὶ τοῦ μετοπώρου διὰ τὰ καύματα καὶ τὴν ἀφθονίαν τῶν ὡραίων· καὶ δὴ καὶ τὰ τοιαῦτα διηγημάτια θρυλεῖται, ὅτι Στρατόνικος ὁ κιθαριστὴς ἰδὼν ἐπιμελῶς[1] χλωροὺς τοὺς Καυνίους, τοῦτ' εἶναι ἔφη τὸ τοῦ ποιητοῦ·

οἵη περ φύλλων γενεή, τοιήδε καὶ ἀνδρῶν.

μεμφομένων δέ, ὡς σκώπτοιτο αὐτῷ[2] ἡ πόλις ὡς νοσερά, Ἐγώ, ἔφη, ταύτην θαρρήσαιμ' ἂν λέγειν C 652 νοσεράν, ὅπου καὶ οἱ νεκροὶ περιπατοῦσιν; ἀπέστησαν δέ ποτε Καύνιοι τῶν Ῥοδίων· κριθέντες δ' ἐπὶ τῶν Ῥωμαίων ἀπελήφθησαν πάλιν· καὶ ἔστι λόγος Μόλωνος κατὰ Καυνίων. φασὶ δ' αὐτοὺς ὁμογλώττους μὲν εἶναι τοῖς Καρσίν, ἀφῖχθαι δ' ἐκ Κρήτης[3] καὶ χρῆσθαι νόμοις ἰδίοις.

4. Ἑξῆς δὲ Φύσκος πολίχνη, λιμένα ἔχουσα καὶ ἄλσος Λητῷον· εἶτα Λώρυμα, παραλία τραχεῖα, καὶ ὄρος ὑψηλότατον τῶν ταύτῃ· ἐπ' ἄκρῳ δὲ φρούριον ὁμώνυμον τῷ ὄρει Φοῖνιξ· πρόκειται δ' ἡ Ἐλαιοῦσσα[4] νῆσος ἐν τέτρασι σταδίοις κύκλον ἔχουσα ὅσον ὀκτωστάδιον.

---

[1] ἐπιμελῶς seems to be corrupt. For various conjectures, see Müller, *Ind. Var. Lect.*, p. 1030.
[2] αὐτῷ, the editors (except Corais), for αὐτῶν.
[3] δ' ἐκ Κρήτης (from Herod. 1. 172), Corais, for δὲ Κρήτης.
[4] Ἐλαιοῦσσα, Tzschucke, for Ἐλεοῦσσα; so Corais and Meineke.

---

[1] An attempt to translate ἐπιμελῶς, which seems to be

Imbrus, a stronghold. Although the country is fertile, the city is agreed by all to have foul air in summer, as also in autumn, because of the heat and the abundance of fruits. And indeed little tales of the following kind are repeated over and over, that Stratonicus the citharist, seeing that the Caunians were pitiably[1] pale,[2] said that this was the thought of the poet in the verse, "Even as is the generation of leaves, such is that also of men"; and when people complained that he was jeering at the city as though it were sickly, he replied, "Would I be so bold as to call this city sickly, where even the corpses walk about?" The Caunians once revolted from the Rhodians, but by a judicial decision of the Romans they were restored to them. And there is extant a speech of Molon[3] entitled *Against the Caunians*. It is said that they speak the same language as the Carians, but that they came from Crete and follow usages of their own.[4]

4. Next one comes to Physcus, a small town, which has a harbour and a sacred precinct of Leto; and then to Loryma, a rugged coast, and to the highest mountain in that part of the country; and on top of the mountain is Phoenix, a stronghold bearing the same name as the mountain; and off the mountain, at a distance of four stadia, lies Elaeussa, an island, which is about eight stadia in circuit.

---

corrupt. Others translate the word either "somewhat" or "very."

[2] Or more strictly, "pale green."

[3] Apollonius Molon of Alabanda, the rhetorician and orator; ambassador of the Rhodians at Rome (81 B.C.), and teacher of Cicero and Julius Caesar.

[4] On their origin, language, and usages, cf. Herodotus 1. 172.

5. Ἡ δὲ τῶν Ῥοδίων πόλις κεῖται μὲν ἐπὶ τοῦ ἑωθινοῦ ἀκρωτηρίου, λιμέσι δὲ καὶ ὁδοῖς καὶ τείχεσι καὶ τῇ ἄλλῃ κατασκευῇ τοσοῦτον διαφέρει τῶν ἄλλων, ὥστ᾽ οὐκ ἔχομεν εἰπεῖν ἑτέραν, ἀλλ᾽ οὐδὲ πάρισον, μή τί γε κρείττω ταύτης τῆς πόλεως. θαυμαστὴ δὲ καὶ ἡ εὐνομία καὶ ἡ ἐπιμέλεια πρός τε τὴν ἄλλην πολιτείαν καὶ τὴν περὶ τὰ ναυτικά, ἀφ᾽ ἧς ἐθαλαττοκράτησε πολὺν χρόνον καὶ τὰ λῃστήρια καθεῖλε καὶ Ῥωμαίοις ἐγένετο φίλη καὶ τῶν βασιλέων τοῖς φιλορωμαίοις τε καὶ φιλέλ- λησιν· ἀφ᾽ ὧν αὐτόνομός τε διετέλεσε καὶ πολλοῖς ἀναθήμασιν ἐκοσμήθη, ἃ κεῖται τὰ μὲν πλεῖστα ἐν τῷ Διονυσίῳ καὶ τῷ γυμνασίῳ, ἄλλα δ᾽ ἐν ἄλλοις τόποις. ἄριστα δὲ ὅ τε τοῦ Ἡλίου κολοσ- σός, ὅν φησιν ὁ ποιήσας τὸ ἰαμβεῖον, ὅτι

ἑπτάκις δέκα
Χάρης ἐποίει πηχέων ὁ Λίνδιος.

κεῖται δὲ νῦν ὑπὸ σεισμοῦ πεσών, περικλασθεὶς ἀπὸ τῶν γονάτων· οὐκ ἀνέστησαν δ᾽ αὐτὸν κατά τι λόγιον. τοῦτό τε δὴ τῶν ἀναθημάτων κράτισ- τον (τῶν γοῦν ἑπτὰ θεαμάτων ὁμολογεῖται), καὶ αἱ τοῦ Πρωτογένους γραφαί, ὅ τε Ἰάλυσος καὶ ὁ Σάτυρος παρεστὼς στύλῳ, ἐπὶ δὲ τῷ στύλῳ πέρδιξ ἐφειστήκει· πρὸς ὃν οὕτως ἐκεχήνεσαν, ὡς ἔοικεν, οἱ ἄνθρωποι, νεωστὶ ἀνακειμένου τοῦ πίνακος, ὥστ᾽ ἐκεῖνον ἐθαύμαζον, ὁ δὲ Σάτυρος παρεωρᾶτο, καίτοι σφόδρα κατωρθωμένος· ἐξέ- πληττον δ᾽ ἔτι μᾶλλον οἱ περδικοτρόφοι, κομί-

---

[1] The god of the Sun. [2] Unknown.
[3] Tutelary hero of Rhodes and reputed grandson of Helius.

5. The city of the Rhodians lies on the eastern promontory of Rhodes; and it is so far superior to all others in harbours and roads and walls and improvements in general that I am unable to speak of any other city as equal to it, or even as almost equal to it, much less superior to it. It is remarkable also for its good order, and for its careful attention to the administration of affairs of state in general; and in particular to that of naval affairs, whereby it held the mastery of the sea for a long time and overthrew the business of piracy, and became a friend to the Romans and to all kings who favoured both the Romans and the Greeks. Consequently it not only has remained autonomous, but also has been adorned with many votive offerings, which for the most part are to be found in the Dionysium and the gymnasium, but partly in other places. The best of these are, first, the Colossus of Helius,[1] of which the author[2] of the iambic verse says, "seven times ten cubits in height, the work of Chares the Lindian"; but it now lies on the ground, having been thrown down by an earthquake and broken at the knees. In accordance with a certain oracle, the people did not raise it again. This, then, is the most excellent of the votive offerings (at any rate, it is by common agreement one of the Seven Wonders); and there are also the paintings of Protogenes, his Ialysus[3] and also his Satyr, the latter standing by a pillar, on top of which stood a male partridge. And at this partridge, as would be natural, the people were so agape when the picture had only recently been set up, that they would behold him with wonder but overlook the Satyr, although the latter was a very great

269

ζοντες τοὺς τιθασοὺς καὶ τιθέντες καταντικρύ·
ἐφθέγγοντο γὰρ πρὸς τὴν γραφὴν οἱ πέρδικες καὶ
ὠχλαγώγουν. ὁρῶν δὲ ὁ Πρωτογένης τὸ ἔργον
πάρεργον γεγονὸς ἐδεήθη τῶν τοῦ τεμένους προε-
στώτων ἐπιτρέψαι παρελθόντα ἐξαλεῖψαι τὸν
ὄρνιν, καὶ ἐποίησε. δημοκηδεῖς δ' εἰσὶν οἱ Ῥόδιοι,
καίπερ οὐ δημοκρατούμενοι, συνέχειν δ' ὅμως
C 653 βουλόμενοι τὸ τῶν πενήτων πλῆθος. σιταρχεῖται
δὴ ὁ δῆμος καὶ οἱ εὔποροι τοὺς ἐνδεεῖς ὑπολαμ-
βάνουσιν ἔθει τινὶ πατρίῳ, λειτουργίαι τέ τινές
εἰσιν ὀψωνιζόμεναι,[1] ὥσθ' ἅμα τόν τε πένητα
ἔχειν τὴν διατροφὴν καὶ τὴν πόλιν τῶν χρειῶν
μὴ καθυστερεῖν, καὶ μάλιστα πρὸς τὰς ναυ-
στολίας. τῶν δὲ ναυστάθμων τινὰ καὶ κρυπτὰ
ἦν καὶ ἀπόρρητα τοῖς πολλοῖς, τῷ δὲ κατοπτεύ-
σαντι ἢ παρελθόντι εἴσω θάνατος ὥριστο ἡ
ζημία. κἀνταῦθα δέ, ὥσπερ ἐν Μασσαλίᾳ καὶ
Κυζίκῳ, τὰ περὶ τοὺς ἀρχιτέκτονας καὶ τὰς
ὀργανοποιίας καὶ θησαυροὺς ὅπλων τε καὶ τῶν
ἄλλων ἐσπούδασται διαφερόντως, καὶ ἔτι γε τῶν
παρ' ἄλλοις μᾶλλον.

6. Δωριεῖς δ' εἰσίν, ὥσπερ καὶ Ἁλικαρνασεῖς
καὶ Κνίδιοι καὶ Κῷοι, οἱ γὰρ Δωριεῖς οἱ τὰ
Μέγαρα[2] κτίσαντες μετὰ τὴν Κόδρου τελευτήν,
οἱ μὲν ἔμειναν αὐτόθι, οἱ δὲ σὺν Ἀλθαιμένει τῷ
Ἀργείῳ τῆς εἰς Κρήτην ἀποικίας ἐκοινώνησαν, οἱ

---

[1] ὀψωνιζόμεναι F and Corais; ὀψωνιαζόμενοι other MSS.
[2] Μέγαρα, Xylander, for μεγάλα; so the later editors.

---

[1] Public offices to which the richer citizens were appointed.
These citizens were usually appointed by rotation, according

270

success. But the partridge-breeders were still more amazed, bringing their tame partridges and placing them opposite the painted partridge; for their partridges would make their call to the painting and attract a mob of people. But when Protogenes saw that the main part of the work had become subordinate, he begged those who were in charge of the sacred precinct to permit him to go there and efface the partridge, and so he did. The Rhodians are concerned for the people in general, although their rule is not democratic; still, they wish to take care of their multitude of poor people. Accordingly, the people are supplied with provisions and the needy are supported by the well-to-do, by a certain ancestral custom; and there are certain liturgies[1] that supply provisions, so that at the same time the poor man receives his sustenance and the city does not run short of useful men, and in particular for the manning of the fleets. As for the roadsteads, some of them were kept hidden and forbidden to the people in general; and death wa the penalty for any person who spied on them or passed inside them. And here too, as in Massalia and Cyzicus, everything relating to the architects, the manufacture of instruments of war, and the stores of arms and everything else are objects of exceptional care, and even more so than anywhere else.

6. The Rhodians, like the people of Halicarnassus and Cnidus and Cos, are Dorians; for of the Dorians who founded Megara after the death of Codrus, some remained there, others took part with Althaemenes the Argive in the colonisation of Crete, and

to their wealth, and they personally paid all the expenses connected with their offices.

δ' εἰς τὴν Ῥόδον καὶ τὰς λεχθείσας ἀρτίως πόλεις ἐμερίσθησαν. ταῦτα δὲ νεώτερα τῶν ὑφ' Ὁμήρου λεγομένων ἐστί· Κνίδος μὲν γὰρ καὶ Ἁλικαρνασὸς οὐδ' ἦν πω, Ῥόδος δ' ἦν καὶ Κῶς, ἀλλ' ᾠκεῖτο ὑφ' Ἡρακλειδῶν. Τληπόλεμος μὲν οὖν ἀνδρωθεὶς

αὐτίκα πατρὸς ἑοῖο φίλον μήτρωα κατέκτα
ἤδη γηράσκοντα, Λικύμνιον.
αἶψα δὲ νῆας ἔπηξε, πολὺν δ' ὅ γε λαὸν ἀγείρας
βῆ φεύγων.

εἶτά φησιν·

εἰς Ῥόδον ἷξεν ἀλώμενος,
τριχθὰ δὲ ᾤκηθεν καταφυλαδόν.

καὶ τὰς πόλεις ὀνομάζει τὰς τότε,

Λίνδον, Ἰηλυσόν τε καὶ ἀργινόεντα Κάμειρον,

τῆς Ῥοδίων πόλεως οὔπω συνῳκισμένης. οὐδαμοῦ δὴ ἐνταῦθα Δωριέας ὀνομάζει, ἀλλ' εἰ[1] ἄρα Αἰολέας ἐμφαίνει καὶ Βοιωτούς, εἴπερ ἐκεῖ ἡ κατοικία τοῦ Ἡρακλέους καὶ τοῦ Λικυμνίου· εἰ δ', ὥσπερ καὶ ἄλλοι φασίν, ἐξ Ἄργους καὶ Τίρυνθος ἀπῆρεν ὁ Τληπόλεμος, οὐδ' οὕτω Δωρικὴ γίνεται ἡ ἐκεῖθεν ἀποικία· πρὸ γὰρ τῆς Ἡρακλειδῶν καθόδου γεγένηται. καὶ τῶν Κᾴων δὲ

Φείδιππός τε καὶ Ἄντιφος ἡγησάσθην,
Θεσσαλοῦ υἷε δύω Ἡρακλείδαο ἄνακτος·

καὶ οὗτοι τὸ Αἰολικὸν μᾶλλον ἢ τὸ Δωρικὸν γένος ἐμφαίνοντες.

7. Ἐκαλεῖτο δ' ἡ Ῥόδος πρότερον Ὀφιοῦσσα καὶ Σταδία, εἶτα Τελχινίς, ἀπὸ τῶν οἰκησάντων

others were distributed to Rhodes and to the cities just now mentioned. But these events are later than those mentioned by Homer, for Cnidus and Halicarnassus were not yet in existence, although Rhodes and Cos were; but they were inhabited by Heracleidae. Now when Tlepolemus had grown to manhood, "he forthwith slew his own father's dear uncle, Licymnius, who was then growing old; and straightway he built him ships, and when he had gathered together a great host he went in flight."[1] The poet then adds, "he came to Rhodes in his wanderings, where his people settled in three divisions by tribes"; and he names the cities of that time, "Lindus, Ialysus, and Cameirus white with chalk,"[2] the city of the Rhodians having not yet been founded. The poet, then, nowhere mentions Dorians by name here, but perhaps indicates Aeolians and Boeotians, if it be true that Heracles and Licymnius settled there. But if, as others say, Tlepolemus set forth from Argos and Tiryns, even so the colonisation thence could not have been Dorian, for it must have taken place before the return of the Heracleidae. And of the Coans, also, Homer says, "these were led by Pheidippus and Antiphus, the two sons of lord Thessalus, son of Heracles";[3] and these names indicate the Aeolian stock of people rather than the Dorian.

7. In earlier times Rhodes was called Ophiussa and Stadia, and then Telchinis, after the Telchines,

[1] *Iliad* 2. 662.   [2] *Iliad* 2. 656.   [3] *Iliad* 2. 678.

---

[1] εἰ, Corais, for ἤ.

C 654 Τελχίνων τὴν νῆσον· οὓς οἱ μὲν βασκάνους φασὶ
καὶ γόητας, θείῳ[1] καταρραίνοντας[2] τὸ τῆς
Στυγὸς ὕδωρ ζᾴων τε καὶ φυτῶν ὀλέθρου χάριν·
οἱ δὲ τέχναις διαφέροντας τοὐναντίον ὑπὸ τῶν
ἀντιτέχνων βασκανθῆναι καὶ τῆς δυσφημίας
τυχεῖν ταύτης· ἐλθεῖν δ' ἐκ Κρήτης εἰς Κύπρον
πρῶτον, εἶτ' εἰς Ῥόδον· πρώτους δ' ἐργάσασθαι
σίδηρόν τε καὶ χαλκόν, καὶ δὴ καὶ τὴν ἅρπην
τῷ Κρόνῳ δημιουργῆσαι. εἴρηται μὲν οὖν καὶ
πρότερον περὶ αὐτῶν, ἀλλὰ ποιεῖ τὸ πολύμυθον
ἀναλαμβάνειν πάλιν ἀναπληροῦντας, εἴ τι παρε-
λίπομεν.

8. Μετὰ δὲ τοὺς Τελχῖνας οἱ Ἡλιάδαι μυθεύον-
ται κατασχεῖν τὴν νῆσον, ὧν ἑνὸς Κερκάφου καὶ
Κυδίππης γενέσθαι παῖδας τοὺς τὰς πόλεις
κτίσαντας ἐπωνύμους αὐτῶν,

Λίνδον Ἰηλυσόν τε καὶ ἀργινόεντα Κάμειρον·

ἔνιοι δὲ τὸν Τληπόλεμον κτίσαι φασί, θέσθαι
δὲ τὰ ὀνόματα ὁμωνύμως τῶν Δαναοῦ θυγατέρων
τισίν.

9. Ἡ δὲ νῦν πόλις ἐκτίσθη κατὰ τὰ Πελο-
ποννησιακὰ ὑπὸ τοῦ αὐτοῦ ἀρχιτέκτονος, ὥς
φασιν, ὑφ' οὗ καὶ ὁ Πειραιεύς· οὐ συμμένει δ'
ὁ Πειραιεύς, κακωθεὶς ὑπό τε Λακεδαιμονίων
πρότερον τῶν τὰ σκέλη καθελόντων καὶ ὑπὸ
Σύλλα τοῦ Ῥωμαίων ἡγεμόνος.

10. Ἱστοροῦσι δὲ καὶ ταῦτα περὶ τῶν Ῥοδίων,
ὅτι οὐ μόνον ἀφ' οὗ χρόνου συνῴκισαν τὴν νῦν

---

[1] θείῳ (sulphur) is strongly suspected. Meineke conj. φθόνῳ, and Forbiger so translates.

who took up their abode in the island. Some say that the Telchines are "maligners" and "sorcerers," who pour the water of the Styx mixed with sulphur[1] upon animals and plants in order to destroy them. But others, on the contrary, say that since they excelled in workmanship they were "maligned" by rival workmen and thus received their bad reputation; and that they first came from Crete to Cypros, and then to Rhodes; and that they were the first to work iron and brass, and in fact fabricated the scythe for Cronus. Now I have already described them before,[2] but the number of the myths about them causes me to resume their description, filling up the gaps, if I have omitted anything.

8. After the Telchines, the Heliadae, according to the mythical story, took possession of the island; and to one of these, Cercaphus, and to his wife Cydippê, were born children who founded the cities that are named after them, "Lindus, Ialysus, and Cameirus white with chalk." But some say that Tlepolemus founded them and gave them the same names as those of certain daughters of Danäus.

9. The present city was founded at the time of the Peloponnesian War by the same architect, as they say, who founded the Peiraeus. But the Peiraeus no longer endures, since it was badly damaged, first by the Lacedaemonians, who tore down the two walls, and later by Sulla, the Roman commander.

10. It is also related of the Rhodians that they have been prosperous by sea, not merely since the

---

[1] See critical note.   [2] 10. 3, 7, 19.

πόλιν εὐτύχουν κατὰ θάλατταν, ἀλλὰ καὶ πρὸ
τῆς Ὀλυμπικῆς θέσεως συχνοῖς ἔτεσιν ἔπλεον
πόρρω τῆς οἰκείας ἐπὶ σωτηρίᾳ τῶν ἀνθρώπων·
ἀφ' οὗ καὶ μέχρι Ἰβηρίας ἔπλευσαν, κἀκεῖ μὲν
τὴν Ῥόδον[1] ἔκτισαν, ἣν ὕστερον Μασσαλιῶται
κατέσχον, ἐν δὲ τοῖς Ὀπικοῖς τὴν Παρθενόπην,
ἐν δὲ Δαυνίοις μετὰ Κώων Ἐλπίας. τινὲς δὲ
μετὰ τὴν ἐκ Τροίας ἄφοδον τὰς Γυμνησίας νήσους
ὑπ' αὐτῶν κτισθῆναι λέγουσιν, ὧν τὴν μείζω φησὶ
Τίμαιος μεγίστην εἶναι μετὰ τὰς ἑπτά, Σαρδώ,
Σικελίαν, Κύπρον, Κρήτην, Εὔβοιαν, Κύρνον,
Λέσβον, οὐ τἀληθῆ λέγων· πολὺ γὰρ ἄλλαι
μείζους. φασὶ δὲ τοὺς γυμνήτας ὑπὸ Φοινίκων
βαλεαρίδας λέγεσθαι, διότι τὰς Γυμνησίας
Βαλεαρίδας λεχθῆναι.[2] τινὲς δὲ τῶν Ῥοδίων
καὶ περὶ Σύβαριν ᾤκησαν κατὰ τὴν Χωνίαν.
ἔοικε δὲ καὶ ὁ ποιητὴς μαρτυρεῖν τὴν ἐκ παλαιοῦ
παροῦσαν τοῖς Ῥοδίοις εὐδαιμονίαν εὐθὺς ἀπὸ τῆς
πρώτης κτίσεως τῶν τριῶν πόλεων·

τριχθὰ δὲ ᾤκηθεν καταφυλαδόν, ἠδ' ἐφίληθεν
ἐκ Διός, ὅστε θεοῖσι καὶ ἀνθρώποισιν ἀνάσσει,
καί σφιν θεσπέσιον πλοῦτον κατέχευε Κρονίων.

C 655 οἱ δ' εἰς μῦθον ἀνήγαγον τὸ ἔπος καὶ χρυσὸν
ὑσθῆναί φασιν ἐν τῇ νήσῳ κατὰ τὴν Ἀθηνᾶς
γένεσιν ἐκ τῆς κεφαλῆς τοῦ Διός, ὡς εἴρηκε
Πίνδαρος. ἡ δὲ νῆσος κύκλον ἔχει σταδίων
ἐννακοσίων εἴκοσιν.

---

[1] On Ῥόδον (which Meineke emends to Ῥόδην), see Vol. II,
p. 92, footnote 2.
[2] φασὶ δὲ . . . λεχθῆναι, Meineke ejects.

---

[1] Cf. 3. 4. 8.   [2] "Light-armed foot-soldiers."

time when they founded the present city, but that even many years before the establishment of the Olympian Games they used to sail far away from their homeland to insure the safety of their people. Since that time, also, they have sailed as far as Iberia; and there they founded Rhodes,[1] of which the Massaliotes later took possession; among the Opici they founded Parthenopê; and among the Daunians they, along with the Coans, founded Elpiae. Some say that the islands called the Gymnesiae were founded by them after their departure from Troy; and the larger of these, according to Timaeus, is the largest of all islands after the seven—Sardinia, Sicily, Cypros, Crete, Euboea, Cyrnos, and Lesbos, but this is untrue, for there are others much larger. It is said that "gymnetes"[2] are called "balearides"[3] by the Phoenicians, and that on this account the Gymnesiae were called Balearides. Some of the Rhodians took up their abode round Sybaris in Chonia. The poet, too, seems to bear witness to the prosperity enjoyed by the Rhodians from ancient times, forthwith from the first founding of the three cities: "and there his[4] people settled in three divisions by tribes, and were loved of Zeus, who is lord over gods and men; and upon them wondrous wealth was shed by the son of Cronus."[5] Other writers refer these verses to a myth, and say that gold rained on the island at the time when Athena was born from the head of Zeus, as Pindar[6] states. The island has a circuit of nine hundred and twenty stadia.

[3] Also spelled "baliarides" (see 3. 5. 1).
[4] Referring to Heracles.   [5] *Iliad* 2. 668.
[6] *Olympian Odes* 7. 61.

11. Ἔστι δὲ πρώτη μὲν Λίνδος ἀπὸ τῆς πόλεως πλέουσιν ἐν δεξιᾷ ἔχουσι τὴν νῆσον, πόλις ἐπὶ ὄρους ἱδρυμένη, πολὺ πρὸς μεσημβρίαν ἀνατείνουσα καὶ πρὸς Ἀλεξάνδρειαν μάλιστα· ἱερὸν δέ ἐστιν Ἀθηνᾶς Λινδίας αὐτόθι ἐπιφανές, τῶν Δαναΐδων ἵδρυμα. πρότερον μὲν οὖν καθ' αὑτοὺς ἐπολιτεύοντο οἱ Λίνδιοι, καθάπερ καὶ Καμειρεῖς καὶ Ἰαλύσιοι, μετὰ ταῦτα δὲ συνῆλθον ἅπαντες εἰς τὴν Ῥόδον. ἐντεῦθεν δ' ἐστὶν εἷς τῶν ἑπτὰ σοφῶν, Κλεόβουλος.

12. Μετὰ δὲ Λίνδον Ἰξία χωρίον καὶ Μνασύριον. εἶθ' ὁ Ἀτάβυρις, ὄρος τῶν ἐνταῦθα ὑψηλότατον, ἱερὸν Διὸς Ἀταβυρίου· εἶτα Κάμειρος· εἶτ' Ἰαλυσὸς κώμη, καὶ ὑπὲρ αὐτὴν ἀκρόπολίς ἐστιν Ὀχύρωμα καλουμένη· εἶθ' ἡ τῶν Ῥοδίων πόλις ἐν ὀγδοήκοντά που σταδίοις. μεταξὺ δ' ἐστὶ τὸ Θοάντιον, ἀκτή τις, ἧς μάλιστα πρόκεινται αἱ Σποράδες αἱ περὶ τὴν Χαλκίαν, ὧν ἐμνήσθημεν πρότερον.

13. Ἄνδρες δ' ἐγένοντο μνήμης ἄξιοι πολλοὶ στρατηλάται τε καὶ ἀθληταί, ὧν εἰσὶ καὶ οἱ Παναιτίου τοῦ φιλοσόφου πρόγονοι· τῶν δὲ πολιτικῶν καὶ τῶν περὶ λόγους καὶ φιλοσοφίαν[1] ὅ τε Παναίτιος αὐτὸς καὶ Στρατοκλῆς καὶ Ἀνδρόνικος ὁ ἐκ τῶν περιπάτων καὶ Λεωνίδης ὁ στωικός· ἔτι δὲ πρότερον Πραξιφάνης καὶ Ἱερώνυμος καὶ Εὔδημος. Ποσειδώνιος δ' ἐπολιτεύσατο μὲν ἐν Ῥόδῳ καὶ ἐσοφίστευσεν, ἦν δ' Ἀπαμεὺς ἐκ τῆς Συρίας, καθάπερ καὶ Ἀπολ-

---

[1] φιλοσοφίαν, Corais, for φιλοσοφίας; so Meineke.

11. As one sails from the city, with the island on the right, one comes first to Lindus, a city situated on a mountain and extending far towards the south and approximately towards Alexandria.[1] In Lindus there is a famous temple of Athena Lindia, founded by the daughters of Danäus. Now in earlier times the Lindians were under a separate government of their own, as were also the Cameirians and the Ialysians, but after this they all came together at Rhodes. Cleobulus, one of the Seven Wise Men, was a native of Lindus.

12. After Lindus one comes to Ixia, a stronghold, and to Mnasyrium; then to Atabyris, the highest of the mountains there, which is sacred to Zeus Atabyrius; then to Cameirus; then to Ialysus, a village, above which there is an acropolis called Ochyroma; then to the city of the Rhodians, at a distance of about eighty stadia. Between these lies Thoantium, a kind of promontory; and it is off Thoantium, generally speaking, that Chalcia and the Sporades in the neighbourhood of Chalcia lie, which I have mentioned before.[2]

13. Many men worthy of mention were native Rhodians, both commanders and athletes, among whom were the ancestors of Panaetius the philosopher; and, among statesmen and rhetoricians and philosophers, Panaetius himself and Stratocles and Andronicus, one of the Peripatetics, and Leonides the Stoic; and also, before their time, Praxiphanes and Hieronymus and Eudemus. Poseidonius engaged in affairs of state in Rhodes and taught there, although he was a native of Apameia in Syria, as

[1] According to Strabo (1. 4. 1 ff.), Rhodes and Alexandria lie on the same meridian.   [2] 10. 5. 14.

STRABO

λώνιος ὁ Μαλακὸς καὶ Μόλων· ἦσαν γὰρ
Ἀλαβανδεῖς, Μενεκλέους μαθηταὶ τοῦ ῥήτορος.
ἐπεδήμησε δὲ πρότερον Ἀπολλώνιος, ὀψὲ δ᾽
ἧκεν ὁ Μόλων, καὶ ἔφη πρὸς αὐτὸν ἐκεῖνος·
ὀψὲ μολών, ἀντὶ τοῦ ἐλθών· καὶ Πείσανδρος
δ᾽ ὁ τὴν Ἡράκλειαν γράψας ποιητὴς Ῥόδιος,
καὶ Σιμμίας ὁ γραμματικὸς καὶ Ἀριστοκλῆς ὁ
καθ᾽ ἡμᾶς· Διονύσιος δὲ ὁ Θρᾷξ καὶ Ἀπολλώνιος
ὁ τοὺς Ἀργοναύτας ποιήσας, Ἀλεξανδρεῖς μέν,
ἐκαλοῦντο δὲ Ῥόδιοι. περὶ μὲν Ῥόδου ἀπο-
χρώντως εἴρηται.

14. Πάλιν δὲ τῆς Καρικῆς παραλίας τῆς
μετὰ τὴν Ῥόδον, ἀπὸ Ἐλεοῦντος καὶ τῶν
Λωρύμων, καμπτήρ τις ἐπὶ τὰς ἄρκτους ἐστί,
καὶ λοιπὸν ἐπ᾽ εὐθείας ὁ πλοῦς μέχρι τῆς
Προποντίδος, ὡς ἂν μεσημβρινήν τινα ποιῶν
γραμμὴν ὅσον πεντακισχιλίων σταδίων ἢ μικρὸν
ἀπολείπουσαν. ἐνταῦθα δ᾽ ἐστὶν ἡ λοιπὴ τῆς
Καρίας καὶ Ἴωνες καὶ Αἰολεῖς καὶ Τροία καὶ
τὰ περὶ Κύζικον καὶ Βυζάντιον. μετὰ δ᾽ οὖν
C 656 τὰ Λώρυμα τὸ Κυνὸς σῆμά ἐστι καὶ Σύμη
νῆσος.

15. Εἶτα Κνίδος, δύο λιμένας ἔχουσα, ὧν τὸν
ἕτερον κλειστὸν τριηρικὸν καὶ ναύσταθμον ναυσὶν
εἴκοσι. πρόκειται δὲ[1] νῆσος ἑπταστάδιός πως
τὴν περίμετρον, ὑψηλή, θεατροειδής, συναπτομένη
χώμασι πρὸς τὴν ἤπειρον καὶ ποιοῦσα δίπολιν

1 δέ, Corais, for δ᾽ ἡ.

[1] He taught rhetoric at Rhodes about 120 B.C.
[2] Apollonius Molon (see 14. 2. 3).
[3] Natives of Alabanda in Caria.

was also the case with Apollonius Malacus[1] and Molon,[2] for they were Alabandians,[3] pupils of Menecles the orator. Apollonius Malacus began his sojourn there earlier than Molon, and when, much later, Molon came, the former said to him, " you are a late ' molon,' " [4] instead of saying, " late ' elthon.' " [5] And Peisander the poet, who wrote the *Heracleia,* was also a Rhodian ; and so was Simmias the grammarian, as also Aristocles of my own time. And Dionysius the Thracian and the Apollonius who wrote the *Argonauts,* though Alexandrians, were called Rhodians. As for Rhodes, I have said enough about it.

14. As for the Carian coast that comes after Rhodes, beginning at Eleus and Loryma, it bends sharply back towards the north, and the voyage thereafter runs in a straight line as far as the Propontis, forming, as it were, a meridian line about five thousand stadia long, or slightly short of that distance. Along this line is situated the remainder of Caria, as are also the Ionians and the Aeolians and Troy and the parts round Cyzicus and Byzantium. After Loryma, then, one comes to Cynos-Sema[6] and to Symê, an island.

15. Then to Cnidus, with two harbours, one of which can be closed, can receive triremes, and is a naval station for twenty ships. Off it lies an island which is approximately seven stadia in circuit, rises high, is theatre-like, is connected by moles with the

---

[4] " Molon " means " comer " (note the word-play).

[5] " Elthon " is the common word for " comer," whereas the other is poetic and comparatively rare.

[6] Cape Volpo. Cf. the reference to the Cynos-Sema at the entrance of the Hellespont, Vol. III, p. 377, *Frag.* 55.

τρόπον τινὰ τὴν Κνίδον· πολὺ γὰρ αὐτῆς μέρος
οἰκεῖ τὴν νῆσον, σκεπάζουσαν ἀμφοτέρους τοὺς
λιμένας. κατ' αὐτὴν δ' ἐστὶν ἡ Νίσυρος πελαγία.
ἄνδρες δ' ἀξιόλογοι Κνίδιοι πρῶτον μὲν Εὔδοξος
ὁ μαθηματικός, τῶν Πλάτωνος ἑταίρων, εἶτ'
Ἀγαθαρχίδης ὁ ἐκ τῶν περιπάτων, ἀνὴρ συγγραφεύς, καθ' ἡμᾶς δὲ Θεόπομπος, ὁ Καίσαρος
τοῦ Θεοῦ φίλος τῶν μεγάλα δυναμένων, καὶ
υἱὸς Ἀρτεμίδωρος. ἐντεῦθεν δὲ καὶ Κτησίας ὁ
ἰατρεύσας μὲν Ἀρταξέρξην, συγγράψας δὲ τὰ
Ἀσσυρικὰ καὶ τὰ Περσικά. εἶτα μετὰ Κνίδον
Κέραμος καὶ Βάργασα πολίχνια ὑπὲρ θαλάττης.

16. Εἶθ' Ἁλικαρνασός, τὸ βασίλειον τῶν τῆς
Καρίας δυναστῶν, Ζεφύρα[1] καλουμένη πρότερον.
ἐνταῦθα δ' ἐστὶν ὅ τε τοῦ Μαυσώλου τάφος,[2]
τῶν ἑπτὰ θεαμάτων, ἔργον,[3] ὅπερ Ἀρτεμισία
τῷ ἀνδρὶ κατεσκεύασε, καὶ ἡ Σαλμακὶς κρήνη,
διαβεβλημένη, οὐκ οἶδ' ὁπόθεν, ὡς μαλακίζουσα
τοὺς πιόντας ἀπ' αὐτῆς. ἔοικε δ' ἡ τρυφὴ τῶν
ἀνθρώπων αἰτιᾶσθαι τοὺς ἀέρας ἢ τὰ ὕδατα·
τρυφῆς δ' αἴτια οὐ ταῦτα, ἀλλὰ πλοῦτος καὶ
ἡ περὶ τὰς διαίτας ἀκολασία. ἔχει δ' ἀκρόπολιν
ἡ Ἁλικαρνασός· πρόκειται δ' αὐτῆς ἡ Ἀρκόν-
νησος. οἰκισταὶ δ' αὐτῆς ἐγένοντο ἄλλοι τε καὶ
Ἄνθης μετὰ Τροιζηνίων. ἄνδρες δὲ γεγόνασιν
ἐξ αὐτῆς Ἡρόδοτός τε ὁ συγγραφεύς, ὃν ὕστερον
Θούριον ἐκάλεσαν διὰ τὸ κοινωνῆσαι τῆς εἰς

---

[1] Stephanus (s.v. Ἁλικαρνασσός) spells the name Ζεφυρία;
so Meineke reads.

[2] Before τῶν Corais and Meineke, following the Epitome,
insert ἕν.

[3] Corais conjectures that Σκόπα has fallen out after ἔργον;

mainland, and in a way makes Cnidus a double city, for a large part of its people live on the island, which shelters both harbours. Opposite it, in the high sea, is Nisyrus. Notable Cnidians were: first, Eudoxus the mathematician, one of the comrades of Plato; then Agatharchides, one of the Peripatetics, a historian; and, in my own time, Theopompus, the friend of the deified Caesar, being a man of great influence with him, and his son Artemidorus. Thence, also, came Ctesias, who served Artaxerxes as physician and wrote the works entitled *Assyrica* and *Persica*. Then, after Cnidus, one comes to Ceramus and Bargasa, small towns situated above the sea.

16. Then to Halicarnassus, the royal residence of the dynasts of Caria, which was formerly called Zephyra. Here is the tomb of Mausolus,[1] one of the Seven Wonders, a monument erected by Artemisia in honour of her husband; and here is the fountain called Salmacis, which has the slanderous repute, for what reason I do not know, of making effeminate all who drink from it. It seems that the effeminacy of man is laid to the charge of the air or of the water; yet it is not these, but rather riches and wanton living, that are the cause of effeminacy. Halicarnassus has an acropolis; and off the city lies Arconnesus. Its colonisers were, among others, Anthes and a number of Troezenians. Natives of Halicarnassus have been: Herodotus the historian, whom they later called a Thurian, because

---

[1] Hence "mausoleum."

Groskurd, Σκόπα καὶ τεχνιτῶν. Meineke indicates a lacuna before ἔργον, conjecturing θαυμαστόν.

STRABO

Θουρίους ἀποικίας, καὶ Ἡράκλειτος ὁ ποιητής, ὁ Καλλιμάχου ἑταῖρος, καὶ καθ᾽ ἡμᾶς Διονύσιος ὁ συγγραφεύς.

17. Ἔπταισε δὲ καὶ αὕτη ἡ πόλις βίᾳ ληφθεῖσα ὑπὸ Ἀλεξάνδρου. Ἑκατόμνω γὰρ τοῦ Καρῶν βασιλέως ἦσαν υἱοὶ τρεῖς, Μαύσωλος καὶ Ἰδριεὺς καὶ Πιξώδαρος, καὶ θυγατέρες δύο, ὧν τῇ πρεσβυτέρᾳ Ἀρτεμισίᾳ Μαύσωλος συνῴκησεν, ὁ πρεσβύτατος τῶν ἀδελφῶν, ὁ δὲ δεύτερος Ἰδριεὺς Ἄδᾳ, τῇ ἑτέρᾳ ἀδελφῇ· ἐβασίλευσε δὲ Μαύσωλος· τελευτῶν δ᾽ ἄτεκνος τὴν ἀρχὴν κατέλιπε τῇ γυναικί, ὑφ᾽ ἧς αὐτῷ κατεσκευάσθη ὁ λεχθεὶς τάφος· φθίσει δ᾽ ἀποθανούσης διὰ πένθος τοῦ ἀνδρός, Ἰδριεὺς ἦρξε· καὶ τοῦτον ἡ γυνὴ Ἄδα διεδέξατο νόσῳ τελευτήσαντα· ἐξέβαλε δὲ ταύτην Πιξώδα-
C 657 ρος, ὁ λοιπὸς τῶν Ἑκατόμνω παίδων. περσίσας δὲ μεταπέμπεται σατράπην ἐπὶ κοινωνίᾳ τῆς ἀρχῆς· ἀπελθόντος δ᾽ ἐκ τοῦ ζῆν καὶ τούτου, κατεῖχεν ὁ σατράπης τὴν Ἁλικαρνασόν· ἐπελθόντος δὲ Ἀλεξάνδρου, πολιορκίαν ὑπέμεινεν, ἔχων Ἄδαν γυναῖκα, ἥτις θυγάτηρ ἦν Πιξωδάρου ἐξ Ἀφνηΐδος, Καππαδοκίσσης γυναικός. ἡ δὲ τοῦ Ἑκατόμνω θυγάτηρ Ἄδα, ἣν ὁ Πιξώδαρος ἐξέβαλεν, ἱκετεύει τὸν Ἀλέξανδρον καὶ πείθει κατάγειν αὐτὴν εἰς τὴν ἀφαιρεθεῖσαν βασιλείαν, ὑποσχομένη ἐπὶ τὰ ἀφεστῶτα συμπράξειν αὐτῷ· τοὺς γὰρ ἔχοντας οἰκείους ὑπάρχειν αὐτῇ· παρεδίδου δὲ καὶ τὰ Ἄλινδα, ἐν ᾧ διέτριβεν αὐτή· ἐπαινέσας δὲ καὶ βασίλισσαν ἀναδείξας, ἁλούσης τῆς πόλεως πλὴν τῆς ἄκρας (διττὴ δ᾽ ἦν), ἐκείνῃ πολιορκεῖν ἔδωκεν· ἑάλω δὲ ὀλίγῳ

284

he took part in the colonisation of Thurii; and
Heracleitus the poet, the comrade of Callimachus;
and, in my time, Dionysius the historian.

17. This city, too, met a reverse when it was forcibly
seized by Alexander. For Hecatomnus, the king of
the Carians, had three sons, Mausolus and Hidrieus
and Pixodarus, and two daughters. Mausolus, the
eldest of the brothers, married Artemisia, the elder of
the daughters, and Hidrieus, the second son, married
Ada, the other sister. Mausolus became king and
at last, childless, he left the empire to his wife, by
whom the above-mentioned tomb was erected. But
she pined away and died through grief for her
husband, and Hidrieus then became ruler. He died
from a disease and was succeeded by his wife Ada;
but she was banished by Pixodarus, the remaining
son of Hecatomnos. Having espoused the side of
the Persians, he sent for a satrap to share the
empire with him; and when he too departed from
life, the satrap took possession of Halicarnassus. And
when Alexander came over, the satrap sustained a
siege. His wife was Ada, who was the daughter of
Pixodarus by Aphenis, a Cappadocian woman. But
Ada, the daughter of Hecatomnos, whom Pixodarus
had banished, entreated Alexander and persuaded
him to restore her to the kingdom of which she had
been deprived, having promised to co-operate with
him against the parts of the country which were in
revolt, for those who held these parts, she said, were
her own relations; and she also gave over to
him Alinda, where she herself was residing. He assented
and appointed her queen; and when the city, except
the acropolis (it was a double city), had been
captured, he assigned to her the siege of the acro-

ὕστερον[1] καὶ ἡ ἄκρα, πρὸς ὀργὴν ἤδη καὶ ἀπέχθειαν τῆς πολιορκίας γενομένης.

18. Ἑξῆς δ' ἐστὶν ἄκρα Τερμέριον Μυνδίων, καθ' ἣν ἀντίκειται τῆς Κῴας ἄκρα Σκανδαρία, διέχουσα τῆς ἠπείρου σταδίους τετταράκοντα· ἔστι δὲ καὶ χωρίον Τέρμερον ὑπὲρ τῆς Κῴας.

19. Ἡ δὲ τῶν Κῴων πόλις ἐκαλεῖτο τὸ παλαιὸν Ἀστυπάλαια, καὶ ᾠκεῖτο ἐν ἄλλῳ τόπῳ ὁμοίως ἐπὶ θαλάττῃ· ἔπειτα διὰ στάσιν μετῴκησαν εἰς τὴν νῦν πόλιν περὶ τὸ Σκανδάριον,[2] καὶ μετωνόμασαν Κῶν ὁμωνύμως τῇ νήσῳ. ἡ μὲν οὖν πόλις οὐ μεγάλη, κάλλιστα δὲ πασῶν συνῳκισμένη καὶ ἰδέσθαι τοῖς καταπλέουσιν ἡδίστη. τῆς δὲ νήσου τὸ μέγεθος ὅσον πεντακοσίων σταδίων καὶ πεντήκοντα· εὔκαρπος δὲ πᾶσα, οἴνῳ δὲ καὶ ἀρίστη, καθάπερ Χίος καὶ Λέσβος· ἔχει δὲ πρὸς νότον μὲν ἄκραν τὸν Λακητῆρα, ἀφ' οὗ ἑξήκοντα εἰς Νίσυρον (πρὸς δὲ τῷ Λακητῆρι χωρίον[3] Ἀλίσαρνα), ἀπὸ δύσεως δὲ τὸ Δρέκανον καὶ κώμην καλουμένην Στομαλίμνην· τοῦτο μὲν οὖν ὅσον διακοσίους τῆς πόλεως διέχει σταδίους· ὁ δὲ Λακητὴρ προσλαμβάνει πέντε καὶ τριάκοντα τῷ μήκει τοῦ πλοῦ. ἐν δὲ τῷ προαστείῳ τὸ Ἀσκληπιεῖόν ἐστι, σφόδρα ἔνδοξον καὶ πολλῶν ἀναθημάτων μεστὸν ἱερόν,[4] ἐν οἷς ἐστι καὶ ὁ Ἀπελλοῦ Ἀντίγονος. ἦν δὲ καὶ ἡ ἀναδυομένη Ἀφροδίτη,

---

[1] The MSS. read ὀλίγῳ δ' ὕστερον.
[2] Σκανδάριον, Tzschucke, for Σκάνδαλον E, Σκανδύλιον other MSS ; so the later editors.
[3] Λακητῆρι χωρίον, Corais, for Λακτητηρίῳ χωρίῳ ; so the later editors.

286

polis. This too was captured a little later, the siege having now become a matter of anger and personal enmity.

18. Next one comes to a promontory, Termerium, belonging to the Myndians, opposite which lies Scandaria, a promontory of Cos, forty stadia distant from the mainland. And there is a place called Termerum above the promontory of Cos.

19. The city of the Coans was in ancient times called Astypalaea; and its people lived on another site, which was likewise on the sea. And then, on account of a sedition, they changed their abode to the present city, near Scandarium, and changed the name to Cos, the same as that of the island. Now the city is not large, but it is the most beautifully settled of all, and is most pleasing to behold as one sails from the high sea to its shore. The size [1] of the island is about five hundred and fifty stadia. It is everywhere well supplied with fruits, but like Chios and Lesbos it is best in respect to its wine. Towards the south it has a promontory, Laceter, whence the distance to Nisyros is sixty stadia (but near Laceter there is a place called Halisarna), and on the west it has Drecanum and a village called Stomalimnê. Now Drecanum is about two hundred stadia distant from the city, but Laceter adds thirty-five stadia to the length of the voyage. In the suburb is the Asclepïeium, a temple exceedingly famous and full of numerous votive offerings, among which is the Antigonus of Apelles. And Aphrodite

---

[1] *i.e.* the circuit.

---

[4] ἱερόν is perhaps rightly omitted by F and Meineke.

ἡ νῦν ἀνάκειται τῷ θεῷ Καίσαρι ἐν Ῥώμῃ,
τοῦ Σεβαστοῦ ἀναθέντος τῷ πατρὶ τὴν ἀρχηγέτιν
τοῦ γένους αὐτοῦ· φασὶ δὲ τοῖς Κῴοις ἀντὶ τῆς
γραφῆς ἑκατὸν ταλάντων ἄφεσιν γενέσθαι τοῦ
προσταχθέντος φόρου. φασὶ δ᾽ Ἱπποκράτην
μάλιστα ἐκ τῶν ἐνταῦθα ἀνακειμένων θεραπειῶν
γυμνάσασθαι τὰ περὶ τὰς διαίτας· οὗτός τε δή
ἐστι τῶν ἐνδόξων Κῷος ἀνὴρ καὶ Σῖμος ὁ ἰατρός,
Φιλητᾶς τε ποιητὴς ἅμα καὶ κριτικός, καὶ καθ᾽
C 653 ἡμᾶς Νικίας ὁ καὶ τυραννήσας Κῴων, καὶ
Ἀρίστων ὁ ἀκροασάμενος τοῦ περιπατητικοῦ
καὶ κληρονομήσας ἐκεῖνον· ἦν δὲ καὶ Θεόμνηστος
ὁ ψάλτης ἐν ὀνόματι, ὃς καὶ ἀντεπολιτεύσατο
τῷ Νικίᾳ.

20. Ἐν δὲ τῇ παραλίᾳ τῆς ἠπείρου κατὰ τὴν
Μυνδίαν Ἀστυπάλαιά [1] ἐστιν ἄκρα καὶ Ζεφύριον·
εἶτ᾽ εὐθὺς ἡ Μύνδος, λιμένα ἔχουσα, καὶ μετὰ
ταύτην Βαργύλια, καὶ αὕτη πόλις· ἐν δὲ τῷ
μεταξὺ Καρύανδα λιμὴν καὶ νῆσος ὁμώνυμος,[2]
ἣν ᾤκουν Καρυανδεῖς. ἐντεῦθεν δ᾽ ἦν καὶ Σκύλαξ
ὁ παλαιὸς συγγραφεύς. πλησίον δ᾽ ἐστὶ τῶν
Βαργυλίων τὸ τῆς Ἀρτέμιδος ἱερὸν τῆς Κινδυάδος,
ὃ πεπιστεύκασι περιίεσθαι· ἦν δέ ποτε καὶ
χωρίον Κινδύη. ἐκ δὲ τῶν Βαργυλίων ἀνὴρ
ἐλλόγιμος ἦν ὁ Ἐπικούρειος Πρώταρχος ὁ
Δημητρίου καθηγησάμενος τοῦ Λάκωνος προσα-
γορευθέντος.

[1] Ἀστυπάλαια, the editors, for Ἀστυπαλεία E, Ἀστυπαλία
other MSS.
[2] ταύτῃ after ὁμώνυμος, is omitted by F and by Stephanus
(s.v. Καρύανδα).

[1] Emerging from the sea.

Anadyomenê[1] used to be there,[2] but it is now dedicated to the deified Caesar in Rome, Augustus thus having dedicated to his father the female founder of his family. It is said that the Coans got a remission of one hundred talents of the appointed tribute in return for the painting. And it is said that the dietetics practised by Hippocrates were derived mostly from the cures recorded on the votive tablets there. He, then, is one of the famous men from Cos; and so is Simus the physician; as also Philetas, at the same time poet and critic; and, in my time, Nicias, who also reigned as tyrant over the Coans; and Ariston, the pupil and heir of the Peripatetic;[3] and Theomnestus, a renowned harper, who was a political opponent of Nicias, was a native of the island.

20. On the coast of the mainland near the Myndian territory lies Astypalaea, a promontory; and also Zephyrium. Then forthwith one comes to Myndus, which has a harbour; and after Myndus to Bargylia, which is also a city; between the two is Caryanda, a harbour, and also an island bearing the same name, where the Caryandians lived. Here was born Scylax, the ancient historian. Near Bargylia is the temple of Artemis Cindyas, round which the rain is believed to fall without striking it. And there was once a place called Cindyê. From Bargylia there was a man of note, the Epicurean Protarchus, who was the teacher of Demetrius called Lacon.[4]

---

[2] This, too, was a painting by Apelles.
[3] Ariston the Peripatetic (fl. third century B.C.), of Iulis in Ceos (see 10. 5. 6). See Pauly-Wissowa.
[4] *i.e.* the Laconian.

STRABO

21. Εἶτ᾽ Ἰασὸς ἐπὶ νήσῳ κεῖται προσκειμένη τῇ ἠπείρῳ, ἔχει δὲ λιμένα, καὶ τὸ πλεῖστον τοῦ βίου τοῖς ἐνθάδε ἐκ θαλάττης· εὐοψεῖ γὰρ χώραν τ᾽ ἔχει παράλυπρον. καὶ δὴ καὶ διηγήματα τοιαῦτα πλάττουσιν εἰς αὐτήν· κιθαρῳδοῦ γὰρ ἐπιδεικνυμένου, τέως μὲν ἀκροᾶσθαι πάντας, ὡς δ᾽ ὁ κώδων ὁ κατὰ τὴν ὀψοπωλίαν ἐψόφησε, καταλιπόντας ἀπελθεῖν ἐπὶ τὸ ὄψον, πλὴν ἑνὸς δυσκώφου· τὸν οὖν κιθαρῳδὸν προσιόντα εἰπεῖν, ὅτι, Ὦ ἄνθρωπε, πολλήν σοι χάριν οἶδα τῆς πρός με τιμῆς καὶ φιλομουσίας· οἱ μὲν γὰρ ἄλλοι ἅμα τῷ κώδωνος ἀκοῦσαι ἀπιόντες οἴχονται. ὁ δέ, Τί λέγεις; ἔφη, ἤδη γὰρ ὁ κώδων ἐψόφηκεν; εἰπόντος δέ, Εὖ σοι εἴη, ἔφη καὶ ἀναστὰς ἀπῆλθε καὶ αὐτός. ἐντεῦθεν δ᾽ ἦν ὁ διαλεκτικὸς Διόδωρος ὁ Κρόνος προσαγορευθείς, κατ᾽ ἀρχὰς μὲν ψευδῶς· Ἀπολλώνιος γὰρ ἐκαλεῖτο ὁ Κρόνος, ὁ ἐπιστατήσας ἐκείνου· μετήνεγκαν δ᾽ ἐπ᾽ αὐτὸν διὰ τὴν ἀδοξίαν τοῦ κατ᾽ ἀλήθειαν Κρόνου.

22. Μετὰ δ᾽ Ἰασὸν τὸ τῶν Μιλησίων Ποσείδιόν ἐστιν. ἐν δὲ τῇ μεσογαίᾳ τρεῖς εἰσὶ πόλεις ἀξιόλογοι, Μύλασα, Στρατονίκεια, Ἀλάβανδα· αἱ δὲ ἄλλαι περιπόλιοι τούτων ἢ τῶν παραλίων, ὧν εἰσιν Ἀμυζών, Ἡράκλεια, Εὔρωμος, Χαλκήτωρ[1] τούτων μὲν οὖν ἐλάττων λόγος.

[1] Χαλκήτωρ is emended by Meineke to Χαλκήτορες (cp. 14. 1. 8).

[1] One who played the cithara and sang to its accompaniment.
[2] "Cronus" was a nickname for "Old Timer," "Old

21. Then one comes to Iasus, which lies on an island close to the mainland. It has a harbour; and the people gain most of their livelihood from the sea, for the sea here is well supplied with fish, but the soil of the country is rather poor. Indeed, people fabricate stories of this kind in regard to Iasus: When a citharoede [1] was giving a recital, the people all listened for a time, but when the bell that announced the sale of fish rang, they all left him and went away to the fish-market, except one man who was hard of hearing. The citharoede, therefore, went up to him and said: "Sir, I am grateful to you for the honour you have done me and for your love of music, for all the others except you went away the moment they heard the sound of the bell." And the man said, "What's that you say? Has the bell already rung?" And when the citharoede said "Yes," the man said, "Fare thee well," and himself arose and went away. Here was born the dialectician Diodorus, nicknamed Cronus, falsely so at the outset, for it was Apollonius his master who was called Cronus, but the nickname was transferred to him because of the true Cronus' lack of repute. [2]

22. After Iasus one comes to the Poseidium of the Milesians. In the interior are three noteworthy cities: Mylasa, Stratoniceia, and Alabanda. The others are dependencies of these or else of the cities on the coast, among which are Amyzon, Heracleia, Euromus, and Chalcetor. As for these, there is less to be said.

Dotard." Diodorus is said to have been given the nickname by Ptolemy Soter because he was unable immediately to solve some dialectic problem put forth by Stilpo. He became the head of the Megarian school of philosophy.

23. Τὰ δὲ Μύλασα ἵδρυται ἐν πεδίῳ σφόδρα
εὐδαίμονι· ὑπέρκειται δὲ κατὰ κορυφὴν ὄρος
αὐτοῦ,[1] λατόμιον λευκοῦ λίθου κάλλιστον ἔχον·
τοῦτο μὲν οὖν ὄφελός ἐστιν οὐ μικρόν, τὴν λιθίαν
πρὸς τὰς οἰκοδομίας ἄφθονον καὶ ἐγγύθεν ἔχον,
καὶ μάλιστα πρὸς τὰς τῶν ἱερῶν καὶ τῶν ἄλλων
δημοσίων ἔργων κατασκευάς· τοιγάρτοι στοαῖς
C 659 τε καὶ ναοῖς, εἴ τις ἄλλη, κεκόσμηται παγκάλως.
θαυμάζειν δ᾽ ἔστι τῶν ὑποβαλόντων οὕτως
ἀλόγως τὸ κτίσμα ὀρθίῳ καὶ ὑπερδεξίῳ κρημνῷ·
καὶ δὴ τῶν ἡγεμόνων τις εἰπεῖν λέγεται, θαυμάσας
τὸ πρᾶγμα· Ταύτην γάρ, ἔφη, τὴν πόλιν ὁ
κτίσας, εἰ μὴ ἐφοβεῖτο, ἆρ᾽ οὐδ᾽ ᾐσχύνετο;
ἔχουσι δ᾽ οἱ Μυλασεῖς ἱερὰ δύο τοῦ Διός, τοῦ
τε Ὀσογῶ καλουμένου, καὶ Λαβρανδηνοῦ· τὸ
μὲν ἐν τῇ πόλει, τὰ δὲ Λάβρανδα κώμη ἐστὶν
ἐν τῷ ὄρει κατὰ τὴν ὑπέρθεσιν τὴν ἐξ Ἀλαβάν-
δων εἰς τὰ Μύλασα, ἄπωθεν τῆς πόλεως· ἐνταῦθα
νεώς ἐστιν ἀρχαῖος καὶ ξόανον Διὸς Στρατίου·
τιμᾶται δὲ ὑπὸ τῶν κύκλῳ καὶ ὑπὸ τῶν
Μυλασέων, ὁδός τε ἔστρωται σχεδόν τι καὶ
ἑξήκοντα σταδίων μέχρι τῆς πόλεως, ἱερὰ καλουμένη, δι᾽ ἧς πομποστολεῖται τὰ ἱερά· ἱερῶνται δ᾽ οἱ ἐπιφανέστατοι τῶν πολιτῶν ἀεὶ διὰ
βίου. ταῦτα μὲν οὖν ἴδια[2] τῆς πόλεως, τρίτον
δ᾽ ἐστὶν ἱερὸν τοῦ Καρίου Διὸς κοινὸν ἁπάντων
Καρῶν, οὗ μέτεστι καὶ Λυδοῖς καὶ Μυσοῖς ὡς
ἀδελφοῖς. ἱστορεῖται δὲ κώμη ὑπάρξαι τὸ

---

[1] For αὐτοῦ C. Müller (*Ind. Var. Lect.* p. 1030) cleverly
conj. αἰπύ.
[2] ἴδια, Casaubon, for διό ; so the later editors.

23. But as for Mylasa: it is situated in an exceedingly fertile plain; and above the plain, towering into a peak, rises a mountain, which has a most excellent quarry of white marble. Now this quarry is of no small advantage, since it has stone in abundance and close at hand, for building purposes and in particular for the building of temples and other public works;[1] accordingly this city, as much as any other, is in every way beautifully adorned with porticoes and temples. But one may well be amazed at those who so absurdly founded the city at the foot of a steep and commanding crag. Accordingly, one of the commanders, amazed at the fact, is said to have said, "If the man who founded this city, was not afraid, was he not even ashamed?" The Mylasians have two temples of Zeus, Zeus Osogo, as he is called, and Zeus Labrandenus. The former is in the city, whereas Labranda is a village far from the city, being situated on the mountain near the pass that leads over from Alabanda to Mylasa. At Labranda there is an ancient shrine and statue of Zeus Stratius. It is honoured by the people all about and by the Mylasians; and there is a paved road of almost sixty stadia from the shrine to Mylasa, called the Sacred Way, on which their sacred processions are conducted. The priestly offices are held by the most distinguished of the citizens, always for life. Now these temples belong peculiarly to the city; but there is a third temple, that of the Carian Zeus, which is a common possession of all Carians, and in which, as brothers, both Lydians and Mysians have a share. It is

---

[1] *i.e.* "works" of art (see Vol. II, p. 349 and footnote 5, and p. 407 and footnote 4).

παλαιόν, πατρὶς δὲ καὶ βασίλειον τῶν Καρῶν τῶν περὶ τὸν Ἑκατόμνω· πλησιάζει δὲ μάλιστα τῇ κατὰ Φύσκον θαλάττῃ ἡ πόλις, καὶ τοῦτ᾽ ἐστὶν αὐτοῖς ἐπίνειον.

24 Ἀξιολόγους δ᾽ ἔσχεν ἄνδρας καθ᾽ ἡμᾶς τὰ Μύλασα, ῥήτοράς τε ἅμα καὶ δημαγωγοὺς τῆς πόλεως, Εὐθύδημόν τε καὶ Ὑβρέαν. ὁ μὲν οὖν Εὐθύδημος ἐκ προγόνων παραλαβὼν οὐσίαν τε μεγάλην καὶ δόξαν, προσθεὶς καὶ τὴν δεινότητα, οὐκ ἐν τῇ πατρίδι μόνον μέγας ἦν, ἀλλὰ καὶ ἐν τῇ Ἀσίᾳ τῆς πρώτης ἠξιοῦτο τιμῆς. Ὑβρέᾳ δ᾽ ὁ πατήρ, ὡς αὐτὸς διηγεῖτο ἐν τῇ σχολῇ καὶ παρὰ τῶν πολιτῶν ὡμολόγητο, ἡμίονον κατέλιπε ξυλοφοροῦντα καὶ ἡμιονηγόν· διοικούμενος δ᾽ ὑπὸ τούτων ὀλίγον χρόνον Διοτρέφους τοῦ Ἀντιοχέως ἀκροασάμενος ἐπανῆλθε καὶ τῷ ἀγορανομίῳ παρέδωκεν αὐτόν· ἐνταῦθα δὲ κυλινδηθεὶς καὶ χρηματισάμενος μικρὰ ὥρμησεν ἐπὶ τὸ πολιτεύεσθαι καὶ τοῖς ἀγοραίοις συνακολουθεῖν. ταχὺ δὲ αὔξησιν ἔσχε καὶ ἐθαυμάσθη[1] ἔτι μὲν καὶ Εὐθυδήμου ζῶντος, ἀλλὰ τελευτήσαντος μάλιστα, κύριος γενόμενος τῆς πόλεως. ζῶν δ᾽ ἐπεκράτει πολὺ ἐκεῖνος, δυνατὸς ὢν ἅμα καὶ χρήσιμος τῇ πόλει, ὥστ᾽, εἰ καί τι τυραννικὸν προσῆν, τοῦτ᾽ ἀπελύετο τῷ παρακολουθεῖν τὸ χρήσιμον. ἐπαινοῦσι γοῦν τοῦτο τοῦ Ὑβρέου, ὅπερ δημηγορῶν ἐπὶ τελευτῆς εἶπεν· Εὐθύδημε, κακὸν εἶ τῆς πόλεως ἀναγκαῖον· οὔτε γὰρ μετὰ σοῦ δυνάμεθα ζῆν οὔτ᾽ ἄνευ σοῦ. αὐξηθεὶς οὖν ἐπὶ πολὺ καὶ δό-

C 660

---

[1] μάλιστα, after ἐθαυμάσθη, is ejected by Meineke.

related that Mylasa was a mere village in ancient times, but that it was the native land and royal residence of the Carians of the house of Hecatomnos. The city is nearest to the sea at Physcus; and this is their seaport.

24. Mylasa has had two notable men in my time, who were at once orators and leaders of the city, Euthydemus and Hybreas. Now Euthydemus, having inherited from his ancestors great wealth and high repute, and having added to these his own cleverness, was not only a great man in his native land, but was also thought worthy of the foremost honour in Asia. As for Hybreas, as he himself used to tell the story in his school and as confirmed by his fellow-citizens, his father left him a mule-driver and a wood-carrying mule. And, being supported by these, he became a pupil of Diotrephes of Antiocheia for a short time, and then came back and "surrendered himself to the office of market-clerk." But when he had been "tossed about" in this office and had made but little money, he began to apply himself to the affairs of state and to follow closely the speakers of the forum. He quickly grew in power, and was already an object of amazement in the lifetime of Euthydemus, but in particular after his death, having become master of the city. So long as Euthydemus lived he strongly prevailed, being at once powerful and useful to the city, so that even if there was something tyrannical about him, it was atoned for by the fact that it was attended by what was good for the city. At any rate, people applaud the following statement of Hybreas, made by him towards the end of a public speech: "Euthydemus: you are an evil necessary to the city, for we

295

ξας καὶ πολίτης ἀγαθὸς εἶναι καὶ ῥήτωρ ἔπταισεν
ἐν τῇ πρὸς Λαβιῆνον ἀντιπολιτείᾳ. οἱ μὲν γὰρ
ἄλλοι μεθ᾽ ὅπλων ἐπιόντι καὶ Παρθικῆς συμμαχίας, ἤδη τῶν Παρθυαίων τὴν Ἀσίαν ἐχόντων,
εἶξαν, ἅτε ἄοπλοι καὶ εἰρηνικοί· Ζήνων δ᾽ ὁ
Λαοδικεὺς καὶ Ὑβρέας οὐκ εἶξαν, ἀμφότεροι
ῥήτορες, ἀλλὰ ἀπέστησαν τὰς ἑαυτῶν πόλεις·
ὁ δ᾽ Ὑβρέας καὶ προσπαρώξυνε φωνῇ τινὶ
μειράκιον εὐερέθιστον καὶ ἀνοίας πλῆρες. ἐκείνου γὰρ ἀνειπόντος ἑαυτὸν Παρθικὸν αὐτοκράτορα, Οὐκοῦν, ἔφη, κἀγὼ λέγω ἐμαυτὸν Καρικὸν
αὐτοκράτορα. ἐκ τούτου δὲ ἐπὶ τὴν πόλιν
ὥρμησε, τάγματα ἔχων ἤδη συντεταγμένα
Ῥωμαίων τῶν ἐν τῇ Ἀσίᾳ· αὐτὸν μὲν οὖν οὐ
κατέλαβε, παραχωρήσαντα εἰς Ῥόδον, τὴν δ᾽
οἰκίαν αὐτοῦ διελυμήνατο, πολυτελεῖς ἔχουσαν
κατασκευάς, καὶ διήρπασεν· ὡς δ᾽ αὕτως καὶ
τὴν πόλιν ὅλην ἐκάκωσεν. ἐκλιπόντος δ᾽ ἐκείνου
τὴν Ἀσίαν, ἐπανῆλθε καὶ ἀνέλαβεν ἑαυτόν τε
καὶ τὴν πόλιν. περὶ μὲν οὖν Μυλάσων ταῦτα.
25. Στρατονίκεια δ᾽ ἐστὶ κατοικία Μακεδόνων·
ἐκοσμήθη δὲ καὶ αὕτη κατασκευαῖς πολυτελέσιν
ὑπὸ τῶν βασιλέων. ἔστι δ᾽ ἐν τῇ χώρᾳ τῶν
Στρατονικέων δύο ἱερά, ἐν μὲν Λαγίνοις τὸ τῆς
Ἑκάτης ἐπιφανέστατον, πανηγύρεις μεγάλας συν-
άγον κατ᾽ ἐνιαυτόν· ἐγγὺς δὲ τῆς πόλεως τὸ τοῦ
Χρυσαορέως Διὸς κοινὸν ἁπάντων Καρῶν, εἰς ὃ
συνίασι θύσοντές τε καὶ βουλευσόμενοι περὶ τῶν

---

[1] The Greek word might mean "legions" rather than
"cohorts."

[2] Of the golden sword.

can live neither with you nor without you." However, although he had grown very strong and had the repute of being both a good citizen and orator, he stumbled in his political opposition to Labienus; for while the others, since they were without arms and inclined to peace, yielded to Labienus when he was coming against them with an army and an allied Parthian force, the Parthians by that time being in possession of Asia, yet Zeno of Laodiceia and Hybreas, both orators, refused to yield and caused their own cities to revolt. Hybreas also provoked Labienus, a lad who was irritable and full of folly, by a certain pronouncement; for when Labienus proclaimed himself Parthian Emperor, Hybreas said, "Then I too call myself Carian Emperor." Consequently Labienus set out against the city with cohorts [1] of Roman soldiers in Asia that were already organised. Labienus did not seize Hybreas, however, since he had withdrawn to Rhodes, but he shamefully maltreated his home, with its costly furnishings, and plundered it. And he likewise damaged the whole of the city. But though Hybreas abandoned Asia, he came back and rehabilitated both himself and the city. So much, then, for Mylasa.

25. Stratoniceia is a settlement of Macedonians. And this too was adorned with costly improvements by the kings. There are two temples in the country of the Stratoniceians, of which the most famous, that of Hecatê, is at Lagina; and it draws great festal assemblies every year. And near the city is the temple of Zeus Chrysaoreus,[2] the common possession of all Carians, whither they gather both to offer sacrifice and to deliberate on their common interests.

κοινῶν· καλεῖται δὲ τὸ σύστημα αὐτῶν Χρυ-
σαορέων, συνεστηκὸς ἐκ κωμῶν· οἱ δὲ πλείστας
παρεχόμενοι κώμας προέχουσι τῇ ψήφῳ, καθάπερ
Κεραμιῆται· καὶ Στρατονικεῖς δὲ τοῦ συστήματος
μετέχουσιν, οὐκ ὄντες τοῦ Καρικοῦ γένους, ἀλλ'
ὅτι κώμας ἔχουσι τοῦ Χρυσαορικοῦ συστήματος.
κἀνταῦθα δ' ἀνὴρ ἀξιόλογος γεγένηται ῥήτωρ
Μένιππος κατὰ τοὺς πατέρας ἡμῶν, Κατόκας
ἐπικαλούμενος, ὃν μάλιστα ἐπαινεῖ τῶν κατὰ τὴν
Ἀσίαν ῥητόρων, ὧν ἠκροάσατο, Κικέρων, ὥς
φησιν ἔν τινι γραφῇ αὐτός, συγκρίνων Ξενοκλεῖ
καὶ τοῖς κατ' ἐκεῖνον ἀκμάζουσιν. ἔστι δὲ καὶ
ἄλλη Στρατονίκεια, ἡ πρὸς τῷ Ταύρῳ καλουμένη,
πολίχνιον προσκείμενον τῷ ὄρει.

26. Ἀλάβανδα δὲ καὶ αὐτὴ μὲν ὑπόκειται
λόφοις δυσὶ συγκειμένοις οὕτως, ὥστ' ὄψιν παρέ-
χεσθαι κανθηλίου κατεστρωμένου. καὶ δὴ κα
ὁ Μαλακὸς Ἀπολλώνιος σκώπτων τὴν πόλιν εἴς
τε ταῦτα καὶ εἰς τὸ τῶν σκορπίων πλῆθος, ἔφη
αὐτὴν εἶναι σκορπίων κανθήλιον κατεστρωμένον·[1]
μεστὴ δ' ἐστὶ καὶ αὕτη καὶ ἡ τῶν Μυλασέων
πόλις τῶν θηρίων τούτων καὶ ἡ μεταξὺ πᾶσα
C 661 ὀρεινή. τρυφητῶν δ' ἐστὶν ἀνθρώπων καὶ καπυ-
ριστῶν, ἔχουσα ψαλτρίας πολλάς. ἄνδρες δ'
ἐγένοντο λόγου ἄξιοι δύο ῥήτορες ἀδελφοὶ Ἀλαβανδεῖς, Μενεκλῆς τε, οὗ ἐμνήσθημεν μικρὸν
ἐπάνω, καὶ Ἱεροκλῆς καὶ οἱ μετοικήσαντες εἰς
τὴν Ῥόδον ὅ τε Ἀπολλώνιος καὶ ὁ Μόλων.

---

[1] κατεστρωμένον, Casaubon, for κατεστραμμένον; so the
editors in general.

---

[1] Cf. the votes of the Lycian cities, 14. 3. 3.

Their League, which consists of villages, is called "Chrysaorian." And those who present the most villages have a preference in the vote,[1] like, for example, the people of Ceramus. The Stratoniceians also have a share in the League, although they are not of the Carian stock, but because they have villages belonging to the Chrysaorian League. Here, too, in the time of our fathers, was born a noteworthy man, Menippus, surnamed Catocas, whom Cicero, as he says in one of his writings,[2] applauded above all the Asiatic orators he had heard, comparing him with Xenocles and with the other orators who flourished in the latter's time. But there is also another Stratoniceia, "Stratoniceia near the Taurus," as it is called; it is a small town situated near the mountain.

26. Alabanda is also situated at the foot of hills, two hills that are joined together in such a way that they present the appearance of an ass laden with panniers. And indeed Apollonius Malacus, in ridiculing the city both in regard to this and in regard to the large number of scorpions there, said that it was an "ass laden with panniers of scorpions." Both this city and Mylasa are full of these creatures, and so is the whole of the mountainous country between them. Alabanda is a city of people who live in luxury and debauchery, containing many girls who play the harp. Alabandians worthy of mention are two orators, brothers, I mean Menecles, whom I mentioned a little above,[3] and Hierocles, and also Apollonius and Molon,[4] who changed their abode to Rhodes.

[2] *Brutus* 91 (315).   [3] § 13.   [4] See § 13.

27. Πολλῶν δὲ λόγων εἰρημένων περὶ Καρῶν, ὁ μάλισθ' ὁμολογούμενός ἐστιν οὗτος, ὅτι οἱ Κᾶρες ὑπὸ Μίνω ἐτάττοντο, τότε Λέλεγες καλούμενοι, καὶ τὰς νήσους ᾤκουν· εἶτ' ἠπειρῶται γενόμενοι, πολλὴν τῆς παραλίας καὶ τῆς μεσογαίας κατέσχον, τοὺς προκατέχοντας ἀφελόμενοι· καὶ οὗτοι δ' ἦσαν οἱ πλείους Λέλεγες καὶ Πελασγοί· πάλιν δὲ τούτους ἀφείλοντο μέρος οἱ Ἕλληνες, Ἴωνές τε καὶ Δωριεῖς. τοῦ δὲ περὶ τὰ στρατιωτικὰ ζήλου τά τε ὄχανα ποιοῦνται τεκμήρια καὶ τὰ ἐπίσημα καὶ τοὺς λόφους· ἅπαντα γὰρ λέγεται Καρικά· Ἀνακρέων μέν γε φησίν·

δία δηῦτε Καρικευργέος
ὀχάνοιο χεῖρα τιθέμεναι.

ὁ δ' Ἀλκαῖος,

λόφον τε σείων Καρικόν.

28. Τοῦ ποιητοῦ δ' εἰρηκότος οὑτωσί·

Μάσθλης[1] αὖ Καρῶν ἡγήσατο βαρβαροφώνων,

οὐκ ἔχει λόγον, πῶς τοσαῦτα εἰδὼς ἔθνη βάρβαρα μόνους εἴρηκε βαρβαροφώνους τοὺς Κᾶρας, βαρβάρους δ' οὐδένας. οὔτ' οὖν Θουκυδίδης ὀρθῶς· οὐδὲ γὰρ λέγεσθαί φησι βαρβάρους διὰ τὸ μηδὲ Ἕλληνάς πω ἀντίπαλον εἰς ἓν ὄνομα ἀποκεκρίσθαι· τό τε γὰρ μηδὲ Ἕλληνάς πω ψεῦδος αὐτὸς ὁ ποιητὴς ἀπελέγχει·

ἀνδρός, τοῦ κλέος εὐρὺ καθ' Ἑλλάδα καὶ μέσον Ἄργος.

___
[1] Μάσθλης, Corais emends to Νάστης.

300

27. Of the numerous accounts of the Carians, the one that is generally agreed upon is this, that the Carians were subject to the rule of Minos, being called Leleges at that time, and lived in the islands; then, having migrated to the mainland, they took possession of much of the coast and of the interior, taking it away from its previous possessors, who for the most part were Leleges and Pelasgians. In turn these were deprived of a part of their country by the Greeks, I mean Ionians and Dorians. As evidences of their zeal for military affairs, writers adduce shield-holders, shield-emblems, and crests, for all these are called "Carian." At least Anacreon says, "Come, put thine arm through the shield-holder, work of the Carians." And Alcaeus [1] says, "shaking the Carian crest."

28. When the poet says, "Masthles [2] in turn led the Carians, of barbarian speech," [3] we have no reason to inquire how it is that, although he knew so many barbarian tribes, he speaks of the Carians alone as "of barbarian speech," but nowhere speaks of "barbarians." Thucydides,[4] therefore, is not correct, for he says that Homer "did not use the term 'barbarians' either, because the Hellenes on their part had not yet been distinguished under one name as opposed to them"; for the poet himself refutes the statement that the Hellenes had not yet been so distinguished when he says, "My husband, whose fame is wide through Hellas and

[1] *Frag.* 22 (Bergk).
[2] An error, apparently, for "Nastes."
[3] *Iliad* 2. 867 (note "Mesthles" in line 864).
[4] 1. 3.

301

καὶ πάλιν·

εἴτ' ἐθέλεις τραφθῆναι[1] ἀν' Ἑλλάδα καὶ μέσον
Ἄργος.

μὴ λεγομένων τε βαρβάρων, πῶς ἔμελλεν εὖ
λεχθήσεσθαι τὸ βαρβαροφώνων; οὔτε δὴ οὗτος
εὖ, οὔτ' Ἀπολλόδωρος ὁ γραμματικός, ὅτι τῷ
κοινῷ ὀνόματι ἰδίως καὶ λοιδόρως ἐχρῶντο οἱ
Ἕλληνες κατὰ τῶν Καρῶν, καὶ μάλιστα οἱ
Ἴωνες, μισοῦντες αὐτοὺς διὰ τὴν ἔχθραν καὶ τὰς
συνεχεῖς στρατείας· ἐχρῆν γὰρ οὕτως βαρβάρους
ὀνομάζειν. ἡμεῖς δὲ ζητοῦμεν, διὰ τί βαρβαροφώνους καλεῖ, βαρβάρους δ' οὐδ' ἅπαξ. ὅτι,
φησί, τὸ πληθυντικὸν εἰς τὸ μέτρον οὐκ ἐμπίπτει,
διὰ τοῦτ' οὐκ εἴρηκε βαρβάρους. ἀλλ' αὕτη μὲν
ἡ πτῶσις οὐκ ἐμπίπτει, ἡ δ' ὀρθὴ οὐ διαφέρει τῆς
C 662 Δάρδανοι·

Τρῶες καὶ Λύκιοι καὶ Δάρδανοι.

τοιοῦτον δὲ καὶ τὸ

οἷοι Τρώιοι ἵπποι.

οὐδέ γε ὅτι τραχυτάτη ἡ γλῶττα τῶν Καρῶν· οὐ
γάρ ἐστιν, ἀλλὰ καὶ πλεῖστα Ἑλληνικὰ ὀνόματα
ἔχει καταμεμιγμένα, ὥς φησι Φίλιππος ὁ τὰ
Καρικὰ γράψας. οἶμαι δέ, τὸ βάρβαρον κατ'
ἀρχὰς ἐκπεφωνῆσθαι οὕτως κατ' ὀνοματοποιίαν
ἐπὶ τῶν δυσεκφόρως καὶ σκληρῶς καὶ τραχέως
λαλούντων, ὡς τὸ βατταρίζειν καὶ τραυλίζειν καὶ
ψελλίζειν· εὐφυέστατοι γάρ ἐσμεν τὰς φωνὰς

---

[1] τραφθῆναι, Corais, for ταρφθῆναι CDFhis, τερφθῆναι other
MSS.

---

[1] i.e. throughout the whole of Greece.

mid-Argos." [1]   And again, "And if thou dost wish
to journey through Hellas and mid-Argos."
Further, if they were not called "barbarians," how
could they properly be called a people "of barbarian speech"? So neither Thucydides is correct,
nor Apollodorus the grammarian, who says that the
general term was used by the Hellenes in a
peculiar and abusive sense against the Carians, and
in particular by the Ionians, who hated them because of their enmity and the continuous military
campaigns; for it was right to name them barbarians
in this sense. But I raise the question, Why does he
call them people "of barbarian speech," but not even
once calls them barbarians? "Because," Apollodorus
replies, "the plural does not fall in with the metre;
this is why he does not call them barbarians." But
though this case [2] does not fall in with metre, the
nominative case [3] does not differ metrically from that
of "Dardanians":[4] "Trojans and Lycians and
Dardanians."[5] So, also, the word "Trojan," in
"of what kind the Trojan horses are."[6] Neither
is he correct when he says that the language of
the Carians is very harsh, for it is not, but even has
very many Greek words mixed up with it, according
to the Philip who wrote *The Carica*.[7] I suppose that
the word "barbarian" was at first uttered onomatopoetically in reference to people who enunciated
words only with difficulty and talked harshly and
raucously, like our words "battarizein," "trau-
lizein," and "psellizein";[8] for we are by nature

[2] The genitive (βαρβάρων).   [3] βάρβαροι.   [4] Δάρδανοι.
[5] *Iliad* 11 286.   [6] *Iliad* 5. 222.   [7] *The History of Caria.*
[8] Meaning respectively, "stutter," "lisp," and "speak
falteringly."

ταῖς ὁμοίαις φωναῖς κατονομάζειν διὰ τὸ ὁμογενές·
ᾗ δὴ[1] καὶ πλεονάζουσι[2] ἐνταῦθα αἱ ὀνοματο-
ποιίαι, οἷον τὸ κελαρύζειν καὶ κλαγγὴ δὲ καὶ
ψόφος καὶ βοὴ καὶ κρότος, ὧν τὰ πλεῖστα ἤδη
καὶ κυρίως ἐκφέρεται· πάντων δὴ τῶν παχυστο-
μούντων οὕτως βαρβάρων λεγομένων, ἐφάνη τὰ
τῶν ἀλλοεθνῶν στόματα τοιαῦτα, λέγω δὲ τὰ
τῶν μὴ Ἑλλήνων. ἐκείνους οὖν ἰδίως ἐκάλεσαν[3]
βαρβάρους, ἐν ἀρχαῖς μὲν κατὰ τὸ λοίδορον, ὡς
ἂν παχυστόμους ἢ τραχυστόμους, εἶτα κατεχρη-
σάμεθα ὡς ἐθνικῷ κοινῷ ὀνόματι, ἀντιδιαιροῦντες
πρὸς τοὺς Ἕλληνας. καὶ γὰρ δὴ τῇ πολλῇ
συνηθείᾳ καὶ ἐπιπλοκῇ[4] τῶν βαρβάρων οὐκέτι
ἐφαίνετο κατὰ παχυστομίαν καὶ ἀφυΐαν τινὰ τῶν
φωνητηρίων ὀργάνων τοῦτο συμβαῖνον, ἀλλὰ κατὰ
τὰς τῶν διαλέκτων ἰδιότητας. ἄλλη δέ τις ἐν τῇ
ἡμετέρᾳ διαλέκτῳ ἀνεφάνη κακοστομία καὶ οἷον
βαρβαροστομία, εἴ τις ἑλληνίζων μὴ κατορθοίη,
ἀλλ᾽ οὕτω λέγοι τὰ ὀνόματα, ὡς οἱ βάρβαροι οἱ
εἰσαγόμενοι εἰς τὸν ἑλληνισμόν, οὐκ ἰσχύοντες
ἀρτιστομεῖν, ὡς οὐδ᾽ ἡμεῖς ἐν ταῖς ἐκείνων διαλέκ-
τοις. τοῦτο δὲ μάλιστα συνέβη τοῖς Καρσί·
τῶν γὰρ ἄλλων οὔτ᾽ ἐπιπλεκομένων πω[5] σφόδρα
τοῖς Ἕλλησιν, οὐδ᾽ ἐπιχειρούντων Ἑλληνικῶς ζῆν
ἢ μανθάνειν τὴν ἡμετέραν διάλεκτον, πλὴν εἴ τινες

---

[1] ᾗ δή, Corais, for ἤδη ; so the later editors.
[2] μέν. after πλεονάζουσι, Corais and Meineke omit.
[3] ἐκάλεσαν, Xylander, for ἐκάλεσε ; so the later editors.
[4] τῇ πολλῇ συνηθείᾳ καὶ ἐπιπλοκῇ F, ἡ πολλὴ συνήθεια καὶ
ἐπιπλοκή other MSS. ; so the editors.
[5] πω (omitted by F), Corais and Meineke, for πως.

very much inclined to denote sounds by words that sound like them, on account of their homogeneity. Wherefore onomatopoetic words abound in our language, as, for example, "celaryzein," and also "clangê," "psophos," "boê," and "crotos,"[1] most of which are by now used in their proper sense. Accordingly, when all who pronounced words thickly were being called barbarians onomatopoetically, it appeared that the pronunciations of all alien races were likewise thick, I mean of those that were not Greek. Those, therefore, they called barbarians in the special sense of the term, at first derisively, meaning that they pronounced words thickly or harshly; and then we misused the word as a general ethnic term, thus making a logical distinction between the Greeks and all other races. The fact is, however, that through our long acquaintance and intercourse with the barbarians this effect was at last seen to be the result, not of a thick pronunciation or any natural defect in the vocal organs, but of the peculiarities of their several languages. And there appeared another faulty and barbarian-like pronunciation in our language, whenever any person speaking Greek did not pronounce it correctly, but pronounced the words like barbarians who are only beginning to learn Greek and are unable to speak it accurately, as is also the case with us in speaking their languages. This was particularly the case with the Carians, for, although the other peoples were not yet having very much intercourse with the Greeks nor even trying to live in Greek fashion or to learn our language—with the exception, perhaps, of rare

[1] Meaning respectively, "gurgle," "clang," "empty sound," "outcry," and "rattling noise."

STRABO

σπάνιοι καὶ κατὰ τύχην ἐπεμίχθησαν καὶ κατ᾽
ἄνδρα ὀλίγοις¹ τῶν Ἑλλήνων τισίν, οὗτοι δὲ
καθ᾽ ὅλην ἐπλανήθησαν τὴν Ἑλλάδα, μισθοῦ
στρατεύοντες. ἤδη οὖν τὸ βαρβαρόφωνον ἐπ᾽
ἐκείνων πυκνὸν ἦν, ἀπὸ τῆς εἰς τὴν Ἑλλάδα
αὐτῶν στρατείας· καὶ μετὰ ταῦτα ἐπεπόλασε
πολὺ μᾶλλον, ἀφ᾽ οὗ τάς τε νήσους μετὰ τῶν
Ἑλλήνων ᾤκησαν, κἀκεῖθεν εἰς τὴν Ἀσίαν ἐκπεσόντες, οὐδ᾽ ἐνταῦθα χωρὶς Ἑλλήνων οἰκεῖν ἠδύ-
C 663 ναντο, ἐπιδιαβάντων τῶν Ἰώνων καὶ τῶν Δωριέων.
ἀπὸ δὲ τῆς αὐτῆς αἰτίας καὶ τὸ βαρβαρίζειν
λέγεται· καὶ γὰρ τοῦτο ἐπὶ τῶν κακῶς ἑλληνιζόν-
των εἰώθαμεν λέγειν, οὐκ ἐπὶ τῶν καριστὶ λαλούντων. οὕτως οὖν καὶ τὸ βαρβαροφωνεῖν καὶ
τοὺς βαρβαροφώνους δεκτέον τοὺς κακῶς ἑλλη-
νίζοντας· ἀπὸ δὲ τοῦ καρίζειν καὶ τὸ βαρβαρίζειν
μετήνεγκαν εἰς τὰς περὶ ἑλληνισμοῦ τέχνας καὶ
τὸ σολοικίζειν, εἴτ᾽ ἀπὸ Σόλων, εἴτ᾽ ἄλλως τοῦ
ὀνόματος τούτου πεπλασμένου.
29. Φησὶ δὲ Ἀρτεμίδωρος ἀπὸ Φύσκου τῆς
Ῥοδίων περαίας ἰοῦσιν εἰς Ἔφεσον μέχρι μὲν
Λαγίνων ὀκτακοσίους εἶναι καὶ πεντήκοντα σταδίους, ἐντεῦθεν δ᾽ εἰς Ἀλάβανδα πεντήκοντα
ἄλλους καὶ διακοσίους, εἰς δὲ Τράλλεις ἑκατὸν
ἑξήκοντα· ἀλλ᾽ ἡ εἰς Τράλλεις ἐστὶ διαβάντι τὸν
Μαίανδρον κατὰ μέσην που τὴν ὁδόν, ὅπου τῆς
Καρίας οἱ ὅροι· γίνονται δ᾽ οἱ πάντες ἀπὸ Φύσκου

¹ ὀλίγοις, Kramer, for ὀλίγοι; so Meineke.

¹ The city in Cilicia, if not that in Cyprus.
² Strabo means that grammarians used the word in its
original, or unrestricted sense, i.e. as applying to speech
306

persons who by chance, and singly, mingled with a few of the Greeks—yet the Carians roamed throughout the whole of Greece, serving on expeditions for pay. Already, therefore, the barbarous element in their Greek was strong, as a result of their expeditions in Greece; and after this it spread much more, from the time they took up their abode with the Greeks in the islands; and when they were driven thence into Asia, even here they were unable to live apart from the Greeks, I mean when the Ionians and Dorians later crossed over to Asia. The term "barbarise," also, has the same origin; for we are wont to use this too in reference to those who speak Greek badly, not to those who talk Carian. So, therefore, we must interpret the terms "speak barbarously" and "barbarously-speaking" as applying to those who speak Greek badly. And it was from the term "Carise" that the term "barbarise" was used in a different sense in works on the art of speaking Greek; and so was the term "soloecise," whether derived from Soli,[1] or made up in some other way.[2]

29. Artemidorus says that, as one goes from Physcus, in the Peraea of the Rhodians, to Ephesus, the distance to Lagina is eight hundred and fifty stadia; and thence to Alabanda, two hundred and fifty more; and to Tralleis, one hundred and sixty. But one comes to the road that leads into Tralleis after crossing the Maeander River, at about the middle of the journey,[3] where are the boundaries of Caria. The distance all told from Physcus to

only. In the meantime it had been used in a broad sense, "to behave like, or imitate, barbarians."

[3] Between Alabanda and Tralleis.

ἐπὶ τὸν Μαίανδρον κατὰ τὴν εἰς Ἔφεσον ὁδὸν
χίλιοι ἑκατὸν ὀγδοήκοντα. πάλιν ἀπὸ τοῦ Μαιάνδρου τῆς Ἰωνίας ἐφεξῆς μῆκος ἐπιόντι κατὰ τὴν
αὐτὴν ὁδὸν ἀπὸ μὲν τοῦ ποταμοῦ εἰς Τράλλεις,
ὀγδοήκοντα, εἶτ᾽ εἰς Μαγνησίαν ἑκατὸν τετταράκοντα, εἰς Ἔφεσον δ᾽ ἑκατὸν εἴκοσιν, εἰς δὲ Σμύρναν
τριακόσιοι εἴκοσιν, εἰς δὲ Φώκαιαν καὶ τοὺς ὅρους
τῆς Ἰωνίας ἐλάττους τῶν διακοσίων· ὥστε τὸ ἐπ᾽
εὐθείας μῆκος τῆς Ἰωνίας εἴη ἂν κατ᾽ αὐτὸν[1]
μικρῷ πλέον τῶν ὀκτακοσίων. ἐπεὶ δὲ κοινή
τις ὁδὸς τέτριπται ἅπασι τοῖς ἐπὶ τὰς ἀνατολὰς
ὁδοιποροῦσιν ἐξ Ἐφέσου, καὶ ταύτην ἔπεισιν.[2]
ἐπὶ μὲν τὰ Κάρουρα τῆς Καρίας ὅριον πρὸς τὴν
Φρυγίαν διὰ Μαγνησίας καὶ Τραλλέων, Νύσης,
Ἀντιοχείας ὁδὸς ἑπτακοσίων καὶ τετταράκοντα
σταδίων· ἐντεῦθεν δὲ ἡ Φρυγία διὰ Λαοδικείας
καὶ Ἀπαμείας καὶ Μητροπόλεως καὶ Χελιδονίων·
ἐπὶ μὲν οὖν τὴν ἀρχὴν τῆς Παρωρείου, τοὺς
Ὄλμους, στάδιοι περὶ ἐννακοσίους καὶ εἴκοσιν
ἐκ τῶν Καρούρων· ἐπὶ δὲ τὸ πρὸς τῇ Λυκαονίᾳ
πέρας τῆς Παρωρείου τὸ Τυριαῖον διὰ Φιλομη-
λίου μικρῷ πλείους τῶν πεντακοσίων. εἶθ᾽ ἡ
Λυκαονία μέχρι Κοροπασσοῦ διὰ Λαοδικείας τῆς
κατακεκαυμένης ὀκτακόσιοι τετταράκοντα· ἐκ δὲ
Κοροπασσοῦ τῆς Λυκαονίας εἰς Γαρσάουρα, πολίχνιον τῆς Καππαδοκίας, ἐπὶ τῶν ὅρων αὐτῆς
ἱδρυμένον, ἑκατὸν εἴκοσιν· ἐντεῦθεν δ᾽ εἰς Μάζακα
τὴν μητρόπολιν τῶν Καππαδόκων διὰ Σοάνδου

---

[1] κατ᾽ αὐτόν, Corais, for κατὰ ταὐτὸ ἢ mxz, κατ᾽ αὐτὸ ἢ other
MSS.; so the later editors.
[2] ταύτην ἔπεισιν, Corais, for ταύτῃ μὲν ἔπεστιν; so the later
editors.

the Maeander along the road to Ephesus amounts
to one thousand one hundred and eighty stadia.
Again, from the Maeander, traversing next in order
the length of Ionia along the same road, the distance
from the river to Tralleis is eighty stadia; then to
Magnesia, one hundred and forty; to Ephesus, one
hundred and twenty; to Smyrna, three hundred
and twenty; and to Phocaea and the boundaries of
Ionia, less than two hundred; so that the length
of Ionia in a straight line would be, according to
Artemidorus, slightly more than eight hundred
stadia. Since there is a kind of common road
constantly used by all who travel from Ephesus
towards the east, Artemidorus traverses this too:
from Ephesus to Carura, a boundary of Caria towards Phrygia, through Magnesia, Tralleis, Nysa,
and Antiocheia, is a journey of seven hundred
and forty stadia; and, from Carura, the journey in
Phrygia, through Laodiceia, Apameia, Metropolis
and Chelidonia.[1] Now near the beginning of
Paroreius,[2] one comes to Holmi, about nine hundred
and twenty stadia from Carura, and, near the end
of Paroreius near Lycaonia, through Philomelium,
to Tyriaeum, slightly more than five hundred.
Then Lycaonia, through Laodiceia Catacecaumenê,[3]
as far as Coropassus, eight hundred and forty stadia;
from Coropassus in Lycaonia to Garsaura, a small
town in Cappadocia, situated on its borders, one
hundred and twenty; thence to Mazaca, the
metropolis of the Cappadocians, through Soandum

[1] " Chelidonia" is thought to be corrupt (see C. Müller,
Ind. Var. Lect., p. 1030).
[2] *i.e.* Phrygia " alongside the mountain."
[3] " Burnt."

STRABO

καὶ Σαδακόρων ἑξακόσιοι ὀγδοήκοντα· ἐντεῦθεν
δ᾽ ἐπὶ τὸν Εὐφράτην μέχρι Τομίσων[1] χωρίου τῆς
Σωφηνῆς διὰ Ἡρφῶν πολίχνης χίλιοι τετρακόσιοι
τετταράκοντα. τὰ δ᾽ ἐπ᾽ εὐθείας τούτοις μέχρι
τῆς Ἰνδικῆς τὰ αὐτὰ κεῖται καὶ παρὰ τῷ Ἀρτε-
μιδώρῳ, ἅπερ καὶ παρὰ τῷ Ἐρατοσθένει. λέγει
δὲ καὶ Πολύβιος, περὶ τῶν ἐκεῖ μάλιστα δεῖν
C 664 πιστεύειν ἐκείνῳ. ἄρχεται δὲ ἀπὸ Σαμοσάτων
τῆς Κομμαγηνῆς, ἣ πρὸς τῇ διαβάσει καὶ τῷ
Ζεύγματι κεῖται· εἰς δὲ Σαμόσατα ἀπὸ τῶν ὅρων
τῆς Καππαδοκίας τῶν περὶ Τόμισα ὑπερθέντι
τὸν Ταῦρον σταδίους εἴρηκε τετρακοσίους καὶ
πεντήκοντα.

III

1. Μετὰ δὲ τὴν Ῥοδίων περαίαν, ἧς ὅριον τὰ
Δαίδαλα, ἐφεξῆς πλέουσι πρὸς ἀνίσχοντα ἥλιον
ἡ Λυκία κεῖται μέχρι Παμφυλίας, εἶθ᾽ ἡ Παμφυλία μέχρι Κιλίκων τῶν τραχέων, εἶθ᾽ ἡ τούτων
μέχρι τῶν ἄλλων Κιλίκων τῶν περὶ τὸν Ἰσσικὸν
κόλπον· ταῦτα δ᾽ ἐστὶ μέρη μὲν τῆς χερρονήσου,
ἧς τὸν ἰσθμὸν ἔφαμεν τὴν ἀπὸ Ἰσσοῦ ὁδὸν μέχρι
Ἀμισοῦ, ἢ Σινώπης, ὥς τινες, ἐκτὸς δὲ τοῦ Ταύρου
ἐν στενῇ παραλίᾳ τῇ ἀπὸ Λυκίας μέχρι τῶν περὶ
Σόλους τόπων, τὴν νῦν Πομπηιόπολιν·[2] ἔπειτα
ἤδη εἰς πεδία ἀναπέπταται ἡ κατὰ τὸν Ἰσσικὸν
κόλπον παραλία ἀπὸ Σόλων καὶ Ταρσοῦ ἀρξαμένη. ταύτην οὖν ἐπελθοῦσιν ὁ πᾶς περὶ τῆς

[1] Τομίσων, the editors, for τὸ μισοῦ CD, Τελμισοῦ x, Τομισοῦ
other MSS.
[2] τὴν νῦν Πομπηιόπολιν, Corais, for τῇ νῦν Πομπηιουπόλει; so
the later editors.

and Sadacora, six hundred and eighty; and thence to the Euphrates River, as far as Tomisa, a place in Sophenê, through Herphae, a small town, one thousand four hundred and forty. The places on a straight line with these as far as India are the same in Artemidorus as they are in Eratosthenes. But Polybius says that we should rely most on Artemidorus in regard to the places here. He begins with Samosata in Commagenê, which lies at the river-crossing and at Zeugma, and states that the distance to Samosata, across the Taurus, from the boundaries of Cappadocia round Tomisa is four hundred and fifty stadia.

III

1.[1] AFTER the Peraea of the Rhodians, of which Daedala is a boundary, sailing next in order towards the rising sun, one comes to Lycia, which extends as far as Pamphylia; then to Pamphylia, extending as far as the Tracheian Cilicians;[2] and then to the country of these, extending as far as the other Cilicians living round the Gulf of Issus. These are parts of the peninsula, the isthmus of which, as I was saying, is the road from Issus to Amisus, or, according to some, Sinopê, but they lie outside the Taurus on the narrow coast which extends from Lycia as far as the region of Soli, the present Pompeïopolis. Then forthwith the coast that lies on the Issic Gulf, beginning at Soli and Tarsus, spreads out into plains. So then, when I have traversed this coast, my account of the whole

[1] See map of Asia Minor at end of Vol. V.
[2] Referring to "Cilicia Tracheia" ("Rugged Cilicia").

STRABO

χερρονήσου λόγος ἔσται περιωδευμένος· εἶτα μεταβησόμεθα ἐπὶ τὰ ἄλλα μέρη τῆς Ἀσίας τὰ ἐκτὸς τοῦ Ταύρου. τελευταῖα δ' ἐκθήσομεν τὰ περὶ τὴν Λιβύην.

2. Μετὰ τοίνυν Δαίδαλα τὰ τῶν Ῥοδίων ὄρος ἐστὶ τῆς Λυκίας ὁμώνυμον αὐτοῖς Δαίδαλα, ἀφ' οὗ λαμβάνει τὴν ἀρχὴν ὁ παράπλους ἅπας ὁ Λυκιακός, σταδίων μὲν ὢν χιλίων ἑπτακοσίων εἴκοσι, τραχὺς δὲ καὶ χαλεπός, ἀλλ' εὐλίμενος σφόδρα καὶ ὑπὸ ἀνθρώπων συνοικούμενος σωφρόνων· ἐπεὶ ἥ γε τῆς χώρας φύσις παραπλησία καὶ τοῖς Παμφύλοις ἐστὶ καὶ τοῖς Τραχειώταις Κίλιξιν· ἀλλ' ἐκεῖνοι μὲν ὁρμητηρίοις ἐχρήσαντο τοῖς τόποις πρὸς τὰ λῃστήρια, αὐτοὶ πειρατεύοντες ἢ τοῖς πειραταῖς λαφυροπώλια καὶ ναύσταθμα παρέχοντες· ἐν Σίδῃ γοῦν πόλει τῆς Παμφυλίας τὰ ναυπήγια συνίστατο τοῖς Κίλιξιν, ὑπὸ κήρυκά τε ἐπώλουν ἐκεῖ τοὺς ἁλόντας ἐλευθέρους ὁμολογοῦντες· Λύκιοι δ' οὕτω πολιτικῶς καὶ σωφρόνως ζῶντες διετέλεσαν, ὥστ', ἐκείνων διὰ τὰς εὐτυχίας θαλαττοκρατησάντων μέχρι τῆς Ἰταλίας, ὅμως ὑπ' οὐδενὸς ἐξήρθησαν αἰσχροῦ κέρδους, ἀλλ' ἔμειναν ἐν τῇ πατρίῳ διοικήσει τοῦ Λυκιακοῦ συστήματος.

3. Εἰσὶ δὲ τρεῖς καὶ εἴκοσι πόλεις αἱ τῆς ψήφου μετέχουσαι· συνέρχονται δὲ ἐξ ἑκάστης πόλεως εἰς κοινὸν συνέδριον, ἣν ἂν δοκιμάσωσι πόλιν ἑλόμενοι· τῶν δὲ πόλεων αἱ μέγισται μὲν τριῶν ψήφων ἐστὶν ἑκάστη κυρία, αἱ δὲ μέσαι δυεῖν, αἱ δ' ἄλλαι μιᾶς· ἀνὰ λόγον δὲ καὶ τὰς εἰσφορὰς εἰσφέρουσι καὶ τὰς ἄλλας λειτουργίας.

C 665

312

peninsula will have been completed. Then I shall pass to the other parts of Asia that are outside the Taurus. And lastly I shall set forth my account of Libya.

2. After Daedala of the Rhodians, then, one comes to a mountain in Lycia which bears the same name as the city, Daedala, whence the whole voyage along the Lycian coast takes its beginning; this coast extends one thousand seven hundred and twenty stadia, and is rugged and hard to travel, but is exceedingly well supplied with harbours and inhabited by decent people. Indeed, the nature of the country, at least, is similar to both that of the Pamphylians and the Tracheian Cilicians, but the former used their places as bases of operation for the business of piracy, when they engaged in piracy themselves or offered them to pirates as markets for the sale of booty and as naval stations. In Sidê, at any rate, a city in Pamphylia, the dockyards stood open to the Cilicians, who would sell their captives at auction there, though admitting that these were freemen. But the Lycians continued living in such a civilised and decent way that, although the Pamphylians through their successes gained the mastery of the sea as far as Italy, still they themselves were stirred by no desire for shameful gain, but remained within the ancestral domain of the Lycian League.

3. There are twenty-three cities that share in the vote. They come together from each city to a general congress, after choosing whatever city they approve of. The largest of the cities control three votes each, the medium-sized two, and the rest one. In the same proportion, also, they make

313

ἐξ δὲ τὰς μεγίστας ἔφη ὁ Ἀρτεμίδωρος, Ξάνθον, Πάταρα, Πίναρα, Ὄλυμπον, Μύρα, Τλῶν, κατὰ τὴν ὑπέρθεσιν[1] τὴν εἰς Κίβυραν κειμένην. ἐν δὲ τῷ συνεδρίῳ πρῶτον μὲν Λυκιάρχης αἱρεῖται, εἶτ᾽ ἄλλαι ἀρχαὶ αἱ τοῦ συστήματος· δικαστήριά τε ἀποδείκνυται κοινῇ· καὶ περὶ πολέμου δὲ καὶ εἰρήνης καὶ συμμαχίας ἐβουλεύοντο πρότερον, νῦν δ᾽ οὐκ εἰκός, ἀλλ᾽ ἐπὶ τοῖς Ῥωμαίοις ταῦτ᾽ ἀνάγκη κεῖσθαι, πλὴν εἰ ἐκείνων ἐπιτρεψάντων, ἢ ὑπὲρ αὐτῶν εἴη χρήσιμον· ὁμοίως δὲ καὶ δικασταὶ καὶ ἄρχοντες ἀνὰ λόγον ταῖς ψήφοις ἐξ ἑκάστης προχειρίζονται πόλεως. οὕτω δ᾽ εὐνομουμένοις αὐτοῖς συνέβη παρὰ Ῥωμαίοις ἐλευθέροις διατελέσαι, τὰ πάτρια νέμουσι, τοὺς δὲ λῃστὰς ἐπιδεῖν ἄρδην ἠφανισμένους, πρότερον μὲν ὑπὸ Σερουιλίου τοῦ Ἰσαυρικοῦ, καθ᾽ ὃν χρόνον καὶ τὰ Ἴσαυρα ἐκεῖνος καθεῖλεν, ὕστερον δὲ Πομπηίου τοῦ Μάγνου, πλείω τῶν χιλίων καὶ τριακοσίων σκαφῶν ἐμπρήσαντος, τὰς δὲ κατοικίας ἐκκόψαντος, τῶν δὲ περιγενομένων ἀνθρώπων ἐν ταῖς μάχαις τοὺς μὲν καταγαγόντος εἰς Σόλους, ἣν ἐκεῖνος Πομπηιόπολιν[2] ὠνόμασε, τοὺς δ᾽ εἰς Δύμην[3] λειπανδρήσασαν, ἣν νυνὶ Ῥωμαίων ἀποικία νέμεται. οἱ ποιηταὶ δέ, μάλιστα οἱ τραγικοί, συγχέοντες τὰ ἔθνη, καθάπερ τοὺς Τρῶας καὶ τοὺς Μυσοὺς καὶ τοὺς Λυδοὺς Φρύγας προσαγορεύουσιν, οὕτω καὶ τοὺς Λυκίους Κᾶρας.

4. Μετὰ δ᾽ οὖν τὰ Δαίδαλα, τὸ τῶν Λυκίων

---

[1] ὑπέρθεσιν, Corais, for θέσιν; so the later editors.
[2] Πομπηιούπολιν moxz.
[3] Δύμην, Casaubon, for Δυμηην CDFhw, Δυσμένην i, Διδυμήνην mosxz; so the later editors.

contributions and discharge other liturgies.[1]   Artemidorus said that the six largest were Xanthus,
Patara, Pinara, Olympus, Myra, and Tlos, the last-
named being situated near the pass that leads over
into Cibyra.   At the congress they first choose a
" Lyciarch," and then other officials of the League;
and general courts of justice are designated.   In
earlier times they would deliberate about war and
peace and alliances, but now they naturally do not
do so, since these matters necessarily lie in the
power of the Romans, except, perhaps when the
Romans should give them permission or it should
be for their benefit.   Likewise, judges and magis-
trates are elected from the several cities in the
same proportion.   And since they lived under such
a good government, they remained ever free under
the Romans, thus retaining their ancestral usages;
and they saw the pirates utterly wiped out, first by
Servilius Isauricus, at the time that he demolished
Isaura, and later by Pompey the Great, when he
set fire to more than thirteen hundred boats and
laid waste their settlements.   Of the pirates who
survived the fights,[2] he brought some down to Soli,
which he named Pompeïopolis, and the others to
Dymê, where there was a dearth of population; it is
now occupied by a colony of Romans.   The poets,
however, and especially the tragic poets, confuse
the tribes, as, for example, the Trojans and the
Mysians and the Lydians, whom they call Phrygians;
and likewise the Lycians, whom they call Carians.

4. After Daedala, then, I mean the mountain in

[1] *i.e.* public services performed at private expense.
[2] See 8. 7. 5.

ὄρος, πλησίον ἐστὶ Τελμησσός, πολίχνη Λυκίων,
καὶ Τελμησσὶς ἄκρα, λιμένα ἔχουσα. ἔλαβε δὲ
τὸ χωρίον τοῦτο παρὰ Ῥωμαίων Εὐμένης ἐν τῷ
Ἀντιοχικῷ πολέμῳ, καταλυθείσης δὲ τῆς βασι-
λείας ἀπέλαβον πάλιν οἱ Λύκιοι.

5. Εἶθ' ἑξῆς ὁ Ἀντίκραγος, ὄρθιον ὄρος, ἐφ' ᾧ
Καρμυλησσός, χωρίον ἐν φάραγγι ᾠκημένον,[1] καὶ
μετὰ τοῦτον ὁ Κράγος, ἔχων ἄκρας[2] ὀκτὼ[3] καὶ
πόλιν ὁμώνυμον. περὶ ταῦτα μυθεύεται τὰ ὄρη
τὰ περὶ τῆς Χιμαίρας· ἔστι δ' οὐκ ἄπωθεν καὶ
ἡ Χίμαιρα, φάραγξ τις ἀπὸ τοῦ αἰγιαλοῦ ἀνατείνουσα. ὑπόκειται δὲ τῷ Κράγῳ Πίναρα ἐν
μεσογαίᾳ, τῶν μεγίστων οὖσα πόλεων ἐν τῇ
Λυκίᾳ. ἐνταῦθα δὲ Πάνδαρος τιμᾶται, τυχὸν
ἴσως ὁμώνυμος τῷ Τρωικῷ· ὡς καὶ

Πανδαρέου κούρη χλωρὴς ἀηδών·[4]

καὶ γὰρ τοῦτον ἐκ Λυκίας φασίν.

6. Εἶθ' ὁ Ξάνθος ποταμός, ὃν Σίρβιν ἐκάλουν
οἱ πρότερον·[5] ἀναπλεύσαντι δ' ὑπηρετικοῖς δέκα
σταδίους τὸ Λητῷόν ἐστιν· ὑπὲρ δὲ τοῦ ἱεροῦ
C 666 προελθόντι ἑξήκοντα ἡ πόλις ἡ τῶν Ξανθίων
ἐστί, μεγίστη τῶν ἐν Λυκίᾳ. μετὰ δὲ τὸν Ξάνθον
Πάταρα, καὶ αὕτη μεγάλη πόλις, λιμένα ἔχουσα
καὶ ἱερὸν Ἀπόλλωνος,[6] κτίσμα Πατάρου. Πτολεμαῖος δ' ὁ Φιλάδελφος ἐπισκευάσας Ἀρσινόην
ἐκάλεσε τὴν ἐν Λυκίᾳ, ἐπεκράτησε δὲ τὸ ἐξ ἀρχῆς
ὄνομα.

---

[1] ἐν φάραγγι ᾠκημένον E, ἐν φαραγγεῖον κείμενον F, ἐν
φαραγγίῳ κείμενον other MSS.
[2] ἄκρας, the editors (following Eustathius on *Iliad* 6. 181),
for κράγας.
[3] For ὀκτώ Eustathius (*l.c.*) reads δύο.

Lycia, one comes to a Lycian town near it, Telmessus, and to Telmessis, a promontory with a harbour. Eumenes[1] received this place from the Romans in the Antiochian War, but when his kingdom was dissolved the Lycians got it back again.

5. Then, next, one comes to Anticragus, a steep mountain, where is Carmylessus, an inhabited place situated in a ravine; and, after this, to Cragus, which has eight promontories and a city of the same name. The scene of the myth of Chimaera is laid in the neighbourhood of these mountains. Chimaera, a ravine extending up from the shore, is not far from them. At the foot of Cragus, in the interior, lies Pinara, one of the largest cities in Lycia. Here Pandarus is held in honour, who may, perhaps, be identical with the Trojan hero, as when the poet says, "the daughter of Pandareus, the nightingale of the greenwood," for Pandareus is said to have been from Lycia.

6. Then one comes to the Xanthus River, which the people of earlier times called the Sirbis. Sailing up this river by rowboat for ten stadia one comes to the Letoüm; and proceeding sixty stadia beyond the temple one comes to the city of the Xanthians, the largest city in Lycia. After Xanthus, to Patara, which is also a large city, has a harbour, has a temple of Apollo, and was founded by Patarus. When Ptolemy Philadelphus repaired it, he called it Lycian Arsinoê, but the original name prevailed.

---

[1] King of Pergamum 197–159 B.C.

---

[4] ὡς καὶ . . . ἀηδών, Meineke ejects.
[5] Instead of οἱ πρότερον, F and Meineke read τὸ πρότερον.
[6] ἱερὸν Ἀπόλλωνος, the editors, for ἱερὰ πολλά.

7. Εἶτα Μύρα ἐν εἴκοσι σταδίοις ὑπὲρ τῆς θαλάττης ἐπὶ μετεώρου λόφου. εἶθ' ἡ ἐκβολὴ τοῦ Λιμύρου[1] ποταμοῦ καὶ ἀνιόντι πεζῇ σταδίους εἴκοσι τὰ Λίμυρα πολίχνη. μεταξὺ δ' ἐν τῷ λεχθέντι παράπλῳ νησία πολλὰ καὶ λιμένες, ὧν καὶ Μεγίστη νῆσος καὶ πόλις ὁμώνυμος, καὶ[2] ἡ Κισθήνη. ἐν δὲ τῇ μεσογαίᾳ χωρία Φελλὸς καὶ Ἀντίφελλος καὶ ἡ Χίμαιρα, ἧς ἐμνήσθημεν ἐπάνω.

8. Εἶθ' Ἱερὰ ἄκρα καὶ αἱ Χελιδόνιαι, τρεῖς νῆσοι τραχεῖαι, πάρισοι τὸ μέγεθος, ὅσον πέντε σταδίοις ἀλλήλων διέχουσαι· τῆς δὲ γῆς ἀφεστᾶσιν ἑξαστάδιον· μία δ' αὐτῶν καὶ πρόσορμον ἔχει. ἐντεῦθεν νομίζουσιν οἱ πολλοὶ τὴν ἀρχὴν λαμβάνειν τὸν Ταῦρον, διά τε τὴν ἄκραν ὑψηλὴν οὖσαν καὶ καθήκουσαν ἀπὸ τῶν Πισιδικῶν ὀρῶν τῶν ὑπερκειμένων τῆς Παμφυλίας καὶ διὰ τὰς προκειμένας νήσους, ἐχούσας ἐπιφανές τι σημεῖον ἐν τῇ θαλάττῃ κρασπέδου δίκην. τὸ δ' ἀληθὲς ἀπὸ τῆς Ῥοδίων περαίας ἐπὶ τὰ πρὸς Πισιδίαν μέρη συνεχής ἐστιν ἡ ὀρεινή, καλεῖται δὲ καὶ αὕτη Ταῦρος. δοκοῦσι δὲ καὶ αἱ Χελιδόνιαι κατὰ Κανωβόν πως πίπτειν· τὸ δὲ δίαρμα λέγεται τετρακισχιλίων σταδίων. ἀπὸ δὲ τῆς Ἱερᾶς ἄκρας ἐπὶ τὴν Ὀλβίαν λείπονται στάδιοι τριακόσιοι ἑξήκοντα ἑπτά· ἐν τούτοις δ' ἐστὶν ἥ τε Κράμβουσα καὶ Ὄλυμπος, πόλις μεγάλη καὶ ὄρος ὁμώνυμον, ὃ καὶ Φοινικοῦς καλεῖται· εἶτα Κώρυκος αἰγιαλός.

---

[1] Λιμύρου EF, Λιρύμου other MSS.
[2] καί, before ἡ, Groskurd inserts.

---

[1] i.e. approximately on the same meridian as Canobus in Egypt.

7. Then one comes to Myra, at a distance of twenty stadia above the sea, on a lofty hill. Then to the outlet of the Limyrus River, and then, going twenty stadia inland on foot, to Limyra, a small town. In the intervening distance on the coasting voyage there are numerous isles and harbours, among which are the island Megistê, with a city of the same name, and Cisthenê. And in the interior are places called Phellus and Antiphellus and Chimaera, which last I have mentioned above.

8. Then one comes to the promontory Hiera; and to the Chelidoniae, three rugged islands, which are about equal in size and are about five stadia distant from one another. They lie about six stadia off the shore, and one of them has a landing-place for vessels. Here it is, according to the majority of writers, that the Taurus takes its beginning, not only because of the loftiness of the promontory and because it extends down from the Pisidian mountains that lie above Pamphylia, but also because of the islands that lie off it, presenting, as they do, a sort of conspicuous sign in the sea, like outskirts of a mountain. But in truth the mountainous tract is continuous from the Peraea of the Rhodians to the parts near Pisidia; and this tract too is called the Taurus. The Chelidoniae are likewise thought to lie approximately opposite to Canobus;[1] and the passage thence to Canobus is said to be four thousand stadia. From the promontory Hiera to Olbia there remain three hundred and sixty-seven stadia; and on this stretch lie, not only Crambusa, but also Olympus, a large city and a mountain of the same name, which latter is also called Phoenicus. Then one comes to Corycus, a tract of sea-coast.

9. Εἶτα Φασηλίς,[1] τρεῖς ἔχουσα λιμένας, πόλις
ἀξιόλογος καὶ λίμνη.[2] ὑπέρκειται δ' αὐτῆς τὰ
Σόλυμα ὄρος καὶ Τερμησσός, Πισιδικὴ πόλις ἐπικειμένη τοῖς στενοῖς, δι' ὧν ὑπέρβασίς ἐστιν εἰς
τὴν Μιλυάδα. καὶ ὁ Ἀλέξανδρος διὰ τοῦτο
ἐξεῖλεν αὐτήν, ἀνοῖξαι βουλόμενος τὰ στενά.
περὶ Φασηλίδα[3] δ' ἐστὶ κατὰ θάλατταν στενά, δι'
ὧν Ἀλέξανδρος παρήγαγε τὴν στρατιάν. ἔστι δ'
ὄρος Κλῖμαξ καλούμενον, ἐπίκειται δὲ τῷ Παμφυλίῳ πελάγει, στενὴν ἀπολεῖπον πάροδον ἐπὶ
τῷ αἰγιαλῷ, ταῖς μὲν νηνεμίαις γυμνουμένην,
ὥστε εἶναι βάσιμον τοῖς ὁδεύουσι, πλημμύροντος
δὲ τοῦ πελάγους ὑπὸ τῶν κυμάτων καλυπτομένην
ἐπὶ πολύ· ἡ μὲν οὖν διὰ τοῦ ὄρους ὑπέρβασις
περίοδον ἔχει καὶ προσάντης ἐστί, τῷ δ' αἰγιαλῷ
χρῶνται κατὰ τὰς εὐδίας. ὁ δὲ Ἀλέξανδρος εἰς
χειμέριον ἐμπεσὼν καιρὸν καὶ τὸ πλέον ἐπιτρέπων
C 667 τῇ τύχῃ, πρὶν ἀνεῖναι τὸ κῦμα ὥρμησε, καὶ ὅλην
τὴν ἡμέραν ἐν ὕδατι γενέσθαι τὴν πορείαν συνέβη,
μέχρι ὀμφαλοῦ βαπτιζομένων. ἔστι μὲν οὖν καὶ
αὕτη ἡ πόλις Λυκιακή, ἐπὶ τῶν ὅρων[4] ἱδρυμένη
τῶν πρὸς Παμφυλίαν, τοῦ δὲ κοινοῦ τῶν Λυκίων
οὐ μετέχει, καθ' αὑτὴν δὲ συνέστηκεν.

10. Ὁ μὲν οὖν ποιητὴς ἑτέρους τῶν Λυκίων
ποιεῖ τοὺς Σολύμους· ὑπὸ γὰρ τοῦ τῶν Λυκίων
βασιλέως πεμφθεὶς ὁ Βελλεροφόντης ἐπὶ δεύτερον
τοῦτον ἆθλον

Σολύμοισι μαχέσσατο κυδαλίμοισιν.

οἱ δὲ τοὺς Λυκίους πρότερον καλεῖσθαι Σολύμους

---

[1] Φασηλίς, the editors (following Eustathius on *Dionys.*
855).

9. Then one comes to Phaselis, with three harbours, a city of note, and to a lake. Above it lies Solyma, a mountain, and also Termessus, a Pisidian city situated near the defiles, through which there is a pass over the mountain to Milyas. Alexander destroyed Milyas for the reason that he wished to open the defiles. Near Phaselis, by the sea, there are defiles, through which Alexander led his army. And here there is a mountain called Climax, which lies near the Pamphylian Sea and leaves a narrow pass on the shore; and in calm weather this pass is free from water, so that it is passable for travellers, but when the sea is at flood-tide it is to a considerable extent hidden by the waves. Now the pass that leads over through the mountain is circuitous and steep, but in fair weather people use the pass along the shore. Alexander, meeting with a stormy season, and being a man who in general trusted to luck, set out before the waves had receded; and the result was that all day long his soldiers marched in water submerged to their navels. Now this city too is Lycian, being situated on the borders towards Pamphylia, but it has no part in the common League and is a separate organisation to itself.

10. Now the poet makes the Solymi different from the Lycians, for when Bellerophon was sent by the king of the Lycians to the second struggle, "he fought with the glorious Solymi."[1] But others, who assert that the Lycians were in earlier times

---

[1] *Iliad* 6. 184.

---

[2] Instead of λίμνη, F and Eustathius (*l.c.*) have λίμνην.
[3] CD*hos* spell the word Φασίλιδα, F Φιλίδα.
[4] ὅρων, Kramer, for ὁρῶν.

φάσκοντες, ὕστερον δὲ Τερμίλας, ἀπὸ τῶν ἐκ
Κρήτης συγκατελθόντων τῷ Σαρπηδόνι, μετὰ δὲ
ταῦτα Λυκίους ἀπὸ Λύκου τοῦ Πανδίονος, ὃν
ἐκπεσόντα τῆς οἰκείας ἐδέξατο Σαρπηδὼν ἐπὶ
μέρει τῆς ἀρχῆς, οὐχ ὁμολογούμενα λέγουσιν
Ὁμήρῳ· βελτίους δ' οἱ φάσκοντες λέγεσθαι
Σολύμους ὑπὸ τοῦ ποιητοῦ τοὺς νῦν Μιλύας
προσαγορευομένους, περὶ ὧν εἰρήκαμεν.

IV

1. Μετὰ Φασηλίδα[1] δ' ἐστὶν ἡ Ὀλβία, τῆς
Παμφυλίας ἀρχή, μέγα ἔρυμα, καὶ μετὰ ταύτην ὁ
Καταράκτης λεγόμενος, ἀφ' ὑψηλῆς πέτρας
καταράττων ποταμὸς πολὺς καὶ χειμαρρώδης,
ὥστε πόρρωθεν ἀκούεσθαι τὸν ψόφον. εἶτα
πόλις Ἀττάλεια, ἐπώνυμος τοῦ κτίσαντος Φιλα-
δέλφου, καὶ οἰκίσαντος εἰς Κώρυκον, πολίχνιον
ὅμορον,[2] ἄλλην κατοικίαν καὶ μείζω[3] περίβολον
περιθέντος. φασὶ δ' ἐν τῷ μεταξὺ Φασηλίδος[4]
καὶ Ἀτταλείας δείκνυσθαι Θήβην τε καὶ Λυρνησσόν, ἐκπεσόντων ἐκ τοῦ Θήβης πεδίου τῶν
Τρωικῶν Κιλίκων εἰς τὴν Παμφυλίαν ἐκ μέρους,
ὡς εἴρηκε Καλλισθένης.

2. Εἶθ' ὁ Κέστρος ποταμός, ὃν ἀναπλεύσαντι
σταδίους ἑξήκοντα Πέργη πόλις, καὶ πλησίον ἐπὶ
μετεώρου τόπου τὸ τῆς Περγαίας Ἀρτέμιδος

---

[1] Φασηλίδα E, Φασιλίδα other MSS.
[2] ὅμορον, Kramer and later editors transfer as above from
a position after κατοικίαν.

called Solymi, but in later times were called Termilae [1] from the Termilae who came there from Crete with Sarpedon, and after this were called Lycians, from Lycius the son of Pandion, who, after having been banished from his homeland, was admitted by Sarpedon as a partner in his empire, are not in agreement with Homer. Better is the opinion of those who assert that by "Solymi" the poet means the people who are now called the Milyae, of whom I have already spoken." [2]

IV

1. After Phaselis one comes to Olbia, the beginning of Pamphylia, a large fortress; and after this to the Cataractes River, so called, which dashes down [3] from a lofty rock in such volume and so impetuously that the noise can be heard from afar. Then to a city, Attaleia, so named after its founder Attalus Philadelphus, who also sent a colony to Corycus, a small neighbouring town, and surrounded it with a greater circuit-wall. It is said that both Thebê and Lyrnessus are to be seen between Phaselis and Attaleia, a part of the Trojan Cilicians having been driven out of the plain of Thebê into Pamphylia, as Callisthenes states.

2. Then one comes to the Cestrus River; and, sailing sixty stadia up this river, one comes to Pergê, a city; and near Pergê, on a lofty site, to the temple of

---

[1] See 12. 8. 5.   [2] 12. 8. 5 and 12. 3. 27
[3] The Greek verb is "cataracts."

---

[3] μείζω μικρόν Cⁱⁿ, merely μικρόν other MSS., except F, which has merely μείζω
[4] Φασηλίδος E, Φασιλίδος other MSS.

ἱερόν, ἐν ᾧ πανήγυρις κατ᾽ ἔτος συντελεῖται.
εἶθ᾽ ὑπὲρ τῆς θαλάττης ὅσον τετταράκοντα
σταδίοις Σύλλιον¹ πόλις ἐστὶν ὑψηλὴ τοῖς ἐκ
Πέργης ἔποπτος· εἶτα λίμνη εὐμεγέθης Καπρία,
καὶ μετὰ ταῦτα ὁ Εὐρυμέδων ποταμός, ὃν ἀναπλεύσαντι ἑξήκοντα σταδίους Ἄσπενδος πόλις,
εὐανδροῦσα ἱκανῶς, Ἀργείων κτίσμα· ὑπέρκειται
δὲ ταύτης Πετνηλισσός· εἶτ᾽ ἄλλος ποταμός, καὶ
νησία προκείμενα πολλά· εἶτα Σίδη, Κυμαίων
ἄποικος· ἔχει δ᾽ Ἀθηνᾶς ἱερόν. πλησίον δ᾽ ἐστὶ
καὶ ἡ Κιβυρατῶν παραλία τῶν μικρῶν· εἶθ᾽ ὁ
Μέλας ποταμὸς καὶ ὕφορμος· εἶτα Πτολεμαῒς
πόλις· καὶ μετὰ ταῦθ᾽ οἱ ὅροι τῆς Παμφυλίας καὶ
τὸ Κορακήσιον, ἀρχὴ τῆς τραχείας Κιλικίας. ὁ
δὲ παράπλους ἅπας ὁ Παμφύλιος στάδιοί εἰσιν
ἑξακόσιοι τεσσαράκοντα.

C 668   3. Φησὶ δ᾽ Ἡρόδοτος τοὺς Παμφύλους τῶν
μετὰ Ἀμφιλόχου καὶ Κάλχαντος εἶναι λαῶν,
μιγάδων τινῶν ἐκ Τροίας συνακολουθησάντων·
τοὺς μὲν δὴ πολλοὺς ἐνθάδε καταμεῖναι, τινὰς δὲ
σκεδασθῆναι πολλαχοῦ τῆς γῆς. Καλλῖνος δὲ
τὸν μὲν Κάλχαντα ἐν Κλάρῳ τελευτῆσαι τὸν
βίον φησί, τοὺς δὲ λαοὺς μετὰ Μόψου τὸν Ταῦρον
ὑπερθέντας, τοὺς μὲν ἐν Παμφυλίᾳ μεῖναι, τοὺς
δ᾽ ἐν Κιλικίᾳ μερισθῆναι καὶ Συρίᾳ μέχρι καὶ
Φοινίκης.

¹ Σύλλιον, Jones inserts, following Tzschucke, who first
noted that this was the city meant. Meineke emends
σταδίοις to Σύλλιον.

Artemis Pergaea, where a general festival is celebrated every year. Then, about forty stadia above the sea, one comes to Syllium, a lofty city that is visible from Pergê. Then one comes to a very large lake, Capria; and after this, to the Eurymedon River; and, sailing sixty stadia up this river, to Aspendus, a city with a flourishing population and founded by the Argives. Above Aspendus lies Petnelissus. Then comes another river; and also numerous isles that lie off it. Then Sidê, a colony of the Cymaeans, which has a temple of Athena; and near by is the coast of the Lesser Cibyratae. Then the Melas River and a mooring-place. Then Ptolemaïs, a city. And after this come the boundaries of Pamphylia, and also Coracesium, the beginning of Cilicia Tracheia. The whole of the voyage along the coast of Pamphylia is six hundred and forty stadia.

3. Herodotus[1] says that the Pamphylians are the descendants of the peoples led by Amphilochus and Calchas, a miscellaneous throng who accompanied them from Troy; and that most of them remained here, but that some of them were scattered to numerous places on earth. Callinus says that Calchas died in Clarus, but that the peoples led by Mopsus passed over the Taurus, and that, though some remained in Pamphylia, the others were dispersed in Cilicia, and also in Syria as far even as Phoenicia.

[1] 7. 91.

STRABO

V

1. Τῆς Κιλικίας δὲ τῆς ἔξω τοῦ Ταύρου ἡ μὲν λέγεται τραχεῖα, ἡ δὲ πεδιάς· τραχεῖα μέν, ἧς ἡ παραλία στενή ἐστι, καὶ οὐδὲν ἢ σπανίως ἔχει τι χωρίον ἐπίπεδον, καὶ ἔτι ἧς ὑπέρκειται ὁ Ταῦρος, οἰκούμενος κακῶς, μέχρι καὶ τῶν προσβόρων πλευρῶν τῶν περὶ Ἴσαυρα καὶ τοὺς Ὁμοναδέας μέχρι τῆς Πισιδίας· καλεῖται δ' ἡ αὐτὴ καὶ Τραχειῶτις καὶ οἱ ἐνοικοῦντες Τραχειῶται· πεδιὰς δ' ἡ ἀπὸ Σόλων καὶ Ταρσοῦ μέχρι Ἰσσοῦ, καὶ ἔτι ὧν ὑπέρκεινται κατὰ τὸ πρόσβορον τοῦ Ταύρου πλευρὸν Καππάδοκες· αὕτη γὰρ ἡ χώρα τὸ πλέον πεδίων εὐπορεῖ καὶ χώρας ἀγαθῆς. ἐπεὶ δὲ τούτων τὰ μέν ἐστιν ἐντὸς τοῦ Ταύρου, τὰ δ' ἐκτός, περὶ μὲν τῶν ἐντὸς εἴρηται, περὶ δὲ τῶν ἐκτὸς λέγωμεν, ἀπὸ τῶν Τραχειωτῶν ἀρξάμενοι.

2. Πρῶτον τοίνυν ἐστὶ τῶν Κιλίκων φρούριον τὸ Κορακήσιον, ἱδρυμένον ἐπὶ πέτρας ἀπορρῶγος, ᾧ ἐχρήσατο Διόδοτος ὁ Τρύφων προσαγορευθεὶς ὁρμητηρίῳ, καθ' ὃν καιρὸν ἀπέστησε τὴν Συρίαν τῶν βασιλέων καὶ διεπολέμει πρὸς ἐκείνους, τοτὲ μὲν κατορθῶν τοτὲ δὲ πταίων. τοῦτον μὲν οὖν Ἀντίοχος ὁ Δημητρίου κατακλείσας εἴς τι χωρίον ἠνάγκασε διεργάσασθαι τὸ σῶμα. τοῖς δὲ Κίλιξιν ἀρχὴν [1] τοῦ τὰ πειρατικὰ συνίστασθαι Τρύφων αἴτιος κατέστη, καὶ ἡ τῶν βασιλέων οὐδένεια τῶν τότε ἐκ διαδοχῆς ἐπιστατούντων τῆς Συρίας ἅμα καὶ τῆς Κιλικίας· τῷ γὰρ ἐκείνου νεωτερισμῷ

---

[1] ἀρχήν, Groskurd, for ἀρχή; so the later editors.

V

1. As for Cilicia outside the Taurus, one part of
it is called Tracheia[1] and the other Pedias.[2] As for
Tracheia, its coast is narrow and has no level ground,
or scarcely any; and, besides that, it lies at the foot
of the Taurus, which affords a poor livelihood as far
as its northern side in the region of Isaura and of
the Homonadeis as far as Pisidia; and the same
country is also called Tracheiotis, and its inhabitants
Tracheiotae. But Cilicia Pedias extends from Soli
and Tarsus as far as Issus, and also to those parts
beyond which, on the northern side of the Taurus,
Cappadocians are situated; for this country consists
for the most part of plains and fertile land. Since
some parts of this country are inside the Taurus and
others outside it, and since I have already spoken of
those inside it, let me now speak of those outside it,
beginning with the Tracheiotae.

2. The first place in Cilicia, then, to which one
comes, is a stronghold, Coracesium, situated on an
abrupt rock, which was used by Diodotus, called
Tryphon, as a base of operations at the time when
he caused Syria to revolt from the kings and was
fighting it out with them, being successful at one
time and failing at another. Now Tryphon was
hemmed up in a certain place by Antiochus, son of
Demetrius, and forced to kill himself; and it was
Tryphon, together with the worthlessness of the
kings who by succession were then reigning over
Syria and at the same time over Cilicia, who caused
the Cilicians to organise their gangs of pirates; for
on account of his revolutionary attempts others made

---

[1] *Rugged* Cilicia.   [2] *Level* Cilicia.

συνενεωτέρισαν καὶ ἄλλοι, διχοστατοῦντές τε
ἀδελφοὶ πρὸς ἀλλήλους ὑποχείριον ἐποίουν τὴν
χώραν τοῖς ἐπιτιθεμένοις. ἡ δὲ τῶν ἀνδραπόδων
ἐξαγωγὴ προυκαλεῖτο μάλιστα εἰς τὰς κακουργίας,
ἐπικερδεστάτη γενομένη· καὶ γὰρ ἡλίσκοντο
ῥᾳδίως, καὶ τὸ ἐμπόριον οὐ παντελῶς ἄπωθεν ἦν
μέγα καὶ πολυχρήματον, ἡ Δῆλος, δυναμένη
μυριάδας ἀνδραπόδων αὐθημερὸν καὶ δέξασθαι
καὶ ἀποπέμψαι, ὥστε καὶ παροιμίαν γενέσθαι διὰ
τοῦτο· ἔμπορε, κατάπλευσον, ἐξελοῦ, πάντα
πέπραται. αἴτιον δ', ὅτι πλούσιοι γενόμενοι
Ῥωμαῖοι μετὰ τὴν Καρχηδόνος καὶ Κορίνθου
κατασκαφὴν οἰκετείαις ἐχρῶντο πολλαῖς· ὁρῶντες
δὲ τὴν εὐπέτειαν οἱ λῃσταὶ ταύτην ἐξήνθησαν
C 669 ἀθρόως, αὐτοὶ καὶ λῃζόμενοι καὶ σωματεμπο-
ροῦντες. συνήργουν δ' εἰς ταῦτα καὶ οἱ τῆς
Κύπρου καὶ οἱ τῆς Αἰγύπτου βασιλεῖς, ἐχθροὶ
τοῖς Σύροις ὄντες· οὐδ' οἱ Ῥόδιοι δὲ φίλοι ἦσαν
αὐτοῖς, ὥστ' οὐδὲν ἐβοήθουν· ἅμα δὲ καὶ οἱ λῃσταὶ
προσποιούμενοι σωματεμπορεῖν, ἄλυτον τὴν
κακουργίαν εἶχον. ἀλλ' οὐδὲ Ῥωμαῖοί πω τοσοῦτον ἐφρόντιζον τῶν ἔξω τοῦ Ταύρου, ἀλλ' ἔπεμψαν
μὲν καὶ Σκιπίωνα τὸν Αἰμιλιανόν, ἐπισκεψόμενον
τὰ ἔθνη καὶ τὰς πόλεις, καὶ πάλιν ἄλλους τινάς·
ἔγνωσαν δὲ κακίᾳ τῶν ἀρχόντων συμβαῖνον τοῦτο,
εἰ καὶ τὴν[1] κατὰ γένος διαδοχὴν τὴν ἀπὸ Σελεύκου τοῦ Νικάτορος, αὐτοὶ κεκυρωκότες, ᾐδοῦντο
ἀφαιρεῖσθαι. τοῦτο δὲ συμβὰν τῆς μὲν χώρας
ἐποίησε κυρίους Παρθυαίους, οἳ τὰ πέραν τοῦ

[1] εἰ καὶ τήν z (by correction), εἰ τήν x, εἰς τήν other MSS.

328

like attempts at the same time, and thus the dissensions of brethren with one another put the country
at the mercy of any who might attack it. The
exportation of slaves induced them most of all to
engage in their evil business, since it proved most
profitable; for not only were they easily captured,
but the market, which was large and rich in property,
was not extremely far away, I mean Delos, which
could both admit and send away ten thousand slaves
on the same day; whence arose the proverb,
"Merchant, sail in, unload your ship, everything
has been sold." The cause of this was the fact
that the Romans, having become rich after the
destruction of Carthage and Corinth, used many
slaves; and the pirates, seeing the easy profit
therein, bloomed forth in great numbers, themselves
not only going in quest of booty but also trafficking
in slaves. The kings both of Cyprus and of Egypt
co-operated with them in this, being enemies to
the Syrians. Neither were the Rhodians friendly
to the Syrians, and they therefore afforded them
no assistance. And at the same time the pirates,
pretending to be slave-dealers, carried on their
evil business unchecked. Neither were the Romans
concerning themselves as yet so much about the
peoples outside the Taurus; but they sent Scipio
Aemilianus, and again certain others, to inspect the
tribes and the cities; and they decided that the
above mentioned piracy was due to the incompetence
of the rulers, although they were ashamed, since
they themselves had ratified the hereditary succession
from Seleucus Nicator, to deprive them of it. And
this is what made the Parthians masters of the
country, who got possession of the region on the far

329

Εὐφράτου κατέσχον· τὸ τελευταῖον δὲ καὶ Ἀρμενίους, οἳ καὶ τὴν ἐκτὸς τοῦ Ταύρου προσέλαβον μέχρι καὶ Φοινίκης, καὶ τοὺς βασιλέας κατέλυσαν εἰς δύναμιν καὶ τὸ γένος αὐτῶν σύμπαν, τὴν δὲ θάλατταν τοῖς Κίλιξι παρέδωκαν. εἶτ' αὐξηθέντας ἠναγκάσθησαν καταλύειν Ῥωμαῖοι πολέμῳ καὶ μετὰ στρατιᾶς, οὓς αὐξομένους οὐκ ἐκώλυσαν. ὀλιγωρίαν μὲν οὖν αὐτῶν χαλεπὸν καταγνῶναι· πρὸς ἑτέροις δὲ ὄντες τοῖς ἐγγυτέρω καὶ κατὰ χεῖρα μᾶλλον οὐχ οἷοί τε ἦσαν τὰ ἀπωτέρω σκοπεῖν. ταῦτα μὲν οὖν ἔδοξεν ἡμῖν ἐν παρεκβάσει διὰ βραχέων εἰπεῖν.

3. Μετὰ δὲ τὸ Κορακήσιον Ἀρσινόη [1] πόλις, εἶθ' Ἀμαξία, ἐπὶ βουνοῦ κατοικία τις ὕφορμον ἔχουσα, ὅπου κατάγεται ἡ ναυπηγήσιμος ὕλη. κέδρος δ' ἐστὶν ἡ πλείστη, καὶ δοκεῖ ταῦτα τὰ μέρη πλεονεκτεῖν τῇ τοιαύτῃ ξυλείᾳ· καὶ διὰ τοῦτ' Ἀντώνιος Κλεοπάτρᾳ τὰ χωρία ταῦτα προσένειμεν, ἐπιτήδεια ὄντα πρὸς τὰς τῶν στόλων κατασκευάς. εἶτα Λαέρτης, φρούριον ἐπὶ λόφου μαστοειδοῦς ὕφορμον ἔχον· εἶτα Σελινοῦς πόλις καὶ [2] ποταμός· εἶτα Κράγος, πέτρα περίκρημνος πρὸς θαλάττῃ· εἶτα Χαραδροῦς, ἔρυμα καὶ αὐτὸ ὕφορμον ἔχον (ὑπέρκειται δ' ὄρος Ἄνδρικλος) καὶ παράπλους τραχύς, Πλατανιστὴς [3] καλούμενος· εἶτ' Ἀνεμούριον ἄκρα, καθ' ἣν ἡ ἤπειρος ἐγγυ-

---

[1] Ἀρσινόη appears to be corrupt. Hopper conj. Συδρή, Tzschucke Σύεδρα, C. Müller Αὔνησις.

[2] πόλις καί, Jones inserts, from conj. of C. Müller (*Ind. Var. Lect.* p. 1031). Meineke, following Groskurd, emends ποταμός to πόλις.

[3] Πλατανιστὴς, Meineke, for Πλατανιστής E, Πλατανιστός other MSS.

side of the Euphrates; and at last made also the
Armenians masters, who not only seized the country
outside the Taurus even as far as Phoenicia, but also,
so far as they could, overthrew the kings and the
whole royal stock; the sea, however, they gave over
to the Cilicians. Then, after these people had grown
in power, the Romans were forced to destroy them
by war and with an army, although they had not
hindered their growing power. Now it is hard to
condemn the Romans of negligence, since, being
engaged with matters that were nearer and more
urgent, they were unable to watch those that were
farther away. So much I have decided to say by
way of a brief digression from my geographical
description.

3. After Coracesium, one comes to Arsinoê,[1] a
city; then to Hamaxia, a settlement on a hill, with
a harbour, where ship-building timber is brought
down. Most of this timber is cedar; and it appears
that this region beyond others abounds in cedar-wood
for ships; and it was on this account that Antony
assigned this region to Cleopatra, since it was suited
to the building of her fleets. Then one comes to
Laertes, a stronghold on a breast-shaped hill, with a
mooring-place. Then to Selinus, a city and river.
Then to Cragus, a rock which is precipitous all
round and near the sea. Then to Charadrus, a
fortress, which also has a mooring-place (above it
lies Mt. Andriclus); and the coast alongside it, called
Platanistes, is rugged. Then to Anemurium, a
promontory, where the mainland approaches closest
to Cyprus, in the direction of the promontory of

----

[1] "Arsinoê" is thought to be an error for "Sydriê," or
"Syedra" or "Aunesis" (see critical note).

τάτω τῆς Κυπρίας ἐστὶν ἐπὶ Κρομμύου ἄκραν,
ἐν διάρματι σταδίων τριακοσίων πεντήκοντα. εἰς
μὲν οὖν τὸ Ἀνεμούριον ἀπὸ τῶν ὅρων τῆς Παμφυλίας ὁ Κιλίκιος παράπλους σταδίων ἐστὶν ὀκτακοσίων εἴκοσι, λοιπὸς δ᾽ ἐστὶ μέχρι Σόλων ὅσον
C 670 πεντακοσίων παράπλους σταδίων. τούτου[1] δ᾽
ἐστὶ Νάγιδος[2] πρώτη[3] μετὰ τὸ Ἀνεμούριον
πόλις· εἶτ᾽ Ἀρσινόη πρόσορμον ἔχουσα· εἶτα
τόπος Μελανία καὶ Κελένδερις, πόλις λιμένα
ἔχουσα. τινὲς δὲ ταύτην ἀρχὴν τίθενται τῆς
Κιλικίας, οὐ τὸ Κορακήσιον, ὧν ἐστὶ καὶ ὁ Ἀρτε-
μίδωρος· καί φησιν ἀπὸ μὲν τοῦ Πηλουσιακοῦ
στόματος εἶναι τρισχιλίους ἐννακοσίους[4] σταδίους εἰς Ὀρθωσίαν, ἐπὶ δὲ τὸν Ὀρόντην ποταμὸν
χίλια ἑκατὸν τριάκοντα, ἐπὶ δὲ τὰς πύλας ἑξῆς
πεντακόσια εἰκοσιπέντε, ἐπὶ δὲ τοὺς ὅρους τῶν
Κιλίκων χίλια διακόσια[5] ἑξήκοντα.

4. Εἶθ᾽ Ὄλμοι, ὅπου πρότερον ᾤκουν οἱ νῦν
Σελευκεῖς· κτισθείσης δ᾽ ἐπὶ τῷ Καλυκάδνῳ τῆς
Σελευκείας, ἐκεῖ μετῳκίσθησαν· εὐθὺς γάρ ἐστιν
ἡ τοῦ Καλυκάδνου ἐκβολὴ κάμψαντι ἠιόνα,

---

[1] τούτου, Meineke, for τοῦτο ; others, following Casaubon,
read ἐν τούτῳ.
[2] ἐστὶ Νάγιδος, Tzschucke, for ἐστὶν ἄτιδος Di, ἐστὶν ἄγιδος
other MSS.
[3] πρωτη. Groskurd, for πρῶτοι ; so the later editors.
[4] ἐννακοσίους, Meineke (following Casaubon and Groskurd)
emends to ἑξακοσίους.
[5] διακόσια, Meineke (following Casaubon and Groskurd)
emends to ἐνακόσια.

---

[1] Cp. 14. 6. 3.
[2] Elsewhere (16. 2. 33) referred to as "Melaenae or
Melaniae."

Crommyus,[1] the passage across being three hundred and fifty stadia. Now the coasting-voyage along Cilicia from the borders of Pamphylia to Anemurium is eight hundred and twenty stadia, whereas the rest, as far as Soli, is about five hundred stadia. On this latter one comes to Nagidus, the first city after Anemurium; then to Arsinoê, which has a landing-place; then to a place called Melania,[2] and to Celenderis, a city with a harbour. Some writers, among whom is Artemidorus, make Celenderis, not Coracesium, the beginning of Cilicia. And he says that the distance from the Pelusian mouth [3] to Orthosia is three thousand nine hundred stadia; to the Orontes River, one thousand one hundred and thirty; to the Gates [4] next thereafter, five hundred and twenty-five; and to the borders [5] of the Cilicians, one thousand two hundred and sixty.[6]

4. Then one comes to Holmi, where the present Seleuceians formerly lived; but when Seleuceia on the Calycadnus was founded, they migrated there; for immediately on doubling the shore, which forms a promontory called Sarpedon, one comes to the

---

[3] The mouth of the Nile at Pelusium.

[4] Elsewhere (14. 5. 19), "Pylae" ("Gates") is called "a boundary between the Cilicians and the Syrians."

[5] *i.e.* the *western* borders (Celenderis, according to Artemidorus).

[6] Elsewhere (16. 2. 33) the MSS. give the figures of Artemidorus as follows: "From Orthosia to Pelusium, 3650 stadia, including the sinuosities of the gulfs: from Melaenae, or Melaniae, in Cilicia near Celenderis, to the common boundaries of Cilicia and Syria, 1900; thence to the Orontes, 520; and then to Orthosia, 1130." Groskurd, Forbiger and Meineke (see critical note) accept these figures and emend the present passage correspondingly.

333

ποιοῦσαν ἄκραν, ἣ καλεῖται Σαρπηδών. πλησίον
δ᾽ ἐστὶ τοῦ Καλυκάδνου καὶ τὸ Ζεφύριον, καὶ
αὕτη ἄκρα· ἔχει δὲ ὁ ποταμὸς ἀνάπλουν εἰς τὴν
Σελεύκειαν, πόλιν εὖ συνοικουμένην καὶ πολὺ
ἀφεστῶσαν τοῦ Κιλικίου καὶ Παμφυλίου τρόπου.
ἐνταῦθα ἐγένοντο καθ᾽ ἡμᾶς ἄνδρες ἀξιόλογοι τῶν
ἐκ τοῦ περιπάτου φιλοσόφων Ἀθήναιός τε καὶ
Ξέναρχος, ὧν ὁ μὲν Ἀθήναιος καὶ ἐπολιτεύσατο
καὶ ἐδημαγώγησε χρόνον τινὰ ἐν τῇ πατρίδι· εἶτ᾽
ἐμπεσὼν εἰς τὴν Μουρήνα φιλίαν ἐκείνῳ συνεάλω
φεύγων, φωραθείσης τῆς κατὰ Καίσαρος τοῦ
Σεβαστοῦ συσταθείσης ἐπιβουλῆς· ἀναίτιος δὲ
φανεὶς ἀφείθη ὑπὸ Καίσαρος. ὡς δ᾽ ἐπανιόντα
εἰς Ῥώμην[1] ἠσπάζοντο καὶ ἐπυνθάνοντο οἱ
πρῶτοι ἐντυγχάνοντες, τὸ τοῦ Εὐριπίδου ἔφη·

ἥκω, νεκρῶν κευθμῶνα καὶ σκότου πύλας
λιπών.

ὀλίγον δ᾽ ἐπιβιοὺς χρόνον ἐν συμπτώσει τῆς
οἰκίας, ἐν ᾗ ᾤκει, διεφθάρη, νύκτωρ γενομένη.
Ξέναρχος δέ, οὗ ἠκροασάμεθα ἡμεῖς, ἐν οἴκῳ μὲν
οὐ πολὺ διέτριψεν, ἐν Ἀλεξανδρείᾳ δὲ καὶ
Ἀθήνησι καὶ τὸ τελευταῖον ἐν Ῥώμῃ, τὸν παιδευ-
τικὸν βίον ἑλόμενος· χρησάμενος δὲ καὶ τῇ
Ἀρείου[2] φιλίᾳ καὶ μετὰ ταῦτα τῇ Καίσαρος τοῦ
Σεβαστοῦ διετέλεσε μέχρι γήρως ἐν τιμῇ ἀγό-
μενος· μικρὸν δὲ πρὸ τῆς τελευτῆς πηρωθεὶς τὴν
ὄψιν κατέστρεψε νόσῳ τὸν βίον.
5. Μετὰ δὲ τὸν Καλύκαδνον ἡ Ποικίλη λεγο-

[1] εἰς Ῥώμην appears to be an error for ἐκ Ῥώμης, as Casaubon and Kramer suggest.

outlet of the Calycadnus. Near the Calycadnus is also Zephyrium, likewise a promontory. The river affords a voyage inland to Seleuceia, a city which is well-peopled and stands far aloof from the Cilician and Pamphylian usages. Here were born in my time noteworthy men of the Peripatetic sect of philosophers, Athenaeus and Xenarchus. Of these, Athenaeus engaged also in affairs of state and was for a time leader of the people in his native land ; and then, having fallen into a friendship with Murena, he was captured along with Murena when in flight with him, after the plot against Augustus Caesar had been detected, but, being clearly proven guiltless, he was released by Caesar. And when, on his return to [1] Rome, the first men who met him were greeting him and questioning him, he repeated the following from Euripides : [2] "I am come, having left the vaults of the dead [3] and the gates of darkness." But he survived his return only a short time, having been killed in the collapse, which took place in the night, of the house in which he lived. Xenarchus, however, of whom I was a pupil, did not tarry long at home, but resided at Alexandria and at Athens and finally at Rome, having chosen the life of a teacher ; and having enjoyed the friendship both of Areius and later of Caesar Augustus, he continued to be held in honour down to old age ; but shortly before the end he lost his sight, and then died of a disease.

5. After the Calycadnus one comes to the rock

---

[1] "To" is apparently an error for "from."
[2] *Hecuba* 1.   [3] *i.e.* Hades.

---

[2] 'Αρείου, Tzschucke, for 'Αρίου ; so the later editors.

STRABO

μένη πέτρα, κλίμακα ἔχουσα λατομητὴν ἐπὶ
Σελεύκειαν ἄγουσαν. εἶτ' Ἀνεμούριον ἄκρα,
ὁμώνυμος τῇ προτέρᾳ, καὶ Κράμβουσα νῆσος καὶ
Κώρυκος ἄκρα, ὑπὲρ ἧς ἐν εἴκοσι σταδίοις ἐστὶ
τὸ Κωρύκιον ἄντρον, ἐν ᾧ ἡ ἀρίστη κρόκος
φύεται. ἔστι δὲ κοιλὰς μεγάλη κυκλοτερής,
C 671 ἔχουσα περικειμένην ὀφρὺν πετρώδη, πανταχόθεν
ἱκανῶς ὑψηλήν· καταβάντι δ' εἰς αὐτὴν ἀνώ-
μαλόν ἐστιν ἔδαφος καὶ τὸ πολὺ πετρῶδες, μεστὸν
δὲ τῆς θαμνώδους ὕλης ἀειθαλοῦς τε καὶ ἡμέρου·
παρέσπαρται δὲ καὶ τὰ ἐδάφη τὰ φέροντα τὴν
κρόκον. ἔστι δὲ καὶ ἄντρον αὐτόθι, ἔχον πηγὴν
μεγάλην, ποταμὸν ἐξιεῖσαν καθαροῦ τε καὶ δια-
φανοῦς ὕδατος, εὐθὺς καταπίπτοντα ὑπὸ γῆς·
ἐνεχθεὶς δ' ἀφανὴς ἔξεισιν εἰς τὴν θάλατταν·
καλοῦσι δὲ Πικρὸν ὕδωρ.

6. Εἶθ' ἡ Ἐλαιοῦσσα [1] νῆσος μετὰ τὴν
Κώρυκον, προσκειμένη τῇ ἠπείρῳ, ἣν συνῴκισεν
Ἀρχέλαος καὶ κατεσκευάσατο βασίλειον, λαβὼν
τὴν Τραχειῶτιν Κιλικίαν ὅλην πλὴν Σελευκείας,
καθ' ὃν τρόπον καὶ Ἀμύντας πρότερον εἶχε καὶ
ἔτι πρότερον Κλεοπάτρα. εὐφυοῦς γὰρ ὄντος
τοῦ τόπου πρὸς τὰ λῃστήρια καὶ κατὰ γῆν καὶ
κατὰ θάλατταν (κατὰ γῆν μὲν διὰ τὸ μέγεθος τῶν
ὀρῶν καὶ τῶν ὑπερκειμένων ἐθνῶν, πεδία καὶ
γεώργια ἐχόντων μεγάλα καὶ εὐκατατρόχαστα,
κατὰ θάλατταν δὲ διὰ τὴν εὐπορίαν τῆς τε

---

[1] Ἐλαιοῦσσα, the editors, for Ἐλεοῦσσα (and Ἐλεοῦσα).

---

[1] *i.e.* the *Pictured* Rock.　　　　[2] § 3 above.
[3] *Crocus sativus*, which yields saffron.
[4] Bitter Water.　　　　[5] See 12. 2. 7.

Poecilê,[1] as it is called, which has steps hewn in it that lead to Seleuceia; then to Anemurium, a promontory, bearing the same name as the former,[2] and to Crambusa, an island, and to Corycus, a promontory, above which, at a distance of twenty stadia, is the Corycian cave, in which the best crocus[3] grows. It is a great circular hollow, with a rocky brow situated all round it that is everywhere quite high. Going down into it, one comes to a floor that is uneven and mostly rocky, but full of trees of the shrub kind, both the evergreen and those that are cultivated. And among these trees are dispersed also the plots of ground which produce the crocus. There is also a cave here, with a great spring, which sends forth a river of pure and transparent water; the river forthwith empties beneath the earth, and then, after running invisible underground, issues forth into the sea. It is called Picrum Hydor.[4]

6. Then, after Corycus, one comes to Elaeussa, an island lying close to the mainland, which Archelaüs settled, making it a royal residence,[5] after he had received[6] the whole of Cilicia Tracheia except Seleuceia—the same way in which it was obtained formerly by Amyntas[7] and still earlier by Cleopatra;[8] for since the region was naturally well adapted to the business of piracy both by land and by sea—by land, because of the height of the mountains and the large tribes that live beyond them, tribes which have plains and farm-lands that are large and very easily overrun, and by sea, because of the good

[6] *i.e.* from the Romans (see 12. 1. 4).
[7] See 12. 5. 1.   [8] See § 3 above.

ναυπηγησίμου ὕλης καὶ τῶν λιμένων καὶ ἐρυ-
μάτων καὶ ὑποδυτηρίων), ἐδόκει πρὸς ἅπαν τὸ
τοιοῦτο βασιλεύεσθαι μᾶλλον τοὺς τόπους, ἢ
ὑπὸ τοῖς Ῥωμαίοις ἡγεμόσιν εἶναι, τοῖς ἐπὶ τὰς
κρίσεις πεμπομένοις, οἳ μήτ' ἀεὶ παρεῖναι ἔμελλον,
μήτε μεθ' ὅπλων. οὕτω μὲν Ἀρχέλαος ἔλαβε
πρὸς τῇ Καππαδοκίᾳ τὴν τραχεῖαν Κιλικίαν.
εἰσὶ δ' ὅροι ταύτης μεταξὺ Σόλων τε καὶ
Ἐλαιούσσης ὁ Λάμος[1] ποταμὸς καὶ κώμη
ὁμώνυμος.

7. Κατὰ δὲ τὰς ἀκρωρείας τοῦ Ταύρου τὸ
Ζηνικέτου πειρατήριόν ἐστιν ὁ Ὄλυμπος, ὄρος
τε καὶ φρούριον ὁμώνυμον, ἀφ' οὗ κατοπτεύεται
πᾶσα Λυκία καὶ Παμφυλία καὶ Πισιδία καὶ
Μιλυάς· ἁλόντος δὲ τοῦ ὄρους ὑπὸ[2] τοῦ Ἰσαυρικοῦ, ἐνέπρησεν ἑαυτὸν πανοίκιον. τούτου δ'
ἦν καὶ ὁ Κώρυκος καὶ ἡ Φασηλὶς[3] καὶ πολλὰ
τῶν Παμφύλων χωρία· πάντα δ' εἷλεν ὁ Ἰσαυ-
ρικός.

8. Μετὰ δὲ Λάμον Σόλοι πόλις ἀξιόλογος,
τῆς ἄλλης Κιλικίας ἀρχὴ τῆς περὶ τὸν Ἰσσόν,
Ἀχαιῶν καὶ Ῥοδίων κτίσμα τῶν ἐκ Λίνδου· εἰς
ταύτην λειπανδρήσασαν Πομπήιος Μάγνος κατώ-
κισε τοὺς περιγενομένους τῶν πειρατῶν, οὓς
μάλιστα ἔγνω σωτηρίας καὶ προνοίας τινὸς ἀξίους,
καὶ μετωνόμασε Πομπηιόπολιν.[4] γεγόνασι δ'
ἄνδρες ἐνθένδε τῶν ὀνομαστῶν Χρύσιππός τε ὁ
στωικὸς φιλόσοφος, πατρὸς ὢν Ταρσέως ἐκεῖθεν

[1] Λάμος, Tzschucke, for Λάγμος C, Λάτμος other MSS.; so
the later editors.
[2] ὑπό, Casaubon inserts; so the later editors.
[3] Φασηλίς, the editors, for Φασιλίς.

supply, not only of shipbuilding timber, but also of harbours and fortresses and secret recesses—with all this in view, I say, the Romans thought that it was better for the region to be ruled by kings than to be under the Roman prefects sent to administer justice, who were not likely always to be present or to have armed forces with them. Thus Archelaüs received, in addition to Cappadocia, Cilicia Tracheia; and the boundary[1] of the latter, the river Lamus and the village of the same name, lies between Soli and Elaeussa.

7. Near the mountain ridges of the Taurus[2] lies the piratical stronghold of Zenicetus—I mean Olympus, both mountain and fortress, whence are visible all Lycia and Pamphylia and Pisidia and Milyas; but when the mountain was captured by Isauricus,[3] Zenicetus burnt himself up with his whole house. To him belonged also Corycus and Phaselis and many places in Pamphylia; but all were taken by Isauricus.

8. After Lamus one comes to Soli, a noteworthy city, the beginning of the other Cilicia, that which is round Issus; it was founded by Achaeans and Rhodians from Lindus. Since this city was of scant population, Pompey the Great settled in it those survivors of the pirates whom he judged most worthy of being saved and provided for;[4] and he changed its name to Pompëiopolis. Among the famous natives of Soli were: Chrysippus the Stoic philosopher, whose father had moved there from

---

[1] *i.e.* on the east.   [2] *i.e.* in Lycia.
[3] Servilius Isauricus.   [4] Cf. 8. 7. 5.

---

[4] E has Πομπηιούπολιν.

μετοικήσαντος, καὶ Φιλήμων, ὁ κωμικὸς ποιητής,
καὶ Ἄρατος, ὁ τὰ φαινόμενα συγγράψας ἐν
ἔπεσιν.

9. Εἶτα Ζεφύριον ὁμώνυμον τῷ πρὸς Καλυκάδνῳ[1] εἶτ᾽ Ἀγχιάλη μικρὸν ὑπὲρ τῆς θαλάττης,
κτίσμα Σαρδαναπάλλου, φησὶν Ἀριστόβουλος·
C 672 ἐνταῦθα δ᾽ εἶναι μνῆμα τοῦ Σαρδαναπάλλου καὶ
τύπον λίθινον, συμβάλλοντα τοὺς τῆς δεξιᾶς
χειρὸς δακτύλους, ὡς ἂν ἀποκροτοῦντα,[2] καὶ
ἐπιγραφὴν εἶναι Ἀσσυρίοις γράμμασι τοιάνδε·
Σαρδανάπαλλος ὁ Ἀνακυνδαράξεω παῖς, Ἀγχιάλην καὶ Ταρσὸν ἔδειμεν ἡμέρῃ μιῇ· ἔσθιε, πίνε,
παῖζε, ὡς τἆλλα[3] τούτου οὐκ ἄξια, τοῦ ἀποκροτήματος.[4] μέμνηται δὲ καὶ Χοιρίλος τούτων· καὶ
δὴ καὶ περιφέρεται τὰ ἔπη ταυτί·

ταῦτ᾽ ἔχω, ὅσσ᾽ ἔφαγον καὶ ἀφύβρισα καὶ μετ᾽
    ἔρωτος
τέρπν᾽ ἔπαθον, τὰ δὲ πολλὰ καὶ ὄλβια κεῖνα
    λέλειπται.

10. Ὑπέρκειται δὲ τὰ Κύινδα τῆς Ἀγχιάλης
ἔρυμα, ᾧ ἐχρήσαντό ποτε οἱ Μακεδόνες γαζοφυ-

[1] Καλυκάδνῳ Emowz, Καλύδνῳ other MSS.
[2] Before καί, all MSS except E read ἔνιοι δέ.
[3] After τἆλλα, Ald. adds ἀνθρώπινα, apparently from
Arrian 2. 5.
[4] After ἀποκροτήματος, the following verses (obviously an
interpolation), inserted by all editors from Casaubon to
Corais, are in DFhi found only in the margin and in Cgsr
preceded by the words τὸ ὅλον ἐπίγραμμα:

εὖ εἰδώς, ὅτι θνητὸς ἔφυς, σὸν θυμὸν ἄεξε,
τερπόμενος θαλίῃσι· θανόντι τοι οὔ τις ὄνησις.
καὶ γὰρ ἐγὼ σποδός εἰμι, Νίνου μεγάλης βασιλεύσας·

Tarsus; Philemon, the comic poet; and Aratus, who wrote the work entitled *The Phaenomena*, in verse.

9. Then to Zephyrium, which bears the same name as the place near Calycadnus.[1] Then, a little above the sea, to Anchialê, which, according to Aristobulus, was founded by Sardanapallus. Here, he says, is the tomb of Sardanapallus, and a stone figure which represents the fingers of the right hand as snapping together, and the following inscription in Assyrian letters: "Sardanapallus, the son of Anacyndaraxes, built Anchialê and Tarsus in one day. Eat, drink, be merry, because all things else are not worth this," meaning the snapping of the fingers. Choerilus also mentions this inscription; and indeed the following verses are everywhere known: "Mine are all that I have eaten, and my loose indulgences and the delights of love that I have enjoyed; but those numerous blessings have been left behind."[2]

10. Above Anchialê lies Cyinda, a fortress, which at one time was used as a treasury by the Mace-

---

[1] 14. 5. 4.

[2] The whole of the epigram, as found in some of the MSS. (see critical note), is as follows: "Well aware that thou art by nature mortal, magnify the desires of thy heart, delighting thyself in merriments; there is no enjoyment for thee after death. For I too am dust, though I have reigned over great Ninus. Mine are all the food that I have eaten, and my loose indulgences, and the delights of love that I have enjoyed; but those numerous blessings have been left behind. This to mortal men is wise advice on how to live."

ταῦτ' ἔχω, ὅσσ' ἔφαγον καὶ ἐφύβρισα καὶ μετ' ἔρωτος
τέρπν' ἔπαθον, τὰ δὲ πολλὰ καὶ ὄλβια κεῖνα λέλειπται.
ἥδε σοφὴ βιότοιο παραίνεσις ἀνθρώποισιν.

λακίῳ· ἦρε δὲ τὰ χρήματα Εὐμένης, ἀποστὰς
Ἀντιγόνου. ἔτι δ᾽ ὕπερθεν τούτου τε καὶ τῶν
Σόλων ὀρεινή ἐστιν, ἐν ᾗ Ὄλβη πόλις, Διὸς ἱερὸν
ἔχουσα, Αἴαντος ἵδρυμα τοῦ Τεύκρου· καὶ ὁ
ἱερεὺς δυνάστης ἐγίνετο τῆς Τραχειώτιδος· εἶτ᾽
ἐπέθεντο τῇ χώρᾳ τύραννοι πολλοί, καὶ συνέστη
τὰ ληστήρια. μετὰ δὲ τὴν τούτων κατάλυσιν
ἐφ᾽ ἡμῶν ἤδη τὴν τοῦ Τεύκρου δυναστείαν ταύτην
ἐκάλουν, τὴν δ᾽ αὐτὴν καὶ ἱερωσύνην· καὶ οἱ
πλεῖστοί γε τῶν ἱερασαμένων ὠνομάζοντο Τεῦκροι
ἢ Αἴαντες. εἰσιοῦσα δ᾽ Ἄβα κατ᾽ ἐπιγαμίαν εἰς
τὸν οἶκον τοῦτον, ἡ Ζηνοφάνους θυγάτηρ, ἑνὸς
τῶν τυράννων, αὐτὴ κατέσχε τὴν ἀρχήν, προ-
λαβόντος τοῦ πατρὸς ἐν ἐπιτρόπου σχήματι·
ὕστερον δὲ καὶ Ἀντώνιος καὶ Κλεοπάτρα κατε-
χαρίσαντο ἐκείνῃ, θεραπείαις ἐκλιπαρηθέντες·
ἔπειθ᾽ ἡ μὲν κατελύθη, τοῖς δ᾽ ἀπὸ τοῦ γένους
διέμεινεν ἡ ἀρχή. μετὰ δὲ τὴν Ἀγχιάλην αἱ τοῦ
Κύδνου ἐκβολαὶ κατὰ τὸ Ῥῆγμα καλούμενον.
ἔστι δὲ λιμνάζων τόπος, ἔχων καὶ παλαιὰ νεώρια,
εἰς ὃν ἐκπίπτει ὁ Κύδνος ὁ διαρρέων μέσην τὴν
Ταρσόν, τὰς ἀρχὰς ἔχων ἀπὸ τοῦ ὑπερκειμένου
τῆς πόλεως Ταύρου· καὶ ἔστιν ἐπίνειον ἡ λίμνη
τῆς Ταρσοῦ.

C 673   11. Μέχρι μὲν δὴ δεῦρο ἡ παραλία πᾶσα, ἀπὸ
τῆς Ῥοδίων περαίας ἀρξαμένη, πρὸς ἰσημερινὰς
ἀνατολὰς ἀπὸ τῶν ὁμωνύμων ἐκτείνεται δύσεων·
εἶτ᾽ ἐπὶ τὴν χειμερινὴν ἀνατολὴν ἐπιστρέφει
μέχρι Ἰσσοῦ, κἀντεῦθεν ἤδη καμπὴν λαμβάνει
πρὸς νότον μέχρι Φοινίκης, τὸ δὲ λοιπὸν πρὸς

---

[1] i.e. straight east and west.

342

donians. But the treasures were taken away by
Eumenes, when he revolted from Antigonus. And
still above this and Soli is a mountainous country,
in which is a city Olbê, with a temple of Zeus,
founded by Ajax the son of Teucer. The priest
of this temple became dynast of Cilicia Tracheia;
and then the country was beset by numerous
tyrants, and the gangs of pirates were organised.
And after the overthrow of these they called this
country the domain of Teucer, and called the same
also the priesthood of Teucer; and most of the
priests were named Teucer or Ajax. But Aba,
the daughter of Xenophanes, one of the tyrants,
came into this family by marriage and herself took
possession of the empire, her father having previously received it in the guise of guardian. But
later both Antony and Cleopatra conferred it upon
her as a favour, being moved by her courteous
entreaties. And then she was overthrown, but the
empire remained with her descendants. After
Anchialê one comes to the outlets of the Cydnus,
near the Rhegma, as it is called. It is a place that
forms into a lake, having also ancient arsenals; and
into it empties the Cydnus River, which flows through
the middle of Tarsus and has its sources in the city
Taurus, which lies above Tarsus. The lake is also
the naval station of Tarsus.

11. Now thus far the seaboard as a whole, beginning at the Peraea of the Rhodians, extends towards
the equinoctial east from the equinoctial west,[1] and
then bends in the direction of winter sunrise[2] as
far as Issus, and then forthwith takes a bend
towards the south as far as Phoenicia; and the

[2] South-east (see Vol. I, p. 105, note 2).

δύσιν μέχρι στηλῶν τελευτᾷ. τὸ μὲν οὖν ἀληθὲς
ὁ ἰσθμὸς τῆς περιωδευμένης χερρονήσου οὗτός
ἐστιν ὁ ἀπὸ Ταρσοῦ καὶ τῆς ἐκβολῆς τοῦ Κύδνου
μέχρι Ἀμισοῦ· τὸ γὰρ ἐλάχιστον ἐξ Ἀμισοῦ
διάστημα ἐπὶ τοὺς Κιλίκων ὅρους τοῦτ᾽ ἔστιν·
ἐντεῦθεν δὲ ἑκατὸν εἴκοσίν εἰσιν εἰς Ταρσὸν
στάδιοι, κἀκεῖθεν οὐ πλείους [1] ἐπὶ τὴν ἐκβολὴν
τοῦ Κύδνου. καὶ μὴν ἐπί γε Ἰσσὸν καὶ τὴν κατ᾽
αὐτὴν θάλατταν οὔτ᾽ ἄλλη ὁδὸς συντομωτέρα
ἐστὶν ἐξ Ἀμισοῦ τῆς διὰ Ταρσοῦ, οὔτ᾽ ἐκ Ταρσοῦ
ἐπὶ Ἰσσὸν ἐγγυτέρω ἐστὶν ἢ ἐπὶ Κύδνον, ὥστε
δῆλον, ὅτι ταῖς μὲν ἀληθείαις οὗτος ἂν εἴη ὁ
ἰσθμός, λέγεται δ᾽ ὅμως ὁ μέχρι τοῦ Ἰσσικοῦ
κόλπου, παρακλεπτόντων διὰ τὸ σημειῶδες. διὰ
δὲ τοῦτ᾽ αὐτὸ καὶ τὴν ἐκ τῆς Ῥοδίας γραμμήν, ἣν
μέχρι τοῦ Κύδνου κατηγάγομεν, τὴν αὐτὴν ἀποφαίνομεν [2] τῇ μέχρι Ἰσσοῦ, οὐδὲν παρὰ τοῦτο
ποιούμενοι, καὶ τὸν Ταῦρόν φαμεν διήκειν ἐπ᾽
εὐθείας τῇδε τῇ γραμμῇ μέχρι τῆς Ἰνδικῆς.

12. Ἡ δὲ Ταρσὸς κεῖται μὲν ἐν πεδίῳ, κτίσμα
δ᾽ ἐστὶ τῶν μετὰ Τριπτολέμου πλανηθέντων
Ἀργείων κατὰ ζήτησιν Ἰοῦς· διαρρεῖ δ᾽ αὐτὴν
μέσην ὁ Κύδνος παρ᾽ αὐτὸ τὸ γυμνάσιον τῶν
νέων· ἅτε δὴ τῆς πηγῆς οὐ πολὺ ἄπωθεν οὔσης,
καὶ τοῦ ῥείθρου διὰ φάραγγος βαθείας ἰόντος, εἶτ᾽
εὐθὺς εἰς τὴν πόλιν ἐκπίπτοντος, ψυχρόν τε καὶ

---

[1] πέντε, after πλείους, all MSS. except F. The translator
believes, with C. Müller, that Strabo wrote ἑβδομήκοντα (*i.e.*
o' and not *ε'*).
[2] ἀποφαίνομεν, Groskurd and the later editors, instead of
ἀποφαινόμενοι.

---

[1] *i.e.* the Pillars of Heracles at Gibraltar.

remainder extends towards the west as far as
the Pillars[1] and there ends. Now the truth is
that the actual isthmus of the peninsula which I
have described is that which extends from Tarsus
and the outlet of the Cydnus to Amisus, for this
is the shortest distance from Amisus to the
boundaries of Cilicia; and the distance thence to
Tarsus is one hundred and twenty stadia, and the
distance from there to the outlet of the Cydnus is
no more than that. And in fact to Issus, and the
sea near it, there is no other road from Amisus
which is shorter than that through Tarsus, and
Tarsus is not nearer to Issus than to the Cydnus;[2]
and therefore it is clear that in reality this would
be the isthmus; but still people call that which
extends as far as the Gulf of Issus the true isthmus,
thus betraying the facts because of the significance
of the gulf. And it is because of this very thing that
I, without making any accurate distinctions, represent the line from Rhodes, which I have prolonged
to the Cydnus, to be the same as the line extending
as far as Issus, and also assert that the Taurus
extends in a straight line with that line as far as
India.

12. As for Tarsus, it lies in a plain; and it was
founded by the Argives who wandered with Tripto-
lemus in quest of Io; and it is intersected in the
middle by the Cydnus River, which flows past the
very gymnasium of the young men. Now inasmuch
as the source of the river is not very far away and
its stream passes through a deep ravine and then
empties immediately into the city, its discharge is
both cold and swift; and hence it is helpful both

[2] *i.e.* the *outlet* of the Cydnus, at Rhegma.

ταχὺ τὸ ῥεῦμά ἐστιν, ὅθεν καὶ τοῖς παχυνευροῦσι
ῥοϊζομένοις καὶ κτήνεσι καὶ ἀνθρώποις ἐπικουρεῖ.
13. Τοσαύτη δὲ τοῖς ἐνθάδε ἀνθρώποις σπουδὴ
πρός τε φιλοσοφίαν καὶ τὴν ἄλλην παιδείαν
ἐγκύκλιον ἅπασαν γέγονεν, ὥσθ᾽ ὑπερβέβληνται
καὶ ᾽Αθήνας καὶ ᾽Αλεξάνδρειαν καὶ εἴ τινα ἄλλον
τόπον δυνατὸν εἰπεῖν, ἐν ᾧ σχολαὶ καὶ διατριβαὶ
φιλοσόφων γεγόνασι. διαφέρει δὲ τοσοῦτον, ὅτι
ἐνταῦθα μὲν οἱ φιλομαθοῦντες ἐπιχώριοι πάντες
εἰσί, ξένοι δ᾽ οὐκ ἐπιδημοῦσι ῥᾳδίως· οὐδ᾽ αὐτοὶ
οὗτοι μένουσιν αὐτόθι, ἀλλὰ καὶ τελειοῦνται
ἐκδημήσαντες, καὶ τελειωθέντες ξενιτεύουσιν
ἡδέως, κατέρχονται δ᾽ ὀλίγοι. ταῖς δ᾽ ἄλλαις
πόλεσιν, ἃς ἀρτίως εἶπον, πλὴν ᾽Αλεξανδρείας,
C 674 συμβαίνει τἀναντία· φοιτῶσι γὰρ εἰς αὐτὰς
πολλοὶ καὶ διατρίβουσιν αὐτόθι ἄσμενοι, τῶν δ᾽
ἐπιχωρίων οὐ πολλοὺς οὔτ᾽ ἂν ἔξω φοιτῶντας
ἴδοις κατὰ φιλομάθειαν, οὔτ᾽ αὐτόθι περὶ τοῦτο
σπουδάζοντας· ᾽Αλεξανδρεῦσι δ᾽ ἀμφότερα συμ-
βαίνει· καὶ γὰρ δέχονται πολλοὺς τῶν ξένων
καὶ ἐκπέμπουσι τῶν ἰδίων οὐκ ὀλίγους. καί εἰσι
σχολαὶ παρ᾽ αὐτοῖς παντοδαπαὶ τῶν περὶ λόγους
τεχνῶν, καὶ τἄλλά τ᾽ εὐανδρεῖ καὶ πλεῖστον
δύναται, τὸν τῆς μητροπόλεως ἐπέχουσα λόγον.
14. ῎Ανδρες δ᾽ ἐξ αὐτῆς γεγόνασι τῶν μὲν
στωικῶν ᾽Αντίπατρός τε καὶ ᾽Αρχέδημος καὶ
Νέστωρ· ἔτι δ᾽ ᾽Αθηνόδωροι δύο, ὧν ὁ μέν,
Κορδυλίων καλούμενος, συνεβίωσε Μάρκῳ

---

[1] i.e. to their schools.

to men and to cattle that are suffering from swollen sinews, if they immerse themselves in its waters.

13. The people at Tarsus have devoted themselves so eagerly, not only to philosophy, but also to the whole round of education in general, that they have surpassed Athens, Alexandria, or any other place that can be named where there have been schools and lectures of philosophers. But it is so different from other cities that there the men who are fond of learning are all natives, and foreigners are not inclined to sojourn there; neither do these natives stay there, but they complete their education abroad; and when they have completed it they are pleased to live abroad, and but few go back home. But the opposite is the case with the other cities which I have just mentioned except Alexandria; for many resort to them and pass time there with pleasure, but you would not see many of the natives either resorting to places outside their country through love of learning or eager about pursuing learning at home. With the Alexandrians, however, both things take place, for they admit[1] many foreigners and also send not a few of their own citizens abroad. Further, the city of Tarsus has all kinds of schools of rhetoric; and in general it not only has a flourishing population but also is most powerful, thus keeping up the reputation of the mother-city.[2]

14. The following men were natives of Tarsus: among the Stoics, Antipater and Archedemus and Nestor; and also the two Athenodoruses, one of whom, called Cordylion, lived with Marcus Cato

[2] *i.e.* in spite of the fact that so many able men leave the city and never return.

347

Κάτωνι, καὶ ἐτελεύτα[1] παρ' ἐκείνῳ, ὁ δὲ τοῦ
Σάνδωνος, ὃν καὶ Κανανίτην φασὶν ἀπὸ κώμης
τινός, Καίσαρος καθηγήσατο καὶ τιμῆς ἔτυχε
μεγάλης· κατιών τε εἰς τὴν πατρίδα ἤδη γηραιὸς
κατέλυσε τὴν καθεστῶσαν πολιτείαν, κακῶς
φερομένην ὑπό τε ἄλλων καὶ Βοηθοῦ, κακοῦ
μὲν ποιητοῦ, κακοῦ δὲ πολίτου, δημοκοπίαις
ἰσχύσαντος τὸ πλέον. ἐπῆρε δ' αὐτὸν καὶ
Ἀντώνιος, κατ' ἀρχὰς ἀποδεξάμενος τὸ γραφὲν
εἰς τὴν ἐν Φιλίπποις νίκην ἔπος, καὶ ἔτι μᾶλλον
ἡ εὐχέρεια ἡ ἐπιπολάζουσα παρὰ τοῖς Ταρσεῦσιν,
ὥστ' ἀπαύστως σχεδιάζειν παρὰ χρῆμα πρὸς
τὴν δεδομένην ὑπόθεσιν· καὶ δὴ καὶ γυμνασιαρ-
χίαν ὑποσχόμενος Ταρσεῦσι τοῦτον ἀντὶ γυμνασιάρχου[2] κατέστησε, καὶ τὰ ἀναλώματα ἐπίσ-
τευσεν αὐτῷ. ἐφωράθη δὲ νοσφισάμενος τά τε
ἄλλα καὶ τοὔλαιον· ἐλεγχόμενος δ' ὑπὸ τῶν
κατηγόρων ἐπὶ τοῦ Ἀντωνίου, παρῃτεῖτο τὴν
ὀργήν, σὺν ἄλλοις καὶ ταῦτα λέγων, ὅτι, "Ὥσπερ
Ὅμηρος ἐξύμνησεν Ἀχιλλέα καὶ Ἀγαμέμνονα
καὶ Ὀδυσσέα, οὕτως ἐγὼ σέ· οὐ δίκαιος οὖν
εἰμὶ εἰς τοιαύτας ἄγεσθαι διαβολὰς ἐπὶ σοῦ.
παραλαβὼν οὖν ὁ κατήγορος τὸν λόγον, "Ἀλλ'
Ὅμηρος μέν, ἔφη, ἔλαιον[3] Ἀγαμέμνονος οὐκ
ἔκλεψεν, ἀλλ' οὐδὲ Ἀχιλλέως, σὺ δέ· ὥστε
δώσεις δίκην. διακρουσάμενος δ' οὖν θεραπείαις
τισὶ τὴν ὀργήν, οὐδὲν ἧττον διετέλεσεν ἄγων
καὶ φέρων τὴν πόλιν μέχρι τῆς καταστροφῆς
τοῦ Ἀντωνίου. τοιαύτην δὲ τὴν πόλιν κατα-

---

[1] ἐτελεύτα, Corais, for τελεύτα.
[2] ἀντὶ γυμνασιάρχου sw, ἀντιγυμνασίαρχον other MSS.
[3] μέν, after ἔλαιον, omitted by mowxz.

and died at his house; and the other, the son of
Sandon, called Cananites after some village, was
Caesar's teacher and was greatly honoured by him;
and when he returned to his native land, now an
old man, he broke up the government there established, which was being badly conducted by Boethus,
among others, who was a bad poet and a bad citizen,
having prevailed there by currying the favour of
the people. He had been raised to prominence by
Antony, who at the outset received favourably the
poem which he had written upon the victory at
Philippi, but still more by that facility prevalent
among the Tarsians whereby he could instantly
speak offhand and unceasingly on any given subject.
Furthermore, Antony promised the Tarsians an office
of gymnasiarch, but appointed Boethus instead of a
gymnasiarch, and entrusted to him the expenditures.
But Boethus was caught secreting, among other
things, the olive-oil; and when he was being proven
guilty by his accusers in the presence of Antony he
deprecated Antony's wrath, saying, among other
things, that "Just as Homer had hymned the
praises of Achilles and Agamemnon and Odysseus,
so I have hymned thine. It is not right, therefore,
that I should be brought before you on such
slanderous charges." When, however, the accuser
caught the statement, he said, "Yes, but Homer
did not steal Agamemnon's oil, nor yet that of
Achilles, but you did; and therefore you shall be
punished." However, he broke the wrath of
Antony by courteous attentions, and no less than
before kept on plundering the city until the overthrow of Antony. Finding the city in this plight,

λαβὼν ὁ Ἀθηνόδωρος, τέως μὲν ἐπεχείρει λόγῳ
μετάγειν κἀκεῖνον καὶ τοὺς συστασιώτας· ὡς δ᾽
οὐκ ἀπείχοντο ὕβρεως οὐδεμιᾶς, ἐχρήσατο τῇ
δοθείσῃ ὑπὸ τοῦ Καίσαρος ἐξουσίᾳ καὶ ἐξέβαλεν
αὐτούς, καταγνοὺς φυγήν. οἱ δὲ πρῶτον μὲν
κατετοιχογράφησαν αὐτοῦ τοιαῦτα·

C 675   ἔργα νέων, βουλαὶ δὲ μέσων, πορδαὶ δὲ γερόν-
των.

ἐπεὶ δ᾽ ἐκεῖνος ἐν παιδιᾶς μέρει δεξάμενος
ἐκέλευσε παρεπιγράψαι "— βρονταὶ δὲ γερόν-
των," καταφρονήσας δέ τις τοῦ ἐπιεικοῦς,
εὔλυτον τὸ κοιλίδιον ἔχων, προσέρρανε πολὺ
τῇ θύρᾳ καὶ τῷ τοίχῳ, νύκτωρ παριὼν τὴν
οἰκίαν. ὁ δὲ τῆς στάσεως κατηγορῶν ἐν ἐκ-
κλησίᾳ, τὴν νόσον τῆς πόλεως, ἔφη, καὶ τὴν
καχεξίαν πολλαχόθεν σκοπεῖν ἔξεστι, καὶ δὴ
καὶ ἐκ τῶν διαχωρημάτων. οὗτοι μὲν στωικοὶ
ἄνδρες· ἀκαδημαϊκὸς δὲ Νέστωρ ὁ καθ᾽ ἡμᾶς, ὁ
Μαρκέλλου καθηγησάμενος, τοῦ Ὀκταουίας
παιδός, τῆς Καίσαρος ἀδελφῆς. καὶ οὗτος δὲ
προέστη τῆς πολιτείας, διαδεξάμενος τὸν Ἀθη-
νόδωρον, καὶ διετέλεσε τιμώμενος παρά τε τοῖς
ἡγεμόσι καὶ ἐν τῇ πόλει.

15. Τῶν δ᾽ ἄλλων φιλοσόφων,

οὕς κεν ἐΰ γνοίην καὶ τοὔνομα μυθησαίμην,

Πλουτιάδης τε ἐγένετο καὶ Διογένης τῶν περι-
πολιζόντων καὶ σχολὰς διατιθεμένων εὐφυῶς·
ὁ δὲ Διογένης καὶ ποιήματα ὥσπερ ἀπεφοίβαζε,
τεθείσης ὑποθέσεως, τραγικὰ ὡς ἐπὶ πολύ· γραμματικοὶ δέ, ὧν καὶ συγγράμματά ἐστιν, Ἀρτε-
μίδωρός τε καὶ Διόδωρος· ποιητὴς δὲ τραγῳδίας
350

Athenodorus for a time tried to induce both Boethus
and his partisans to change their course; but since
they would abstain from no act of insolence, he
used the authority given him by Caesar, condemned
them to exile, and expelled them. These at first
indicted him with the following inscription on the
walls: "Work for young men, counsels for the
middle-aged, and flatulence for old men"; and
when he, taking the inscription as a joke, ordered the
following words to be inscribed beside it, "thunder
for old men," someone, contemptuous of all decency
and afflicted with looseness of the bowels, pro-
fusely bespattered the door and wall of Athenodorus'
house as he was passing by it at night. Athenodorus, while bringing accusations in the assembly
against the faction, said: "One may see the sickly
plight and the disaffection of the city in many ways,
and in particular from its excrements." These men
were Stoics; but the Nestor of my time, the teacher
of Marcellus, son of Octavia the sister of Caesar,
was an Academician. He too was at the head of
the government of Tarsus, having succeeded Athenodorus; and he continued to be held in honour both
by the prefects and in the city.

15. Among the other philosophers from Tarsus,
"whom I could well note and tell their names,"[1]
are Plutiades and Diogenes, who were among those
philosophers that went round from city to city and
conducted schools in an able manner. Diogenes
also composed poems, as if by inspiration, when a
subject was given him—for the most part tragic
poems; and as for grammarians whose writings are
extant, there are Artemidorus and Diodorus; and

[1] *Iliad* 3. 235.

ἄριστος τῶν τῆς Πλειάδος καταριθμουμένων
Διονυσίδης. μάλιστα δ᾽ ἡ Ῥώμη[1] δύναται δι-
δάσκειν τὸ πλῆθος τῶν ἐκ τῆσδε τῆς πόλεως
φιλολόγων· Ταρσέων γὰρ καὶ Ἀλεξανδρέων ἐστὶ
μεστή. τοιαύτη μὲν ἡ Ταρσός.

16. Μετὰ δὲ τὸν Κύδνον ὁ Πύραμος ἐκ τῆς
Καταονίας ῥέων, οὗπερ καὶ πρότερον ἐμνήσθημεν·
φησὶ δ᾽ Ἀρτεμίδωρος, ἐντεῦθεν εἰς Σόλους εὐθυπλοίᾳ σταδίους εἶναι πεντακοσίους. πλησίον
δὲ καὶ Μαλλός, ἐφ᾽ ὕψους κειμένη, κτίσμα
Ἀμφιλόχου καὶ Μόψου, τοῦ Ἀπόλλωνος καὶ
Μαντοῦς,[2] περὶ ὧν πολλὰ μυθολογεῖται· καὶ
δὴ καὶ ἡμεῖς ἐμνήσθημεν αὐτῶν ἐν τοῖς περὶ
Κάλχαντος λόγοις καὶ τῆς ἔριδος, ἣν ἤρισαν
περὶ τῆς μαντικῆς ὅ τε Κάλχας καὶ ὁ Μόψος·
ταύτην τε γὰρ τὴν ἔριν μεταφέρουσιν ἔνιοι,
καθάπερ καὶ Σοφοκλῆς, εἰς τὴν Κιλικίαν, καλέσας
ἐκεῖνος αὐτὴν Παμφυλίαν τραγικῶς, καθάπερ
καὶ τὴν Λυκίαν Καρίαν καὶ τὴν Τροίαν καὶ
Λυδίαν[3] Φρυγίαν· καὶ τὸν θάνατον δὲ τοῦ
Κάλχαντος ἐνταῦθα παραδιδόασιν ἄλλοι τε καὶ
Σοφοκλῆς. οὐ μόνον δὲ τὴν περὶ τῆς μαντικῆς
ἔριν μεμυθεύκασιν, ἀλλὰ καὶ τῆς ἀρχῆς. τὸν
γὰρ Μόψον φασὶ καὶ τὸν Ἀμφίλοχον ἐκ Τροίας
C 676 ἐλθόντας κτίσαι Μαλλόν· εἶτ᾽ Ἀμφίλοχον εἰς
Ἄργος ἀπελθεῖν, δυσαρεστήσαντα δὲ τοῖς ἐκεῖ
πάλιν ἀναστρέψαι δεῦρο, ἀποκλειόμενον δὲ τῆς
κοινωνίας συμβαλεῖν εἰς μονομαχίαν πρὸς τὸν

---

[1] ἡ Ῥώμη, Sihler (*American Journal of Philology*, 1923,
p. 141) would emend to τὴν Ῥώμην.
[2] Μαντοῦς, Xylander, for Λητοῦς; so the later editors.
[3] καί, before Φρυγίαν, Groskurd omits, so Meineke.

the best tragic poet among those enumerated in the
" Pleias " [1] was Dionysides.   But it is Rome that is
best able to tell us the number of learned men from
this city ; [2] for it is full of Tarsians and Alexandrians.
Such is Tarsus.

16. After the Cydnus River one comes to the
Pyramus River, which flows from Cataonia, a river
which I have mentioned before. [3]   According to
Artemidorus, the distance thence to Soli in a straight
voyage is five hundred stadia.   Near by, also, is
Mallus, situated on a height, founded by Amphilochus
and Mopsus, the latter the son of Apollo and Manto,
concerning whom many myths are told.   And indeed
I, too, have mentioned them in my account of
Calchas [4] and of the quarrel between Calchas and
Mopsus about their powers of divination.   For some
writers transfer this quarrel, Sophocles, for example,
to Cilicia, which he, following the custom of tragic
poets, calls Pamphylia, just as he calls Lycia " Caria " [5]
and Troy and Lydia " Phrygia."   And Sophocles,
among others, tells us that Calchas died there.   But,
according to the myth, the contest concerned,
not only the power of divination, but also the
sovereignty ; for they say that Mopsus and
Amphilochus went from Troy and founded Mallus,
and that Amphilochus then went away to Argos,
and, being dissatisfied with affairs there, returned to
Mallus, but that, being excluded from a share in the
government there, he fought a duel with Mopsus,

---

[1] *i.e.* the "Seven (Alexandrian) Stars," referring to the
Pleiades, the seven daughters of Atlas, who were placed by
Zeus among the stars and became one of the oldest Greek
constellations.
  [2] See critical note.   [3] 12. 2. 4.
  [4] 14. 1. 27.   [5] See 14. 3. 3.

Μόψον, πεσόντας δ' ἀμφοτέρους ταφῆναι μὴ ἐν
ἐπόψει ἀλλήλοις· καὶ νῦν οἱ τάφοι δείκνυνται
περὶ Μάγαρσα τοῦ Πυράμου πλησίον. ἐντεῦθεν
δ' ἦν Κράτης ὁ γραμματικός, οὗ φησὶ γενέσθαι
μαθητὴς Παναίτιος.

17. Ὑπέρκειται δὲ τῆς παραλίας ταύτης
Ἀλήιον πεδίον, δι' οὗ Φιλώτας διήγαγεν Ἀλεξάνδρῳ τὴν ἵππον, ἐκείνου τὴν φάλαγγα ἀγαγόντος ἐκ τῶν Σόλων διὰ τῆς παραλίας καὶ τῆς
Μαλλώτιδος ἐπί τε Ἰσσὸν καὶ τὰς Δαρείου
δυνάμεις. φασὶ δὲ καὶ ἐναγίσαι τῷ Ἀμφιλόχῳ
τὸν Ἀλέξανδρον διὰ τὴν ἐξ Ἄργους συγγένειαν.
Ἡσίοδος δ' ἐν Σόλοις ὑπὸ Ἀπόλλωνος ἀναιρεθῆναι τὸν Ἀμφίλοχόν φησιν, οἱ δὲ περὶ τὸ
Ἀλήιον πεδίον, οἱ δ' ἐν Συρίᾳ, ἀπὸ τοῦ Ἀληίου
ἀπιόντα διὰ τὴν ἔριν.

18. Μετὰ δὲ Μαλλὸν Αἰγαῖαι πολίχνιον,
ὕφορμον ἔχον· εἶτ' Ἀμανίδες πύλαι, ὕφορμον
ἔχουσαι, εἰς ἃς τελευτᾷ τὸ Ἀμανὸν ὄρος ἀπὸ
τοῦ Ταύρου καθῆκον, ὃ τῆς Κιλικίας ὑπέρκειται
κατὰ τὸ πρὸς ἔω μέρος, ἀεὶ μὲν ὑπὸ πλειόνων
δυναστευόμενον τυράννων, ἐχόντων ἐρύματα· καθ'
ἡμᾶς δὲ κατέστη κύριος πάντων ἀνὴρ ἀξιόλογος
καὶ βασιλεὺς ὑπὸ Ῥωμαίων ὠνομάσθη διὰ τὰς
ἀνδραγαθίας Ταρκονδίμοτος,[1] καὶ τὴν διαδοχὴν
τοῖς μετ' αὐτὸν παρέδωκε.

19. Μετὰ δὲ Αἰγαίας Ἰσσὸς πολίχνιον ὕφορμον ἔχον καὶ ποταμὸς Πίναρος.[2] ἐνταῦθα ὁ
ἀγὼν συνέπεσεν Ἀλεξάνδρῳ καὶ Δαρείῳ· καὶ ὁ

[1] Ταρκονδίμοτος, Casaubon, for Ταρκοδίμεντος CF, Ταρκδή-
μεντος other MSS.
[2] Πίναρος, Tzschucke, for Πίδνος D, Πίνδος other MSS.

and that both fell in the duel and were buried in
places that were not in sight of one another. And
to-day their tombs are to be seen in the neighbourhood of Magarsa near the Pyramus River. This [1]
was the birthplace of Crates the grammarian, of
whom Panaetius is said to have been a pupil.

17. Above this coast lies the Aleïan Plain, through
which Philotas led the cavalry for Alexander, when
Alexander led his phalanx from Soli along the coast
and the territory of Mallus against Issus and the
forces of Dareius. It is said that Alexander performed sacrifices to Amphilochus because of his
kinship with the Argives. Hesiod says that
Amphilochus was slain by Apollo at Soli; but others
say that he was slain in the neighbourhood of the
Aleïan Plain, and others in Syria, when he was
quitting the Aleïan Plain because of the quarrel.

18. After Mallus one comes to Aegaeae, a small
town, with a mooring-place; and then to the
Amanides Gates, with a mooring-place, where ends
the mountain Amanus, which extends down from
the Taurus and lies above Cilicia towards the east.
It was always ruled by several powerful tyrants, who
possessed strongholds; but in my time a notable
man established himself as lord of all, and was named
king by the Romans because of his manly virtues—
I refer to Tarcondimotus, who bequeathed the
succession to his posterity.

19. After Aegaeae, one comes to Issus, a small
town with a mooring-place, and to the Pinarus
River. It was here that the struggle between
Alexander and Dareius occurred; and the gulf is

---

[1] Mallus.

κόλπος εἴρηται Ἰσσικός· ἐν αὐτῷ δὲ πόλις
Ῥωσὸς καὶ Μυρίανδρος πόλις καὶ Ἀλεξάνδρεια
καὶ Νικόπολις καὶ Μόψου ἑστία καὶ Πύλαι
λεγόμεναι, ὅριον Κιλίκων τε καὶ Σύρων. ἐν δὲ
τῇ Κιλικίᾳ ἐστὶ καὶ τὸ τῆς Σαρπηδονίας
Ἀρτέμιδος ἱερὸν καὶ μαντεῖον, τοὺς δὲ χρησμοὺς
ἔνθεοι προθεσπίζουσιν.

20. Μετὰ δὲ τὴν Κιλικίαν πρώτη πόλις ἐστὶ
τῶν Σύρων Σελεύκεια ἡ ἐν Πιερίᾳ, καὶ πλησίον
Ὀρόντης ἐκδίδωσι ποταμός. ἔστι δ' ἀπὸ
Σελευκείας εἰς Σόλους ἐπ' εὐθείας πλοῦς ὀλίγον
ἀπολείπων τῶν χιλίων σταδίων.

21. Τῶν δ' ἐν Τροίᾳ Κιλίκων, ὧν Ὅμηρος
μέμνηται, πολὺ διεστώτων ἀπὸ τῶν ἔξω τοῦ
Ταύρου Κιλίκων, οἱ μὲν ἀποφαίνουσιν ἀρχηγέτας
τοὺς ἐν τῇ Τροίᾳ τούτων καὶ δεικνύουσί τινας
τόπους κἀνταῦθα, ὥσπερ ἐν τῇ Παμφυλίᾳ
Θήβην καὶ Λυρνησσόν, οἱ δ' ἔμπαλιν καὶ Ἀλήιόν
τι πεδίον κἀκεῖ δεικνύουσι.

Περιωδευμένων δὲ καὶ τῶν ἔξω τοῦ Ταύρου
μερῶν τῆς προειρημένης χερρονήσου, προσθετέον
ἐστὶ καὶ ταῦτα.

C 677   22. Ὁ γὰρ Ἀπολλόδωρος ἐν τοῖς περὶ νεῶν
ἔτι καὶ τοιαῦτα λέγει· τοὺς γὰρ ἐκ τῆς Ἀσίας
ἐπικούρους τῶν Τρώων ἅπαντας καταριθμεῖσθαί
φησιν ὑπὸ τοῦ ποιητοῦ τῆς χερρονήσου κατοίκους
ὄντας, ἧς ὁ στενώτατος ἰσθμός ἐστι τὸ μεταξὺ
τοῦ κατὰ Σινώπην μυχοῦ καὶ Ἰσσοῦ· αἱ δ' ἐκτὸς
πλευραί, φησί, τριγωνοειδοῦς οὔσης, εἰσὶ μὲν
ἄνισοι, παρήκουσι δὲ ἡ μὲν ἀπὸ Κιλικίας ἐπὶ
Χελιδονίας, ἡ δ' ἐνθένδε ἐπὶ τὸ στόμα τοῦ
Εὐξείνου, ἡ δ' ἐπὶ Σινώπην πάλιν ἐνθένδε. τὸ

called the Issic Gulf. On this gulf are situated the city Rhosus, the city Myriandrus, Alexandreia, Nicopolis, Mopsuestia, and Pylae, as it is called, which is the boundary between the Cilicians and the Syrians. In Cilicia is also the temple and oracle of the Sarpedonian Artemis; and the oracles are delivered by persons who are divinely inspired.

20. After Cilicia the first Syrian city is Seleuceia-in-Pieria, near which the Orontes River empties. The voyage from Seleuceia to Soli, on a straight course, is but little short of one thousand stadia.

21. Since the Cilicians in the Troad whom Homer mentions are far distant from the Cilicians outside the Taurus, some represent those in Troy as original colonisers of the latter, and point out certain places of the same name there, as, for example, Thebê and Lyrnessus in Pamphylia, whereas others of contrary opinion point out also an Aleïan Plain in the former.

Now that the parts of the aforesaid peninsula outside the Taurus have been described, I must add what follows.

22. Apollodorus, in his work *On the Catalogue of Ships*, goes on to say to this effect, that all the allies of the Trojans from Asia were enumerated by the poet as being inhabitants of the peninsula, of which the narrowest isthmus is that between the innermost recess at Sinopê and Issus. And the exterior sides of this peninsula, he says, which is triangular in shape, are unequal in length, one of them extending from Cilicia to the Chelidonian Islands, another from the Chelidonian Islands to the mouth of the Euxine, and the third thence back to Sinopê. Now the assertion that the allies were

357

μὲν οὖν μόνους τοὺς ἐν τῇ χερρονήσῳ διὰ τῶν
αὐτῶν ἐλέγχοιτ' ἂν ψεῦδος ὄν, δι' ὧν ἠλέγξαμεν
πρότερον, μὴ μόνους τοὺς ἐντὸς Ἅλυος. οἱ γὰρ
περὶ Φαρνακίαν τόποι, ἐν οἷς τοὺς Ἁλιζώνους
ἔφαμεν, ὥσπερ ἔξω τοῦ Ἅλυός εἰσιν, οὕτω καὶ
ἔξω τοῦ ἰσθμοῦ, εἴπερ καὶ τῶν στενῶν τῶν
μεταξὺ Σινώπης καὶ Ἰσσοῦ, καὶ οὐ τούτων γε
μόνων, ἀλλὰ καὶ τῶν κατ' ἀλήθειαν στενῶν τῶν
μεταξὺ Ἀμισοῦ τε καὶ Ἰσσοῦ· οὐδὲ γὰρ ἐκεῖνος
ὀρθῶς ἀφώρισται τὸν ἰσθμὸν καὶ τὰ κατ' αὐτὸν
στενά, ἐκεῖνα ἀντὶ τούτων τιθείς. πάντων δ'
εὐηθέστατον τὸ τὴν χερρόνησον τριγωνοειδῆ
φήσαντα τρεῖς ἀποφήνασθαι τὰς ἔξω πλευράς·
ὁ γὰρ τὰς ἔξω λέγων πλευρὰς ἔοικεν ὑπεξαι-
ρουμένῳ τὴν κατὰ τὰ στενά, ὡς καὶ ταύτην
οὖσαν πλευράν, οὐκ ἔξω δὲ οὐδ' ἐπὶ θαλάττῃ.
εἰ μὲν τοίνυν τὰ στενὰ ταῦτα οὕτως ἦν συνηγ-
μένα, ὥστε μικρὸν ἀπολείπειν τοῦ συνάπτειν ἐπ'
ἀλλήλαις τήν τε ἐπὶ Ἰσσὸν καὶ τὴν ἐπὶ Σινώπην
πίπτουσαν πλευράν, συνεχώρει ἂν τριγωνοειδῆ
λέγεσθαι τὴν χερρόνησον· νῦν δέ γε τρισχιλίους
σταδίους ἀπολειπόντων μεταξὺ τῶν ὑπ' αὐτοῦ
λεγομένων στενῶν, ἀμαθία τὸ λέγειν τριγωνοειδὲς
τὸ τοιοῦτον τετράπλευρον, οὐδὲ χωρογραφικόν.
ὁ δὲ καὶ χωρογραφίαν ἐξέδωκεν ἐν κωμικῷ
μέτρῳ, γῆς περίοδον ἐπιγράψας. μένει δ' ἡ
αὐτὴ ἀμαθία, κἂν εἰς τοὐλάχιστον καταγάγῃ
διάστημά τις τὸν ἰσθμόν, ὅσον εἰρήκασιν οἱ
πλεῖστον ψευσάμενοι τὸ ἥμισυ τοῦ παντός, ὅσον
εἴρηκε καὶ Ἀρτεμίδωρος, χιλίους καὶ πεντακο-

---

[1] 12. 3. 24.   [2] Iambic verse.

alone those who lived in the peninsula can be
proved wrong by the same arguments by which I
have previously shown that the allies were not alone
those who lived this side the Halys River.[1] For
just as the places round Pharnacia, in which, as I
said, the Halizoni lived, are outside the Halys River,
so also they are outside the isthmus, if indeed they
are outside the narrows between Sinopê and Issus ;
and not outside these alone, but also outside the
true narrows between Amisus and Issus, for he too
incorrectly defines the isthmus and its narrows,
since he substitutes the former for the latter. But
the greatest absurdity is this, that, after calling the
peninsula triangular in shape, he represents the
" exterior sides " as three in number ; for when he
speaks of the " exterior sides " he seems privily to
exclude the side along the narrows, as though this
too were a side, but not " exterior " or on the sea.
If, then, these narrows were so shortened that the
exterior side ending at Issus and that ending at
Sinopê lacked but little of joining one another, one
might concede that the peninsula should be called
triangular ; but, as it is, since the narrows mentioned
by him leave a distance of three thousand stadia
between Issus and Sinopê, it is ignorance and not
knowledge of chorography to call such a four-sided
figure triangular. Yet he published in the metre
of comedy[2] a work on chorography entitled *A
Description of the Earth*. The same ignorance still
remains even though one should reduce the isthmus
to the minimum distance, I mean, to one-half of the
whole distance, as given by those who have most
belied the facts, among whom is also Artemidorus,

σίους σταδίους· οὐδὲ γὰρ τοῦτο συναγωγήν πω
τριγωνοειδοῦς ποιεῖ σχήματος. ἀλλ' οὐδὲ τὰς
πλευρὰς ὀρθῶς διήρηται τὰς ἔξω, τὴν ἀπὸ Ἰσσοῦ
μέχρι Χελιδονίων εἰπών· λοιπὴ γάρ ἐστιν ὅλη
ἐπ' εὐθείας ἡ Λυκιακὴ παραλία ταύτῃ, καὶ ἡ
τῶν Ῥοδίων περαία μέχρι Φύσκου· ἐντεῦθεν δὲ
καμπὴν λαβοῦσα ἡ ἤπειρος ἄρχεται τὴν δευτέραν
καὶ δυσμικὴν ποιεῖν πλευρὰν ἄχρι Προποντίδος
καὶ Βυζαντίου.

C 678   23. Φήσαντος δὲ τοῦ Ἐφόρου, διότι τὴν
χερρόνησον κατοικεῖ ταύτην ἑκκαίδεκα γένη,
τρία μὲν Ἑλληνικά, τὰ δὲ λοιπὰ βάρβαρα
χωρὶς τῶν μιγάδων, ἐπὶ θαλάττῃ μὲν Κίλικες
καὶ Πάμφυλοι καὶ Λύκιοι καὶ Βιθυνοὶ καὶ
Παφλαγόνες καὶ Μαριανδυνοὶ καὶ Τρῶες καὶ
Κᾶρες, Πισίδαι δὲ καὶ Μυσοὶ καὶ Χάλυβες καὶ
Φρύγες καὶ Μιλύαι ἐν τῇ μεσογαίᾳ, διαιτῶν[1]
ταῦτα ὁ Ἀπολλόδωρος ἑπτακαιδέκατόν φησιν
εἶναι τὸ τῶν Γαλατῶν, ὃ νεώτερόν ἐστι τοῦ
Ἐφόρου, τῶν δ' εἰρημένων τὰ μὲν Ἑλληνικὰ
μήπω κατὰ[2] τὰ Τρωικὰ κατῳκίσθαι, τὰ δὲ
βάρβαρα πολλὴν ἔχειν[3] σύγχυσιν διὰ τὸν
χρόνον· καταλέγεσθαι δ' ὑπὸ τοῦ ποιητοῦ τό
τε τῶν Τρώων[4] καὶ τῶν νῦν ὀνομαζομένων
Παφλαγόνων καὶ Μυσῶν καὶ Φρυγῶν καὶ
Καρῶν καὶ Λυκίων,[5] Μῄονάς τε ἀντὶ Λυδῶν
καὶ ἄλλους ἀγνῶτας, οἷον Ἁλιζῶνας καὶ Καύ-
κωνας· ἐκτὸς δὲ τοῦ καταλόγου Κητείους τε καὶ

---

[1] διαιτῶν, Corais, for διαιρῶν.
[2] κατά, Casaubon, for καὶ τά.
[3] ἔχειν F, ἔχει other MSS.
[4] Τρώων moz, Τρωικῶν other MSS.

that is, fifteen hundred stadia; for even this does not contract the side along the narrows enough to make the peninsula a triangular figure. Neither does Artemidorus correctly distinguish the exterior sides when he speaks of "the side that extends from Issus as far as the Chelidonian Islands," for there still remains to this side the whole of the Lycian coast, which lies in a straight line with the side he mentions, as does also the Peraea of the Rhodians as far as Physcus. And thence the mainland bends and begins to form the second, or westerly, side extending as far as the Propontis and Byzantium.

23. But though Ephorus said that this peninsula was inhabited by sixteen tribes, of which three were Hellenic and the rest barbarian, except those that were mixed, adding that the Cilicians, Pamphylians, Lycians, Bithynians, Paphlagonians, Mariandynians, Trojans, and Carians lived on the sea, but the Pisidians, Mysians, Chalybians, Phrygians, and Milyans in the interior, Apollodorus, who passes judgment upon this matter, says that the tribe of the Galatians, which is more recent than the time of Ephorus, is a seventeenth, and that, of the aforesaid tribes, the Hellenic had not yet, in the time of the Trojan War, settled there, and that the barbarian tribes are much confused because of the lapse of time; and that the poet names in his *Catalogue* the tribes of the Trojans and of the Paphlagonians, as they are now named, and of the Mysians and Phrygians and Carians and Lycians, as also the Meïonians, instead of the Lydians, and other unknown peoples, as, for example, the Halizones and Caucones; and, outside the *Catalogue*,

---

⁵ Λυκίων, Corais, for Λικίων F, Κιλίκων other MSS.

Σολύμους καὶ Κίλικας τοὺς ἐκ Θήβης πεδίου
καὶ Λέλεγας· Παμφύλους δὲ καὶ Βιθυνοὺς καὶ
Μαριανδυνοὺς καὶ Πισίδας καὶ Χάλυβας καὶ
Μιλύας καὶ Καππάδοκας μηδ᾽ ὠνομάσθαι, τοὺς
μὲν διὰ τὸ μηδέπω τοὺς τόπους κατῳκηκέναι
τούτους, τοὺς δὲ διὰ τὸ ἑτέροις γένεσι περιέχεσθαι, ὡς Ἰδριεῖς μὲν καὶ Τερμίλαι[1] Καρσί,
Δολίονες δὲ καὶ Βέβρυκες Φρυξί.

24. Φαίνεται δ᾽ οὔτε τοῦ Ἐφόρου τὴν ἀπόφασιν διαιτῶν ἱκανῶς, τά τε τοῦ ποιητοῦ ταράτ-
των καὶ καταψευδόμενος. Ἐφόρου τε γὰρ τοῦτο
πρῶτον ἀπαιτεῖν ἐχρῆν, τί δὴ τοὺς Χάλυβας
τίθησιν ἐντὸς τῆς χερρονήσου, τοσοῦτον ἀφε-
στῶτας καὶ Σινώπης καὶ Ἀμισοῦ πρὸς ἕω; οἱ
γὰρ λέγοντες τὸν ἰσθμὸν τῆς χερρονήσου ταύτης
τὴν ἀπὸ Ἰσσοῦ γραμμὴν ἐπὶ τὸν Εὔξεινον, ὡς
ἂν μεσημβρινήν τινα τιθέασι ταύτην, ἣν[2] οἱ
μὲν εἶναι νομίζουσι τὴν ἐπὶ Σινώπης, οἱ δὲ τὴν
ἐπ᾽ Ἀμισοῦ, ἐπὶ δὲ τῶν Χαλύβων οὐδείς· λοξὴ
γάρ ἐστι τελέως. ὁ γὰρ δὴ διὰ Χαλύβων μεσημ-
βρινὸς διὰ τῆς μικρᾶς Ἀρμενίας γράφοιτ᾽ ἂν
καὶ τοῦ Εὐφράτου, τὴν Καππαδοκίαν ὅλην ἐντὸς
ἀπολαμβάνων καὶ τὴν Κομμαγηνὴν καὶ τὸν
Ἀμανὸν καὶ τὸν Ἰσσικὸν κόλπον. εἰ δ᾽ οὖν
καὶ τὴν λοξὴν γραμμὴν ὁρίζειν τὸν ἰσθμὸν
συγχωρήσαιμεν, τὰ πλεῖστά γε τούτων, καὶ
μάλιστα ἡ Καππαδοκία, ἐντὸς ἀπολαμβάνοιτ᾽
ἂν καὶ ὁ νῦν ἰδίως λεγόμενος Πόντος, τῆς
Καππαδοκίας μέρος ὢν τὸ πρὸς τῷ Εὐξείνῳ·
ὥστ᾽ εἰ τοὺς Χάλυβας τῆς χερρονήσου θετέον

---

[1] Τερμίλαι, Xylander, for Τερμίδαι.

the Ceteians and the Solymi and the Cilicians from the plain of Thebê and the Leleges, but nowhere names the Pamphylians, Bithynians, Mariandynians, Pisidians, Chalybians, Milyans, or Cappadocians—some because they had not yet settled in this region, and others because they were included among other tribes, as, for example, the Hidrieis and the Termilae among the Carians, and the Doliones and Bebryces among the Phrygians.

24. But obviously Apollodorus does not pass a fair judgment upon the statement of Ephorus, and also confuses and falsifies the words of the poet; for he ought first to have asked Ephorus this question : Why he placed the Chalybians inside the peninsula when they were so far distant towards the east from both Sinopê and Amisus ? For those who say that the isthmus of this peninsula is the line from Issus to the Euxine make this line a kind of meridian, which some think should be the line to Sinopê, and others, that to Amisus, but no one that to the land of the Chalybians, which is absolutely oblique ; in fact, the meridian through the land of the Chalybians would be drawn through Lesser Armenia and the Euphrates, cutting off on this side of it the whole of Cappadocia, Commagenê, Mt. Amanus, and the Issic Gulf. If, however, we should concede that the oblique line bounds the isthmus, at least most of these places, and Cappadocia in particular, would be cut off on this side, as also the country now called Pontus in the special sense of the term, which is a part of Cappadocia towards the Euxine ; so that, if the land of the Chalybians

---

¹ ἤν, Corais inserts.

μέρος, πολὺ μᾶλλον τοὺς Κατάονας καὶ Καππάδοκας ἀμφοτέρους καὶ Λυκάονας δέ, οὓς καὶ
αὐτοὺς παρῆκε. διὰ τί δ' ἐν τοῖς μεσογαίοις
C 679 ἔταξε τοὺς Χάλυβας, οὓς ὁ ποιητὴς Ἁλιζώνας[1]
ἐκάλεσεν, ὥσπερ καὶ ἡμεῖς ἀπεδείξαμεν; ἄμεινον
γὰρ ἦν διελεῖν καὶ τοὺς μὲν ἐπὶ τῇ θαλάττῃ
φάναι, τοὺς δὲ ἐν τῇ μεσογαίᾳ· ὅπερ καὶ ἐπὶ
τῆς Καππαδοκίας ποιητέον καὶ τῆς Κιλικίας. ὁ
δὲ τὴν μὲν οὐδ' ὠνόμακε, τοὺς Κίλικας δὲ τοὺς
ἐπὶ τῇ θαλάττῃ μόνον εἴρηκεν. οἱ οὖν ἐπ'
Ἀντιπάτρῳ τῷ Δερβήτῃ καὶ οἱ Ὁμοναδεῖς καὶ
ἄλλοι πλείους οἱ συνάπτοντες τοῖς Πισίδαις,

οἳ οὐκ ἴσασι θάλατταν
ἀνέρες, οὐδέ θ'[2] ἅλεσσι μεμιγμένον εἶδαρ
ἔδουσι,

τίνα λάβωσι τάξιν; ἀλλ' οὐδὲ Λυδοὺς οὐδὲ
Μήονας εἴρηκεν, εἴτε δύο εἴθ' οἱ αὐτοί εἰσι, καὶ
εἴτε καθ' ἑαυτοὺς εἴτ' ἐν ἑτέρῳ γένει περιεχο-
μένους. οὕτω γὰρ ἐπίσημον ἔθνος οὐκ ἀπο-
κρύψαι δυνατόν, ὅ τε μὴ λέγων περὶ αὐτοῦ μηδὲν
οὐκ ἂν δόξειε παραλιπεῖν τι τῶν κυριωτάτων;
25. Τίνες δ' εἰσὶν οἱ μιγάδες; οὐ γὰρ ἂν
ἔχοιμεν εἰπεῖν παρὰ τοὺς λεχθέντας τόπους ἢ
ὠνομάσθαι ὑπ' αὐτοῦ ἢ παραλελεῖφθαι ἄλλους,
οὓς ἀποδώσομεν τοῖς μιγάσιν, οὐδέ γε αὐτῶν τινας
τούτων, ὧν ἢ εἶπεν ἢ παρέλιπε. καὶ γὰρ εἰ
κατεμίχθησαν, ἀλλ' ἡ ἐπικράτεια πεποίηκεν ἢ
Ἕλληνας ἢ βαρβάρους· τρίτον δὲ γένος οὐδὲν
ἴσμεν τὸ μικτόν.

---

[1] Ἁλιζώνους CEFsw.
[2] οὐδέ θ' F, οὐδ' ἔθ' other MSS.

must be set down as a part of the peninsula, much more should Cataonia and both Cappadocias, as also Lycaonia, which is itself omitted by him. Again, why did Ephorus place in the interior the Chalybians, whom the poet called Halizones, as I have already demonstrated?[1] For it would have been better to divide them and set one part of them on the sea and the other in the interior, as should also be done in the case of Cappadocia and Cilicia; but Ephorus does not even name Cappadocia, and speaks only of the Cilicians on the sea. Now as for the people who were subject to Antipater Derbetes, and the Homonadeis and several other peoples who border on the Pisidians, "men who do not know the sea and even do not eat food mingled with salt,"[2] where are they to be placed? Neither does he say in regard to the Lydians or Meïones whether they are two peoples or the same, or whether they live separately by themselves or are included within another tribe. For it would be impossible to lose from sight so significant a tribe; and if Ephorus says nothing about it, would he not seem to have omitted something most important?

25. And who are the "mixed" tribes? For we would be unable to say that, as compared with the aforesaid places, others were either named or omitted by him which we shall assign to the "mixed" tribes; neither can we call "mixed" any of these peoples themselves whom he has mentioned or omitted; for, even if they had become mixed, still the predominant element has made them either Hellenes or barbarians; and I know nothing of a third tribe of people that is "mixed."

[1] 12. 3. 20.　　　　[2] *Odyssey* 11. 122.

26. Πῶς δὲ τρία γένη τῶν Ἑλλήνων ἐστὶ τὰ τὴν χερρόνησον οἰκοῦντα; εἰ γάρ, ὅτι τὸ παλαιὸν οἱ αὐτοὶ ἦσαν Ἴωνες καὶ Ἀθηναῖοι, λεγέσθωσαν καὶ οἱ Δωριεῖς καὶ οἱ Αἰολεῖς οἱ αὐτοί, ὥστε δύο ἔθνη γίνοιτ' ἄν· εἰ δὲ διαιρετέον κατὰ τὰ ὕστερα ἔθη, καθάπερ καὶ τὰς διαλέκτους, τέτταρα ἂν εἴη καὶ τὰ ἔθνη, καθάπερ καὶ αἱ διάλεκτοι. οἰκοῦσι δὲ τὴν χερρόνησον ταύτην, καὶ μάλιστα κατὰ τὸν τοῦ Ἐφόρου διορισμόν, οὐκ Ἴωνες μόνον, ἀλλὰ καὶ Ἀθηναῖοι, καθάπερ ἐν τοῖς καθ' ἕκαστα δεδήλωται.[1] τοιαῦτα μὲν δὴ πρὸς τὸν Ἔφορον διαπορεῖν ἄξιον, Ἀπολλόδωρος δὲ τούτων μὲν ἐφρόντισεν οὐδέν· τοῖς δὲ ἑκκαίδεκα ἔθνεσι προστίθησιν ἑπτακαιδέκατον, τὸ τῶν Γαλατῶν, ἄλλως μὲν χρήσιμον λεχθῆναι, πρὸς δὲ τὴν δίαιταν τῶν ὑπὸ τοῦ Ἐφόρου λεγομένων ἢ παραλειπομένων οὐ δέον· εἴρηκε δὲ τὴν αἰτίαν αὐτός, ὅτι ταῦτα πάντα νεώτερα τῆς ἐκείνου ἡλικίας.

27. Μεταβὰς δ' ἐπὶ τὸν ποιητὴν τοῦτο μὲν ὀρθῶς λέγει, διότι πολλὴ σύγχυσις γεγένηται τῶν βαρβάρων ἐθνῶν ἀπὸ τῶν Τρωικῶν εἰς τὰ νῦν διὰ τὰς μεταπτώσεις· καὶ γὰρ προσγέγονέ τινα καὶ ἐλλέλοιπε καὶ διέσπασται καὶ συνῆκται εἰς ἕν. οὐκ εὖ δὲ τὴν αἰτίαν διττὴν ἀποφαίνει, δι' ἣν οὐ μέμνηταί τινων ὁ ποιητής· ἢ τῷ μήπω C 680 τότ' οἰκεῖσθαι ὑπὸ τοῦ ἔθνους τούτου, ἢ τῷ ἐν ἑτέρῳ γένει περιέχεσθαι. τὴν γὰρ Καππαδοκίαν οὐκ εἴρηκεν, οὐδὲ τὴν Καταονίαν, ὡς δ' αὕτως τὴν

---

[1] Cf. 8. 1. 2.   [2] 14. 1. 3 ff.

26. And how can there be three Hellenic tribes that live on the peninsula? For if it is because the Athenians and the Ionians were the same people in ancient times, let also the Dorians and the Aeolians be called the same people; and thus there would be only two tribes. But if one should make distinctions in accordance with the customs of later times, as, for example, in accordance with dialects, then the tribes, like the dialects, would be four in number.[1] But this peninsula, particularly in accordance with the division of Ephorus, is inhabited, not only by Ionians, but also by Athenians, as I have shown in my account of the several places.[2] Now although it is worth while to raise such questions as these with reference to Ephorus, yet Apollodorus took no thought for them and also goes on to add to the sixteen tribes a seventeenth, that of the Galatians—in general a useful thing to do, but unnecessary for the passing of judgment upon what is said or omitted by Ephorus. But Apollodorus states the reason himself, that all this is later than the time of Ephorus.

27. Passing to the poet, Apollodorus rightly says that much confusion of the barbarian tribes has taken place from the Trojan times to the present because of the changes, for some of them have been added to, others have vanished, others have been dispersed, and others have been combined into one tribe. But he incorrectly sets forth as twofold the reason why the poet does not mention some of them; either because a country was not yet inhabited by this or that tribe or because this or that tribe was included within another; for instance, the poet fails to mention Cappadocia, Cataonia, and

Λυκαονίαν, δι᾽ οὐδέτερον τούτων· οὐ γὰρ ἔχομεν
τοιαύτην ἱστορίαν ἐπ᾽ αὐτῶν οὐδεμίαν. γελοῖόν
τε τὸ τοὺς Καππάδοκας καὶ Λυκάονας διὰ τί μὲν
Ὅμηρος παρέλιπε, φροντίσαι καὶ ἀπολογήσασθαι,
διὰ τί δ᾽ Ἔφορος παρῆλθε, παρελθεῖν καὶ αὐτόν,
καὶ ταῦτα παραθέμενον πρὸς αὐτὸ τοῦτο τὴν
ἀπόφασιν τἀνδρός, πρὸς τὸ ἐξετάσαι καὶ διαι-
τῆσαι· καί, διότι μὲν Μήονας ἀντὶ Λυδῶν Ὅμηρος εἶπε, διδάξαι, ὅτι δ᾽ οὔτε Λυδοὺς οὔτε Μήονας
εἴρηκεν Ἔφορος, μὴ ἐπισημήνασθαι.
28. Φήσας δὲ ἀγνώτων τινῶν μεμνῆσθαι τὸν
ποιητήν, Καύκωνας μὲν ὀρθῶς λέγει καὶ Σολύμους
καὶ Κητείους [1] καὶ Λέλεγας καὶ Κίλικας τοὺς ἐκ
Θήβης πεδίου, τοὺς δ᾽ Ἀλιζῶνας αὐτὸς πλάττει,
μᾶλλον δ᾽ οἱ πρῶτοι τοὺς Ἀλιζῶνας ἀγνοήσαντες,
τίνες εἰσί, καὶ μεταγράφοντες πλεοναχῶς καὶ
πλάττοντες τὴν τοῦ ἀργύρου γενέθλην καὶ ἄλλα
πολλὰ μέταλλα,[2] ἐκλελειμμένα ἅπαντα. πρὸς
ταύτην δὲ τὴν φιλοτιμίαν κἀκείνας συνήγαγον
τὰς ἱστορίας, ἃς ὁ Σκήψιος τίθησι παρὰ Καλλι-
σθένους λαβὼν καὶ ἄλλων τινῶν, οὐ καθαρευόντων
τῆς περὶ τῶν Ἁλιζώνων ψευδοδοξίας· ὡς ὁ μὲν
Ταντάλου πλοῦτος καὶ τῶν Πελοπιδῶν ἀπὸ τῶν
περὶ Φρυγίαν καὶ Σίπυλον μετάλλων ἐγένετο· ὁ
δὲ Κάδμου ἐκ τῶν [3] περὶ Θρᾴκην καὶ τὸ Παγγαῖον
ὄρος· ὁ δὲ Πριάμου ἐκ τῶν ἐν Ἀστύροις [4] περὶ
Ἄβυδον χρυσείων, ὧν καὶ νῦν ἔτι μικρὰ λείπεται·

---

[1] Κητείους, Xylander, for Κητίους; so later editors.
[2] μέταλλα, Corais, for μεγάλα; so later editors.
[3] ἐκ τῶν, Corais inserts: so later editors.
[4] Ἀστύροις, Xylander, for Ἀσυρίοις CDF*iw*, περὶ Ἄβυδον
moz.

likewise Lycaonia, but for neither of these reasons, for we have no history of this kind in their case. Further, it is ridiculous that Apollodorus should concern himself about the reason why Homer omitted the Cappadocians and Lycaonians and speak in his defence, and yet should himself omit to tell the reason why Ephorus omitted them, and that too when he had cited the statement of the man for the very purpose of examining it and passing judgment upon it ; and also to teach us why Homer mentioned Meïonians instead of Lydians, but not to remark that Ephorus mentions neither Lydians nor Meïonians.

28. After saying that the poet mentions certain unknown tribes, Apollodorus rightly names the Cauconians, the Solymi, the Ceteians, the Leleges, and the Cilicians of the plain of Thebê; but the Halizones are a fabrication of his own, or rather of the first men who, not knowing who the Halizones were, wrote the name in several different ways [1] and fabricated the " birthplace of silver " [2] and many other mines, all of which have given out. And in furtherance of their emulous desire they also collected the stories cited by Demetrius of Scepsis from Callisthenes and certain other writers, who were not free from the false notions about the Halizones. Likewise the wealth of Tantalus and the Pelopidae arose from the mines round Phrygia and Sipylus ; that of Cadmus from those round Thrace and Mt. Pangaeus ; that of Priam from the gold mines at Astyra near Abydus (of which still to-day there are small remains ; here the amount of earth thrown out is considerable, and the excava-

[1] See 12. 3. 21.   [2] See 12. 3. 24.

πολλὴ δ' ἡ ἐκβολὴ καὶ τὰ ὀρύγματα σημεῖα τῆς
πάλαι μεταλλείας· ὁ δὲ Μίδου ἐκ τῶν περὶ τὸ
Βέρμιον ὄρος· ὁ δὲ Γύγου καὶ Ἀλυάττου καὶ
Κροίσου ἀπὸ τῶν ἐν Λυδίᾳ καὶ[1] τῆς μεταξὺ
Ἀταρνέως τε καὶ Περγάμου, ὅπου[2] πολίχνη
ἐρήμη, ἐκμεμεταλλευμένα ἔχουσα τὰ χωρία.

29. Ἔτι καὶ ταῦτα μέμψαιτο ἄν τις τοῦ
Ἀπολλοδώρου, ὅτι τῶν νεωτέρων καινοτομούντων
πολλὰ παρὰ τὰς Ὁμηρικὰς ἀποφάσεις, εἰωθὼς
ταῦτ' ἐλέγχειν ἐπὶ πλέον, ἐνταῦθα οὐκ ὠλιγώρηκε
μόνον, ἀλλὰ καὶ τἀναντία εἰς ἓν συνάγει τὰ μὴ
ὡσαύτως λεγόμενα. ὁ μὲν γὰρ Ξάνθος ὁ Λυδὸς
μετὰ τὰ Τρωικά φησιν ἐλθεῖν τοὺς Φρύγας ἐκ τῆς
Εὐρώπης καὶ τῶν ἀριστερῶν τοῦ Πόντου, ἀγαγεῖν
δ' αὐτοὺς Σκαμάνδριον ἐκ Βερεκύντων καὶ Ἀσκανίας, ἐπιλέγει δὲ τούτοις ὁ Ἀπολλόδωρος, ὅτι τῆς
Ἀσκανίας ταύτης μνημονεύει καὶ Ὅμηρος, ἧς ὁ
Ξάνθος·

C 681   Φόρκυς δὲ Φρύγας ἦγε καὶ Ἀσκάνιος θεοειδὴς
         τῆλ' ἐξ Ἀσκανίης.

ἀλλ' εἰ οὕτως ἔχει, ἡ μὲν μετανάστασις ὕστερον
ἂν εἴη τῶν Τρωικῶν γεγονυῖα, ἐν δὲ τοῖς Τρωικοῖς
τὸ λεγόμενον ὑπὸ τοῦ ποιητοῦ ἐπικουρικὸν ἦκεν
ἐκ τῆς περαίας ἐκ τῶν Βερεκύντων καὶ τῆς Ἀσκανίας. τίνες οὖν Φρύγες ἦσαν,

οἵ ῥα τότ' ἐστρατόωντο παρ' ὄχθας Σαγγαρίοιο,
ὅτε ὁ Πρίαμος,

        ἐπίκουρος ἐὼν μετὰ τοῖσιν ἐλέγμην,[3]

---

[1] καί, before τῆς, Corais inserts.
[2] ὅπου, before πολίχνη, Jones inserts. Tzschucke and Corais
emend πολίχνη ἐρήμη . . . ἔχουσα to πολίχνης ἐρήμης . . .
ἐχούσης.

tions are signs of the mining in olden times); and that of Midas from those round Mt. Bermius; and that of Gyges and Alyattes and Croesus from those in Lydia and from the region between Atarneus and Pergamum, where is a small deserted town, whose lands have been exhausted of ore.

29. Still further one might find fault with Apollodorus, because, when the more recent writers make numerous innovations contrary to the statements of Homer, he is wont frequently to put these innovations to the test, but in the present case he not only has made small account of them, but also, on the contrary, identifies things that are not meant alike; for instance, Xanthus the Lydian says that it was after the Trojan War that the Phrygians came from Europe and the left-hand side of the Pontus, and that Scamandrius led them from the Berecyntes and Ascania, but Apollodorus adds to this the statement that Homer refers to this Ascania that is mentioned by Xanthus: "And Phorcys and godlike Ascanius led the Phrygians from afar, from Ascania." [1] However, if this is so, the migration must have taken place later than the Trojan War, whereas the allied force mentioned by the poet came from the opposite mainland, from the Berecyntes and Ascania. Who, then, were the Phrygians, "who were then encamped along the banks of the Sangarius," [2] when Priam says, "for I too, being an ally, was numbered among these"? [3] And how could Priam have sent

---

[1] *Iliad* 2. 862.   [2] *Iliad* 3. 187.   [3] *Iliad* 3. 188.

[3] ἐλέγμην is emended by Tzschucke and Corais to ἐλέχθην (as in the Homeric text).

φησί; πῶς δὲ ἐκ μὲν Βερεκύντων μετεπέμπετο
Φρύγας ὁ Πρίαμος, πρὸς οὓς οὐδὲν ἦν αὐτῷ
συμβόλαιον, τοὺς δ' ὁμόρους καὶ οἷς αὐτὸς
πρότερον ἐπεκούρησε παρέλιπεν; οὕτω δὲ περὶ
τῶν Φρυγῶν εἰπὼν ἐπιφέρει καὶ τὰ περὶ τῶν
Μυσῶν οὐχ ὁμολογούμενα τούτοις· λέγεσθαι γάρ
φησι καὶ τῆς Μυσίας κώμην Ἀσκανίαν περὶ
λίμνην ὁμώνυμον, ἐξ ἧς καὶ τὸν Ἀσκάνιον ποταμὸν ῥεῖν, οὗ μνημονεύει καὶ Εὐφορίων·

Μυσοῖο παρ' ὕδασιν Ἀσκανίοιο·

καὶ ὁ Αἰτωλὸς Ἀλέξανδρος·

οἳ[1] καὶ ἐπ' Ἀσκανίῳ δώματ' ἔχουσι ῥόῳ,
λίμνης Ἀσκανίης ἐπὶ χείλεσιν· ἔνθα Δολίων
υἱὸς Σιληνοῦ νάσσατο καὶ Μελίης.

καλοῦσι δέ, φησί, Δολιονίδα καὶ Μυσίαν τὴν
περὶ Κύζικον ἰόντι εἰς Μιλητούπολιν. εἰ οὖν
οὕτως ἔχει ταῦτα, καὶ ἐκμαρτυρεῖται ὑπὸ τῶν
δεικνυμένων νῦν καὶ ὑπὸ τῶν ποιητῶν, τί ἐκώλυε
τὸν Ὅμηρον ταύτης μεμνῆσθαι τῆς Ἀσκανίας,
ἀλλὰ μὴ τῆς ὑπὸ Ξάνθου λεγομένης; εἴρηται δὲ
καὶ πρότερον περὶ τούτων ἐν τῷ περὶ Μυσῶν καὶ
Φρυγῶν λόγῳ, ὥστε ἐχέτω πέρας.

VI

1. Λοιπὸν δὲ τὴν πρὸς νότου παρακειμένην τῇ
χερρονήσῳ ταύτῃ περιοδεῦσαι νῆσον τὴν Κύπρον.
εἴρηται δ', ὅτι ἡ περιεχομένη θάλαττα ὑπὸ τῆς
Αἰγύπτου καὶ Φοινίκης καὶ Συρίας καὶ τῆς λοιπῆς
παραλίας μέχρι τῆς Ῥοδίας σύνθετός πώς ἐστιν

---

[1] εἰ CDEF*h*; but see same passage in 12. 4. 8.

for Phrygians from the Berecyntes, with whom he had no compact, and yet leave uninvited those who lived on his borders and to whom he had formerly been ally? And after speaking in this way about the Phrygians he adds also an account of the Mysians that is not in agreement with this; for he says that there is also a village in Mysia which is called Ascania, near a lake of the same name, whence flows the Ascanius River, which is mentioned by Euphorion, "beside the waters of the Mysian Ascanius," and by Alexander the Aetolian, "who have their homes on the Ascanian streams, on the lips of the Ascanian Lake, where dwelt Dolion, the son of Silenus and Melia." And he says that the country round Cyzicus, as one goes to Miletupolis, is called Dolionis and Mysia. If this is so, then, and if witness thereto is borne both by the places now pointed out and by the poets, what could have prevented Homer from mentioning this Ascania, and not the Ascania spoken of by Xanthus? I have discussed this before, in my account of the Mysians and Phrygians;[1] and therefore let this be the end of that subject.

VI

1. It remains for me to describe the island which lies alongside this peninsula on the south, I mean Cyprus. I have already said that the sea surrounded by Egypt, Phoenicia, Syria, and the rest of the coast as far as Rhodia[2] consists approximately of

---

[1] 7. 3. 2–3; 12. 3. 3; 12. 4. 5.
[2] The Peraea of the Rhodians.

ἔκ τε τοῦ Αἰγυπτίου πελάγους καὶ τοῦ Παμφυλίου καὶ τοῦ κατὰ τὸν Ἰσσικὸν κόλπον. ἐν δὲ
ταύτῃ ἐστὶν ἡ Κύπρος, τὰ μὲν προσάρκτια μέρη
συνάπτοντα ἔχουσα τῇ Τραχείᾳ Κιλικίᾳ, καθ᾽ ἃ
δὴ καὶ προσεχεστάτη τῇ ἠπείρῳ ἐστί, τὰ δὲ ἑῷα
τῷ Ἰσσικῷ κόλπῳ, τὰ δ᾽ ἑσπέρια τῷ Παμφυλίῳ
κλυζόμενα πελάγει, τὰ δὲ νότια τῷ Αἰγυπτίῳ.
τοῦτο μὲν οὖν σύρρουν ἐστὶν ἀπὸ τῆς ἑσπέρας τῷ
Λιβυκῷ καὶ τῷ Καρπαθίῳ πελάγει, ἀπὸ δὲ τῶν
νοτίων καὶ τῶν ἑῴων μερῶν ἥ τε Αἴγυπτός ἐστι
καὶ ἡ ἐφεξῆς παραλία μέχρι Σελευκείας τε καὶ
Ἰσσοῦ, πρὸς ἄρκτον δ᾽ ἥ τε Κύπρος καὶ τὸ Παμ-
φύλιον πέλαγος. τοῦτο δὲ ἀπὸ μὲν τῶν ἄρκτων
περιέχεται τοῖς τε ἄκροις τῆς Τραχείας Κιλικίας
καὶ τῆς Παμφυλίας καὶ Λυκίας μέχρι τῆς Ῥοδίας,
ἀπὸ δὲ τῆς δύσεως τῇ Ῥοδίων νήσῳ, ἀπὸ δὲ τῆς
C 682 ἀνατολῆς τῇ Κύπρῳ τῇ κατὰ Πάφον καὶ τὸν
Ἀκάμαντα, ἀπὸ δὲ τῆς μεσημβρίας σύρρουν ἐστὶ
τῷ Αἰγυπτίῳ πελάγει.
2. Ἔστι δ᾽ ὁ μὲν κύκλος τῆς Κύπρου σταδίων
τρισχιλίων καὶ τετρακοσίων εἴκοσι κατακολ-
πίζοντι· μῆκος δὲ ἀπὸ Κλειδῶν ἐπὶ τὸν Ἀκάμαντα
πεζῇ σταδίων χιλίων τετρακοσίων ὁδεύοντι ἀπ᾽
ἀνατολῆς ἐπὶ δύσιν. εἰσὶ δὲ αἱ μὲν Κλεῖδες
νησία δύο προκείμενα[1] τῇ Κύπρῳ κατὰ τὰ ἑωθινὰ
μέρη τῆς νήσου, τὰ διέχοντα τοῦ Πυράμου σταδίους ἑπτακοσίους· ὁ δ᾽ Ἀκάμας ἐστὶν ἄκρα δύο
μαστοὺς ἔχουσα καὶ ὕλην πολλήν, κείμενος μὲν
ἐπὶ τῶν ἑσπερίων τῆς νήσου μερῶν, ἀνατείνων δὲ
πρὸς ἄρκτους, ἐγγυτάτω μὲν πρὸς Σελινοῦντα τῆς
Τραχείας Κιλικίας ἐν διάρματι χιλίων σταδίων,
πρὸς Σίδην δὲ τῆς Παμφυλίας χιλίων καὶ ἑξακο-

the Aegyptian and Pamphylian Seas and of the sea
at the gulf of Issus. In this last sea lies Cypros; its
northern parts closely approach Cilicia Tracheia,
where they are closest to the mainland, and its
eastern parts border on the Issic Gulf, and its
western on the Pamphylian Sea, being washed by
that sea, and its southern by the Aegyptian Sea.
Now the Aegyptian Sea is confluent on the west
with the Libyan and Carpathian Seas, but in its
southern and eastern parts borders on Aegypt and
the coast next thereafter as far as Seleuceia and
Issus, and towards the north on Cypros and the
Pamphylian Sea; but the Pamphylian Sea is surrounded on the north by the extremities of Cilicia
Tracheia, of Pamphylia, and of Lycia, as far as
Rhodia, and on the west by the island of the
Rhodians, and on the east by the part of Cypros
near Paphos and the Acamas, and on the south is
confluent with the Aegyptian Sea.

2. The circuit of Cypros is three thousand four
hundred and twenty stadia, including the sinuosities
of the gulfs. The length from Cleides to the Acamas
by land, travelling from east to west, is one thousand
four hundred stadia. The Cleides are two isles
lying off Cypros opposite the eastern parts of the
island, which are seven hundred stadia distant from
the Pyramus. The Acamas is a promontory with two
breasts and much timber. It is situated at the
western part of the island, and extends towards the
north; it lies closest to Selinus in Cilicia Tracheia,
the passage across being one thousand stadia,
whereas the passage across to Sidê in Pamphylia is

---

[1] Instead of προκείμενα, Corais and Meineke, following F,
read προσκείμενα.

σίων, πρὸς δὲ Χελιδονίας χιλίων ἐννακοσίων. ἔστι
δὲ ἑτερομήκης τὸ ὅλον τῆς νήσου σχῆμα, καί που
καὶ ἰσθμοὺς ποιεῖ κατὰ τὰς τὸ πλάτος διοριζούσας
πλευράς· ἔχει δὲ καὶ τὰ καθ' ἕκαστα, ὡς ἐν
βραχέσιν εἰπεῖν, οὕτως, ἀρξαμένοις ἀπὸ τοῦ προσ-
εχεστάτου σημείου τῇ ἠπείρῳ.

3. Ἔφαμεν δέ[1] που κατὰ τὸ Ἀνεμούριον,
ἄκραν τῆς Τραχείας Κιλικίας, ἀντικεῖσθαι τὸ
τῶν Κυπρίων ἀκρωτήριον τὴν Κρομμύου ἄκραν ἐν
τριακοσίοις καὶ πεντήκοντα σταδίοις· ἐντεῦθεν δ'
ἤδη δεξιὰν τὴν νῆσον ἔχουσιν, ἐν ἀριστερᾷ δὲ τὴν
ἤπειρον, πρὸς ἄρκτον ὁ πλοῦς ἐστι καὶ πρὸς ἔω
καὶ πρὸς τὰς Κλεῖδας εὐθυπλοίᾳ σταδίων ἑπτακοσίων. ἐν δὲ τῷ μεταξὺ Λάπαθός τέ ἐστι πόλις,
ὕφορμον ἔχουσα καὶ νεώρια, Λακώνων κτίσμα
καὶ Πραξάνδρου, καθ' ἣν ἡ Νάγιδος.[2] εἶτ' Ἀφροδίσιον, καθ' ὃ στενὴ ἡ νῆσος· εἰς γὰρ Σαλαμῖνα
ὑπέρβασις σταδίων ἑβδομήκοντα· εἶτ' Ἀχαιῶν
ἀκτή,[3] ὅπου Τεῦκρος προσωρμίσθη πρῶτον ὁ[4]
κτίσας Σαλαμῖνα τὴν ἐν Κύπρῳ, ἐκβληθείς, ὥς
φασιν, ὑπὸ τοῦ πατρὸς Τελαμῶνος· εἶτα Καρ-
πασία πόλις, λιμένα ἔχουσα. κεῖται δὲ κατὰ τὴν
ἄκραν τὴν Σαρπηδόνα· ἐκ δὲ τῆς Καρπασίας
ὑπέρβασίς ἐστιν ἰσθμοῦ τριάκοντα σταδίων πρὸς
τὰς νήσους τὰς Καρπασίας καὶ τὸ νότιον πέλαγος·
εἶτ' ἄκρα καὶ ὅρος· ἡ δ' ἀκρώρεια καλεῖται Ὄλυμπος, ἔχουσα Ἀφροδίτης Ἀκραίας ναόν, ἄδυτον
γυναικὶ καὶ ἀόρατον. πρόκεινται δὲ πλησίον αἱ

[1] δέ, Corais emends to δή.
[2] ἡ Νάγιδος, Corais, for ἣν ἄγιδος; so the later editors.
[3] εἶτ' Ἀχαιῶν ἀκτή moxz, εἶτα χάρων ἀκτή other MSS.; so
the editors.

376

sixteen hundred and to the Chelidonian islands one
thousand nine hundred. The shape of the island
as a whole is oblong; and in some places it forms
isthmuses on the sides which define its breadth.
But the island also has its several parts, which I
shall describe briefly, beginning with the point that
is nearest to the mainland.

3. I have said somewhere[1] that opposite to
Anemurium, a cape of Cilicia Tracheia, is the
promontory of the Cyprians, I mean the promontory
of Crommyus, at a distance of three hundred and
fifty stadia. Thence forthwith, keeping the island
on the right and the mainland on the left, the
voyage to the Cleides lies in a straight line towards
the north-east, a distance of seven hundred stadia.
In the interval is the city Lapathus, with a mooring-
place and dockyards; it was founded by Laconians
and Praxander, and opposite it lies Nagidus. Then
one comes to Aphrodisium, where the island is
narrow, for the passage across to Salamis is only
seventy stadia. Then to the beach of the Achaeans,
where Teucer, the founder of Salamis in Cypros,
first landed, having been banished, as they say, by
his father Telamon. Then to a city Carpasia, with
a harbour. It is situated opposite the promontory
Sarpedon; and the passage from Carpasia across
the isthmus to the Carpasian Islands and the
southern sea is thirty stadia. Then to a promontory and mountain. The mountain peak is called
Olympus; and it has a temple of Aphroditê Acraea,
which cannot be entered or seen by women. Off

---

[1] 14. 5. 3.

---

[4] ὁ, before κτίσας, Kramer inserts; so the later editors.

Κλεῖδες καὶ ἄλλαι δὲ πλείους, εἶθ᾽ αἱ Καρπάσιαι
νῆσοι, καὶ μετὰ ταύτας ἡ Σαλαμίς, ὅθεν ἦν
Ἄριστος ὁ συγγραφεύς· εἶτ᾽ Ἀρσινόη πόλις καὶ
λιμήν· εἶτ᾽ ἄλλος λιμὴν Λεύκολλα·[1] εἶτ᾽ ἄκρα
Πηδάλιον, ἧς[2] ὑπέρκειται λόφος τραχύς, ὑψηλός,
τραπεζοειδής, ἱερὸς Ἀφροδίτης, εἰς ὃν ἀπὸ Κλειδῶν στάδιοι ἑξακόσιοι ὀγδοήκοντα· εἶτα κολπώ-
δης καὶ τραχὺς παράπλους ὁ πλείων εἰς Κίτιον·
ἔχει δὲ λιμένα κλειστόν· ἐντεῦθέν ἐστι Ζήνων τε,
ὁ τῆς στωικῆς αἱρέσεως ἀρχηγέτης, καὶ Ἀπολ-
C 683 λώνιος ἰατρός· ἐντεῦθεν εἰς Βηρυτὸν στάδιοι χίλιοι
πεντακόσιοι. εἶτ᾽ Ἀμαθοῦς πόλις καὶ μεταξὺ
πολίχνη, Παλαιὰ καλουμένη, καὶ ὄρος μαστοειδὲς
Ὄλυμπος· εἶτα Κουριὰς χερρονησώδης, εἰς ἣν
ἀπὸ Θρόνων στάδιοι ἑπτακόσιοι. εἶτα πόλις
Κούριον, ὅρμον ἔχουσα, Ἀργείων κτίσμα. ἤδη
οὖν πάρεστι σκοπεῖν τὴν ῥαθυμίαν τοῦ ποιήσαντος
τὸ ἐλεγεῖον τοῦτο, οὗ ἡ ἀρχή·

ἱραὶ τῷ Φοίβῳ, πολλὸν διὰ κῦμα θέουσαι,
    ἤλθομεν αἱ ταχιναὶ τόξα φυγεῖν ἔλαφοι·

εἶθ᾽ Ἡδύλος[3] ἐστίν, εἴθ᾽ ὁστισοῦν· φησὶ[4] μὲν γὰρ
ὁρμηθῆναι τὰς ἐλάφους Κωρυκίης ἀπὸ δειράδος,
ἐκ δὲ Κιλίσσης ἠιόνος εἰς ἀκτὰς διανήξασθαι
Κουριάδας, καὶ ἐπιφθέγγεται, διότι

μυρίον ἀνδράσι θαῦμα νοεῖν πάρα, πῶς ἀνόδευ-
    τον
χεῦμα δι᾽ εἰαρινῷ[5] ἐδράμομεν ζεφύρῳ.[6]

---

[1] Λεύκολλα, Casaubon, for Λεύκολα ; so the later editors.
[2] ἧς F, εἰς ἥν other MSS.
[3] Ἡδύλος F, εἴθ᾽ ἡ δῆλος other MSS.   [4] φασί CDhiosz.
[5] δι᾽ εἰαρινῷ, Meineke, for δ᾽ ἀερινίων moz, δι᾽ ἐρίνων other
MSS.

it, and near it, lie the Cleides, as also several other islands; and then one comes to the Carpasian Islands; and, after these, to Salamis, where Aristus the historian was born. Then to Arsinoê, a city and harbour. Then to another harbour, Leucolla. Then to a promontory, Pedalium, above which lies a hill that is rugged, high, trapezium-shaped, and sacred to Aphroditê, whereto the distance from the Cleides is⁶ six hundred and eighty stadia. Then comes the coasting-voyage to Citium, which for the most part is sinuous and rough. Citium has a harbour that can be closed; and here were born both Zeno, the original founder of the Stoic sect, and Apollonius, a physician. The distance thence to Berytus is one thousand five hundred stadia. Then to the city Amathus, and, in the interval, to a small town called Palaea, and to a breast-shaped mountain called Olympus. Then to Curias, which is peninsula-like, whereto the distance from Throni is seven hundred stadia. Then to a city Curium, which has a mooring-place and was founded by the Argives. One may therefore see at once the carelessness of the poet who wrote the elegy that begins, "we hinds, sacred to Phoebus, racing across many billows, came hither in our swift course to escape the arrows of our pursuers," whether the author was Hedylus or someone else; for he says that the hinds set out from the Corycian heights and swam across from the Cilician shore to the beach of Curias, and further says that "it is a matter of untold amazement to men to think how we ran across the impassable stream by the aid of a vernal west wind"; for while

---

⁶ ζεφύρῳ, Meineke, for ζεφύρων.

STRABO

ἀπὸ γὰρ Κωρύκου περίπλους μέν ἐστιν εἰς Κουριάδα ἀκτήν, οὔτε ζεφύρῳ δέ, οὔτε ἐν δεξιᾷ ἔχοντι τὴν νῆσον, οὔτ' ἐν ἀριστερᾷ, δίαρμα δ' οὐδέν. ἀρχὴ δ' οὖν τοῦ δυσμικοῦ παράπλου τὸ Κούριον τοῦ βλέποντος πρὸς Ῥόδον, καὶ εὐθύς ἐστιν ἄκρα, ἀφ' ἧς ῥίπτουσι τοὺς ἁψαμένους τοῦ βωμοῦ τοῦ Ἀπόλλωνος· εἶτα Τρῆτα καὶ Βοόσουρα καὶ Παλαίπαφος, ὅσον ἐν δέκα σταδίοις ὑπὲρ τῆς θαλάττης ἱδρυμένη, ὕφορμον ἔχουσα, καὶ ἱερὸν ἀρχαῖον τῆς Παφίας Ἀφροδίτης· εἶτ' ἄκρα Ζεφυρία, πρόσορμον ἔχουσα, καὶ ἄλλη Ἀρσινόη, ὁμοίως πρόσορμον ἔχουσα καὶ ἱερὸν καὶ ἄλσος· μικρὸν δ' ἀπὸ τῆς θαλάττης καὶ ἡ Ἱεροκηπίς. εἶθ' ἡ Πάφος, κτίσμα Ἀγαπήνορος, καὶ λιμένα ἔχουσα καὶ ἱερὰ εὖ κατεσκευασμένα. διέχει δὲ πεζῇ σταδίους ἑξήκοντα τῆς Παλαιπάφου, καὶ πανηγυρίζουσι διὰ τῆς ὁδοῦ ταύτης κατ' ἔτος ἐπὶ τὴν Παλαίπαφον ἄνδρες ὁμοῦ γυναιξὶν συνιόντες καὶ[1] ἐκ τῶν ἄλλων πόλεων. φασὶ δ' εἰς Ἀλεξάνδρειάν τινες ἐκ Πάφου σταδίους εἶναι τρισχιλίους ἑξακοσίους. εἶθ' ὁ Ἀκάμας ἐστὶ μετὰ Πάφον· εἶτα πρὸς ἕω μετὰ τὸν Ἀκάμαντα πλοῦς εἰς Ἀρσινόην πόλιν καὶ τὸ τοῦ Διὸς ἄλσος· εἶτα Σόλοι[2] πόλις, λιμένα ἔχουσα καὶ ποταμὸν καὶ ἱερὸν Ἀφροδίτης καὶ Ἴσιδος· κτίσμα δ' ἐστὶ Φαλήρου καὶ Ἀκάμαντος Ἀθηναίων· οἱ δ' ἐνοικοῦντες Σόλιοι καλοῦνται. ἐντεῦθεν ἦν Στασάνωρ τῶν Ἀλεξάνδρου ἑταίρων, ἀνὴρ ἡγεμονίας ἠξιωμένος· ὑπέρκειται δ' ἐν μεσογαίᾳ Λιμενία πόλις· εἶθ' ἡ Κρομμύου ἄκρα.

[1] καί is omitted by all MSS. except DF.
[2] Σόλοι, Tzschucke, for Σόλους.

380

there is a voyage round the island from Corycus to the beach Curias, which is made neither by the aid of a west wind nor by keeping the island on the right nor on the left, there is no passage across the sea between the two places. At any rate, Curium is the beginning of the westerly voyage in the direction of Rhodes; and immediately one comes to a promontory, whence are flung those who touch the altar of Apollo. Then to Treta, and to Boosura, and to Palaepaphus, which last is situated at about ten stadia above the sea, has a mooring-place, and an ancient temple of the Paphian Aphroditê. Then to the promontory Zephyria, with a landing-place, and to another Arsinoê, which likewise has a landing-place and a temple and a sacred precinct. And at a little distance from the sea is Hierocepis. Then to Paphus, which was founded by Agapenor, and has both a harbour and well-built temples. It is sixty stadia distant from Palaepaphus by land; and on this road men together with women, who also assemble here from the other cities, hold an annual procession to Palaepaphus. Some say that the distance from Paphus to Alexandria is three thousand six hundred stadia. Then, after Paphus, one comes to the Acamas. Then, after the Acamas, towards the east, one sails to a city Arsinoê and the sacred precinct of Zeus. Then to a city Soli, with a harbour and a river and a temple of Aphroditê and Isis. It was founded by Phalerus and Acamas, Athenians; and the inhabitants are called Solians; and here was born Stasanor, one of the comrades of Alexander, who was thought worthy of a chief command; and above it, in the interior, lies a city Limenia. And then to the promontory of Crommyus.

381

4. Τί δὲ δεῖ τῶν ποιητῶν θαυμάζειν, καὶ μάλιστα τῶν τοιούτων, οἷς ἡ πᾶσα περὶ τὴν

C 684 φράσιν ἐστὶ σπουδή, τὰ τοῦ Δαμάστου συγκρίνοντας, ὅστις τῆς νήσου τὸ μῆκος ἀπὸ τῶν ἄρκτων πρὸς μεσημβρίαν ἀποδίδωσιν, ἀπὸ Ἱεροκηπίας, ὥς φησιν, εἰς Κλείδας; οὐδὲ ὁ Ἐρατοσθένης εὖ· αἰτιώμενος γὰρ τοῦτον, οὐκ ἀπ' ἄρκτων φησὶν εἶναι τὴν Ἱεροκηπίαν, ἀλλ' ἀπὸ νότου· οὐδὲ γὰρ ἀπὸ νότου, ἀλλ' ἀπὸ δύσεως, εἴπερ ἐν τῇ δυσμικῇ πλευρᾷ κεῖται, ἐν ᾗ καὶ ἡ Πάφος καὶ ὁ Ἀκάμας. διάκειται μὲν οὕτως ἡ Κύπρος τῇ θέσει.

5. Κατ' ἀρετὴν δ' οὐδεμιᾶς τῶν νήσων λείπεται· καὶ γὰρ εὔοινός ἐστι καὶ εὐέλαιος, σίτῳ τε αὐτάρκει χρῆται· μέταλλά τε χαλκοῦ ἐστιν ἄφθονα τὰ ἐν Ταμασσῷ,[1] ἐν οἷς τὸ χαλκανθὲς γίνεται, καὶ ὁ ἰὸς τοῦ χαλκοῦ, πρὸς τὰς ἰατρικὰς δυνάμεις χρήσιμα. φησὶ δ' Ἐρατοσθένης τὸ παλαιὸν ὑλομανούντων τῶν πεδίων, ὥστε κατέχεσθαι δρυμοῖς καὶ μὴ γεωργεῖσθαι, μικρὰ μὲν ἐπωφελεῖν πρὸς τοῦτο τὰ μέταλλα, δενδροτομούντων πρὸς τὴν καῦσιν τοῦ χαλκοῦ καὶ τοῦ ἀργύρου, προσγενέσθαι δὲ καὶ τὴν ναυπηγίαν τῶν στόλων, ἤδη πλεομένης ἀδεῶς τῆς θαλάττης καὶ μετὰ δυνάμεων· ὡς δ' οὐκ ἐξενίκων, ἐπιτρέψαι τοῖς βουλομένοις καὶ δυναμένοις ἐκκόπτειν καὶ ἔχειν ἰδιόκτητον καὶ ἀτελῆ τὴν διακαθαρθεῖσαν γῆν.

6. Πρότερον μὲν οὖν κατὰ πόλεις ἐτυραννοῦντο οἱ Κύπριοι, ἀφ' οὗ δ' οἱ Πτολεμαϊκοὶ βασιλεῖς

---

[1] Ταμασσῷ, Xylander, for Ταμασῷ E, Τανασσῷ other MSS.

4. But why should one wonder at the poets, and particularly at writers of the kind that are wholly concerned about style, when we compare the statements of Damastes, who gives the length of the island as from north to south, "from Hierocepias," as he says, "to Cleides"? Neither is Eratosthenes correct, for, although he censures Damastes, he says that Hierocepias is not on the north but on the south; for it is not on the south either, but on the west, since it lies on the western side, where are also Paphus and the Acamas. Such is the geographical position of Cypros.

5. In fertility Cyprus is not inferior to any one of the islands, for it produces both good wine and good oil, and also a sufficient supply of grain for its own use. And at Tamassus there are abundant mines of copper, in which is found chalcanthite[1] and also the rust of copper, which latter is useful for its medicinal properties. Eratosthenes says that in ancient times the plains were thickly overgrown with forests, and therefore were covered with woods and not cultivated; that the mines helped a little against this, since the people would cut down the trees to burn the copper and the silver, and that the building of the fleets further helped, since the sea was now being navigated safely, that is, with naval forces, but that, because they could not thus prevail over the growth of the timber, they permitted anyone who wished, or was able, to cut out the timber and to keep the land thus cleared as his own property and exempt from taxes.

6. Now in the earlier times the several cities of the Cyprians were under the rule of tyrants,

[1] Sulphate of copper.

κύριοι τῆς Αἰγύπτου κατέστησαν, εἰς ἐκείνους καὶ
ἡ Κύπρος περιέστη, συμπραττόντων πολλάκις
καὶ τῶν Ῥωμαίων. ἐπεὶ δ' ὁ τελευταῖος ἄρξας
Πτολεμαῖος, ἀδελφὸς τοῦ Κλεοπάτρας πατρός,
τῆς καθ' ἡμᾶς βασιλίσσης, ἔδοξε πλημμελής τε
εἶναι καὶ ἀχάριστος εἰς τοὺς εὐεργέτας, ἐκεῖνος
μὲν κατελύθη, Ῥωμαῖοι δὲ κατέσχον τὴν νῆσον,
καὶ γέγονε στρατηγικὴ ἐπαρχία καθ' αὑτήν.
μάλιστα δ' αἴτιος τοῦ ὀλέθρου κατέστη τῷ
βασιλεῖ Πόπλιος Κλαύδιος Πούλχερ· ἐμπεσὼν
γὰρ εἰς τὰ ληστήρια, τῶν Κιλίκων ἀκμαζόντων
τότε, λύτρον αἰτούμενος ἐπέστειλε τῷ βασιλεῖ,
δεόμενος πέμψαι καὶ ῥύσασθαι αὐτόν· ὁ δ'
ἔπεμψε μέν, μικρὸν δὲ τελέως, ὥστε καὶ τοὺς
λῃστὰς αἰδεσθῆναι λαβεῖν, ἀλλὰ ἀναπέμψαι
πάλιν, τὸν δ' ἄνευ λύτρων ἀπολῦσαι. σωθεὶς δ'
ἐκεῖνος ἀπεμνημόνευσεν ἀμφοτέροις τὴν χάριν,
καὶ γενόμενος δήμαρχος, ἴσχυσε τοσοῦτον, ὥστε
ἐπέμφθη Μάρκος Κάτων, ἀφαιρησόμενος τὴν
Κύπρον τὸν κατέχοντα. ἐκεῖνος μὲν οὖν ἔφθη
διαχειρισάμενος αὑτόν, Κάτων δὲ ἐπελθὼν παρέ-
C 685 λαβε τὴν Κύπρον, καὶ τὴν βασιλικὴν οὐσίαν
διέθετο, καὶ τὰ χρήματα εἰς τὸ δημόσιον ταμεῖον
τῶν Ῥωμαίων ἐκόμισεν· ἐξ ἐκείνου δ' ἐγένετο
ἐπαρχία ἡ νῆσος, καθάπερ καὶ νῦν ἐστί, στρα-
τηγική· ὀλίγον δὲ χρόνον τὸν μεταξὺ Ἀντώνιος
Κλεοπάτρᾳ καὶ τῇ ἀδελφῇ αὐτῆς Ἀρσινόῃ παρέ-
δωκε· καταλυθέντος δὲ ἐκείνου, συγκατελύθησαν
καὶ αἱ διατάξεις αὐτοῦ πᾶσαι.

but from the time the Ptolemaïc kings became established as lords of Egypt Cyprus too came into their power, the Romans often co-operating with them. But when the last Ptolemy that reigned, the brother of the father of Cleopatra, the queen in my time, was decreed to be both disagreeable and ungrateful to his benefactors, he was deposed, and the Romans took possession of the island ; and it has become a praetorian province by itself. The chief cause of the ruin of the king was Publius Claudius Pulcher; for the latter, having fallen into the hands of the bands of pirates, the Cilicians then being at the height of their power, and, being asked for a ransom, sent a message to the king, begging him to send and rescue him. The king indeed sent a ransom, but so utterly small that the pirates disdained to take it and sent it back again, but released him without ransom. Having safely escaped, he remembered the favour of both ; and, when he became tribune of the people, he was so powerful that he had Marcus Cato sent to take Cypros away from its possessor. Now the king killed himself beforehand, but Cato went over and took Cypros and disposed of the king's property and carried the money to the Roman treasury. From that time the island became a province, just as it is now—a praetorian province. During a short intervening time Antony gave it over to Cleopatra and her sister Arsinoê, but when he was overthrown his whole organisation was overthrown with him.

A PARTIAL DICTIONARY OF PROPER NAMES[1]

A

ABA, queen of Olbê, 343

Abydus, 5, 19, 23, 37, 41, 43

Acamas, the promontory, 375, 381

Achilles, 15, 61, 105, 107, 119, 121, 129, 149, 151

Adeimantus of Lampsacus (see footnote 3 on p. 36), 37

Aega, the promontory, 133, 135

Aeneias, 19, 65, 105, 107, 119

Adramyttium, 9, 103, 123, 127, 129

Adramyttium, Gulf of, 13, 97, 103

Adrasteia, 27, 29

Adrestus, builder of altar to Nemesis, 31

Aeolians, the, 7, 23

Aeolis, 7, 23

Aepytus, son of Neleus, founder of Priene, 199

Aeschines the orator, contemporary of Cicero, native of Miletus, 207

Aeschylus, on the Caïcus River, 139

Aesepus River, the, 3, 7, 85

Agamemnon, 55, 97, 223, 233

Agapenor, on return from Troy founded Paphus, 381

Agatharchides the Peripatetic and historian (fl. apparently about 130 B.C.), native of Cnidus, 283

Agathocles, son of Lysimachus, slain by his father, 165

Agrippa, transported a work of Lysippus from Lampsacus to Rome, 37

Alabanda, 27, 299

Alcaeus the poet, threw away his arms in battle, 77; on Antandrus, 101; native of Mitylenê, 141; author of *Stasiotic* poems. 143; interpreted by Callias, 147

Alexander the Great, defeated satraps

of Dareius, 27; visited Ilium, 51; friendly to Ilium, 55, 57; offered to restore temple of Artemis at Ephesus, 227; extended limits of refuge, 229; sacred precinct of, 239; seized Halicarnassus, 285; destroyed Milyas, 321; led phalanx against Dareius from Soli, 355

Alexander Lychnus the orator, native of Ephesus, 231

Althaemenes the Argive, coloniser of Crete, Rhodes, and other cities, 271

Alyattes, mound of, built by prostitutes, 177, 179

Amphilochus, founder of Mallus, 353; tomb of, near Magarsa, 355

Amyntas (see *Dictionary* in vol. v), received a part of Cilicia Tracheia from the Romans, 337

Anacreon the melic poet (see *Dictionary* in vol. ii), calls Teos "Athamantis," 199; lived with tyrant Polycrates, 217; native of Teos, 237; on warlike zeal of the Carians, 301

Anaxagoras the natural philosopher, a Clazomenian, 245

Anaxarchus, companion of Alexander on Asiatic expedition, 55

Anaxenor the citharoede, exalted by Antony and consecrated to Zeus by his native land, 255

Anaximander (see *Dictionary* in vol. i), native of Miletus, 207

Anaximenes of Lampsacus, accompanied Alexander on Asiatic expedition, wrote histories of Philip and Alexander, a history of Greece in twelve books; on places called Colonae, 35; a rhetorician, 37; on the colonies of Miletus, 207

Anaximenes the philosopher, native

A PARTIAL DICTIONARY OF PROPER NAMES

of Miletus, 207; associate of Anaxagoras, 245

Anchialê, founded by Sardanapallus and the site of his tomb, according to Aristobulus, 341, 343

Androclus, son of Codrus the king of Athens, leader of the Ionian colonisation and founder of Ephesus (according to Pherecydes), 199; drove Carians and Leleges out of Ephesus, 225

Andromachê, native of Thebê, 17

Andronicus the Peripatetic, native of Rhodes, 279

Antandrus, 101, 103, 123

Antigonus the son of Philip (see *Dictionary* in vol. v), founder of Alexandreia in Troad, 53; founder of Antigonia (Alexandreia), 65; incorporated Scepsians into Alexandreia, 105; builder of new Smyrna, 245; revolted from, by Eumenes, 343

Antimachus (see *Dictionary* in vol. iv), on the goddess Nemesis, 31

Antimenidas, brother of Alcaeus, native of Mytilenê, 141

Antiocheia on the Maeander, 189

Antiochus the Great (see *Dictionary* in vol. v); expelled by the Romans, 53; fought by Eumenes, 167

Antiochus Soter (see *Dictionary* in vol. v); conquered by Eumenes, 165

Antipater Derbetes, the tyrant, 365

Antipater the Stoic, native of Tarsus, 347

Antony (see *Dictionary* in vol. v), carried off statue of Aias to Aegypt, 59; carried off statues from the Heraeum, 213; increased limits of refuge at Ephesus, 229; assigned part of Cilicia to Cleopatra, 331; conferred queenship on Aba, 343; friendly to Boethus, ruler of Tarsus, 349; gave Cypros to Cleopatra amd her sister Arsinoê, 385

Apelles the painter (see *Dictionary* in vol. i), native of Ephesus, 231; painted portrait of Antigonus and the Aphroditê Anadyomenê, 287, 289

Apellicon of Teos, bought libraries of Aristotle and Theophrastus, 111; "a Teian," 239

Aphroditê Acraca, 377

Aphroditê the Paphian, 381

Apoecus, the Athenian, founder of Teos, 201

Apollo, 159, 243, 245, 317, 381; Actaeus, 29; Cillaean, 123, 127; Clarius, 233; Didymeus, 205; Hecatus, 147; Larisaean, 155; Sminthian, 21, 123; Thymbraean, 69; "Ulius," 207

Apollodorus, of Athens (see *Dictionary* in vol. i), author of works *On the Catalogue of Ships* and *A Description of the Earth*; on the term "barbarians," 303; on the Trojan allies, 357, 359; on the number of tribes in Asia Minor, 361, 363, 367; on the Trojan allies according to Homer, 369; wrongly interprets Homer's "Ascania," 371

Apollodorus the rhetorician and philosopher, native of Pergamum, 171

Apollonius the physician, native of Citium, 379

Apollonius the Stoic, best of the disciples of Panaetius, native of Nysa, 263

Apollonius Malacus (teacher of rhetoric at Rhodes about 120 B.C.), native of Alabanda, 281; ridiculed Alabanda, 299

Apollonius Molon of Alabanda, author of speech entitled *Against the Caunians*, 267; pupil of Menecles the orator, 281; changed his abode to Rhodes, 299

Apollonius Mus, fellow-pupil with Heracleides the physician in time of Strabo, 243

Apollonius Rhodius, author of the *Argonauts*, an Alexandrian but called a Rhodian, 281

Aratus the poet, author of *The Phaenomena*, native of Soli, 341

Arcesilaüs, of the Academy, and fellow-student of Zeno, 131

Archedemus the Stoic, native of Tarsus, 347

Archeläus, king of Cappadocia, received the whole of Cilicia Tracheia except Seleuceia (from Augustus), 337, 339

Archeläus the natural philosopher (fl. about 450 B.C.), pupil of Anaxagoras, 245

Archilochus, on the Magnetans, 253

A PARTIAL DICTIONARY OF PROPER NAMES

Areius, contemporary of Augustus, friend of Xenarchus the philosopher, 335

Archaeanax of Mitylenê, reputed builder of wall round Sigeium, 75

Arion, the citharist, native of Methymna, 145

Aristarchus (see *Dictionary* in vol. i), teacher of Menecrates, 263

Aristeas of Proconnesus (see *Dictionary* in vol. i), 33; reputed teacher of Homer, 219

Aristobulus (see *Dictionary* in vol. v), says that Anchialê was founded by, and was the site of tomb of, Sardanapallus, 341

Aristocles the grammarian, contemporary of Strabo, native of Rhodes, 281

Aristodemus, son of Menecrates, teacher of Strabo at Nysa, 263

Ariston the Peripatetic (see footnote 3 on p. 289), 289

Ariston, pupil and heir of Ariston the Peripatetic, native of Cos, 289

Aristonicus, caused Leucae to revolt after death of his brother Attalus Philometor, 247; ended life in prison at Rome, 249

Aristotle, on the Trojan walls, 1; teacher of Neleus, 111; tarried at Assus, 115; teacher and friend of Hermeias the tyrant, 117; teacher of Theophrastus and Phanias, 145

Artemidorus (see *Dictionary* in vol. ii), on distances between certain Aeolian cities, 159; on the restoration of temple of Ephesian Artemis, 227; ambassador to Rome, honoured at Ephesus, 233; on certain distances in Asia Minor, 307, 309, 311; on cities in the Lycian League, 315; makes Celenderis, not Coracesium, the beginning of Cilicia, 333; on the distance from the Pyramus River to Soli, 353; falsifier of distances, 359; on the number of the tribes in Asia Minor, 361

Artemidorus, son of Theopompus the contemporary of Strabo, native of Cnidus 283

Artemidorus the grammarian, native of Tarsus, 351

Artemis, 29, 207, 221; the Astyrene, 129; Cindyas, 289; Ephesian, 223,

225; Leucophryene, 251; Munychia, 223; Pergaea, 325; Sarpedonian, 357

Artemisia, wife of Mausolus the king of Caria, 283

Asander the king, slayer of Pharnaces and king of the Bosporus, 169

Asclepius, born near Triccê, 249

Assus, 101, 115, 129

Astyra, 45, 129, 131

Athena, 81, 83, 135, 215, 277, 325

Athena Lindia, 279

Athenaeus the Peripatetic, contemporary of Strabo, native of Seleuceia, 335

Athenaïs the prophetess (contemporary of Alexander), native of Erythrae, 243

Athenians, the, voted, but rescinded, disgraceful decree against the Mitylenaeans, 145; founders of Elaea, 159

Athenodorus Cananites (see *Dictionary* in vol. i), teacher of Augustus, native of Tarsus, 349; restored good government at Tarsus, 351

Athenodorus Cordylion, lived with Marcus Cato, native of Tarsus, 347

Attalic kings, the, 31, 159, 163

Attalus I, king of Pergamum (reigned 241–197 B.C.), on the Beautiful Pine, 89; transferred Gergithians of the Troad to Gergitha, 139; son of Attalus and Antiochis, 165; friend of the Romans, 167

Attalus II, Philadelphus, king of Pergamum (reigned 159–138 B.C.), deceived in regard to mole at mouth of Ephesian harbour, 229; settled the " Dionysiac artists " in Myonnesus, 237; Attaleia named after him, 323

Attalus III, Philometor, king of Pergamum (reigned 138–133 B.C.), left the Romans his heirs, 169; after his death Leucae revolted, 247

B

Bacchylides, on the source of the Caïcus River, 137

Bellerophon, Palisade of, 191

Bias, one of the Seven Wise Men, native of Prienê, 211

389

A PARTIAL DICTIONARY OF PROPER NAMES

Boethus, bad poet, bad citizen, and ruler of Tarsus, 349

C

Caesar Augustus, gave back statue of Aias to Rhoeteians, 59; appointed Marcus Pompey procurator of Asia, 145; pupil of Apollodorus, 171; restored statues to the Heraeum, 215; nullified extension of limits of refuge at Ephesus, 229; dedicated a painting of Apelles to his father, 289; friend of Xenarchus the philosopher, 335

Caesar, Julius, friendly to Ilium, 55, 57; friend to Mithridates of Pergamum, 169; Trebonius one of his murderers, 247; sold wealth of Pythodorus, 257; painting by Apelles dedicated to him by his son Augustus, 289

Caïcus River, the, 5, 103, 133, 137, 153, 169

Calchas the prophet, died of grief as result of contest with Mopsus the prophet, 233, 325, 353

Callias, interpreter of Sappho and Alcaeus, 147

Callimachus (see *Dictionary* in vol. i), on Creophilus of Samos, 219; comrade of the poet Heracleitus, 285

Callinus the elegiac poet, on the Teucrians, 95; on the capture of Sardeis, 179; calls Ephesians "Smyrnaeans," 201; on the Magnetans, 251; on the early invasion of the Cimmerians, 253; on the death of Calchas at Clarus, 325

Callisthenes (see *Dictionary* in vol. v), on the name "Adrasteia," 29; companion of Alexander, 55; on the cities united by Mausolus, 119; on the Arimi, 177; on Sardeis, 179; on Phrynichus the tragic poet, 209; had false notions about the Halizones, 369

Cameirus, 275, 279

Canae, 5, 13, 105, 133, 141

Caresenê, 87, 89

Carians, the, 117, 119, 197, 199, 215, 225, 263, 293, 301

Cato, Marcus, sent from Rome to seize Cyprus, 385

Cauconians, the 151

Cayster Plain, the, 155, 185

Celaenae, 137

Chares the Lindian, built the Colossus of Rhodes, 269

Charon the historian, on the boundaries of the Troad, 9; native of Lampsacus, 37

Cheirocrates the architect, completed the temple of Artemis at Ephesus and proposed to Alexander to fashion Mt. Athos in his likeness, 227

Chelidonian Islands, the, 263, 319

Chersiphron, first architect of temple of Artemis at Ephesus, 225

Chios, founded by Egertius, 201, 243

Chrysa, 93, 121, 123

Chrysippus, successor of Cleanthes as head of the Stoic school of philosophy, 115; native of Soli, 339

Cibyra, 189, 193

Cicero, applauded Menippus Catocas above all Asiatic orators, 299

Cilicia Pedias, 327

Cilicia Tracheia, 311, 313, 325, 327, 337, 375

Cilicians, the, 121, 149, 153, 331

Citium, home of Zeno, 379

Clazomenae, founded by Paralus, 201, 239, 245

Cleanthes of Assus, the Stoic philosopher, successor of Zeno, 115

Cleides, the, two isles off Cyprus, 375, 379

Cleobulus, one of the Seven Wise Men, native of Lindus, 279

Cleopatra, assigned by Antony a part of Cilicia Tracheia for the building of her fleets, 331; joined Antony in conferring queenship upon Aba, 343; presented Cyprus by Antony, 385

Codrus, king of Athens, 199

Colophon, 199, 203, 233, 235

Colossus of Rhodes, the. 269

Coriscus, Socratic philosopher, 111

Cos, 287

Crates the grammarian, native of Mallus, 355

Cratippus, sons of, tyrants at Tralleis, 257

Creophilus of Samos, reputed teacher of Homer, and by Callimachus called author of the poem entitled *The Capture of Oechalia*, 219

A PARTIAL DICTIONARY OF PROPER NAMES

Crinagoras (fl. in Strabo's time), author of fifty epigrams in the Greek Anthology, native of Mitylenê, 143

Croesus, 173; origin of wealth of, 371

Crommyus, the promontory, 333, 377, 381

Ctesias, physician of Artaxerxes and author of works entitled *Assyrica* and *Persica*, native of Cnidus, 283

Curetes, the, frightened Hera, 223; special college of, 225

Curium, 379, 381

Cycnus, king of Colonae, 35

Cydnus River, the, 343, 345, 353

Cymê, 5, 153, 155 161

Cyprus, 373, 383, 385

Cyzicenê, 5, 7, 11

Cyzicus, 23, 33

D.

Daës of Colonae, on the temple of Cillaean Apollo, 123

Damastes (see *Dictionary* in vol. i), on the boundaries of the Troad, 9; wrong on the geographical position of Cypros, 383

Damasus, the Athenian, founder of Teos, 201

Damasus Scombrus the orator, native of Tralleis, 257

Daphitas the grammarian, reputed to have been crucified because he reviled the kings in a distich, 249

Dardania, 47, 65, 99

Dardanians, the, 19, 101

Dareius, father of Xerxes, burned the cities on the Propontis, 43; gave Syloson the tyranny over Samos, 219

Delos, great slave market, 329

Demetrius Lacon, pupil of the Epicurean Protarchus, 289

Demetrius, son of Seleucus, helped by Attalus to defeat Alexander the son of Antiochus, 169

Demetrius of Scepsis (see *Dictionary* in vol. i), visited Ilium, 53; on territory subject to Hector, 65; on spurs of Mt. Ida, 67; cites Hestiaea of Alexandreia, 73; calls Timaeus a falsifier 77; on Mt. Ida, 85; on the Rhesus River, 87; his commentary on the *Catalogue of the Trojans*, 91; on Antandrus, 101; on Scepsis, 105; author of *The Marshalling of the Trojan Forces*, 113; calls the Gargarians semi-barbarians, 117; on the Arimi, 177; on the Asioneis, 179; borrowed stories from Callisthenes, 369

Diodorus the dialectician, nicknamed Cronus, contemporary of Ptolemy Soter, 291

Diodorus the general (see footnote 2 on p. 129), 129

Diodorus the grammarian, native of Tarsus, 351

Diodorus the younger, of Sardeis, friend of Strabo, and author of poems and historical treatises, 181

Diodoruses, the; two orators, both natives of Sardeis, 179, 181

Diodotus Tryphon, caused Syria to revolt, but was forced by Antiochus the son of Demetrius to kill himself, 327

Diogenes the poet and itinerant philosopher, native of Tarsus, 351

Dionysides the tragic poet, native of Tarsus, 353

Dionysius the historian and rhetorician, contemporary of Strabo, native of Halicarnassus, 285

Dionysius Thrax, Alexandrian but called Rhodian, 281

Dionysocles the orator, native of Tralleis, 257

Dionysus, Games in honour of, 237

Dionysus Pyrigenes, 183

Diophanes the rhetorician, native of Mitylenê, 143

Diotrephes of Antiocheia, teacher of Hybreas of Mylasa, 295

Diotrephes the sophist, native of Antiocheia on the Maeander, 191

Dolabella, captured at Smyrna, and slew, Trebonius, one of the murderers of Caesar, 247

Dometius Ahenobarbus (see *Dictionary* in vol. ii), opponent and slayer of Menodarus, 257

E

Egertius, founder of Chios, 201

Elaea, 105, 133, 159

Elaeussa, the island, royal residence of Archelaüs, 267, 337

A PARTIAL DICTIONARY OF PROPER NAMES

Elaïtic Gulf, the, 5, 103, 133

Ephesus, 155, 199, 201, 205, 221, 225, 237

Ephorus (see *Dictionary* in vol. i), on the extent of Aeolis, 9; on the name " Aeolis," 79; native of Cymê, 161; object of ridicule, 163; on the founding of Miletus, 205; on the number of tribes in Asia Minor, 361, 363; does not name Cappadocia, 365; on Homer's Trojan allies, 369

Epicurus the philosopher, in a sense a Lampsacenian, 37; became an ephebus at Athens, 219

Erastus, Socratic philosopher, 111

Eratosthenes (see *Dictionary* in vol. i), wrong on the geographical position of Cyprus, 38; on certain distances in Asia Minor, 311

Erythrae, founded by Cnopus the son of Codrus, 201, 239, 241

Eudemus the philosopher, native of Rhodes, 279

Eudoxus of Cnidus (see *Dictionary* in vol. i), on places on the Propontis, 9; mathematician and comrade of Plato, 283

Eumenes I, brother of Lysimachus and king of Pergamum, 165

Eumenes II, king of Pergamum, 165; received Telmessus from the Romans but later was forced to give it back to the Lycians, 317

Eumenes of Cardia (see *Dictionary* in vol. v), removed Macedonian treasures from Cyinda, 343

Euripides, on Augê the mother of Telephus, 135; on Marsyas, 137; pupil of Anaxagoras, 245; quoted by Athenaeus, 335

Euthydemus, orator and statesman, contemporary of Strabo, native of Mylasa, 295

F

Fimbria, Roman quaestor, destroyer of Ilium, 55

G

Gargara, 103, 117

Glaucias, the tyrant, refugee to Sidenê, 83

Granicus River, the, 5, 7, 27, 85

H

Halicarnassus, 119, 209, 283, 285

Halizones, the 365, 369

Hamaxitus, 93, 95, 97, 101

Hecataeus (see *Dictionary* in vol. i), native of Miletus, 207; on the mountain of the Phtheires, 209; native of Teos, 239

Hecatomnos, king of the Carians, father of three sons and two daughters, 285, 295

Hector, 19, 149, 151, 153

Hedylus the elegiac poet, contemporary of Callimachus, 379

Hegesianax, on the visit of the Galatae to Ilium, 53

Hegesias the orator, corrupter of the Attic style, native of Magnesia, 253

Hellanicus (see *Dictionary* in vol. i), speaks to gratify the Ilians, 85; calls Assus an Aeolian city, 117; native of Lesbos, 147

Heracleides the Herophileian physician, contemporary of Strabo, native of Erythrae, 243

Heracleides of Pontus (see *Dictionary* in vol. i), on the temple of Apollo, 95

Heracleitus the poet, comrade of Callimachus, native of Halicarnassus, 285

Heracleitus the Obscure, native of Ephesus, 231

Hermeias, tyrant of Assus and Atarneus, 115, 131

Hermocreon, builder of altar at Parium, 29

Hermodorus, called by Heracleitus " the most useful man of Ephesus," and reputed to have written certain laws for the Romans, 231

Hermus River, the, 5, 13, 159, 173, 197

Herodotus, on the priestess of Athena at Pedasus, 119; on Arion of Methymna, 145; on certain rivers near Sardeis, 173; on the tomb of Alyattes, 177, 179; native of Halicarnassus, 283; on the Pamphylians, 325

Herostratus, an Ephesian who in 356 B.C. set on fire the temple of Artemis at Ephesus to immortalise himself, 225

Hesiod, knew not of the god Priapus, 29; native of Cymê, 161; on the

A PARTIAL DICTIONARY OF PROPER NAMES

contest between Calchas and Mopsus, 233; says that Amphilochus was slain by Apollo at Soli, 355; on the origin of the Asiatic Magnetans, 251

Hestiaea of Alexandreia, author of a work on Homer's *Iliad*, 73

Hidrieus, second son of king Hecatomnos, married his younger sister Ada, 285

Hierapolis, 185, 189

Hierocles the orator, native of Alabanda, 299

Hieronymus the philosopher, native of Rhodes, 279

Hippocrates the great physician, native of Cos, 289

Hipponax (see *Dictionary* in vol. iv), on a place called Smyrna that belonged to Ephesus, 201; on Bias of Priene, 211; native of Ephesus, 231

Homer, 9, 11, 15, 23, 49, 71, 81, 99, 105, 109, 117, 121, 135, 137, 153, 161, 175, 179, 219, 237, 243, 247, 273, 301, 321, 349

Hybreas, orator, statesman, contemporary of Strabo, native of Mylasa, 295, 297

I

Ialysus, 275, 279

Ida, Mt., 9, 65, 85, 97

Ilians, the Village of, reputed site of ancient Ilium, 69, 81

Ilium, territory of, 45; founded by Ilus, 49, 53, 55, 67, 81, 153

Ion the tragic poet, native of Chios, 243

Ionia, 197

Ionian colonisation, the, 5

Ionian League, the, 201

Ionians, the, 197

Isocrates the orator, teacher of Ephorus, 161

L

Labienus, Quintus, seized Mylasa, 297

Larisa, 153, 155

Lectum, 5, 11, 13, 97, 101

Leleges, the, 17, 97, 117, 119, 121, 149, 151, 153, 199, 225, 301

Lesbians, the, 157

Lesbocles, native of Mitylene, 143

Lesbos, 7, 139, 149

Leto, the mother of Apollo and Artemis 223, 265, 267

Lindus, 275, 279

Lycia, 265, 311

Lycians, the, 19, 179

Lycian League, the, 313, 315

Lycurgus the orator, on the rasing of Ilium, 83

Lydians, the, 181

Lyrnessus, 17, 105, 107, 121, 323

Lysimachus (see *Dictionary* in vol. v, and footnote 3 on p. 203 of vol. iii), devoted especial attention to Ilium and Alexandreia, 53; permitted Scepsians to return home from Alexandreia, 65; founder of the Asclepieium, 89; king of Pergamum, 163, 165; built wall round Ephesus, 225; builder of the new Smyrna, 245; ridiculed in distich composed by Daphitas, 251

M

Maeander River, the, 185, 211, 249

Magnesia, 159

Magnesia on the Maeander, 249

Mallus, 353, 355

Manius Aquillius the consul (129 B.C.), personally organised a province in Asia Minor, 249

Marcus Perpernas, made campaign against Aristonicus and captured him alive, 249

Mausolus, king of Caria, 119; tomb of, 283; married his elder sister Artemisia, 285

Malenchrus, tyrant of Mitylene, 143

Memnon of Rhodes, served Persians as general, 117

Menander (see *Dictionary* in vol. v), says "it (*Samos*) produces even bird's milk," 217; became an ephebus at Athens, 219

Menecles the orator, teacher of Apollonius Malacus and Apollonius Molon, 281; native of Alabanda, 299

Menecrates, pupil of Aristarchus, native of Nysa, 263

Menecrates of Elaea (see *Dictionary* in vol. v), author of *On the Founding of Cities*, on the Pelasgians, 157

Menippus Catocas, the Asiatic orator,

A PARTIAL DICTIONARY OF PROPER NAMES

applauded by Cicero and native of Stratoniceia, 299

Menodorus, contemporary of Strabo, scholar and priest, 257

Mesogis, Mt., 213, 255, 257

Methymna, 139, 141, 145

Metrodorus of Lampsacus, comrade of Epicurus, 37

Metrodorus of Scepsis, philosopher, statesman, and rhetorician, 113

Midas, origin of wealth of, 371

Miletus, founded by Neleus of Pylus, 199, 209, 211

Milyas, destroyed by Alexander, 321

Mimnermus, says that Colophon was founded by Andraemon of Pylus, 199; on Colophon, 203; native of Colophon, 235

Minos the king, 301

Mithridates Eupator (the Great), friend to Metrodorus, 113; the king, 181; extended limits of refuge at Ephesus, 229

Mithridates of Pergamum, friend of Julius Caesar, 169

Mitylenê, 141

Mopsus the prophet, victor over Calchas in contest, 233; led peoples over the Taurus, 325, 353; tomb of, near Magarsa, 355

Murena, ended tyranny at Cibyra, 193; friend of Athenaeus the Peripatetic (contemporary of Strabo), and captured because of plot against Augustus, 335

Mylasa, 291, 293, 295, 299

Myrina, 159, 163

Myron (fl. about 430 B.C.), one of the greatest Greek sculptors, 213

Myrsilus, the historian, of Methymna, on the founders of Assus, 117

Myrsilus, tyrant of Mitylenê, 143

Mysia, 181

Myus, founded by Cydrelus, 199, 211

N

Neleus, Socratic philosopher, pupil of Aristotle and Theophrastus, and heir to libraries of Aristotle and Theophrastus, 111

Neocles the schoolmaster, father of Epicurus, sent by Athenians to Samos, 219

Neoptolemus the glossographer of

Parium (see footnote 1 on p. 36), 37

Nestor the Academician, teacher of Marcellus the nephew of Augustus, native of Tarsus and successor of Athenodorus as ruler there, 351

Nestor, the Stoic, native of Tarsus, 347

Nicias, contemporary of Strabo, tyrant over the Coans, 289

Nicomedes the Bithynian, helped to overcome Aristonicus (131 B.C.), 247

P

Pamphylia, 311

Panaetius the philosopher, native of Rhodes, 279; reputed to have been a pupil of Crates of Mallus, 355

Paris, tomb of, 65

Parrhasius the painter, native of Ephesus, 231

Peiraeus, the, torn down by Sulla, 275

Peisander the poet, author of the *Heracleia* and native of Rhodes, 281

Pelasgians, the, 153, 155, 157, 301

Peraea of the Rhodians, the, 263, 265, 311

Pergamum, library of, 111, 163

Pericles, statesman and general, subdued Samos (440 B.C.), 219

Phanias the Peripatetic, native of Eressus, 145

Pherecydes of Leros (see *Dictionary* in vol. v), on the Ionian seaboard, 197; on the contest between Calchas and Mopsus, 235

Philataerus of Tïeium, treasurer of Pergamum, 165

Philemon the comic poet, native of Soli, 341

Philetas, the poet and critic, native of Cos, 289

Philip, author of *The Carica*, on the Carian language, 303

Philotas of Thebes, coloniser of Prienê, 199, 211; leader of Alexander's cavalry, 355

Phocaea, 5, 201

Phoenix, Mt., 265

Phrygia, 23

Phrynon, Olympian victor, 75; Athenian general, 77

Pinarus River, the; scene of the struggle between Alexander and Dareius, 355

A PARTIAL DICTIONARY OF PROPER NAMES

Pindar, on the Pithecussae, 177; on Polymnastus the musician, 235; on the Homeridae of Chios, 245; says that gold rained on Rhodes, 277

Pittacus of Mitylenê, one of the Seven Wise Men, 77; born at Mitylenê, 141; one of the tyrants, 143

Pixodarus, third son of king Hecatomnos of Caria, 285

Plato, on the stages of civilisation, 47; teacher of Hermeias the tyrant, 117

Plutiades the itinerant philosopher, native of Tarsus, 351

Plutonium, the, near Acharaca, 259; at Hierapolis, 187

Polemon, teacher of Zeno and Arcesilaüs, 131

Polycrates (hanged 522 B.C.), tyrant of Samos, 217

Polymedium, 101, 139

Polymnastus, mentioned by Pindar as a famous musician and as a native of Colophon, 237

Pompey the Great, insulted by Aeschines the orator, 209; friend of Pythodorus, 257; wiped out piracy, 315; colonised Soli, 315; friend of Theophanes the historian, 143

Pompey, Marcus, the son of Theophanes of Mitylenê, appointed Procurator of Asia by Augustus, 145

Poseidon, 81, 213; the Heliconian, 221

Poseidonius (see *Dictionary* in vol. i), on brick-making in Iberia, 133; statesman at Rhodes, 279

Potamon the rhetorician, native of Mitylenê, 143

Praxander the Laconian, founder of Lapathus, 377

Praxiphanes, native of Rhodes, 279

Praxiteles the great sculptor, works of in the temple of Artemis at Ephesus, 229

Priam, the sway of, 13, 17, 63, 81, 107, 369

Prienê, 199, 211

Procles, founder of Samos, 201

Proconnesus, Old and New, 33

Propontis, the, 3 5

Protarchus the Epicurean, native of Bargylia and teacher of Demetrius Lacon, 289

Protesiläus, temple of, 61

Protogenes the painter; his *Ialysus* and his *Satyr* at Rhodes, 269

Ptolemy, the last that reigned and uncle of Cleopatra, ruined by Publius Claudius Pulcher, 385

Ptolemy Philadelphus, repaired Patara and called it Lycian Arsinoê, 317

Publius Crassus, made campaign against Aristonicus, 249

Pulcher, Publius Claudius, ruined Ptolemy the uncle of Cleopatra, 385

Pylaeus, commander of the Lesbians, 157

Pyrrha, 141, 145, 211

Pythodoris, queen of the Pontus, daughter of Pythodorus the "Asiarch," 257

Pythodorus, native of Nysa, "Asiarch" at Tralleis, friend of Pompey, extremely wealthy, and father of Queen Pythodoris, 257

R

Rhodes, 269, 273, 275

Rhoeteium, 59, 67, 83, 85

S

Samos, founded by Tembrion and Procles, 201, 213, 215

Sappho, on the promontory called Aega, 135; native of Mitylenê, 143; interpreted by Callias, 147

Sardeis, 171, 173, 177

Scamander River, the, 65, 67, 73, 85, 87

Scepsis, 85, 101, 105, 109

Scipio Aemilianus, sent by Romans to inspect Cilicia, 329

Scopas the great sculptor, maker of image of Apollo, 95; maker of work containing statues of Leto and Ortygia (the nurse) with a child in each arm of the latter 223

Scylax of Caryanda (see *Dictionary* in vol. v), on the boundaries of the Troad, 8; born at Caryanda, 289

Seleuceia, 333, 335, 337

Seleuceia-in-Pieria, first Syrian city after Cilicia, 357

Seleucus Nicator, overthrew Lysimachus and was slain by Ptolemy Ceraunus 165; incompetent hereditary succession of, 329

Servilius Isauricus, demolished Isaura

A PARTIAL DICTIONARY OF PROPER NAMES

(75 B.C.), 315; captured Olympus, the fortress of Zenicetus the pirate, 339

Sestus, 5, 41, 43

Sibylla the prophetess, native of Erythrae, 241

Sigeium, 61, 67, 73, 75, 79, 85

Sigrium, promontory of Lesbos, 139, 141, 145

Simonides, the poet, on " pordacian " clothes, 147

Simus the physician, native of Cos, 289

Simus the melic poet, corrupter of the traditional style, 253

Simmias the grammarian (fl. about 300 B.C.), native of Rhodes, 281

Sipylus, ruler of Magnesia, 159

Smyrna, 201, 203, 245

Soli (Pompeïopolis), 315, 339, 355

Solmissus, Mt., 223

Sophocles the tragic poet, on the immunity of Antenor's home, 107; helped Pericles to subdue Samos, 219; on the contest between Calchas and Mopsus, 235, 353

Sostratus, grammarian and teacher of Pompey the Great, 263

Stratocles the philosopher, native of Rhodes, 279

Stratoniceia, 297, 299

Stratonicus the citharist, on Assus, 115; on the paleness of the Caunians, 267

Sulla, overthrew Fimbria and came to agreement with Mithridates, 55, 59; carried off Apellicon's library to Rome, 113; tore down the Peiraeus, 275

Syloson, brother and assistant of his brother Polycrates the tyrant of Samos, 217; later became tyrant of of Samos by gift of Dareius, 219

Syrians, the, 177

T

Tamassus in Cyprus, site of copper mines, 383

Tantalus, origin of wealth of, 369

Tarcondimotus, named by the Romans king of Mt. Amanus, 355

Tarsus, 343, 345, 347

Taurus, Mt., the extremities of, 263

Telephus the king, 135

Temnus, birthplace of Hermagoras, author of an *Art of Rhetoric*, 159

Teos, founded at first by Athamas, 199, 237

Teuthras, king of the Cilicians and Mysians, 135

Terpander the musical artist, 147

Thales, one of the Seven Wise Men, native of Miletus, 207

Thebê, 121, 129, 149, 323

Themistocles; his wife, or daughter, a priestess in temple of Dindymenê, 251

Theocritus the sophist, native of Chios, 243

Theophanes the historian, of Mitylenê, contemporary of Strabo, 143

Theophrastus, teacher of Neleus, 111; native of Eressus, 145

Theopompus (see *Dictionary* in vol. i), on Sestus, 45; on Mt. Mesogis, 185; native of Chios, 243

Theopompus, contemporary of Strabo, friend of Julius Caesar, native of Cnidus, 283

Thrason, sculptor of chapel of Hecatê and other works at the temple of Artemis at Ephesus, 229

Thucydides, on the seizure of Troy by the Athenians, 79; on the term " barbarians," 301, 303

Thyateira, 171, 247

Tiberius, friend to Marcus Pompey, 145; restorer of Sardeis, 179

Tigranes the Armenian, 115

Timaeus the historian (see *Dictionary* in vol. ii), called falsifier by Demetrius, 77; on the size of the largest of the Gymnesian Isles, 277

Timosthenes (see *Dictionary* in vol. i), on islands between Asia and Lesbos, 147

Tmolus, Mt., 173, 183

Tralleis, 255

Trebonius, one of the murderers of Caesar, slain by Dolabella at Smyrna, 247

Treres, the, 179, 251

Troad, the, 3, 7, 21, 77

Trojan Plain, the, 65, 67

Trojans, the, sway and dynasties of, 5, 19, 149

Troy, 7, 9, 15

Typhon the giant, 177, 183

Tyrranion the grammarian, got possession of Apellicon's library at Rome, 113

A PARTIAL DICTIONARY OF PROPER NAMES

MAP

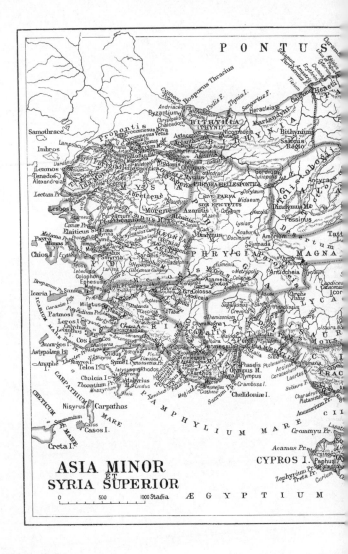

ASIA MINOR
ET
SYRIA SUPERIOR

0   500   1000 Stadia

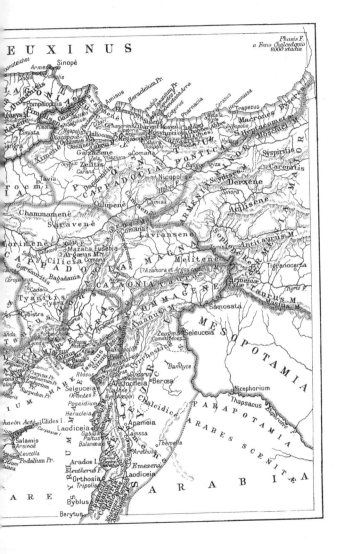

PONTUS EUXINUS

Phasis F.
a Fano Chalcedonio
8000 stadia

Sinopē

Armenē

Amisus

Heracleum Pr.

Trapezus

Hermonassa

Pharnacia

Cerasus

Macrones

Byzere

Zygopolis

Colchi

Moschici

CAPPADOCIA

PONTUS

SYSPIRITIS

Carenitis

Zelitis

Nicopolis

ARMENIA

Derxene

MAIOR

Culupenē

ARMENIA

Acilisene

Chammanenē

Sirauenē

Comana

Laviansenē

Antitaurus M.

Mazaca Eusebia

Melitenē

Tigranocerta

CAPPADOCIA

Argaeus M.

Cilicia

Comana

CATAONIA

Taurus M.

Masius M.

COMMAGENE

Tigris F.

Armeniae

Cybistra

Samosata

MESOPOTAMIA

Amanus M.

SYRIA

Zeugma

Seleucia

Commagenes

Tarsus

Issus

Nicopolis

Alexandrea

Rhosus

Myriandrus

Bambyce

Beroea

Seleucia

Antiochia

Orontes F.

Nicephorium

Thapsacus

PARAPOTAMIA

Daphne

Poseidium

Chalcidice

ARABES SCENITAE

Heraclea

Salamis

Laodiceia

Apameia

Arsinoē

Gabala

Larissa

Leucolla

Paltus

Themella

Pedalium Pr.

Balanea

Arethusa

Arados I.

Emesa

SYRIA

Eleutherus F.

Laodiceia

Orthosia

Tripolis

Byblus

Berytus

MARE